A Short History of
CLASSICAL
CIVILIZATION

A Short History of
CLASSICAL CIVILIZATION

Michael Grant

Weidenfeld and Nicolson
London

THE BRITISH MUSEUM

50104   6 10644810

Copyright © 1991 by Michael Grant Publications Ltd
Maps drawn by Andras Bereznay

First published 1991 by
George Weidenfeld & Nicolson Ltd
91 Clapham High Street
London SW4 7TA

British Library Cataloguing in Publication Data
available upon request

All rights reserved. No part of this publication may
be reproduced, stored in a retrieval system, or
transmitted in any form or by any means,
electronic, mechanical, photocopying, recording
or otherwise, without the prior permission of the
copyright owner.

Printed and bound in Great Britain by
Butler & Tanner Ltd,
Frome & London

BEXLEY LIBRARY SERVICE

LOC. CLXX	CL No. 930,4 GRA	
PRICE 8·99	ACC DATE 13 FEB 1992	BKS OP
COLL CODE	ITEM LOAN TYPE	
KEYER MB	LANG	CH	PB SAF

THE BRITISH MUSEUM
THE PAUL HAMLYN LIBRARY
WITHDRAWN

930. 4 GRA

Contents

List of maps   *vii*

Acknowledgment   *viii*

Introduction   I

THE GREEKS

PART I: THE RISE OF THE GREEKS

Chapter 1: The Early Greeks   8
  1 The Early Greeks and the Near East   8
  2 Greece takes shape   11

Chapter 2: Greece   18
  1 Central Greece   18
  2 The Peloponnese   27

Chapter 3: East, North-East and West   35
  1 Ionia, Aeolis, Cyprus   35
  2 The North-East   45
  3 The West   48

PART II: THE CLASSICAL GREEKS

Chapter 4: Against Persia and Carthage   56

Chapter 5: The Classical City-States   63
  1 Climax and Eclipse   63
  2 Poetry and Drama   75
  3 Philosophy   88
  4 Art   101
  5 The Classical Achievement   110

PART III: THE HELLENISTIC GREEKS

Chapter 6: Alexander and his Successors   114

Chapter 7: Hellenistic Man and Woman   122
  1 Reality and the Individual   122
  2 The Search for Peace of Mind   129
  3 Epilogue   133

THE ROMANS

PART IV: EARLY ROME AND THE REPUBLIC

Chapter 8: The Etruscans and the Rise of Rome   142

Chapter 9: The Imperial Republic   156
   1 Rome as a Mediterranean Power   156
   2 The Fall of the Republic   162

PART V: ROME UNDER THE EMPERORS

Chapter 10: The Augustan Age   176
   1 Augustus   176
   2 Architects, Sculptors, Writers   182

Chapter 11: Rome After Augustus   191
   1 The Empire and its Transformation   191
   2 Recovery and Fall   205
   3 The Roman Achievement   216
   4 The Aftermath   221

Appendices   225
   I The Plots of Homer and Hesiod   225
   II The East   228
   III The Principal Greek Shrines   232
   IV Corinth's Neighbours: Megara and Sicyon   235
   V Solon and Cleisthenes of Athens   238
   VI Jews and Christians   241
   VII List of Roman Emperors   244

References   245

Notes   247

Table of Dates: 266
   I The Greeks and Others   266
   II The Romans and Others   287

Bibliography: 300
   I Ancient Writers   300
   II Modern Writers   304

Maps   311

Index   326

Maps

1 Central and Northern Greece
2 The Peloponnese
3 The Aegean and its east coast
4 The Near and Middle East
5 Central Europe and northern Balkans
6 South Italy
7 Central and Northern Italy
8 Western Europe
9 Early Greek colonisation
10 The conquests of Alexander the Great
11 The Hellenistic kingdoms in 185 BC
12 The Roman provinces in 100 BC
13 The Roman Empire in AD 161
14 The Empire of Diocletian, AD 284–305, and his successors
15 The barbarian invasions of the fifth century AD

Acknowledgment

The author and publishers are grateful to Penguin Books Ltd for permission to quote from Kenneth Wellesley's translation of Tacitus, *Histories* (Penguin Classics, 1975).

Introduction

The experience of the Greeks and Romans demands our attention for two reasons. First of all, in itself and in its own right, without any consideration whatever of modern comparisons and echoes. It is overwhelmingly worthwhile to attempt to recreate this phenomenon just as it was, without paying any deliberate attention at all to our own late twentieth-century concerns. The study of such an unparalleled historical process is justified purely and simply on its own account.

Yet, at the same time, this interest does assume an imperative further dimension when it is recalled that we ourselves, whether we like it or not, are the heirs of the Greeks and Romans. In a thousand different ways, they are permanently and indestructibly woven into the fabric of our own existences. This has been occasionally questioned, in recent times, owing to our lately increased knowledge of other ancient civilizations as well. However, in the end, it does not emerge that in the light of them we owe the Greeks and Romans any less. True, it is now clear how much more the Greeks themselves owed to near-eastern civilizations than we had thought, and this will become clear in the chapters that follow. But it is through the Greeks that these near-eastern elements have been filtered through to us, and, once again, the Greco-Roman contribution to our own ways of living and thinking is not diminished by such knowledge. Without that massive contribution we should not be what we are. Its influences crowd in upon us insistently from many sides, having reached us in numerous different times and ways, and at every level of consciousness and profundity. The Greeks and Romans lived through a variety of events and developments – political, social, literary, artistic – which prefigured and prompted what has subsequently happened, what is still happening, and what will happen in the future, to our own lives and our own communities.

Circumstances and backgrounds, of course, have come to differ radically over the centuries. Yet to be able to see no relevant lessons or warnings in this Greco-Roman world would be strangely mistaken. For it is a world that can show us the good and bad things of which humanity has been capable, and may therefore be capable of again. And besides, a knowledge of history will save us (and would have saved many politicians in our own lifetimes) from making appalling mistakes: those who cannot remember the past, it has rightly been said, are condemned to repeat it – and particularly to repeat its mistakes. Or, in other words, without some awareness of this background we are blindfolded in our efforts to grapple with the future. We can only confront the human and intellectual and practical problems that this future will bring if we know something of our roots, and so many of those roots lie in the civilization of the ancient Greeks and Romans. Let those who sometimes try to forget about their existence – for example by excluding them from school curricula – bear in mind that their traditions are behind us, whether we want them or not. If we remain unconscious of those traditions, we are their victims all the same. If we understand them, on the other hand, they free us from the bonds of this historical necessity: they enhance our lives instead of deadening them, for we have become the masters of our past rather than its slaves.

After all, in our own daily lives, we, as individuals, manage to learn from what we ourselves have done or had done to us during the previous years of our existences, and it is only natural that we should try to improve on our own personal earlier performances or experiences. Is it not logical, then, that we should also learn from the experiences and achievements and decisions and errors of those who lived in earlier times as well? And Greece and Rome are uniquely able to help us in this way, since not only were they our spiritual ancestors but theirs are the only past civilizations spread out for our detailed inspection all the way from beginning to end – from the birth of the historical west in c.1000 BC until its convulsion, fifteen hundred years later, which led directly into our own world. All of us who look at the Greeks and Romans will find that it reveals not only many things about those remarkable communities, but also much about the conditions of our own times, and about the men and women who form part of them, and about ourselves.

This book sets out to group the Greeks and Romans together. That is not very often attempted, but I believe that it can be done (however inadequately), and indeed that it is necessary. Certainly, the deeds, aims, characters and temperaments of the two peoples operated on very different lines. Yet Greece and Rome were inextricably intermingled, in a wide variety of ways, as I hope that the pages which lie ahead will make clear. Theirs was a single world, in which the Romans took up the inheritance of the Greeks, and adapted it to their own language

2

and national traditions. Such was the phenomenon that we call classical civilization, a joint product of Greece and Rome, and if that civilization is to be given its full, significant meaning, Greece and Rome have to be considered in conjunction.

I have, in earlier volumes, dealt with each of the periods and themes, which will here be discussed, in separate, illustrated books, *The Rise of the Greeks*, *The Classical Greeks*, *From Alexander to Cleopatra (The Hellenistic Greeks)*, and *History of Rome*. In a sense, therefore, the present book consists of a shortened version of those four studies. But only in a sense, because the process of abbreviation has also involved extensive recasting, as well as consideration of recent writings and points of view. Obviously, some readers will feel that I owe them an apology, because this is a selective, personal presentation and interpretation, which cannot correspond with everyone's ideas. Nevertheless, I have ventured to present my personal interpretation, and here it is.

I have added appendices and notes, at the end of the book, for the benefit of those who wish to pursue some of the subjects further. I offer my warmest thanks to Mr Nick Williams and Mr Malcolm Gerratt, who have edited the volume, and to Mrs Maria Ellis, whose comments have been valuable.

Michael Grant

1990

THE GREEKS

Part I
THE RISE OF THE GREEKS

1

The Early Greeks

1 The Early Greeks and the Near East

In about 2000–1900 BC invaders, speaking a language which later developed into Greek, came into Greece from the north, and ravaged most of the settlements that they found there. Subsequently, and especially after *c*.1600 BC, the country came under the influence of the advanced 'Minoan' civilization, which centred upon Crete – where Minos was the legendary king – but possessed an outpost on another island which lay between itself and the mainland, Thera (Santorini). Then the sparkling fluency of Minoan art was translated into stiffer and more monumental terms by a Greek mainland culture, which is known as 'Mycenaean' after Mycenae in the Argolid (north-eastern Peloponnese), one of a number of impressive, fortified townships of the epoch. The Mycenaeans were not only formidable soldiers but adventurous seamen, who established trading stations throughout the eastern Mediterranean, and farther to the west as well.

Whether Homer (Appendix 1) was right to believe that these 'Achaeans', as he called them, captured Troy in north-western Asia Minor remains uncertain. But at any rate, from the later thirteenth century, this whole Mycenaean civilization collapsed. It was probably riven by internal disunities; and the belief that a new wave of Greek invaders or immigrants, the Dorians, played a major part in the destruction could well be correct.

Yet the epoch that followed was not wholly 'Dark', as excavations at Lefkandi (Euboea) and Salamis (Cyprus) have revealed. And Athens, too, later claimed not only to have held out against the invaders, but to have led a mass emigration to the west coast of Asia Minor. Athens also initiated the widespread Protogeometric pottery (*c*.1025–900), displaying circular patterned designs. And in the subsequent

8

rectilinear, Geometric period (*c.*900–700), the same city took the lead once again.

The establishment of more stable conditions in the tenth century heralded a period of urbanization when villages developed into defensible towns. In 850–750 these urban concentrations became the nuclei of hundreds of independent Greek city-states (*poleis*), none very large and some extremely small. This *polis* concept partly owed its origin to Phoenician and north Syrian models (Appendix II). Thereafter, it became the most characteristic type of Greek political unit. Aristotle maintained that the new Greek city-states were at first governed by kings[1] – claiming to rule and judge by divine right. Yet if so – and often, if not always, this is indeed apparently what happened – most of the monarchies proved, after a time, unable to maintain their autocratic power in the face of competition from their nobles, who finally substituted rule by themselves, as aristocratic ruling groups.

During the eighth century near-eastern influences revived on a massive scale, inspiring a revolution in Greek tastes and affairs. But, as the Greeks themselves appreciated, they never imitated these external models in any exact or slavish fashion, but adapted and altered what they borrowed in order to suit their own requirements and temperaments.[2] Moreover, they did not limit their borrowings to any single region of the near east. Upon the 'orientalizing', widely circulating Corinthian vases, for example, abstract geometric decoration was cast aside in favour of a seething multitude of animals and monsters and other undulating designs which owed a variety of debts to northern Syria, Phoenicia, Assyria, Egypt and other territories as well.

But the eighth-century revolution extended far beyond the borders of art. Iron had been employed in Greece since before 1000 BC, but its metallurgy developed extensively from *c.*750 onwards, markedly increasing the number of people who were able to gain a livelihood in the country. These much more numerous inhabitants switched from pasturage to arable farming, and food production became far more extensive.

Yet, all the same, it did not, seemingly, increase to a sufficient extent, for there appears, as time went on, to have been serious over-population. Such pressures caused a large number of Greeks, from many cities, to move overseas. After the Mycenaean collapse, as we saw, their world had expanded to Asia Minor, and now, during the eighth century – after the preliminary, exploratory establishment of trading-posts (*emporia*) – the number of city-states was doubled by the creation of new settlements over an enormous additional area. The cities that were now created, known to the Greeks as *apoikiai*, 'away homes', and to ourselves, misleadingly, as 'colonies', rapidly became independent of their founding states. Before sailing and settling, their leaders were accustomed to seek the approval of the Delphic oracle (Appendix III). On arrival at their new destinations, they had to contend not only with the native populations of the hinterlands but with rival colonies established by the Phoenician city-states, Tyre (Sur) and Sidon (Saida).

It was by developing the agricultural products of their new territories that the Greek colonists primarily lived. But they also depended on trade. Colonies sent Greece metals – in great demand among its governments and their armies – and dispatched raw materials and foodstuffs as well, importing finished articles in exchange. Goods circulated from non-commercial motives too, in the form of gift-exchanges and sanctuary dedications which were required by the aristocratic way of life. These nobles who ruled the Greek cities could also afford to equip vessels and send them to sea to convey cargoes, at first employing warships and then, from the sixth century, sail-driven merchantmen.

Yet really efficient trading would have required a cooperation between one city-state and another which rarely existed. As Plato later pointed out,[3] the natural state of affairs between them was war – engaged in by almost every state, in order to enable it to seize better resources for itself.

Confronted by this situation, each city had to improve its military power, and the result was the creation of the soldiers known as hoplites. Replacing, for the most part, knightly horsemen, the hoplites were heavily-armed infantry, employing short, straight, iron swords and nine-foot-long thrusting spears. They fought in phalanxes – close, tight masses of soldiers eight lines deep. The age of individual, heroic, Homeric duels had come to an end, and instead there was corporate action on behalf of the state. Hoplites were men of property, who had to pay for their own weapons and armour. Some of them were of noble birth, but many were not, and their existence contributed largely to the eventual broadening of the city-states' governments – with the result that those governments remained wholly aristocratic no longer.

Commerce, of which the nobles by no means possessed a monopoly, exercised a similar effect, and so did the reintroduction of writing, based on adapted versions of the Phoenician or north Syrian alphabet. People were beginning to want to see and read their city's laws (*nomoi*), set out in written form; the days when monarchs and aristocrats had handed down their 'god-given' ordinances (*thesmoi*) were over. A sight of the written laws, whatever their degree of harshness, could not fail to give citizens a clearer, enlarged concept of their own rights, and consequently lead to demands for reform.

The alphabet came just in time to write down the *Iliad* and *Odyssey* ascribed to Homer, which became the principal educative influences upon all Greeks for evermore. The very different epics attributed to Hesiod and Boeotia, the *Theogony* and *Works and Days*, depict what seems to be a less primitive and heroic form of society, but may not be later in date, since different regions differed widely in customs. As for lyrical poetry, the name and some works of Archilochus of Paros have survived. He and others offer powerful and varied (though sometimes literary rather than personally experienced) expressions of feeling. We cannot, however, speak of this more introspective, 'lyrical' age as chronologically following upon an 'epic' age, since earlier non-epic poems, now lost, had already been referred to in the *Iliad* and *Odyssey*.

The Greeks had taken something over from the Minoan and Mycenaean civilizations, but they had taken over a great deal more from the near-eastern cultures which still adjoined their borders (Appendix II). This was true of their art, architecture, literature, philosophy and religion (see next section), and even, as we saw, of the city-state structure which became so characteristic of Greek life. Yet while absorbing what the near east had to offer in all these fields, the Greeks continued to make everything that they took over into something astonishingly different – and original.

This phenomenon prompts meditations about the whole concept of originality. The assertion that it must necessarily imply total 'newness' is a nineteenth-century idea which is by no means universally applicable. To take a literary or artistic product over and adjust, adapt and transmute it into something that has a novel and brilliant existence all of its own is likewise originality of the highest kind. And that is what the early Greeks succeeded in doing.

2 Greece Takes Shape

Religion is never long absent from any of the works of the Greeks, since it pervaded their whole life. They found room for many gods and goddesses, who, despite multiple overlaps, represented different aspects of existence. As for the principal deities, the Olympians, debts to the non-Greek near-eastern past are perceptible in the cults of Hera and Artemis and Demeter, who recall earlier Earth Mothers and Mistresses of Animals. But Zeus, the chief of the gods and lord of the heavens, was a subsequent importation brought in when the Mycenaean world collapsed. And so was the dread, shining Apollo, the most Greek of the gods despite his non-Greek name.

According to Homer these divinities were human beings writ perilously large, with human vices and foibles. In early times, at least, they scarcely embodied ethical ideals, except that Zeus favoured certain basic forms of human decency, such as hospitality and the protection of suppliants. The assumption that the gods resented over-successful mortals does not explicitly precede the fifth century BC. But the Greeks already believed, much earlier, that their deities could be dangerous if they were not acknowledged and placated. This could best be done by sacrifice, and especially by the guilt-dispersing, exultation-producing blood sacrifice of meat, which stressed life by its encounter with death. Great sanctuaries came into existence (Appendix III), and the Panhellenic character of the festivals that developed round them did something to counterbalance the particularism of individual city-states. Yet at the same time, too, by way of contrast, the contests which were the essential elements of these festivals displayed and exemplified the unfettered competitiveness that so firmly kept the states apart.

Alongside the worship of the principal divinities were many other popular, and often regional, cults, venerating local gods and goddesses and local men or women or legendary heroes, particularly at their actual or supposed graves. And there were also ecstatic, underworld rituals, such as the cult of Dionysus (from Thrace) and the secret Mysteries of Demeter at Eleusis. Initiation into such mystical proceedings was believed to guarantee salvation in the afterlife (which had only been a shadowy affair in Homer). The priests might come from designated families, as at Eleusis, but professional priesthoods did not exist. There was no Church – and no orthodoxy developed either. The mythology of the gods and heroes, one of the most extraordinary imaginative creations of the Greeks, was bewilderingly contradictory. The myths sought to expound natural and social phenomena. They recorded folklore. They explained rituals, or were explained by them. They served many a patriotic or class-directed purpose. Or they just told stories. And they were stories which were remembered forever.

In a number of advanced maritime city-states the aristocratic governments were, in due course, overthrown and superseded by 'tyrants' or dictators.

Their pioneer may have been Pheidon, a ruler of Argos (c.675). He, however, belonged to a somewhat special category, since he was a hereditary monarch, who became a dictatorial autocrat. More readily

12

classifiable as tyrant-dictators were intrusive upstarts at Corinth and Sicyon (Appendix IV) and Sicilian and Ionian centres. These were men, of noble or partly noble origin, who supplanted their city's government with the help of dissident aristocrats and hoplites. Such rulers formed ambitious foreign alliances and dynastic marriages, and developed fleets to increase their power and trade, which was also stimulated by the introduction of coinage. The tyrants liked to engage in heavy expenditure upon public buildings and state cults and festivals, which served to diminish the traditions of older ceremonies based on families and clans. To meet the financial demands made by this lavish outlay, the tyrant-dictators imposed harbour-dues and taxes on sales and on agricultural produce. Since these impositions were, inevitably, unpopular, the leaders sought to broaden their appeal by ingratiating themselves not only with their Dorian subjects but also with the non-Dorian elements of the populations under their control.

In the second or third generation of these dictators, however (except throughout disturbed Sicily, and Asia Minor under the suzerainty of the Persians), their régimes crumbled and were replaced by oligarchies – governments by a few, like the earlier aristocracies, but now composed of men notable for wealth rather than birth. The first signs of democracy also began to emerge. Assemblies had existed before, but without much power, whereas now, in certain cities, these collective bodies started to assert themselves more positively, and began to include a wider range of male citizens in their membership.

Sparta was a democracy of a kind, in that its male citizens were all 'equals' (*homoioi*); but they only formed a small part of the total population. It was Athens, rather, that took the lead shortly before 500 BC, when Cleisthenes (building on the reforms of Solon) introduced many features of the city's future democracy. Yet the processes of constitutional change in the Greek cities were complex and disturbed, because in addition to frequent wars between one and another there was also recurrent warfare between factions within the states themselves: between oligarchs and democrats, privileged and unprivileged, rich and poor.

However, vital advances in both architecture and sculpture were also taking place – as early as the seventh century BC. The Greeks derived the conception of monumental stone architecture from Egypt, but as usual subjected what they found to radical changes (partly suggested by Mycenaean models). The first Greek stone temples to be constructed on this substantial scale were at Corinth (in *c.*700 or a little later), utilizing the Doric Order, solid, symmetrical, strong and reposeful.

Next, in and around the coastlands of Asia Minor, came enormous buildings for which the Ionic Order was employed, displaying far greater decorative lavishness: notably the Temple of Artemis at Ephesus.

Sometimes, above the architraves of these shrines, ran a sculptural frieze, and the frontal pediments, too, contained high sculptural reliefs. But statuary in the round, independent of architecture, also evolved rapidly at about the same time. From *c*.675 BC, 'Daedalic' figurines, mainly female and with wig-like hair, were produced throughout Greek lands, under the influence of Phoenician and Syrian terracotta statuettes. This style contributed something to the large-scale figures that followed, shortly before 650, notably upon the Aegean islands of Naxos and Paros, where marble was conveniently available. But the main impulse behind this new, important development, like the influences that created major Greek architecture, probably came from the Egyptians (Appendix II).

The Greek sculptors' principal theme was the masculine nude (*kouros*), depicting Apollo or his servants but also reflecting the dominant role of naked males in Greek daily life. These statues, serving as grave-markers or votive dedications or cult-images, moved gradually towards naturalism, but not too far, because their artists were mainly concerned not so much to reproduce actual reality, but to express an ideal. Feminine figures (*korai*) were also made in some abundance, representing goddesses or their acolytes and intended for sanctuaries. In such statues attention was concentrated not on the female bodies but on the rippling lines and folds of the drapery they wore, displaying an elegance which, in the later sixth century, owed much, at Athens and elsewhere, to the influx of sculptors from Ionia, whose own cities had been, at this time, subjected to the domination of the Persian empire.

Another sixth-century Greek accomplishment was the rapid and diversified evolution of painting on pottery. Corinth had been the pioneer, but it was now Athens which, as in earlier times, took the lead, and distributed its vases far and wide. First came the two-colour black-figure method, increasingly favouring narrative themes, often derived from mythology. Next (*c*.530), an even larger reputation and circulation were enjoyed by the red-figure style, which left the decoration in the ground colour, while the background was painted black.

Moreover, other arts flourished as well. The designing of both gems and coins, for example, was versatile and often excellent. Gems remained a delicate upper-class art, with a limited production. Coins became much more abundant, as cities displayed eagerness to outbid one another in the beauty of the pieces that they issued.

At the same time the Greeks were establishing the bases of rational and scientific thought. The first 'Pre-Socratic' philosopher-scientists came from Miletus. They were Thales, Anaximander and Anaximenes; men who wanted to know what the universe and the world came from and what they were made of.

Xenophanes of Colophon wrote verse in which he criticized Homer's and Hesiod's anthropomorphic pictures of the gods. Pythagoras of Samos was a pioneer mathematician, guru and founder of a religious society, which gained control of the city of Croton in south-eastern Italy. He and other philosophers began to shift the emphasis from the universal macrocosm to the microcosm of the human soul, ascribing the existence and evolution of both alike to a conflict of opposites.

The aim of each of these thinkers was to relate particular instances to general laws. They also put forward, it is true, a number of pragmatic conclusions based on observations – but not very many. For their questions and arguments, for the most part, continued to be directed towards theoretical rather than practical advances.

The same preference for theoretical argument, as opposed to empirical inventiveness, meant that technological advances were, on the whole, sluggish or lacking. Likewise, in the field of business, the instinct for productive investment was scarcely to be found; wealth was, rather, intended for display. Most Greeks did not like making things for profit, and shunned the mechanical occupations that this activity required. There was no idea of 'work for work's sake', or of labour as a saleable market commodity. This meant that unskilled 'free' workers sometimes tended to be objects of pity or contempt.

All the same, until after 500, they were more numerous than slaves. Nevertheless, the number of slaves had been gradually increasing. All previous non-Greek states, throughout the known world, had been slave-owning, in varying degrees; and so were those of the Greeks. True, slaves, upon their economic scene, were never more than a subsidiary factor. Yet their masters would have fared poorly without them. They were the property of their owners, like tools. And it was sensible, therefore, not to treat them too badly, although in mines, for example, their conditions were wretched.

There were also, in the Greek city-states, various intermediate categories of person who were neither citizens nor slaves: resident aliens (*metoikoi*) at Athens, 'dwellers round about' (*perioikoi*) in a number of territories, and people of more or less serf-like character as well – at Sparta they were called Helots.

All these people lacked political participation in Greek city-states. And so did women. Homer's Ionian women, certainly, fulfilled a significant background role – but they were not decision-makers. Sappho's female society on Lesbos enjoyed a brief, impressive and emotional independence, which her poetry illustrates. Yet Semonides of Amorgos was malevolent towards women, and Hesiod's myth of Pandora shows how they were obsessively feared. For they seemed mysterious, dangerous and polluting, as many an Athenian tragic play confirms. Sparta and Crete, indeed, present relatively liberal pictures. But women everywhere lacked control of their own affairs, remaining under the care, legally speaking, of a male, without the right to possess or dispose of property on their own account.

True, some people – notably the historian Herodotus – were well aware of women's role in the establishment and preservation of the social order. Yet religion was their only public sphere. Festivals and rituals concerned with fertility, such as the Athenian Thesmophoria, were their concern, regarded by the authorities as a sort of safety valve, which enabled the female sex to release its otherwise perilous energies.

These restrictive attitudes to women promoted a Greek society that was markedly homosexual. Again, customs differed considerably from state to state, but in most Greek communities the women were kept at home and the men spent their days with other men or boys. Artists, as we saw, paid special attention to the nude masculine form; and pederasty abounded. It was far more favoured than homosexual relations between men and youths of the same age, and indeed a whole philosophy was built up round the pederastic situation, founded on the concept that the lover was his beloved's educator and military trainer. Official attitudes to the physical, homosexual sex-act varied, although, in general, the younger partner was expected to resist or evade such physical advances for as long as possible.

Towards the end of the sixth century, the entire civilization established in the Greek world was menaced – by the Persians who lay to the east.

Their king Cyrus II the Great, after conquering the kingdom of the Lydians (546), had supplanted them as suzerains over the Greek cities on and beside the shores of Asia Minor. Then Darius I crossed into Europe and annexed Thrace (c.513–512), within easy reach of the Greek mainland. Next, the Ionian cities, and others, rebelled against his rule (499–494) – and two Greek states across the Aegean, Athens

16

and Eretria (in Euboea), sent ships to help them. Herodotus correctly saw that this made the Persian Wars inevitable.[4] And so an epoch was at an end.

2

Greece

1 Central Greece

Euboea, the largest Aegean island (after Crete), must be regarded as virtually part of the Greek mainland, since it was only separated from Boeotia and Attica by the narrow Euboean Gulf or Sea, which at one point, in the Euripus channel, was less than a hundred yards wide. The cities of Chalcis and Eretria were situated on the south-west coast of the island, not far apart; and they permanently disputed the possession of the Lelantine plain that lay between them. The waters of the Lelanton river, after which the plain was named, were close to mines yielding both copper and iron. It is here that exceptional discoveries have recently been made, beside the modern village of Lefkandi.

Occupying a wide peninsula with a convenient anchorage, Lefkandi, in *c.*1150 BC, had been a prosperous Mycenaean (Late Bronze Age) settlement. Unusually, the place continued to flourish after the Mycenaean collapse, during the ensuing transitional period (from *c.*1075) which we describe as the 'Dark Age' – not quite accurately, as this site at Lefkandi now shows. For although it was small, its people were among the earliest in Greece to acquire luxury goods from the near east – and especially from northern Syria and Phoenicia.

Excavations at Lefkandi have also revealed the remains of a large, sophisticated apsidal structure, probably of the tenth century BC. The building was subsequently overlaid by two richly equipped tombs. One is the grave of a warrior who, to judge from his splendour, belonged to a house which was, or had been, of royal status. The second tomb proved to contain the cremated remains of a woman wearing expensive ornaments; and the skeletons of horses were found beside her. An adjacent foundry (*c.*900) shows that the near-eastern metalwork imported to Lefkandi, and still arriving in increasing quantities, was also copied locally. But cremation burials ceased abruptly in *c.*865,

18

although life continued at the place, on a diminished scale, until *c*.700.

Meanwhile Eretria had revived, yielding pottery of *c*.875–825, and the remains of a temple of Apollo Daphnephorus (*c*.750), as well as a hero's shrine. From the same period, too, dated the unification and urbanization of Chalcis, which became a major manufacturing city. And these two Euboean centres, Eretria and Chalcis, profited from their strategic location by leading the resumption of the overseas commercial activities suspended at the end of the Mycenaean epoch. A large part in recapturing these contacts was played by at least three ports in northern Syria (Appendix II), which sent gold and silver to Greece, as well as various kinds of artefacts which their Greek recipients employed as models for their own 'orientalizing' art. Moreover, some of these luxury imports were passed on by the Euboeans to their markets (*emporia*) at Pithecusae and Cumae in south-western Italy, where they were traded with the Etruscans, in return for iron. The Chalcidians also established colonies in Sicily. In addition, too, they collaborated with Eretria to fill the three-pronged promontory of Chalcidice on the Macedonian coast with colonies, which enjoyed access to grain and mines and slaves obtainable from their hinterland.

Shortly before 700, however, Chalcis and Eretria came to blows over the ownership of the Lelantine plain. This was the earliest Greek war that can be regarded as historical. The prolonged hostilities, in which each side was supported by a variety of Greek cities (providing them, for example, with cavalry), exhausted both the Euboean combatants. Yet their collapse only proved temporary, since Eretria subsequently built imposing fortifications, and Chalcis resumed its colonization programme and produced a fine silver coinage based on a widespread 'Euboic standard'.

However, as the Athenians, on the mainland, increasingly came to the fore, Chalcis felt alarmed that they were encroaching upon its freedom of action, and joined Sparta in an attack on Athens in 507/506. But the Chalcidians, as well as the Boeotian League which rallied to their coalition, suffered a defeat, and part of their territory was annexed and handed over to 4,000 Athenian colonists (cleruchs). The Eretrians, on the other hand, did not become involved, and allied themselves with Athens in its support for the Ionian revolt against Persia (499–498): which meant that they, like the Athenians, were prime targets for the Persian retribution that was shortly to follow.

The territory dominated by Athens, Attica, is a compact triangular promontory about one thousand square miles in size. It forms the easternmost part of central Greece, bounded by Megara to the west, by Boeotia to the north, by the Aegean Sea to the south-east, by the island of Euboea to the east, and by the Saronic Gulf to the south.

Within Attica itself, four lines of mountains created geographical subdivisions. Only one quarter of the territory's surface was cultivated, and the unusually dense population found, as time went on, that it was obliged to import a substantial amount of grain, although it was better off for wine and oil, since during the hot summers the deep roots of vines and olives could draw on the moisture stored up in the lower soil. Special assets, when they came to be exploited, included the silver of Laurium, the marble of Mount Pentelicus, and the clay of the River Cephisus. Anchorages on the sand beach of Phaleron and within the deep-water inlets of Piraeus and Zea facilitated maritime communications.

The Athenians claimed that they were 'autochthonous' (indigenous), and their city could look back on a Bronze Age existence. The Dorian invaders, as we saw, had failed to capture Athens, and new fortifications were built at that time. Stories were also told of refugees from the invasions flocking within these city walls; and, indeed, the Athenians were evidently of mixed race. It had been they, reputedly, who, in the sixth generation after the Fall of Troy, led the Ionian migration to western Asia and its isles. Moreover, during the same period, at home, Athens may also have retained control over at least the eastern part of Attica itself, and in the years before and after 1100 the region was fairly thickly settled.

Although life remained anxious and precarious, this was the first mainland zone in which iron (probably of eastern origin) was to be seen, as well as the practice of cremation, which became common at Athens in c.1050. Protogeometric pottery (c.1025–900), with its rectilinear patterns, displayed a more meticulous finish than its Sub-Mycenaean predecessors, and was no longer drawn by hand, but executed with compasses and multiple brushes, on a faster wheel. Athens led this development, and during the subsequent Geometric period (c.900–700) it continued to be in the forefront, encouraged, before long, by a widespread external demand for these vases among other Greek city-states.

Near-eastern influences, although weaker than in earlier Mycenaean times, still provided general models, but the disciplined, architectonic command over firmly comprehended principles which these vases displayed is specifically Greek. In due course, diminutive friezes of animals were included in their designs, and then enormous pots were painted with friezes which depicted men and women (the 'Dipylon master', *c.*770–760, was one of their artists), and provided the earliest indications of how the Greeks envisaged the human figure.

The unification, or rather reunification, of Attica seems to have been well advanced by *c.*900. The state which this territory comprised was (for Greece) unusually substantial and stable, effectively coordinating town and countryside, in which the preexistent villages, although now under centralized control, continued to flourish.

The people of Attica were organized in a series of concentric institutions, *oikos* (family), *genos* (clan), *phratria* (brotherhood) and, including all the rest, four tribes. It was the job of the Athenian kings, the Medontids, to hold this complex structure together. As at other Greek centres, however, these monarchs gradually lost their supreme prerogatives to a group of aristocratic leaders. A new official, the polemarch (war-chief), was appointed to share the kings' powers, and then they found themselves under the direction of an archon (later, 'first archon') who controlled civil affairs. Subsequently, one of the kings surrendered his monarchical position altogether to this archon. The latter, and other functionaries, were advised by a council of noblemen (*Eupatridai*), the Areopagus.

An additional body, the Assembly (*Ecclesia*), comprising all citizens, was still shadowy and largely formal. Yet the Athenians, as a whole, grew increasingly reluctant to accept the arbitrary rulings of officials and judges, until in *c.*632, or a little later, a prominent Eupatrid named Cylon – the son-in-law of Theagenes, dictator of Megara – attempted a *coup d'état* at Athens. He was not successful, but in 621–620 a certain Dracon was appointed to codify and publish the city's laws.

Meanwhile Athens had somewhat faded, for the time being, from Greek history. Argos, in the Peloponnese, as well as the island city-state of Aegina, inhibited its seaward development, and the Athenians sent out no colonies – presumably because Attica had seemed large and fertile enough to stave off land hunger. But, if so, things were changing, since the population of the area had increased further, and there was no longer enough grain to go around. The Athenians' solution was to try to control the grain-route from the Black Sea, and with this in mind, at the end of the seventh century, they seized Sigeum at the entry to the Hellespont (Dardanelles).

In order to secure anchorages for this Black Sea route, however, they were also concerned with a problem far nearer at hand. For they coveted the island of Salamis which lay off the coast of Attica itself but belonged to another city-state, Megara (Appendix IV). Evidently efforts to seize the island from the Megarians had not scored any permanent success, since at the turn of the sixth century the Athenian Solon is found urging his discouraged countrymen to launch further efforts to achieve annexation. Belonging to a new breed, a nobleman who may have made himself into a merchant, Solon is the earliest Greek statesman whose own words we are able to read, framed in forceful, oracular poetry.

The agrarian problems of Athens had erupted into a crisis of rivalry between powerful clans. Some of these approached the disaffected poor – who had forfeited their lands because of debts – with sweeping promises; so that other Athenians feared that the clan leaders were bent on revolution, and appealed to Solon to stave it off. He was elected first archon in the later 590s, and used his powers to achieve a bold and subtle solution involving the cancellation of crippling debts, the codification of law, the setting up of property (timocracy) as the framework of the state, and the establishment of a new Council (Boule) of 400 to limit the powers of the old aristocratic Areopagus (Appendix v). Solon, who had first set himself up as the spokesman of the oppressed, caused disappointment by not carrying this attitude to extremes. Nevertheless, his measures moved Athens in the direction of democracy and modernity.

The period that followed the reforms of Solon was an age of artistic ebullience in the city. The long procession of sculptured young men (*kouroi*) culminated in the Moschophorus (Calf-Bearer) of *c*.570–560. The potter Ergotimus and painter Clitias produced large and lavishly decorated ceramical objects, notably the François vase. And soon afterwards the commercial and artistic supersession of Corinth, which the creation of this vase symbolized, was sealed by powerful new developments in Attic black-figure pottery, offering lavish scope to talented artists.

Meanwhile, however, although Solon's law code remained in effect, he lived long enough to discover that his political changes had not achieved equally longstanding effects. For all they had done, instead, was to introduce novel and damaging problems. In particular, the removal of the aristocratic blood criterion had opened the way to a new struggle, in which the rival noble clans competed violently for the help of the middle and lower classes: so that in 590–589 and 586–584 anarchy even prevented the appointment of any archons at all. Three main factions, all guided by nobles, arose in the Assembly.

Amid this rivalry Athenian politics took a turn which had been familiar enough at other Greek cities: that is to say, an autocratic, dictatorial régime ('tyranny') came into being. Its leader was

Pisistratus. Related on his mother's side to Solon, and elected archon in 569–8, he distinguished himself in a war against Megara, assumed leadership of one of his city's factions (the Hill), and twice attempted *coups d'état* without success (561, 555). Finally, however, after establishing a power-base in Macedonia and Thrace, he managed to seize power at Athens (546–527). Backed by a mercenary army, he was also supported by most of the nobility, because he upheld their traditions. Yet he insisted that their internal conflicts among themselves should come to an end: and this restriction of their power remained permanent.

Pisistratus made use of his Thraco-Macedonian connections, supporting a pocket principality of his compatriot Miltiades the elder in the Chersonese (Gallipoli) peninsula, and resuming control of Sigeum, so as to safeguard not only the grain-route but communications with the Macedonian mines of Pangaeum. Nearer home, he finally established Athenian possession of the island of Salamis. But, at the same time, he also cemented closer relations with Aegean islands farther afield, including Delos with its festival of Apollo; and he asserted Athens's claim to be the mother and leader of all Ionian Greeks. In Attica itself, he helped small and medium farmers, by establishing a fund which handed out state loans. Within the city of Athens, too, the destitute element benefited from his attentions, and he encouraged a large-scale expansion of commerce, so that traders (as well as farmers) could henceforward be taxed, as he intended them to be, without suffering undue hardship.

Sculpture, too, flourished under Pisistratus, exemplified by a series of marble maidens (*korai*). He also showed a determination to unify the state through a centralization of religious cults. He founded, or greatly developed, the Panathenaia festival in honour of the city's goddess Athena, as a rival to the four major Panhellenic festivals at other centres (Appendix III). Staged annually, but with special pomp every fourth year, and comprising both athletic and musical contests, the Panathenaic celebrations eventually occupied an eight-day period during the month of July. The second major festival which Pisistratus took over and installed, magnificently, in Athenian cult was the Great or City Dionysia, held in the spring in honour of the god Dionysus – whose worship was active in Attica – and thrown open to all, including slaves and ex-slaves (freedmen).

It was now, too, that the presentation of tragic plays became established as a regular feature of the Great Dionysia. What emerged was a gradually dramatized improvement upon various kinds of entertainments already existing in different parts of Greece; and it was this that developed into Greek tragedy. According to tradition it was a certain Thespis who presented what passed as the first Athenian tragic play in *c*.534, gaining a prize. Earlier choral performances had employed mime and impersonation, and Thespis perhaps added a prologue and set speeches, which were declaimed to the accompaniment of a double flute. A second creator of this tragic drama was Phrynichus, who won his first victory in 511/508 and was remembered for his lyrics and inventive dances, and for the introduction of female characters (acted by men). In these early days, the tragedies may have been staged in a wooden theatre in the Agora (market place). Behind the earthen dancing-floor (*orchestra*), upon which the performances took place, stood a wooden hut or tent, which could also serve as a backcloth for the plays.

Pisistratus had forged the unity of Attica and Athens, amid prolonged peace and widely increased prosperity. And he had tamed the Eupatrid nobility, thus paving the way towards democratic developments. His sons Hippias and Hipparchus, who succeeded him, sent Miltiades the younger to maintain the régime of his uncle and namesake in the Thracian Chersonese (*c*.516). Hipparchus also continued his father's encouragement of the arts, introduced Homeric recitations into the Panathenaic festival, and attracted the poet Simonides of Iulis (Ceos) to his court. It was at about this time, too, that the Athenians inaug-urated their longlived and hugely circulating silver issues which dis-played the head of Athena and an owl. And, meanwhile, the recently introduced red-figure technique of vase-painting perpetuated and enhanced the supremacy that Athens had gained by its earlier black-figure vases. In the red-figure pots that took their place, human and other forms were left in the natural, rich colour of the fine Ceramicus clay, with its content of iron, and the earlier incised designs were replaced by brush-drawing, which made for greater freedom of design and flexibility. The invention of the style is credited to the Andocides painter, who had been a pupil of the black-figure artist Exekias, and the new tradition was carried on by a group known as the 'Pioneers', as well as by many other successors. The artists of these red-figure vases experimented in foreshortening and in reproducing the moment of maximum action.

But the advance of the Persian king Darius I into Europe (*c*.513/512), where he invaded Thrace, crossed the Danube, and threatened Mace-donia, meant that Athens lost Pisistratus's gains in the area, including the Pangaean mines. Faced by economic recession, Hippias and Hip-parchus began to rule more harshly, and in 514 Hipparchus was murdered. Then Cleomenes I of Sparta drove Hippias out, allegedly with the support of the Delphic oracle (510); Cleisthenes, who belonged to the powerful but wayward Athenian clan of the Alcmaeonids and was now in charge at Athens, also backed the *coup*. Shortly afterwards, however, he fell out with Cleomenes, who subsequently, on three occasions, tried to remove him from power – without success. During the second of these attempts (*c*.506), the Athenians defeated Sparta's allies Chalcis and the Boeotian League in separate battles, and confiscated the properties of the landowners of Chalcis, handing them over to 4000 Athenian settlers.

Then Cleisthenes consolidated his power (*c*.506–500), and introduced the most famous constitutional reforms in Greek history. The four antique Attic tribes were superseded by ten deregionalized tribes, containing 140 demes – which replaced the old organization based on aristocratic phratries and clans – and a new Council of 500 was founded on the demes; while the Assembly, too, for the first time was given considerable powers, so that a kind of democracy was brought within the Athenians' reach (Appendix v).

But the external politics of his epoch were overshadowed by the encroaching power of Persia. When Darius I had invaded Thrace in *c*.513/512, he or his advisers may already have had in mind the eventual subjection of all mainland Greece. However, Cleisthenes perhaps found it advisable (though, if so, the idea did not work) to try to enlist Persian assistance against his Greek enemies. Support was needed against Sparta, and against the island city-state of Aegina as well, which had become a successful sea power and was far too close, for comfort, to the Athenians, against whom it waged the 'Heraldless War' (506–before 490).

The Aeginetans did not, in the end, fare well in the war. All the same, however, once the Athenians had displayed enmity to Persia by sending twenty ships to help the Ionian revolt (499–8), it was because of their fear of Aegina that they withdrew their force precipitately from Asia Minor. Yet, despite this withdrawal, the Persians, after stamping out the Ionian rebellion (494), still remembered the earlier hostile intervention of Athens, and were determined to avenge this impudent act: so that the Persian Wars were now imminent. At Athens, Themistocles obtained permission to develop the Piraeus as a fortified port, partly against the Persian threat, but also to keep Aegina at bay.

Attica's neighbour to the north-west was Boeotia, adjoining, on other flanks, the island of Euboea which lay to its east, and the Gulf of Corinth to its south. Thus Euboea formed a strategic passageway between the two chief regions of the mainland, central (with northern)

Greece and the Peloponnese. The core of Boeotian territory comprised relatively fertile plainland, which produced grain and olives and horses and was dominated by Thebes. The Mycenaean (Bronze Age) importance of the territory continued to be mirrored in an array of myths, among which those centred upon Thebes became preeminent, and especially the sagas concerned with Oedipus and his house.

The city's acropolis, the Cadmeia, overlooked the rocky gorges of the Rivers Dirce and Ismenus. The royal Theban palace-fortress of the Mycenaean epoch was sacked, burned and abandoned in *c*.1270 BC. But subsequently the Boeotians, who spoke a Greek dialect of complex affinities, arrived from the north, and Thebes gradually recovered and became a city-state. Yet it did not at first control the whole of Boeotia, since in the eighth century BC there were still a dozen or more other cities in Boeotia which likewise retained their independence.

One of them was Thespiae, the principal centre of the southern part of the territory, near the eastern foot of Mount Helicon.

Among the places controlled by the Thespians was the small town or village of Ascra. It was there that the poet Hesiod was born, his father having emigrated from Cyme in Aeolis (north-western Asia Minor). Hesiod probably composed the *Works and Days* and the *Theogony* in the later eighth century BC (Appendix I). The poems display extensive near-eastern borrowing, and recall better than any other Greek writings the debts that the Greeks owed to that part of the world, before converting what they learnt to their own uses. For the *Works and Days* reproduce old, traditional themes derived from many oriental literatures, whereas in Greek there is no known precedent for such a work. The tales in the *Theogony*, too, show strong connections with various beliefs held in countries farther to the east, notably among the Hurrians and Hittites of Asia Minor and its borderlands (Appendix II).

Both poems tell of forms of Greek society that seem later than those described in Homer's *Iliad* and *Odyssey* (Chapter 3, section I), although, as was pointed out earlier, that does not necessarily mean that Hesiod lived later than Homer. In any case, whether he did so or not, Hesiod was the founder and principal exponent of the second, non-Homeric, epic tradition of the Greeks, which originated not in Ionia but upon the Hellenic mainland. Belonging to an epoch when Greek writing had only lately been created or revived, it appears likely that, while retaining a style characteristic of oral poetry, Hesiod (like Homer) dictated his poems to scribes. His forceful, vivid and, at times, somewhat crude verses reflect a distinctive character, which has been acclaimed as the earliest personality in western literature. He is the first man who speaks to us about himself in his own words.

The rivalry and hostility between the city-states of Boeotia, each seeking to grab the region's agricultural resources for themselves, remained endemic. However, they needed to stand together against Thessaly and Athens, and as early as c.550 the evolution of some sort of political Boeotian confederacy is indicated by a federal coinage.

Within the confederacy, however, Thebes was the dominant power, under a narrowly aristocratic government, in which birth and wealth combined forces. In c.519 war broke out against the Athenians, over the border-city of Plataea. Thebes lost, and lost again when it joined Sparta and Chalcis against Athens in 507–6.

2 The Peloponnese

Within the Peloponnese, the mainly mountainous peninsula of southern Greece – separated from the rest of the mainland by the Isthmus of Corinth – its north-eastern region was the triangular Argolid. The city of Argos was situated near the ruins of the Bronze Age palace-fortresses of Mycenae and Tiryns. Argos itself, too, had been a Bronze Age centre, and shared in the widespread disruption in c.1200 when the Mycenaean civilization collapsed. After the Dorian invasion (c.1075/1050), Argos initially became the centre of Dorian power in the Peloponnese. What remained of its earlier population was subordinated but not enslaved, becoming *perioikoi*, dwellers around.

The early Argives learnt, and adapted, the Protogeometric and Geometric styles of pottery from Athens. They were also skilled in metalwork, owning their own silver refinery from the later tenth century, and specializing in the manufacture of bronze cauldrons ornamented with the heads of griffins. These cauldrons were often dedicated in the Argive Heraeum, an adjacent shrine of Hera to which the city owed much of its renown. Her eighth-century temple, which stood at the top of a series of hillside terraces rising from the plain, was one of the first Greek shrines to assume a peripteral form (i.e. surrounded by columns: of which the bases, at least, were already made of stone). And the temple also had a roof of terracotta tiles instead of the customary timber and thatch.

The creation, or reconstruction, of this sanctuary was probably the work of Argos's outstanding monarch and personage Pheidon. Although sources are legendary and obscure, a date in the early seventh century seems to suit him best. He was described as the first Greek 'tyrant' (dictator), but differed from the upstarts who came after him in a number of cities, since he was, unlike them, a hereditary monarch, who, at a time when monarchies were declining, converted this process to his own ends by seizing the new, dynamic form of absolute power described as tyranny. He completed the reunification of the Argive plain, occupied the island of Aegina, led his city, it appears, in a victorious battle against the Spartans at Hysiae (c.669), and took over the organization of the Olympic Games from Elis. His successes were no doubt due to his pioneer possession of the hoplite (heavy infantry) troops which revolutionized Greek history. The hoplites' double-gripped shield was known as 'Argive' or 'Argolic', and Pheidon may well have created or perfected the phalanx formation in which they learned to fight so successfully. Moreover, these hoplites too, partly of middle-class origin, are likely to have helped him to maintain his authority over the Argive nobles.

The aristocratic or oligarchic government which succeeded to Pheidon, after his death, could not maintain Argive political power against the rise of Corinth, though Argos succeeded in taking charge of the Nemean Games, which achieved Panhellenic status in 573 (Appendix IV). Not long afterwards, however, Sparta took its revenge for Hysiae, by winning the Battle of the Champions at Thyrea (c.546). In this engagement, three hundred chosen Argives fought against three hundred Spartans. Nearly all the combatants, on both sides, were killed, but each of the two contesting cities claimed the victory, so that, in order to decide the issue, a general battle had to follow – which the Argives lost. And they were once again defeated by Sparta at Sepeia in c.494. So their claims to Peloponnesian supremacy came to nothing, and they were never a major power again.

Corinth stood beside the isthmus at the north-eastern extremity of the Peloponnese, dominating its communications with the rest of mainland Greece, and overshadowing nearby Megara and Sicyon (so that many Megarians emigrated as colonists, Appendix IV). On the eastern shore of the isthmus lay the Saronic Gulf, an indentation of the Aegean Sea, and upon the isthmus' west coast was the Gulf of Corinth, leading to the Ionian and Adriatic Seas.

The 'wealthy Corinth' of the *Iliad*5 had perhaps been coastal Korakou, but after the Dorians (organized, as usual, in three tribes) occupied the region in about the eleventh century BC, they established a monarchy – reducing the non-Dorian inhabitants to a serf-like subordination, under the name of 'Wearers of dogskin caps'. then, not long

28

long after 800, Corinth, under the protection of its acropolis Acrocorinth, became urbanized by the amalgamation of eight villages.

Expanding the export of its Geometric pottery, Corinth established colonies on the island of Corcyra (Corfu) off Epirus, and at Syracuse in eastern Sicily. These foundations, carried out with the approval of the Delphic oracle in c.733 (?) BC, were the nuclei of an extensive colonial programme undertaken by the Corinthians, who moreover, once their colonies had been founded, succeeded in retaining unusually intimate relations with them throughout subsequent years.

The sixth Corinthian king bore the name of Bacchis, and five monarchs of his Bacchiad line came after him. These reigns, however, were followed by the establishment of an aristocratic administration (c.747), which based its success upon profitable commerce (entrusted for the most part to resident aliens), supplemented by transit tolls for freight across the isthmus.

Early Corinth also led the way in architecture and art. There is evidence for prototype buildings of eighth-century date, and soon after 700 the Corinthians seem to have invented the Doric architectural order. They also produced ivory, bronze and perhaps stone statuettes – and there was a theory that they invented line-drawing.

This tradition did not go uncontested. But the city produced an unrivalled series of pottery styles, known successively as Protocorinthian and Corinthian, which were initiated in the later eighth century and reached their zenith early in the sixth. The whitish clay of Corinth, burnt pale green or buff, was coated with a lustrous pigment, painted with silhouette designs, and decorated with swirling curvilinear patterns. The numerous motifs, often depicting animals, which these vases displayed were often eclectically adapted from the arts of various near-eastern regions, and typefied the orientalizing movement diffused through Greece by the revival of communications with Syrian ports (Appendix II). Already before 600 the Corinthians were flooding the west with these products, receiving, in exchange, Egyptian terracottas, scarabs and amulets, which they then reexported to the west in exchange for Sicilian wheat and Etruscan metals. And, indeed, their wares pervaded the entire Greek world. It was not until the commercial lead passed to Athens, in c.550, that Corinth's drive to produce and export its own pottery began to flag.

An impetus towards these developments had been given by a family of 'tyrants' (dictators). This north-eastern corner of the Peloponnese specialized in autocrats of such a type (Appendix IV). But the Corinthian dynasty is the earliest known to us, with the exception of Pheidon of Argos (who, as we saw, was in a special category of his own, 'king turned tyrant'). The founder of the Corinthian ruling house, Cypselus (c.658/7–c.628) – taking advantage of his city's disarray after a defeat inflicted by Corcyra off Sybota (c.664) – superseded the local Bacchiad aristocracy (of which he himself was a fringe member), and killed or exiled some of its leaders, confiscating their lands for distribution among his supporters. Moreover Cypselus (or his son) organized the citizens of Corinth in eight territorial tribes, cutting across the hereditary Doric tribal structure. Cypselus also codified his city's laws, to do away with the arbitrary, archaic interpretations prevalent in past aristocratic epochs. Hoplite support may have helped him gain the throne and certainly kept him there; following the example of Pheidon he developed and exploited the middle-class hoplite phalanx. He also planted Corinthian colonies on the Adriatic coast of northern Greece – and this western expansion proved the most lasting legacy that the dictators of Corinth left behind them.

Under Cypselus's son Periander (c.628–586), exports continued to increase, and the city reached the zenith of its prosperity. He laid down a draw-way (diolkos) across the isthmus, in order to enable ships to be hauled from one sea to the other – from the Saronic Gulf to the Gulf of Corinth, and vice versa.

Corinth also invented at least one, and perhaps all three, of the principal successive forms of Greek warship, the penteconter, bireme and trireme. At what dates these inventions took place is uncertain, but they contributed to the power of Cypselus and Periander. The long penteconters moved rapidly, but were hard to manoeuvre. The biremes could achieve even more rapid speeds. The trireme that followed, explicitly described by Thucydides as a Corinthian innovation,[6] added a third to the previous two levels of oarsmen, and each man at the new level worked his individual oar through a laterally projecting outrigger (parexeiresia). Sacrificing weight to mobility, this multi-purpose vessel, although cramped in space and vulnerable to weather, was light, easy to draw up on shore, and well suited for amphibious operations, so that it was able to dominate naval warfare for centuries to come (especially in the hands of the Athenians, when they inherited Corinth's maritime supremacy).

Periander brought Corcyra to order, and founded new colonies at Apollonia (Pojani) in Illyricum and Potidaea in Macedonia (on the way to the grain-producing Black Sea area). He also established a network of political alliances, and attracted cultural leaders to his court, gaining himself a place, according to some accounts, among the Seven

Sages. But he was a violent man, who earned for the term 'tyrant' the sinister significance it has borne ever since.

Some five years after Periander's death the dominance of his family came to an end, succeeded by a long-lasting oligarchy. It was perhaps at this stage that the leading families established the Isthmian Games held in honour of Poseidon beside the god's seventh-century sanctuary at Isthmia (Appendix III).

In c.570, Corinth had inaugurated its famous series of silver coins, known as 'colts' (*poloi*) because of their representations of the winged horse Pegasus (c.570), which were accepted far and wide. Then, in c.560–540 the reconstruction of the city's temple of Apollo confirmed its leadership in the evolution of Doric architecture.

In its foreign policy, the Corinthian oligarchy was cautious, and kept a close eye on the growing Peloponnesian power of the Spartans. And this they were right to do, since, as the sixth century ran its course, Corinth had, in fact, entered upon a gradual decline from its glorious past: the future of the Peloponnese lay with Sparta instead.

Laconia, of which Sparta (Lacedaemon) was the capital, comprised the south-eastern region of the Peloponnese, bounded on the west by Messenia, on the north by Arcadia, and on the south and east by the Aegean Sea. The territory includes two parallel mountain chains running from north to south, Taygetus and Parnon, separated by the fertile Eurotas valley and plain, which contains Sparta.

The prosperous Bronze Age (Mycenaean) town on the site crumbled gradually in about the twelfth century BC. And then, in a time of general disturbance, came the Dorians, settling in four or five villages round what later became the Spartan acropolis. The earliest Laconian Protogeometric pottery (c.1000–950) seems to mark the beginning of more settled conditions, and in the ninth century the villages had united to become the town of Sparta. This lacked the usual features and amenities of a Greek city (as the historian Thucydides observed)[7], but possessed not only valuable agricultural land but iron mines as well.

Despite retrospective propaganda and legend, the peculiar features of the Spartan constitution which gradually developed are identifiable. There were always two kings reigning together, one of the Agiad and the other of the Eurypontid family. There were also annually appointed ephors (overseers), eventually five in number, who enjoyed executive, administrative and judicial authority. The Council of Elders (*Gerousia*) consisted of thirty elected members over sixty years of age. But there was also an Assembly (*Apella*), conducting business prepared by the

31

Council of Elders. All 9,000 Spartiates (free-born Spartans) were members of this Assembly: they were the *homoioi*, Equals or Like Ones. These Equals, each owning his own allotment of land, made Sparta a democracy, the earliest in Greece or in the world – as far as they, the citizens, were concerned. Yet everyone else was excluded, not only women and slaves, as elsewhere, but also two categories of persons living in Laconia who may have been of pre-Dorian origin, the *perioikoi*, dwellers around – who engaged in trade but had to renounce any degree of political independence – and the Helots, who led a serf-like existence like comparable subject populations in other Greek states.

The Equals comprised the bulk of Sparta's hoplite army, organized in five companies (*lochoi*) synonymous with the five tribes (successors of the three archaic Dorian tribes, which were retained for religious purposes only). The Spartans, improving on Argive models, were said to have been the major developers of the phalanx, and their army was by far the best in Greece. Indeed, it was military developments by which the gradual creation of this complex system was stimulated. These developments involved Laconia's western neighbour Messenia, which Sparta subjected in the First and Second Messenian Wars (*c*.740/730–720/710 and *c*.650–620 [?]). After the first of the two wars Sparta had founded one of its very few colonies, at Taras (Taranto) in south-east Italy, perhaps settled by dissidents whom the homeland wanted to get out of the way.

Sparta's successful wars contributed to its reputation for uncultured militarism. Yet its people, from *c*.700 to *c*.550, had not only imported a wide range of luxury products but themselves excelled in bronze, ivory and terracotta work, and made fine and original pottery. Moreover, the city was also the chief centre of Greek choral poetry and music, producing at least two major masters. One was the seventh-century elegist Tyrtaeus (although other cities, too, claimed his birthplace), who wrote marching songs to rally the Spartans in the Second Messenian War, and praised the beginnings of the civic, collective hoplite phalanx. After enumerating a list of desirable personal advantages – royal blood, handsome looks, athletic talent, eloquent speech – Tyrtaeus concluded that courage in the face of the enemy ranks highest of all. Like him, another seventh-century poet, Alcman, played a pioneer part in the creation of the choral lyric. His *Song of Maidens* (*Partheneion*), of which a hundred verses survive – glorifying the religious initiations of young women – was chanted and danced by ten of these girls to a goddess before dawn, at a Spartan festival.

But it was also, probably, the same seventh century, under the pressure of the Messenian Wars (and the secret policing which their results imposed upon the Spartans), that witnessed decisive developments in the *agoge*. This was the complex of communal, totalitarian, socio-military institutions (associated with the name of the perhaps mythical lawgiver Lycurgus) which gave the Spartans their subsequent austere reputation. Examined soon after birth, all Spartan infants, if weak or deformed, were thrown over a cliff and killed. Those who survived, at the age of seven or eight, were removed from their families and drafted into a 'herd', under the control of a senior Spartiate. And for the next two decades they worked their way through a brutalizing series of state-oriented training programmes. During the course of this period, at the age of about twenty, they became eligible for one of the Spartan messes or dining clubs, each of which possessed about fifteen members. Their food was awful, but each member had to pay a mess-bill; and failure to pay – or, for that matter, to endure the severities of the training curriculum – resulted in deprivation of Spartiate status.

When these young men joined the Assembly, at the age of thirty, they had become ruthless, taciturn and unquestioning. Their predominant ethos was homosexual, but they were expected to marry, in order to produce children. Their brides had to undergo a macabre wedding ceremony. Subsequently, however, the barrack-room existence to which their husbands were tied left these women a good deal to themselves. Moreover, their biological role as bearers of Sparta's children did not go unrecognized, so that they enjoyed unusual day-by-day and legal freedom. Yet in other respects, the city's rigorous, archaic, disciplinary system kept it lagging behind the rest of Greece not only in art and literature, which ceased, but also in economic development. For example, money was held to be corrupting, so that primitive spits of iron, mined on the adjacent mountains, were utilized in its place – and trade was carried on by barter.

Yet in the sixth century Sparta became a major power. This was due not only to its citizens' military capacity, but also to the personal efforts of Chilon – later regarded as one of the Seven Sages – who was the most famous of all Spartan ephors, and reshaped that office to rival the dual kingship. It was in his time that his people became dominant in the Peloponnese, turning the tables on the Arcadian city of Tegea (which had defeated them in c.560–550) and proclaiming the liberation of other city-states from dictatorial 'tyrants' – which meant, in practical terms, using them as a counterpoise first to Tegea and then to Argos, defeated in the Battle of the Champions at Thyrea (546).

After these developments Sparta presided, without a rival, over the coalition known as the Peloponnesian League. And then King Cleomenes I (c.519–490) pursued an even more positive policy, seeking to extend Spartan suzerainty beyond the Peloponnese into other parts of Greece as well. However, after expelling Hippias from Athens (510), his efforts to establish a pro-Spartan régime in that city proved unsuccessful. Within the Peloponnese itself, however, his achievement was greater, since he stamped out Argive attempts to achieve a comeback by his victory at Sepeia (c.494).

3

East, North-East and West

1 Ionia, Aeolis and Cyprus

Before the end of the second millennium BC the west coast of Asia Minor and the adjoining islands was settled by migrants from Greece: Ionians in the central sector, Aeolians to their north, and Dorians to their south.

The Ionians, occupying large islands and fertile valleys of the peninsula beside three rivers, had apparently fled from invaders of Greece at various times after *c.*1100. Athens is likely to have played a prominent part in the migration, but not perhaps quite so prominent as its later writers maintained, since early Ionians had lived, too, in various other parts of Greece, and these also provided some of the new arrivals in western Asia Minor.

At all events, by the late eighth century, twelve Ionian city-states had emerged across the Aegean: one each on the islands of Chios and Samos, and ten on the mainland of Asia Minor. These twelve *poleis*, each preserving its original Ionian structure of four tribes, formed a loose religious confederation, the Pan-Ionian League, which sent representatives to gatherings on Mount (Cape) Mycale at the southern extremity of Ionia. But the individual Ionian states remained separate from one another, and independent. Some of them, if not all, were initially ruled by monarchs. But in due course, as in Greece itself, they were superseded by aristocratic republican governments.

Chios, measuring thirty miles by eight (or at certain points fifteen), lay five miles off the principal promontory of mainland Ionia. In *c.*1000 BC the immigrants from Attica and other parts of Greece settled in a plain upon the east coast of Chios, beneath the place where, later on, the island's principal town was established. On that first site and at Emporio, to the south, archaic remains have been excavated.

35

Chios and Smyrna are the most convincing claimants to Homer's birthplace; probably he was born at the latter, and dwelt and worked at the former. A *Hymn to Apollo* calls him a supreme poet who 'lived in rocky Chios' and was blind.[8] Singing was regarded as a suitable occupation for the blind. But the term could also be a metaphorical description of a poet who fastened his gaze on inward things.

The Homeric poems appear to have nearly reached their final form in c.750–700 BC. The *Iliad* describes the fighting during the last year of the Trojan War, whereas the *Odyssey* tells of the prolonged, adventurous return of Odysseus from the war to his native Ithaca (Appendix 1). These two epics amalgamated shorter works by illiterate bards, whose songs, orally transmitted from one generation to another, included recurrent formulas which served as mnemonic landmarks to guide the impromptu singers. But Homer's lifetime seems to have coincided with the reintroduction of writing into the Greek world; so that he was able either to write down his poems himself, or, more probably (like Hesiod, see above, Chapter 2, section 1), to dictate them to others. Yet Homer himself had composed his poetry for reciting or chanting aloud, while he accompanied his words on a simple kind of lyre. These performances may have taken place at noblemen's banquets or at festivals, such as the Pan-Ionian meetings on Mount Mycale.

The language of the *Iliad* and *Odyssey* was a blend of dialects in which Ionic (resembling the Attic-Ionic of Athens) predominates, though other forms also occur. The poems contain some of the most exciting and moving passages ever composed by a poet, in addition to delicate touches of humour. The Homeric verses are notable for their clarity, directness and speed, and can rise to every mood and occasion. The poems were not concerned, however, to reproduce the features of any actual society belonging to any specific date, since they include elements both from the Mycenaean epoch – when, as excavations confirm, Troy was destroyed in c.1250–1200, perhaps by attackers from the Greek mainland – and from the contemporary eighth century (more numerous), and, in addition, from a wide variety of intermediate periods that lie between those two epochs: so that the scenes described in the poems cannot be chronologically pinned down. It has often been argued that the *Iliad* and *Odyssey*, reflecting such different ways of life, must be the work of different poets. But they may well, instead, have been composed by one man, Homer, in which case their background differences are explainable not by multiple authorship, but by the multiple tradition which their single poet had inherited.

These stories, and the heroes Achilles and Odysseus, have proved memorable for ever. Once composed, the *Iliad* and *Odyssey* became, before long, the properties of a guild or clan of reciters, the Homeridae, who in turn formed the models of the rhapsodes, professional reciters of poetry who took their name from their *rhabdos* (baton).

Then, throughout the whole of the subsequent thousand years of ancient history, these two poems, perhaps slightly altered during the sixth century BC – and then, in the third century, divided into twenty-four books each – provided the Greeks with their supreme civilizing influence, and formed the foundation of many of their attitudes, attracting universal admiration as sources of wisdom, and providing models for the heroic yet human dignity and action to which Greeks, at their best, aspired.

Chios was rich in grain, figs, gum-mastic, and widely exported wine, which was also the speciality of its colony Maronea (Maronia) on the coast of Thrace, founded before 650 BC. The Thracian hinterland and other regions provided slaves for the Chians, who created the principal receiving-station for the slave-trade of the eastern Mediterranean region.

For the rights of their free citizens, on the other hand, the people of Chios showed an unusually high degree of respect. Their narrowly aristocratic government, based on a Council of Three Hundred, was replaced by a system which displayed democratic elements comparable to the reforms of Solon of Athens, or even in advance of them. Incorporated into the Persian empire by Cyrus II the Great, Chios joined the Ionian Revolt (499–4). Its defeat, however, led to severe Persian repression.

Samos is another island, mountainous but also fertile, twenty-seven miles long and fourteen wide, less than two miles from Cape Mycale. Ionian immigrants seem to have arrived before 1000 BC. Semonides, reputedly the son-in-law of Homer, wrote a poetic *Archaeology of the Samians*, as well as a more famous, vituperative attack on women.

The position of Samos as the maritime terminal of the only relatively safe all-weather Aegean crossing gave its population profitable access to the commercial land-routes traversing Asia Minor – and enabled them to intercept the maritime trade of their rival Miletus as well. Moreover, in *c*.640–638 a merchant vessel under the command of Colaeus of Samos was driven by storms right across the western waters of the Mediterranean Sea and through the Pillars of Heracles (Straits of Gibraltar), making contact with the rich, non-Greek Tartessians of southern Spain and returning home with a lucrative cargo of metals. Samian colonists were also sent to many strategically placed ports in other distant regions, including Perinthus (Marmaraereğlisi, *c*.602) and Bisanthe (Rhadaestus, Rodosto) in Thrace, and Dicaearchia (Puteoli, Pozzuoli) in south-west Italy.

The temple of Hera, the Heraeum, four miles west of the city of Samos, became famous throughout the Greek world. Built soon after 700, upon a site which had housed a long series of prehistoric cult-centres, it was notable for its unprecedentedly large size, which required the innovation of internal wooden posts; and the building was sur-rounded by wooden columns set on rectangular stone bases. Next, after this original temple had been destroyed by a flood, an even larger Heraeum was constructed in *c*.660, and yet another in *c*.560. These enterprises stimulated the production of excellent Samian sculpture in bronze, marble and ivory; and a poet from the island, Asius, wrote about the colourful gatherings and fashionable clothes at the Heraeum, in these days of the island's outstanding prosperity.[9]

Early on, a junta of aristocratic Samian landlords (*geomoroi*) had superseded the monarchical régime. But in the sixth century their government, as so often happened elsewhere, succumbed to tyrant-dictators. One of them, Polycrates (*c*.540–522), became exceptionally powerful. He recruited local archers, borrowed mercenaries from Naxos, and mobilized a fleet of penteconters and triremes, with which he launched aggressive raids against other states – the first Greek, it was said, to understand the importance of sea-power. In *c*.525 Polycrates annexed the island of Siphnos, taking over its silver-mines. Moreover, in addition, he occupied another island, Rheneia, beside Delos, as part of a scheme to control the Delian festival (Appendix III), thus asserting his leadership of the Ionian Greeks against the claims of the Athenians.

At home, he imported Milesian sheep – in order to improve the local stock – and he encouraged his Samian subjects to become preeminent in scientific and technological progress as well. Thus Eupalinus of Megara, working for Polycrates, designed and carried out, in its final form, a tunnel which conveyed water from a spring to the city's harbour. It appears also to have been at this time that the Heraeum was once again reconstructed, on so enormous a scale – with double external colonnades, and three internal aisles – that the work could never be completed.

Polycrates also found it possible to attract poets to his court. One of them, Anacreon of Teos, was the last important Greek composer and performer of solo song; and at the same time he became a new sort of lyric poet, no longer geographically rooted but an itinerant professional, although for a time he remained as Polycrates's guest. His reputation as poet of love and wine and song caused his verses to continue to be imitated for more than three centuries to come. Ibycus of Rhegium (Reggio di Calabria) was more mannered than Anacreon, but also more immediate and passionate. One of his poems, complimenting a young Polycrates who was probably the ruler's son, seems to have been a metaphorical farewell to his own earlier narrative poetry, which he had previously composed, in favour of the erotic themes that were fashionable, in this new era, at Samos.

For a time, despite vicissitudes, Polycrates was able to hold the balance between the massive Persian and Egyptian powers that threatened to encroach on him. But in c.522 he was treacherously captured by Oroetes, the Persian satrap at Sardis (Sart), and put to death. After two subsequent Samian rulers had likewise come to unhappy ends, the Persians repeopled the island with enfranchised slaves. Nevertheless, it joined the Ionian Revolt. But at the battle of Lade (495) its flotilla deserted the doomed rebels' cause.

Miletus (Yeniköy), the southernmost of the mainland cities of Ionia, was situated at the mouth of the fertile valley of the River Maeander (Menderes), but is now five miles from the sea. After the destruction of the Late Bronze Age (Mycenaean) city's walls in c.1200 BC, the place became the earliest foundation of the Ionian immigrants.

Miletus's ruling nobility exercised decisive influence over Apollo's neighbouring oracular sanctuary at Didyma (Appendix III). Moreover, they bred sheep which provided the finest wool in the Greek world. But the city's territory was of limited dimensions, and the rising mercantile class possessed little share of such acres as there were, so that many people were eager to get away. That was why, and how, they created the outstanding phenomenon in the history of Miletus – the dominant part, with the aid of the city's four natural harbours, that its adventurous seamen and businessmen played in the foundation of Greek colonies in distant lands.

The region upon which the Milesian emigrants concentrated was the Black Sea, together with its exits, the Propontis (Sea of Marmara) and Hellespont (Dardanelles). Their aims were to acquire the limitless grain supplies of the Ukraine, and to catch the tunny-fish moving down into the Mediterranean every year. Miletus's colonies in these areas must have numbered nearly a hundred, so that for a considerable period the Black Sea and its approaches became virtually a preserve of its seamen. They also founded a Fort of the Milesians in Egypt (c.650), and fulfilled a leading rôle in creating the Greek marketing centre of Naucratis in the same country (Appendix II).

The Milesian government, based on a Council known as the Aeinautai ('perpetual sailors'), sought to extract the maximum profit from the city's overseas ventures, although, at the same time, managing to gain a reputation for commercial honesty. Nevertheless, internal political convulsions were frequent, and one such upheaval resulted in the rule of a powerful tyrant-dictator, Thrasybulus (c.600). He successfully resisted onslaughts from the king of inland, non-Greek Lydia (Appendix II), but succumbed to his own city's endemic internal strife, in which the hitherto dominant Aeinautai, known as the Faction of Wealth, were now being challenged by the Faction of the Barefists. The moderate, though still oligarchic, government which emerged from these struggles could not avoid becoming a dependency of Lydia.

Nevertheless, Miletus still contrived to enjoy a somewhat privileged status, which enabled it to avoid a formal alliance with Lydia's last king Croesus (c.560–546 BC), reputedly on the advice of Thales.

This was the man who, although he left no writings, came to be hailed as one of the Seven Sages of antiquity. The earliest of the pre-Socratic philosophers, he was also the first known Greek geometrician, employing his knowledge of Egypt to measure the heights of pyramids from their shadows. But above all he became famous for his cosmology, his theory of the constitution of the universe and the earth. For seeing water pervading everything, he believed that water was what the world had evolved from, and was destined to return to. Arbitrary though this assertion could not fail to be, its insistence on a single unifying principle in the physical world marked a major, fruitful departure from the complex, mythological Greek cosmogonies of the past, and entitles Thales to be regarded as the founder of physical science.

Unlike Thales – who had perhaps been his teacher – Anaximander (c.610–soon after 546) identified the basic material of the universe not as water, but as something of a more indeterminate character, which he called the Boundless or Indefinite (apeiron): an echo, in a sense, of the near-eastern unfathomable deep, yet at the same time the product of pure reasoning – a more logical sort of reasoning than the theories of Thales. Moreover, improving, once again, on Thales's conception of an earth resting upon water, he believed that the world in which we live is freely suspended in space. It is one of numberless worlds comprising the universe, he maintained, and they are all constructed out of contrasting, conflicting opposites such as wet and dry, or hot and cold. Furthermore, Anaximander was also interested in the original evolution of human beings, which he sought to reconstruct by employing personal observation to support his conclusions. His work *About*

Nature (*c.*550) appears to have been the earliest philosophical essay ever to have been written in prose.

Anaximenes (590s–528/5), believed to have been Anaximander's student, preferred to define and interpret his master's 'Boundless' or 'Indefinite' as air – a substance whose capacity for self-transformation can be experimentally seen, so that he felt able to declare all changes to be 'condensation or rarefaction'.[10] And he was said to have envisaged even the human soul (*pneuma*) as forming a part of this same basic material composed of air, thus linking and uniting a man or woman's individual personality with the universe that lies around them in a fashion which attained great significance in the hands of later philosophers.

These three men, Thales, Anaximander and Anaximenes, were still curious rather than truly scientific. Yet their attempt to apply rationally comprehensible criteria to the facts of physical existence has proved one of the Greeks' most imposing claims to remembrance and renown. And then a further new aspect of this broader way of thinking was opened up by another Milesian, Hecataeus (born before 525), whose *Journey Round the World* made him a pioneer geographer, while his *Histories* (or *Genealogy* or *Heroology*) subjected Greek myths and legends to a new critical attention, as a sort of pseudo-history which, despite a good deal of over-credulity on the part of the author, turned out to be the forerunner and prototype of later historical writing, initiating the analysis of human societies on a more systematic basis than had ever been attempted before.

After Cyrus II the Great of Persia had supplanted Lydia as the suzerain of the coastal Greek cities (546), it was Miletus, now in economic difficulties from which it sought to escape, that spearheaded the Ionian Revolt (499–4). The rebellion's disastrous outcome led to the sacking of the city, amid casualties and deportations, an event which caused horror throughout the Greek world – and meant the permanent eclipse of Ionian political power.

Phocaea (Foca), named after *phoke*, a seal – because of the shape of islands nearby – lay at the opposite, northern extremity of coastal Ionia, near the tip of a promontory. But, as at Miletus, the arable soil available to its Ionian settlers proved inadequate for their needs, and, in consequence, their descendants exploited the advantages presented by the town's two harbours, one on either flank of the inhabited area. These harbours attracted the interest of the kings of Lydia in the interior, for whose commerce, by way of the valley of the River Hermus (Gediz), they provided a maritime outlet. But above all Phocaea's

41

harbours also enabled its own Greek inhabitants to rival the Milesians in enterprising seamanship and colonization.

Unlike them, however, the Phocaeans achieved their most extraordinary results in the remote west. They followed up Samos's contacts with the Tartessians of southern Spain, and in *c.*550 a Phocaean, Midacritus, imported a cargo of tin (an essential constituent of bronze) from Cornwall in south-western Britain. Moreover, the Phocaeans created the city of Massalia (Marseille, see section 3 below) in southern Gaul (*c.*600); and a little later Phocaea and Massalia between them colonized Emporion (Emporiae, Ampurias) on the north-east coast of Spain.

Then, in *c.*565, the Phocaeans founded a colony at Alalia (Aleria) in Corsica, near the mines of mainland Etruria (Appendix v); and after the Persians took control in Asia Minor the settlement was reinforced by further Phocaeans, taking refuge from the conqueror. But the naval 'battle of Alalia' in *c.*540–535 against Etruscan Caeretans and Carthaginians, although indecisive, inflicted such heavy losses on the Greeks that many of them set sail for south-western Italy, where they established a new colony at Elea (Velia, Castellamare di Brucia).

Subsequently Phocaea itself – to which some of its refugees had returned – joined the Ionian Revolt against the Persians, and a Phocaean, Dionysius, was in command at the battle of Lade which was the death-knell of the revolt (495).

Surrounded by orchards, the city of Ephesus (Selçuk) stood upon the south bank of the narrow estuary of the River Cayster (Küçük Menderes), which is now a good deal farther to the west. Its monarchs gave way, in due course, to the aristocratic regime of the Basilidae. The citizens whom they ruled were at first grouped into the usual four Ionian tribes, but these were later supplemented by two others, incorporating Greek settlers of various origins whose ancestors had arrived later than the original Ionian colonists.

Three-quarters of a mile east of the city of Ephesus, upon a mountain slope, stood the world-famous temple of Artemis, the Artemisium. This shrine developed from an altar of early seventh-century date, but also bore witness to pre-Greek origins through the curious, archaizing figure of the goddess, studded with twenty-four egg-shaped protuberances (later interpreted, probably wrongly, as breasts). When, in *c.*600, the Basilidae were superseded by a tyrant-dictator, Pythagoras, the temple was reconstructed, and then, in *c.*560–550, work began (and continued for many decades) on yet another Artemisium, a huge, long, narrow building believed to be the first monumental edifice ever made almost entirely of marble. The new Artemisium equalled or excelled the Samian Heraeum as the largest of all Greek buildings, and ranked as one of the Seven Wonders of the World. Its interior displayed a forest of colonnades, and the exterior was apparently surrounded by a double row of slender, fluted, Ionic columns, supplemented by a third row across the front of the temple.

Ephesus formed increasingly close ties with the Lydian kingdom, and when this had been overthrown by the Persians their king, Darius I (521–486), laid down a Royal Road from his homeland to the city, enabling its merchants, under the rule of Persian protégés, to receive consignments of eastern products, especially slaves, for transmission to other parts of the Greek world.

During this period, too, Ephesus produced a satirical poet, Hipponax, and a critical, lonely philosopher, Heraclitus. Seizing upon a suggestion by Anaximander of Miletus, Heraclitus saw the transformations of the universe as a ceaseless series of changes and exchanges, conflicts and tentions, between opposites; and he was credited, in consequence, with the saying *panta rhei*, all things are in a state of flux: 'You cannot step into the same river twice.'[11] Nevertheless, Heraclitus also conceded, in the universe, the existence of an over-riding unity, in which opposites coalesce into a single, regular, cohesive order. He describes this transcendental, controlling unity as the Word (*Logos*) – call it Zeus if you like, he says – which takes the form of an eternal, elemental Fire or, in psychological terms, of Reason: for Heraclitus (like Anaximenes) believed the individual soul to consist of the same material as the macrocosm of the universe. We must make an enormous effort, he stresses, if we are to understand this all-enveloping order, and the part that we play in its unfolding. He was a thoroughly original thinker, but the abrupt, peremptory, paradoxical nature of his surviving sayings explains why he was known as the Obscure (*skoteinos*).

Ephesus, reluctantly, joined the Ionian Revolt against the Persians, with whom, however, it ingratiated itself after the disastrous battle of Lade (495), by capturing the survivors of crews from its fellow-rebel Chios and slaughtering them all.

North of Ionia was Aeolis, settled gradually from *c.*1300 to *c.*1000 BC by immigrants from Boeotia and Thessaly, who belonged to the Aeolian linguistic and ethnological branch of the Greek race. They came to Lesbos, the largest island off western Asia Minor, and spread slowly over the coastal mainland, founding a number of cities there, of which eleven in the southern sector formed a religious league.

On Lesbos itself, where the soil was fertile and climate favourable, five more city-states were founded, ruled by hereditary princely families which reproduced, on a smaller scale, the grandeur of earlier Mycenaean (Bronze Age) times. The strongest of these centres was Mytilene, which enjoyed the possession of two harbours, one of which dominated the in-shore sea route from north to south. Local monarchs of the Penthilid clan were succeeded by an aristocratic government composed of the same clan's members, after which a tyranny or dictatorship emerged in the late seventh century under Melanchrus, who fought the Athenians for the possession of Sigeum. Then, in *c*.590, Pittacus obtained a ten-year 'elective tyranny' in which he defined his supreme position by the term *aesymnetes* (arbitrator or umpire).

The lyric poet Alcaeus, an extrovert of unrelenting animosity, reviled Pittacus, and was exiled. Much of his work had been recited at the feasting-clubs (*hetaireiai*) which played such an important part in Greek aristocratic life. He composed hymns, and poems about the Trojan War, and possessed a keen eye for beauty, employing a variety of lyric metres to communicate his feelings. Sappho, almost his contemporary, was likewise born on Lesbos, perhaps at the town of Eresus, but after a period devoted to travel made her residence at Mytilene. She wrote love songs, accompanied by the lyre, of which the surviving fragments, and the completely extant *Prayer to Aphrodite*, display an intimate talent for the communications of scorching emotions – even if, as seems probable, they are not necessarily autobiographical, but the expression of literary, poetic reactions and standpoints. Her verses breathe a delicate, incantatory sensuousness, which must have accurately reflected the lives and loves of her small, self-regarding and (for Greece) unusually liberated group of unmarried women. The modern term 'Lesbian' is derived from her intense feelings for her own sex, although she got married, and composed choral wedding songs for other couples.

After the peaceful reign of Pittacus, the Mytilenaeans were defeated, first by Pisistratus of Athens – who finally dislodged them from Sigeum – and then again by Polycrates of Samos. The Persians installed a puppet tyrant-dictator, Coes, who was stoned to death, however, at the outset of the Ionian Revolt (499).

Cyprus, the largest island in the eastern Mediterranean, formed an important point of communication from one part of the near-eastern and Aegean region to another. Upon its surface, between mountain ranges, the central plain of Mesaoria provided timber for shipbuilding and for the smelting of copper ores from local mines.

During the Late Bronze (Mycenaean) Age, groups of migrants had come from the Greek mainland and settled on Cyprus: which subsequently, too – even after the fall of Mycenae – remained notable (like Euboea, and to some extent Crete) for its continuity with the standards of the past Mycenaean world, thus belying, for this region at least, the term 'Dark Age', which is so often applied to the period. In due course, however, the island underwent strong Syrian influence (c.1000) and subsequent Phoenician penetration (c.800).

Salamis, founded in c.1075 as the successor of Mycenaean Enkomi, became the leading city of Cyprus, situated beside its east coast, five miles to the north of the modern Famagusta. Its acropolis overlooked a sandy bay providing a natural harbour (now silted up) at the mouth of the River Pediaeus (Pidias). The earliest political life of the post-Mycenaean town centred round the local kings and their aristocratic followers. Its relations with the near east, as well as connections with Greek centres, especially the cities of Euboea, are attested by various finds and influences. Metallurgy, which had already been prominent at Salamis in earlier times, now flourished more than ever before, and it may have been from here that Greek knowledge of ironwork originated. The city established itself very quickly on a stable and prosperous basis; and its 'royal' tombs, reflecting not only local craftsmanship but also many external influences, date from the eighth and seventh centuries. One of their features, already encountered at Euboean Lefkandi, was the sacrifice of pairs of yoked horses (with or without their chariots) in honour of the dead – recalling the funeral of Patroclus in the *Iliad*.[12] Indeed, the analogies to the Homeric poems in the tombs of Salamis are multiple and numerous.

Remains of the early habitation centre of the city, on the other hand, have scarcely come to light. A place bearing the name of Sillua or Sillume, mentioned among tributaries of the Assyrian king Esarhaddon (c.672, Appendix II), seems to be identifiable with Salamis. Later, a king of the place, Euelthon (c.560–525), claimed to be the independent ruler of the entire island. But in 545 he came under Persian control.

The second city of Cyprus was Paphos, which had the most famous temple of Aphrodite (Cypris) in the Greek world, inherited from the Mycenaean Great Goddess.

2 The North-East

North of the continental homeland of Greece lay the partially Hellenized kingdom of Macedonia – of which more will be heard later (Chapter 5, section 1).

Its coastland early became a target for colonization by the Greek city-states. One of their objects was the acquisition of agricultural land, and another was the desire to gain possession of Macedonian animal products and timber. Here, as elsewhere, the lead was taken by the cities of Euboea. Before 700 BC Eretrians, from that island, came to found Methone on Macedonia's Thermaic Gulf, and the three-pronged peninsula further to the east carries the name of Chalcidice, bearing witness to the colonizing activities of another Euboean city, Chalcis. But the foremost Greek colony of the northern Aegean was to be the offshore island of Thasos, settled by men from Paros (c.650?), and conveniently placed to exploit the gold and silver mines of Mount Pangaeum in mainland Thrace. In that country, on its mainland, stood further Greek colonies, notably Abdera, founded by the people of Teos (Sığacık) in Ionia.

All eyes were turned, however, towards the fertile Black Sea region and its threefold succession of approaches, consisting of the Hellespont (Dardanelles) strait, the Propontis (Sea of Marmara), and the Thracian Bosphorus. The waters of the Hellespont seethed with currents and gales, and Greek ships often liked to disembark their cargoes just before the strait began (on the southern [Asian], more welcoming, coast), to be carried overland to a re-embarkation point farther on. Colonies at Abydus (Nağara point), Lampsacus (Lapseki) and Sigeum, planted by Miletus, Phocaea and Athens respectively (c.680–652, c.654 and c.600–590), bear witness to this intention. But the northern (European) bank of the strait, too, despite its greater hazards, attracted settlers, and in c.555 Miltiades the elder occupied the whole of the Thracian Chersonese (Gallipoli peninsula), with the support of his fellow-Athenian Pisistratus. Then in c.520 the younger Miltiades took over, and married the daughter of a local Thracian king. He accompanied the Persian monarch Darius I on his expedition into Thrace (and then Scythia, c.513–512), but later took part in the Ionian Revolt against the Persians (499–4), and subsequently returned to Athens to command its army against the Persian invaders at Marathon.

Cyzicus (Belkis) was a Milesian colony beside the Propontis, dating from c.679, a few years after the Megarians had established a settlement at Calchedon (Kadıköy) farther to the east, upon the Asian shore of the strategic Thracian Bosphorus (c.685). Some seventeen (or twenty-eight) years later the Milesians founded Byzantium (Istanbul) on the other, European, bank of the Bosphorus. An easily defensible site, served by the elongated, silt-free natural harbour of the fish-filled Golden Horn, Byzantium became a halting point for ships before or after they tackled the hazardous waters of the Bosphorus, which led to the Black

Sea and the natural wealth of its hinterland. The reigning tyrant of Byzantium (like his colleague at Cyzicus) refused to defect from Darius I while the latter was returning from his expedition into Europe (c.512), but during the subsequent Ionian Revolt many Byzantines fled, with people from Calchedon, to their joint Black Sea colony Mesambria (Nessebur).

Nevertheless, the many advantages of Byzantium ensured its future, and a millennium later, as the bridge between Europe and Asia, it was destined to become, under the name of Constantinople, the greatest city in the western world.

The Greeks called the Black Sea 'Euxine' – friendly to travellers, which it was not; or perhaps the term was a corruption of a non-Greek word meaning 'dark' or 'north'.

In mythology, the sea was famous for the story of the Argonauts from Thessaly. But then, in historical times, the Milesians made it virtually a private lake of their own. On its south coast, they and others established a marketing post (*emporion*) at Sinope (Sinop) in c.756, which they converted into a colony in c.631. Trapezus (Trabzon), too, was perhaps another eighth-century *emporion*, and the Milesians and Phocaeans together settled at Amisus (Samsun) in c.564.

Long before that, however, in c.657 BC, the Milesians had sailed far up the west coast of the same Black Sea, establishing a colony at Istrus (Histria) in what is now the Rumanian Dobrogea, just south of the delta of the River Ister (Danube), which gave the place its name. The Istrians established a row of their own market-harbours along the coast, and traded with eastern Greek centres, as well as with the surrounding non-Greek population – so that their wares reached far into continental Europe. These exports included gold and silver, to which they had access from mountains across the Danube.

Only a decade after their foundation of Istrus, another group of Milesians, joined by people from other cities, moved further north to establish the colony of Olbia (Olvia, near Parutino), upon the Black Sea coast of what is now the Soviet Republic of the Ukraine. The selected site was on the right (west) bank of the River Hypanis (Bug), near the entrance of its large estuary gulf (*liman*), twenty-three miles west of another river, the Borysthenes (Danapris, Dnieper) which gave the colony its earliest name before it assumed the designation of Olbia. Thus the new foundation was excellently placed to control the traffic on the massive waterways which dominate Ukrainian life.

Olbia, of which the original population of about 6,000 seems to have doubled before long, comprised an upper town, of which the public buildings date from $c.550–500$, and a lower town, which now lies partly under water. The colony's goldwork was mainly intended for sale to the Scythian peoples of the hinterland, with whom Olbia maintained a close relationship as commercial partner and perhaps, to some extent, dependent. Conversely, however, the city was at the same time at pains to emphasize its Greekness, and in this capacity it became the ruler or suzerain of a number of other Greek Black Sea settlements or marketing centres which helped it to trade with other parts of the Greek world.

The Olbians were also in direct control of a substantial territory of their own, some forty miles wide and thirty miles deep. The name of the city means happiness or prosperity. For fish swarmed in the great river-mouths, and Olbia played a major, lucrative part in the transmission to other Greek lands of grain obtained from the fertile 'Black Earth' of the hinterland. Moreover, cattle, honey, wax, furs, timbers and slaves were exported by the Olbians as well. In exchange, the Greek ships calling at the port brought and unloaded wine and oil. Light is thrown on the region's business life by a letter of $c.500$, found in a crack of a wall at Berezan, an important peninsular site in Olbian territory. The letter outlines a complicated dispute, which illustrates the lives of a professional class of businessmen at the place.[13]

Before 500, however, Olbia was sacked by Scythian raiders. It recovered some of its importance later on. But the leadership of Hellenism in the northern Black Sea area passed to Panticapaeum (Kerch) on the Cimmerian Bosphorus (Strait of Kerch), which had been founded by Miletus in $c.600$ and, early in the fifth century, became the capital of the long-lived Bosphoran kingdom.

3 The West

The most adventurous and far-reaching series of enterprises undertaken by the Greeks was their early expansion into south Italy ('Great Greece') and Sicily. Within a brief space of time colonies were founded not only in Campania and the Gulf of Taras (Taranto) but also upon the Sicilian Strait (Strait of Messina) and in eastern Sicily. These were regions offering the Greeks a familiar environment into which they could import their way of life more or less unchanged, but with better material opportunities, very often, than they could have enjoyed in their own homeland.

The volcanic soil of Campania, the territory upon which their attention initially fell, was particularly productive. But it was for trading purposes that the Greeks established their earliest footholds in the area. The first of these outposts was on Pithecusae (Aenaria, Ischia), a fertile island seven miles from the Campanian mainland, offshore from the north tip of the Gulf of Cumae (Bay of Naples). After Late Bronze Age occupation of the promontory of Monte Vico, at the north-western end of the island (with sheltered harbours on either side, c.1400), a Greek trading-station was established nearby. The traders came from Chalcis and Eretria in Euboea, and their purpose was to make contact with the cities of Etruria, of which the metals, especially iron and copper, were coveted by the Greeks. And the Etruscans wanted, in return, the gold which the Euboeans brought from their other *emporia* in northern Syria (Appendices VI, II).

In about 500 BC Pithecusae was devastated by a volcanic eruption of its Monte Montagnone. Long before that disaster, however, the Pithecusan market had already lost much of its importance, owing to the Euboeans' establishment of a second *emporion* at Cumae (Cyme) on the adjoining mainland (c.750). Guarded by an acropolis which looked down upon a protected harbour, this trading-station at Cumae soon assumed the status of an independent colony and city-state (c.730–725). It possessed not only profitable fisheries but its own agricultural hinterland, and introduced Italy to the cultivation of the vine and olive – as well as transmitting the Greek alphabet to the city-states of the Etruscans, who adapted it to their own tongue.

Cumae soon became a political power, eager to assert control over the strategic Sicilian Strait, where it settled Zancle (Messana, Messina) almost immediately – and later colonies, nearer home, were Dicaearchia (Puteoli, Pozzuoli, c.621) and Neapolis (Naples, c.600). Cumae became famous for the oracle of its Sibyl, and produced an early historical personage in its tyrant-dictator Aristodemus the Effeminate, who found himself at war with the previously friendly Etruscans, whose attack he rebuffed (c.525–4) – repeating the victory some twenty years later.

Another area of Greek colonization was the southernmost tip, or toe, of Italy, known in ancient times as Brettioi (Bruttii) and now as Calabria.

Shortly after the Chalcidians had founded Rhegium (Reggio di Calabria, c.730–720), the Achaeans of the northern Peloponnese settled Sybaris (Sibari) upon the 'instep' of the peninsula (the Gulf of Taras). Sybaris occupied an extensive site which bordered the sea-coast between the Rivers Sybaris and Crathis. Soon after their arrival, by agreement with the local tribe of the Serdaioi, the Sybarites expanded their territory across the neighbouring alluvial plain. They derived wealth from their livestock, including sheep productive of wool that was coveted by many Greeks elsewhere.

Sybaris ruled over four ethnic groups and twenty-five dependent towns. It also supported a new foundation by the Achaeans (of the northern Peloponnese) at Metapontum, upon the gulf to the north, and sent its own colonists across to settlements on the opposite, western (Tyrrhenian) shore of south Italy, including Posidonia (Paestum, c.625–600). The Sybarites also looked east, providing a market and transit-point for the textiles of Miletus, which Sybaris passed on to the Etruscans.

In the early sixth century the place was perhaps larger, wealthier, more addicted to luxury (for which it had become famous), and better administered, than any other Greek city-state. But recurrent hostilities poisoned its relations with its southern neighbour Croton (Crotone), which finally brought the independence of Sybaris to an end (510), though without, archaeology suggests, the total dramatic obliteration that was recorded. Prolonged searches were necessary, in recent times, to locate the ancient city, buried in river-borne mud, and its excavation still remains a task for the future.

Croton, too, had been created by Achaeans, in c.710 BC, upon a promontory flanked by harbours on either side of the River Aesarus (Esaro); and before long this city, too, established colonies on its own account, both beside its borderland, and across the foot of the peninsula.

The most famous man ever to have lived at Croton was Pythagoras, who moved to south Italy from Samos in c.531. He left nothing in writing, but his doctrines, as far as we can reconstruct them, seem to have formed a mixture of religion or superstition, charismatic community guidance, natural science, and mathematical and musical theory. Pythagoras believed that only a numerate, numerical explanation could explain the universe: nature could best be interpreted, that is to say, in terms of measurable and countable numbers. Mathematical science was not new – Pythagoras may have known of Babylonian contributions – but it was he who elevated the subject to universal status.

What inspired these advances was his discovery of the ratios determining the principal intervals of the musical scale. This attitude prompted him to widen his enquiries and interpret the entire universe in relation to similar mathematical ratios. Moreover, like earlier Ionian thinkers, he saw the individual human soul in the same light: as corresponding directly with the orderly construction of the universe. By stressing this link, he helped to teach other, later, thinkers to look at souls as things of real, ethical importance – an attitude destined for a huge philosophical future.

And yet at the same time, in a manner which seems more eccentric, he envisaged the soul as a fallen, polluted divinity imprisoned within the body, as in a tomb, and destined to a cycle of reincarnations (*metempsychosis*). From this cycle, however, it can gain release by ritual purging, accomplished by abstinence and training and study, which he associated with the worship of Apollo. The soul, he believed, is indestructible, but temporarily detachable from the body; a theory of 'bilocation' derived from shamanistic faiths (named after the legendary Orpheus) current in Scythia and Thrace. Here Pythagoras was moving away from science into different spheres altogether; and in doing so he gained a reputation as occultist and miracle-worker, wearing melodramatic clothes and laying down primitive taboos. Incidentally, too, he interpreted the Ionian doctrine of opposites as a way of regarding women as antitheses of men and thus keeping them down (although this did not prevent many of them from becoming his followers).

This Pythagorean design for living amounted to a new religion; and it was practised at Croton by an ascetic society or brotherhood. Three hundred of its youthful, dedicated adherents conspired, successfully, to take over the government of the city, apparently under the direction of Pythagoras himself. In his old age, however, a hostile movement compelled him to withdraw to Metapontum, where he died.

Nevertheless, even after he had gone, Croton continued to remember him, and continued also to rise to a position of power in southern Italy. The Crotoniates experienced setbacks, but in *c*.510, as we have seen, they overwhelmed Sybaris. Extending a network of dominant secret Pythagorean societies far and wide, they preserved for their city a holy aura, derived from dedication to lofty minds and healthy bodies. In relation to the latter, it was probably shortly after 500 that an eminent physician, Alcmaeon, worked at Croton, where he had been born – and his activities displayed a close attachment to the thought of Pythagoras. Nevertheless, the local Pythagorean junta, which had hitherto retained control of the city, finally succumbed to its enemies, and Sybaris fell a prey to internal conflicts, conducted with a ferocity that even exceeded the savage behaviour to which Greek city-states were accustomed.

Sicily, separated from the Italian mainland by the narrow Sicilian Strait (Strait of Messina), is the largest Mediterranean island, measuring over 160 miles across and nearly 100 miles (in its eastern region) from north to south. While other peoples inhabited the interior, many coastal regions were occupied by the Phoenicians and Greeks from the eighth century onwards. The historian Thucydides believed that the Pho-enicians arrived first,[14] but this is uncertain. At any rate, they were ultimately based upon three cities in the west of the island.

As for the Greeks, their earliest colony in Sicily was said to have been Naxos (Giardini Naxos, c.734), on the east coast, settled by the Chalcidians. A year later Syracuse (Siracusa) was founded by migrants from Corinth (like Corcyra [Corfu] at about the same time). Within the next three decades Syracuse had spread from its original settlement, the islet of Ortygia, onto the main island of Sicily itself. Before long, the Syracusans gained control of a section of Sicilian territory, reducing many of its inhabitants to the status of serfs, known as Kyllyrioi. The Doric temple of Apollo on Ortygia may have been the largest ever to have been erected, up to that date (c.575?), anywhere in the Greek world (except possibly the shrine of Artemis at Corcyra).

By the end of the century Syracuse, under its aristocratic ruling class the *gamoroi*, 'dividers of the land', who formed a Council of 600, had succeeded Sybaris as the most imposing of western Greek cities, and perhaps of all Greek centres anywhere else as well. Its prosperity was demonstrated by a long-lived silver coinage. In the same period, too, the city seems to have produced the witty and versatile comic poet and dramatist Epicharmus (although Cos also claimed his birthplace). In c.492, however, Syracuse suffered a military reverse at the hands of Hippocrates, the tyrant-dictator of Gela, whereupon the discredited ruling aristocracy of the defeated city succumbed to a democratic revolution – an event characteristic of Syracusan history, which was cursed by an exceptional series of internal struggles.

Between 730 and 720 Chalcis, which had founded Sicilian Naxos in 734, was joined by other Euboean cities in the establishment of a colony on the Sicilian Strait, bearing the name Zancle (from *zanklon*, a sickel, because of an adjacent curved spit or sandbar), and later known as Messana (now Messina). Subsequently Zancle, in its turn, sent colonists to Himera (Imera, c.648), the westernmost Greek settlement in northern Sicily, opening up contacts with the non-Greek interior of the island. Not long afterwards the south Italian poet Stesichorus went to live at Himera. An outstanding figure in the formative period of lyric verse, it was he who put the western Greeks on the cultural map, so that they could claim to be leading participants in Hellenic civilization. He followed the Epic Cycle of Thebes (based on the vicissitudes of Oedipus and his children), and wrote about the Argonauts, and composed sequels to the *Iliad* and *Odyssey*. Another of his works was a poem named *Helen*. In this he followed the usual story, recounting how, willingly, she was seduced by Paris and taken to Troy. But in his *Palinode* he went back on that version, declaring that Helen had never travelled to Troy at all, but that it was only her phantom who had gone there. This revised tale reflected the masculine view that so great a war could not have been fought about a woman. Moreover, Stesichorus may also have wanted to cease offending Spartans and others who worshipped Helen as a goddess.

A later resident of Zancle itself was the poetic philosopher Xenophanes (c.570–475?), although he had been born elsewhere, at Colophon (Değirmendere) in Ionia, and had spent much of his life wandering about from place to place. But he settled at Zancle and Catana (Catania) in Sicily, and became the poet of the Ionian intellectual enlightenment in the west. Xenophanes was a man who, although reciting his works at noblemen's clubs (hetaireiai), nevertheless denounced accepted standards of aristocratic, militaristic behaviour. But his principal achievement was a demolition of the anthropomorphic pictures of the gods presented by Homer and Hesiod. In contrast, Xenophanes envisaged the divine power in a spiritual sense, endowing it with an eternal, superhuman consciousness and intelligence pervading and regulating all that is and all that happens.

All the same, however, Xenophanes did not forget the more practical interest in natural phenomena displayed by earlier Ionian thinkers, and displayed an unusual gift for scientific observation, noting, for example, the discovery of sea-creatures' fossilized shells in rocks, and deducing from this that the land had once been covered by the sea. Furthermore, while stressing the distinction between what one has actually seen and what one can only infer, he also delivered a warning about the inevitable defectiveness of human knowledge. Yet this defectiveness, he went on to say, could be remedied to a considerable extent, provided that one dedicated oneself to arduous, well-thought-out, first-hand investigation.

At other Greek cities of Sicily, Acragas (Agrigento) and Selinus (Selinunte) – which was the western frontier-town of the Greeks in the south of the island, like Himera in the north – spectacular temples survive, as also at Elymian Segesta.

Massalia (Massilia, Marseille) was a port upon the southern, Mediterranean coast of Gaul, in the Gallic Gulf (Golfe du Lion). After earlier commercial explorations the Greek colony at Massalia was settled by men from Phocaea in c.600, whose leader, it was said, married the daughter of the king of the neighbouring tribe. The colonists settled a rocky spur comprising three low hills near the sea, protected by a landward marsh and flanked by streams.

The Massalian constitution (which later Romans greatly admired) was at first a narrowly aristocratic system, which later, as elsewhere in the Greek world, evolved into an oligarchic régime, based on wealth. It was directed by a Council of Six Hundred, which elected, from its own ranks, a steering committee of fifteen, presided over by three chairmen. The Council was assiduous in maintaining its links with older Greek lands, adopting Apollo and Artemis as Massalia's patron deities in order to ensure contact with their respective Delphic and Ephesian sanctuaries; and Massalia maintained its own Treasury at Delphi.

Upon their small plain, the Massalians grew vines and olives, of which the knowledge thus spread, along the thoroughfare beside the adjacent River Rhodanus (Rhône), up to the rest of Gaul (just as Pithecusae and Cumae had introduced similar cultivation to Italy). And Massalian salt, too, and luxury goods that had reached the city from Greece, fanned out throughout Gaul in the same way, exchanged for grain and amber and tin and slaves. As Strabo pointed out, however,[15] the location of the colony at Massalia was primarily motivated not by this landward Gallic trade, but by the facilities offered by its spacious and well-protected harbour Lacydon (Vieux Port) for commercial enterprises overseas. And so in due course Massalia established colonies of its own not only at other coastal centres of Gaul but also along the Mediterranean shores of north-eastern Spain.

In addition, the Massalians cooperated in a Phocaean colony at Alalia in Corsica; but the partial evacuation of that settlement after a sea-battle (c.540–530[?]) weakened the influence they had gained on the island. This withdrawal was brought about by an alliance between Carthage – which rivalled Massalia with increasing success – and Caere (Cerveteri) in Etruria (Chapter 8), a country with which, nevertheless, the Massalians maintained close relations, as they did with early Rome as well. They were also quick to follow up explorations initiated by Midacritus the Phocaean, when he passed through the Pillars of Hercules (Strait of Gibraltar). Thus in about 550, Euthymenes of Massalia likewise sailed through the strait, and then moved southwards along the African coast, apparently as far down as the River Senegal.

Part II

THE
CLASSICAL GREEKS

4

Against Persia and Carthage

When the Greek cities of Ionia had revolted against the Persian king Darius I, Athens and Eretria (in Euboea) came to their assistance – and helped to sack the capital of Persia's satrapy in western Asia Minor, Sardis (Sart; 498). Their contingents withdrew soon afterwards, but Darius, all the same, decided to take vengeance upon Athens and Eretria. If they both succumbed, as was expected, he would probably propose to extend his conquests to other parts of Greece as well.

In preparation for the expedition, his nephew and son-in-law Mardonius soothed some of the Ionian cities, whose revolt had been suppressed, by deposing their puppet tyrants (set up by the Persians themselves) and permitting the establishment of more or less democratic forms of government in their place (*c*.492). Then Mardonius crossed over to Europe, and, although shipwrecked and wounded, completed the subjugation of Thrace, influencing the kingdom of Macedonia, too, to become Persia's subject ally. This done, the Persian generals Datis and Artaphernes launched their punitive maritime expedition against Athens and Eretria. They were accompanied by the fugitive Athenian ex-tyrant Hippias, who looked forward to reinstatement as the ruler of his former city.

Treachery gave up Eretria to the Persians, who then sailed south and landed their 15,000–20,000 heavy-armed infantry, cavalry and archers upon the Bay of Marathon in Attica, forty-one miles north of Athens itself. The bay provided a protected beach, watering facilities that were unusual in the region, and autumn pastures for horses; and Hippias hoped he would find political adherents in the neighbourhood. The Athenian commander-in-chief was, constitutionally speaking, the polemarch (war archon) Callimachus, but in practice the command was jointly vested in the city's ten generals (*strategoi*), among whom Miltiades the younger took the lead. He and his colleagues decided not to await a Persian attack upon Athens, but to move out and march north to Marathon themselves. This left the city perilously undefended, if the Persians planned to sail on and launch an assault against its walls. But the Athenian generals felt they had to prevent the enemy from establishing a solid base in Attica, which would constitute the gravest of perils (and might attract collaborators). And so they decided to send out their force, which consisted of about ten thousand hoplites.

Six hundred men joined them from Plataea (on the borders of Attica and Boeotia), but no one came from Sparta, ostensibly owing to a local religious festival, yet also, perhaps, because some of that city's leaders did not want to cause offence to the Persians. Nevertheless, Miltiades, at Marathon, decided to attack. Thinning his centre and reinforcing his wings, he ordered his men to charge across the plain. His weak centre was penetrated by its Persian adversaries, but both Greek wings threw back their opponents and then wheeled inwards, putting the hitherto victorious enemy centre to flight. That proved the end of the battle. The Persians had lost 6,400 dead, whereas Athenian casualties only numbered 192. The Spartans arrived after the battle was over.

The defeated Persian soldiers streamed back to the sea, where their ships took them aboard. Then their fleet sailed on round Cape Sunium, in the hope of assaulting Athens before its army came back from Marathon. There were stories that a fifth column within the walls flashed the Persian ships a signal. However, the victorious Athenian force, proceeding rapidly homewards by land, got there first, and the Persians did not venture to attack the city after all. Instead they sailed back to Asia Minor, and for the time being the peril was at an end.

Miltiades and his army had shown the other Greek states that their imperial foes were not invincible, that they could not easily invade Greece by sea, that the Athenian citizen hoplite was more than a match for any soldier in the Persian empire, and that heroic Athens itself was a power for the future.

In the following year, however, Miltiades – like so many other highly successful Greek individuals at various periods – came to an unhappy end, dying of an injury while undergoing prosecution after he had failed to capture the island of Paros.

The sequel was savage rivalry between Athenian politicians, among whom Themistocles (despite unsuccessful attempts to get rid of him by ostracism, Appendix v) gradually came to the fore. Themistocles was unimpressed by the victory of Miltiades on land, advocating a naval policy instead, as more appropriate to Athens' position and aims. His ambitions in this direction were encouraged by a fortunate discovery of rich new veins of silver, beneath Attic soil – in the mines of Laurium –

which he persuaded the Assembly to spend on multiplying the Athenian navy from 70 triremes to 200.

For the Persians did not intend their setback to go unavenged, and Darius's son Xerxes I (486–465), hampered initially by internal rebellions, moved, as soon as he could, into a coordinated invasion of Greece by land and sea: perhaps with 1,000 ships and 100,000 soldiers, a more formidable force than the Mediterranean had ever seen before. His land army crossed the Hellespont (Dardanelles), bridged for the purpose, in late spring 480. Thessaly, Delphi and Argos were among many Greek states which were not prepared to resist him. But Sparta and Athens murdered his envoys, and it was Sparta (despite its poor showing at Marathon by far the greatest land-power in Greece) that had now taken the lead, by summoning a Panhellenic Congress – the earliest ever to be held – at the Isthmus of Corinth in autumn 481. The thirty-one states which sent representatives included thirteen Peloponnesian cities in addition to Athens, which, exceptionally, granted Themistocles supreme command over its forces, although the overall inter-allied command, both on land and sea, remained in Spartan hands.

The initial Greek strategy, designed to hold the narrow valley of Tempe (between Thessaly and Macedonia) with 10,000 men, was quickly abandoned, because the Thessalians were not to be relied upon and, besides, the Persians could have penetrated the mountain barrier elsewhere. So instead the Greeks decided to concentrate their forces on the east coast of the country, stationing an army of 6,000 hoplites, commanded by the Spartan king Leonidas I, brother and successor of Cleomenes I, upon the narrow coastal pass of Thermopylae. At the same time, their combined fleet of 271 triremes was posted off Artemisium in northern Euboea, where its Spartan admiral was advised by Themistocles.

Leonidas and his Spartans fell, gallantly, against overwhelming Persian force. Their resistance had been brief. But it was enough to save the Greek fleet at Artemisium – after three days of fierce fighting – from inevitable annihilation at the hands of the Persian navy, damaged by storms though it was. However, the destruction of Leonidas meant that the Greek fleet's position at Artemisium was no longer tenable. So it had to retreat, hastily and after dark, through the Euripus strait between Boeotia and Euboea.

Accepting grim necessity, most Athenians and their families, on the proposal of Themistocles, evacuated their city, which Xerxes took and burnt. The Athenian wives and children left for Troezen, Aegina and the island of Salamis, to which the government of the city also moved.

Themistocles persuaded the Peloponnesians not to carry out their intention of retreating to the Isthmus of Corinth – since as long as the Persian fleet remained undefeated any such land fortification could easily be turned – but instead induced them to fight well ahead of the Isthmus, upon the narrow strait of Salamis: where a naval victory, one of the most famous of all time, was then won, though the relative parts played by Spartans and Athenians were to be long and acrimoniously disputed in future years.

Xerxes retreated after his defeat, and took most of his army back to Asia. But he left behind a picked force of 30,000 or 40,000 men under Mardonius, to try again in the following year. During the winter Mardonius, employing King Alexander I of Macedonia as his intermediary, endeavoured to win Athens away from the Spartan alliance, but without success. So in spring 479 he marched south, ravaged Attica, and inflicted a second occupation upon the Athenians. However, they still rejected calls to surrender, although no help was yet on the way from Sparta, to which they had appealed. But finally the Spartans set out, under Pausanias of the Agiad royal house. Their force comprised 5,000 Spartiates, 5,000 *perioikoi* (dwellers around) and perhaps 35,000 Helots: the largest Spartan army ever to have been sent outside the Peloponnese. It advanced as far as the Isthmus of Corinth, whereupon Mardonius withdrew from Attica into Boeotia, intending to use his superior cavalry on the Boeotian plain. His Greek opponents, who, swelled by Athenian and Corinthian contingents, now numbered 110,000, confronted him from low hills beside Plataea. One night, however, Pausanias decided to move to higher ground under cover of darkness: and at that juncture Mardonius pounced. But the Greeks counterattacked, charging downhill at the double, and the Persian troops fled. Mardonius was killed, and his second-in-command Artabazus took the survivors home to Asia by land.

This was the greatest land battle the Greeks had ever fought, and, together with Marathon and Salamis, it filled them with a new sense of identity, and immeasurable confidence about their potentialities and their future: confirming in their minds a potent conviction of the difference between themselves and 'barbarians', their natural inferiors and enemies – despots' slaves and no match for themselves, who were free men and the members of free communities.

These sensational events are often hailed as the beginning of European history. Yet they did not result in any strengthening of the Panhellenic political union which the emergency had, partially and temporarily, brought into being. On the contrary, strife between one Greek city-state and another immediately resumed, and persisted.

Meanwhile, stirring events had also taken place in Sicily. In *c*.492 Hippocrates of Gela, the wealthiest and most powerful of the island's tyrant-dictators, defeated the Syracusans. In a battle a year or two later, he met his death at the hands of natives from the hinterland. But then his successor Gelon, founder of the Deinomenid dynasty, seized Syracuse itself (485). This was in response to an appeal from the Syracusan aristocracy or oligarchy (*gamoroi*), who were threatened by internal disaffection. But they did not, to their disappointment, find that Gelon restored their authority, since instead he moved into Syracuse to become its leader himself (leaving his brother Hiero I to assume control of Gela). Under Gelon's rule at Syracuse many people from other parts of Sicily were forcibly drafted into the city, which thus became even larger, and remained extremely rich. Its armed forces were built up by the recruitment of mercenaries, and a new navy was constructed in its harbours.

Early in his reign Gelon became involved in warfare against the Carthaginians, whose leadership of the Phoenician colonies in the west of Sicily he presented to his fellow-Greeks as an imminent foreign threat. At first, he himself intended to invade Carthaginian north Africa, but the assistance he had hoped for from the Spartans failed to materialize, and the plan was abandoned. So it was now the Carthaginians, instead, who proposed to invade Sicily, probably fearing that Gelon would cut off the transportation of the metal supplies they relied upon from Spain. The Carthaginians' pretext for their attack was an appeal they had received from Terillus, the Greek tyrant of Himera (Imera), who had been expelled by Gelon's ally Theron of Acragas (Agrigento).

Carthage responded to the appeal by sending 200 warships and 30,000 soldiers under Hamilcar – the largest expedition that had ever invaded Sicily (480). After landing, Hamilcar marched from his base at Panormus (Palermo) in order to besiege Himera. He had hoped to join forces with Terillus's son-in-law Anaxilas of Rhegium (Reggio di Calabria), but before this could be done Gelon attacked him with 50,000 infantry and 5,000 cavalry. This cavalry, a speciality of Syracuse's horse-breeding nobles, penetrated Hamilcar's stockade (by pretending to be his allies) and killed him and many of his men, setting fire to their ships. Those Carthaginian soldiers who had survived then proceeded to surrender, losing huge quantities of plunder, and their government at home brought an end to hostilities by paying a massive indemnity.

This was the very year in which Xerxes I invaded Greece, and there may well have been a measure of collusion between Carthage (a Phoenician foundation) and the Persians (whose fleet largely consisted of Phoenician ships and men). The result of the Sicilian warfare, however, although it did not eliminate the Phoenician settlements in the west of the island, dealt Carthage such a severe blow that seven decades were to pass before its armies would venture to launch a further invasion. Gelon's victory was celebrated throughout the Greek world, in which he was now the most powerful figure. But in 478 he died, leaving memories of his reign (despite anti-tyrant propaganda) as a period of prosperity and happiness.

After his death, Hiero I moved from Gela to become tyrant of Syracuse in his place. An important part of Hiero's policy was his preoccupation with the Italian mainland.

There, after various interventions, he came into open conflict with the Etruscan city-states, which constituted the second set of powers, after Carthage and its Sicilian associates, which offered a threat to the Greeks of the west (Chapter 8). Strife had already arisen in Campania between the Greek colony at Cumae and Etruscan bases at Capua (Santa Maria Capua Vetere) and Cales (Calvi), reinforced by armies from the city-states of Etruria itself. Cooperation between certain of these states and Carthage, in order to repel the Greeks, was nothing new (it had been seen at the battle of Alalia in c.540–535), and when in c.474 an Etruscan fleet sailed against Cumae Carthaginian support was forthcoming. However, Hiero believed that a defeat of the Greek cause in Campania would be a disaster for himself, and consequently dispatched a flotilla, which gained a victory over the Etruscans in the Gulf of Cumae. The power of the cities of Etruria, both at home and in areas subject to their influence such as Campania, was already waning at this time, and Hiero, by his success, had ensured that it would not revive.

His achievement, before he died in 467–6, had been to secure the western Greeks against one of their two principal menaces, the threat presented by the Etruscans, just as Gelon had driven off the other, which came from Carthage. Like Gelon again, he had created alliances and coalitions which could never have been attained by any less auto-cratic form of government. Moreover, amid a sparkling upsurge of cultural life, the poets Pindar, Bacchylides and Simonides had been mobilized to celebrate the splendours of Syracuse's court.

Both Gelon and Hiero were aristocratic by birth and inclination alike. And yet, paradoxically, their transplantations of populations, as well as large-scale enfranchisements of mercenaries, weakened the conservative traditions that had hitherto bound the people of Syracuse to its nobility. A further problem was created by fierce struggles between old and new citizens, who were failing to live together in this first cosmopolitan Greek centre. In consequence, after the death of Hiero, chronic instability returned to the city.

5

The Classical City-States

1 Climax and Eclipse

After his victory at Plataea, the Spartan Pausanias, commanding a fleet to which various Greek cities contributed ships, captured Byzantium. But his dictatorial arrogance caused his allies to turn against him and appeal to the Athenian commander, the honest Aristides, to take over the leadership instead. And so, by Aristides's initiative, the Athenian confederacy came into being (477). Its purpose was mutual protection against Persia, together with retaliation, when possible, to avenge the Persian invasions that had just ended. The Athenians were to supply the federal commanders-in-chief and decide which city-states should supply ships and which, instead, should provide money (controlled, after it had been paid, by ten Athenian *hellenotamiai*, 'Greek treasurers'). The joint treasury, and meeting-place, was to be on the historic, holy, Ionian island of Delos, so that the confederacy gained the name of the Delian League.

Its leading figure was the Athenian Cimon, who in the years that followed dislodged Pausanias from Byzantium, expelled the Persian garrison from Eion at the mouth of the River Strymon (Struma), occupied the island of Scyros, and probably played a leading part both in forcing Carystus, at the southern tip of Euboea, to join the League, and then in preventing the secession of the Aegean island of Naxos. This coercion of Naxos was the first occasion in which an ally was subjected to such forcible treatment. But Cimon distracted attention by leading an allied fleet to southern Asia Minor, where he won a victory over the Persians, by land and sea, at the River Eurymedon (Köprü Çayı) in Pamphylia (469–8?). This triumph was a climactic aftermath to the Persian Wars; the Persians had lost their Mediterranean bases, and henceforward the members of the Delian League could engage safely in maritime commerce. Cimon went on to deal with a revolt by the islanders of Thasos (465–4) – who felt that the Athenians were threatening their mainland mining interests. But Cimon, in the end, succeeded in bringing them to heel.

At this moment, however, his enemies at Athens turned against him. They were led by the more democratically inclined Ephialtes, who regarded Cimon's attitude as too pro-Spartan: since what the latter really believed in was the joint leadership of Greece by Athens and Sparta, combining forces against the Persians – and it was because of his sympathetic attitude towards themselves that the Spartans had done nothing to hamper the Delian League. Yet now this policy of Cimon was severely put to the test. For in c.465 Sparta was disabled by an earthquake, whereupon its subject Helots in Messenia broke into rebellion, the most serious in living memory. Sparta succeeded in penning them in, but nevertheless felt obliged to appeal to Athens for assistance. In response, Cimon went to help them with 4,000 hoplites. But then, surprisingly, the Spartan government sent all these Athenians back home again. For the anti-Spartan Ephialtes was in the process of launching revolutionary reforms at Athens (462–1), and the Spartans feared that the Athenian soldiers who had arrived in Laconia might have caught this political infection, which could prompt them to intrigue with the Helots. The Spartan government can hardly have expected that Cimon himself would engage in any act which was so contrary to their interests. Nevertheless, it was he who now suffered, since his pro-Spartan policy at Athens was discredited and abandoned, and he himself suffered ostracism (461) – a referendum which meant that he had to go away (Appendix v).

What Ephialtes's reforms had done was to strip the conservative, pro-Spartan Areopagus of its 'guardianship of the laws' and much of its jurisdiction, so that from now onwards the Athenian government depended more closely upon its democratic institutions, the popular Assembly and Council. Ephialtes, after passing these measures, was assassinated – probably by a supporter of the exiled Cimon. Yet his changes did not die with him, and the leadership of the pro-democratic elements in the state gradually passed into the hands of one of his adherents, Pericles – with whom it remained for many decades.

True, he had to be reelected general (*strategos*) every year, so that (although he belonged to a leading Attic family) his authority rested on a democratic basis. Yet, by virtue of this longlasting continuity, it was he who decided policy much more than his ever-changing nine colleagues could ever aspire to do. 'In name it was democracy,' remarked the historian Thucydides, 'but in fact it was rule by one man.'[1] Pericles's wonderful oratory was what helped him along; for this was something to which Greeks were particularly susceptible.

When relations between Athens and Sparta broke down, desultory hostilities followed, in which, nevertheless, not Sparta but Corinth initially proved to be Athens's most determined foe, inspired by commercial rivalry. But the Spartans, too, became active, marching up to Tanagra in Boeotia, where they defeated the Athenians, who got their own back, however, on Sparta's Boeotian allies at Oenophyta (457). Yet at the same time Athens had plunged into an ill-judged war against the Persians in Egypt (460–454), which proved a complete failure, one of the worst the Athenians ever experienced, involving the loss of almost their entire force.

It was probably this grave setback, raising the menace of a new, retaliatory, Persian invasion, which prompted Pericles to move the Delian League's treasury from Delos to Athens (454) – a sign that Athenian imperialism was taking hold: a series of inscriptions, the Tribute Lists, tell us more about this ever-increasing process.[2] Military operations in Greece were brought to an end by the Egyptian catastrophe, the pro-Spartan Cimon was brought back from ostracism, a Five Years' Truce was concluded with Sparta (451), and, in addition, a formal or informal 'Peace of Callias' was concluded with Persia (449).

These agreements protected the Athenians from flank attacks during a subsequent hostile move by Boeotia (whose troops won the battle of Coronea in 447) and an uprising of Euboean cities that followed. Pericles stamped out the Euboean revolt. But when the Five Years' Truce with the Spartans came to an end he found it advisable to conclude a Thirty Years' Peace with their leaders (445), according to which Athens admittedly kept Euboea, but was obliged to accept that the Boeotians were outside its control.

In 443 Pericles had to meet the most determined internal challenge that he had so far encountered, when the conservative leader of the day, Thucydides, the son of Melesias, objected to what he considered the immoral use of League Funds for the construction of magnificent buildings at Athens – a practice which, said the other Thucydides, the historian, Pericles was happy to defend as an education of Greece.[3] Thucydides the son of Melesias failed to dislodge Pericles, and was ostracized. But the latter's intellectual friends, and his mistress Aspasia, were also subjected to attacks.

What other opposition he suffered from is less easy to tell. Athenians, of every class, benefited from the empire – and the majority naturally welcomed his moves towards greater democracy, including the poorer citizens, who had gained importance because they rowed in the fleet. Furthermore, Pericles introduced state pay (*misthosis*), boasting, against his critics, that his measures gave every citizen an opportunity to serve Athens. And he did his best to exalt this citizen status, by restricting the franchise to those who inherited it on both sides of their families.

The allies of Athens, naturally, were more divided about this imperial city that was gradually coercing them into a subject relationship. On the whole, no doubt, the democrats among them were more sympathetic than their oligarchs towards Athens. But troubles occurred. Thus, in 440–439, Samos, a member of the League, fell out with the Athenians, because it did not like the outcome of their arbitration in a Samian dispute with Miletus. So Samos broke out in rebellion – making a pact with Pissuthnes, the Persian satrap of Sardis. But Pericles forced the city to capitulate. And then, in 437–6, he looked further afield, reviving a project to colonize Amphipolis in Macedonia, in order to secure Thracian metals and timber and facilitate the transportation of grain from the ports of the Black Sea; into which he led a naval expedition to emphasize Athenian claims.

But the problems between Athens and Sparta – summed up by the basic question as to which of them should lead Greece – remained too fundamental to be settled by any means except fighting, and in 431 the two states confronted each other in the Peloponnesian War. One of the principal causes of the war was widespread suspicion of the Athenians, because of their aggressively restrictive attitude towards other cities' autonomy. Corinth, hemmed in by Athenian power on both sides, and sometimes directly provoked, felt particular alarm. Its complaints received sympathy from Sparta; and despite reluctance by some of Spartan leaders, its jealousy and its fear of Athens were fundamental factors leading to the struggle that now ensued. As for Pericles, although the Thirty Years' Peace was not nearly due to end, he decided that war had become inevitable. Neither side can be exonerated completely over its outbreak.

And so the conflict began. It was not such a vast and continuously unitary affair as the historian Thucydides declared. But it was the largest war that Greeks had ever fought, and its ultimate consequences were disastrously far-reaching. Neither side had any chance of decisive victory, without external support – that is to say, the support of Persia. The Athenians could collect supplies by sea wherever they liked, while the Spartans were equally unchallengeable at land, and could even devastate Attica itself every year, when its population had to flock into Athens behind its Long Walls, which Pericles had completed.

This annual immigration into the city, however, plunged the Athenians into a crisis which had not been foreseen. For an acute epidemic (not satisfactorily identified) broke out in overcrowded Athens, which lost more than a quarter of its inhabitants from the scourge. Then Pericles himself – two of whose sons had succumbed to the infection – failed to secure reelection as general, and was even fined. True, soon afterwards, in spring 429, he was restored to office. But he, too, had been attacked by the pestilence, and six months later he died. The leaders who competed to take his place became more crudely expert in exploiting the ambitions, fears and prejudices of the Assembly and lawcourts. Prominent among them was Cleon, who, despite his financial gifts, was loathed and reviled by the historian Thucydides and other conservatives – principally because, although rich, he did not belong to the traditional, aristocratic ruling circle.

In the war, both sides scored encouraging military successes, though none of them proved conclusive. The Athenians put down a revolt by Mytilene (Lesbos, 428–427), and in 425 captured the island of Sphacteria (off the Peloponnesian island of Pylos), with the result that 292 prisoners were taken, including the unusual and spectacular total of 120 Spartan citizens (Spartiates). But then an attempt by the Athenians to put Sparta's Boeotian allies out of the war was defeated at Delium (424). And in the same year a Spartan of unusual talent and integrity, Brasidas, carried the war into Macedonia and Thrace, capturing Amphipolis and threatening Athens's imports of metals and timber from the region, and of grain from the Black Sea.

When, however, the war-leaders, Brasidas and Cleon, both fell in battle (422), exhaustion led the two sides, in the following year, to agree to the 'Peace of Nicias'. Yet it was an indecisive compromise, which Sparta's principal adherents Corinth and Boeotia proceeded to repudiate; and during the ensuing period a brilliant but flashy and unreliable Athenian politician, Alcibiades, took the opportunity to form a new coalition against the Spartans. They defeated it, however, at the battle of Mantinea in Arcadia (418), and Alcibiades's initiative had come to nothing.

The Athenians then prepared to launch their expedition against Syracuse in Sicily. The 'tyranny' (dictatorship) at that city, which came to an end in 466, had left a turbulent factional inheritance: despite which the Syracusans were able to attack Aethalia (Elba) and Cyrnus (Corsica), to plunder the coast of Etruria (453), and to defeat hostile natives in the hinterland and Greek enemies at Acragas (Agrigento). During the 450s, too, if not earlier, the Athenians had begun to display an interest in Sicily, as an alternative source of grain in case their Black Sea link was cut. These efforts, however, proved ineffective, because when the Peloponnesian War broke out it was to Sparta, instead, that Syracuse sent its grain.

In 427 and 425 the Athenians sent flotillas to put a stop to this (although ostensibly they were responding to a Sicilian appeal), but in 424 the leading Syracusan statesman Hermocrates summoned the Conference of Gela to persuade the island's states to unite against such interventions. None the less, in 415 the Athenians planned their invasion of Sicily (once again in response to an appeal). The Athenian public thought that the expedition would bring in money, and by now Athens probably intended to take over at least the eastern half of the whole island.

Unforgettably recorded by the historian Thucydides, the expedition ended, after two years, in total triumph for the Syracusans – who thus freed themselves, for ever, from the menace of external domination – matched by correspondingly total disaster for the Athenians. Their commander Nicias, to whose incompetence the defeat was largely due, met his death at the hands of the Syracusans, together with his fellow-general Demosthenes, and their entire force was killed or taken prisoner. Athens had lost one-third of its total military potential and most of its navy. And yet it still managed to struggle on with the Peloponnesian War.

Meanwhile, however, on the traitorous advice of Alcibiades (who defected in order to avoid a trial for blasphemy at home), the Spartans had established a fortified base at Decelea in northern Attica (414), cutting Athens off from its agricultural land and Laurium silver-mines, from which many slaves now proceeded to desert. The effects of this move upon the Athenian economy were serious; and at about this time (c.414/412 – if not earlier), the Athenians took a further step towards their own ruin by backing a dissident, Amorges, in Caria (son of an earlier rebel Pissuthnes), against Darius II Ochus of Persia. At about the same period, too, many of Athens's subject-allies rebelled, imperilling the city's grain supplies from the Black Sea and Egypt; and the states of Euboea joined the rising.

At Athens itself, an oligarchic revolution took place, giving control to the Four Hundred, who were then overthrown, however, by the more moderate 'Five Thousand'. Two naval victories were won against the Spartans (off Cynossema in the Thracian Chersonese and off Cyzicus [Belkis], in 411 and 410). But the Athenian politician Cleophon refused a Spartan offer of peace, and Alcibiades, victor at Cyzicus, returned to the city, for a short time, as commander-in-chief (407).

Now, however, a decisive turning-point occurred, in the shape of a close and unexpected friendship that arose between the Persian prince

Cyrus the younger, son of Darius II, and the Spartan general Lysander. With the aid of Persian money, Lysander defeated an Athenian fleet at Notium, the port of Colophon in Ionia (407). In the following year, Athens managed to fight back, and won a victory off the Aeolian islands of Arginusae. But the Athenians unwisely executed their successful generals (who had failed to rescue drowning men in a heavy sea) and, in 405, were finally and fatally defeated by Lysander at Aegospotami in the Thracian Chersonese (Gallipoli peninsula) on the Hellespont. Their Black Sea grain-route was cut, and the war was over. In 404, Athens unconditionally surrendered.

For our knowledge of fifth-century events we are dependent, all too dependent, on the work of two outstandingly brilliant historical writers, Herodotus and Thucydides.

Their forerunner was Hecataeus of Miletus. Soon after 500 Hecataeus had written prose works which foreshadowed subsequent histori-ography. The 'father' of that art, Herodotus (c.480–425), likewise came from the western coastlands of Asia Minor, his home being Halicarnassus (Bodrum) in Caria, which was under Persian control. A local civil war prompted him to leave his home town, and thereafter he travelled extensively, residing above all at Athens, at whose 'Panhel-lenic' colony at Thurii (Sybaris) in south Italy he died, shortly before his *History* was complete.

This work, later divided into nine books, had been arranged by himself in two main parts. The first, a prelude, tells of the rise of the Persian empire, and the origins of its wars against the Greeks. The second, main, section describes the Persian Wars themselves, comprising the invasions by Darius I (490) and Xerxes I (480–479). These cam-paigns were regarded by Herodotus as the most influential events in world history. And, in particular, he saw the triumphant Greek resist-ance as an unprecedented approach to that Panhellenic cooperation which later so signally failed.

But his purpose went far beyond the actual campaigns, since what he desired was to 'place on record the wonderful achievements both of our own and of the barbarian (Asian) peoples'[4] – a liberal, unchau-vinistic theme well suited to a man who not only came from a region where the two cultures met, but had later travelled widely in exile. At first, perhaps, he had planned a geographical work, like Hecataeus's *Journey Round the World*, and then, at a subsequent date, he turned instead to his ultimate theme of the wars, under the influence of Athens.

The mass of stories that Herodotus collected on his journeys make him the pioneer not only of history, but of comparative anthropology and archaeology as well. His sources were personal contacts, hearsay, and oral tales, supplementing whatever inadequate documentation might happen to be available. The absence of any substantial previous historiographical traditions means that he had to invent new standards of his own. The Persian Wars, which had finished a generation ago, were already encrusted with legend. And 'my job', asserts Herodotus, 'is to write what has been said, but I do not have to believe it'[5] – a tantalizing admission, since we all too often have no second account against which we can check what he tells us. Moreover, in keeping with Homeric practice, he includes speeches – of which he could not have had any personal knowledge: thus providing a disconcerting model for all future historians in the Greco-Roman world.

He was convinced of the prompting and direction of the gods, and believed in the operation of arrogance (*hubris*) to bring down a mighty human being at their hands. This was a doctrine which he shared with the tragic poets, but which weakened analyses based on naturally operative causes and effects: although, under the influence, this time, of contemporary sophists, he sometimes, nevertheless, seeks to subject these divinely inspired patterns to rationalizing explanation. For somewhat paradoxically, despite god-sent interventions, Herodotus does recognize that significant human individuals are the forces that create history – not only men but also women, of whose role he is fully aware. So he devotes to people's personal ambitions, relations and frictions the careful treatment that they deserve.

Viewed as a historian, whatever his limitations, he broke an infinite amount of new ground. As a writer, he was a model for everyone ever since who has tried to write history in an attractive fashion. For his sweeping interest and receptive curiosity expressed itself superabundantly in spicy stories and digressions, which make him a peerless entertainer.

The second major historian of the age, Thucydides (*c.*460/455–*c.*400), was the son of an Athenian with the Thracian name of Olorus, and possessed an estate in Thrace, which was probably why, as one of his city's ten generals in 424, he was placed in command of the fleet in that area. His failure, however, to save Amphipolis from the Spartan Brasidas earned him banishment, which ended only after Athens's final defeat in 404. His *History of the Peloponnesian War* offers an account of the war down to 411, but then terminates – probably because Thucydides died before he could complete his story.

Like Herodotus, he selected a war as his theme. But he innovated by choosing a war of his own epoch. Adapting and correcting Herodotus, who had said the same about the Persian struggle, he declared the Peloponnesian War the greatest war that there had ever been.[6] From a military viewpoint, this seems an exaggerated estimate; and, in any case, hostilities were so intermittent that it is difficult, as we saw, to regard them as continuous and unified. Nevertheless the war, and the widespread degradation that accompanied its solution, did, eventually, destroy the independence of the Greek city-states, and thus undermine their distinctive way of life, giving an entirely new turn to the process of classical civilization: so that in a larger sense Thucydides's claim for his theme is not unjustified.

The Herodotean romantic element, he declares, is lacking from his work, which is intended to be 'a possession for all time',[7] of educational value to the future. Being, himself, a man of imposing intellect, he attaches primary significance to the brain-power of the characters he describes, singling out from this viewpoint, among others, Themistocles and Pericles. However, he also seeks to transcend individual happenings and attain to universal truths, by searching beneath the surface of events in order to detect underlying motivations – in the spirit of the contemporary physician Hippocrates. Moreover, in explaining why the Peloponnesian War broke out in the first place, Thucydides distinguishes between immediate 'causes', or occasions for friction, and the basic underlying realities of power; so that he can be described as the creator of more than two millennia of political history (he knows economic developments are important, but regards them as second ary). No less decisive was his persistent refusal, in contrast with Herodotus, to blame human failures on divine intervention, although his account of the Sicilian expedition, for example, contains strong implications of the *hubris* and Nemesis of tragic drama. However, chance, too, is allowed to have devastating effects, though it must not be blamed, he says, all the time.

Thucydides's grave, intense language, crammed with meaning, is well equipped to portray the collective emotions and over-optimisms and miseries of internal strife (*stasis*) and scenes of battle. His selectivity, however, is rigorous, and it is hard for us nowadays to fill the gaps. Like Herodotus (and the tragedians), he includes many speeches – and admits that he does not, cannot, reproduce them accurately,[8] intending them rather as means of exploring and illustrating psychological and philosophical backgrounds.

After Athens's capitulation at the end of the Peloponnesian War, the Spartan victor Lysander imposed a tough oligarchic government, the Thirty, upon the city, and set up Boards of Ten in the states that had belonged to the Delian (Athenian) League. But the arrangements proved inefficient and unpopular, and the king of Sparta, Pausanias (409-395), allowed democracies to be restored (c.403-402). Any expectation that the Spartans might take over Athens's imperial role was doomed to failure, and by 395 even the Athenians had recovered sufficiently to join Corinth, Thebes and Argos in the 'Corinthian War' against Sparta. The principal casualty of this new war was Lysander himself, killed at Haliartus in Boeotia in the same year.

The Persian king Artaxerxes II Mnemon, annoyed with the Spartans because Pausanias's colleague Agesilaus II (399-360) had engaged in open hostilities against Persia, sent funds to help the confederates who were fighting against them, but later changed sides and compelled all combatants alike to accept the King's Peace or Peace of Antalcidas (387/6). The Spartans, however, did not desist from aggressive activity, embarking on treacherous *coups* at Thebes (382-379) and Athens (379): whereupon Persia intervened once again and sought to enforce a Peace of Callias (371).

Thebes, however, under its outstanding commander Epaminondas, refused to comply, and there followed a brief period of Theban hegemony in Greece. It started with the battle of Leuctra in Boeotia, at which the Spartans were, unprecedentedly, defeated – 'the most famous of all victories won over Greeks'.[9] Epaminondas then invaded the Peloponnese (370/369), and liberated Arcadia and Messenia: whereupon the longlived Peloponnesian Confederacy finally ceased to exist (366). Then he decided to challenge the supremacy of the Athenian League (which had revived) at sea, leading a fleet to Byzantium. But next he and his allies had to confront a coalition of Spartans, Athenians and others at Mantinea (362). The Theban army was winning, when Epaminondas fell, mortally wounded. His death put an end to his city's predominance, and from now on there was no mainland state capable of taking the lead, so that lethal and mutually destructive divisions continued.

This situation brought King Philip II of Macedonia onto the scene.

The nucleus of his state, surrounded by a crescent of mountains, was the fertile Macedonian plain, formed by three substantial rivers debouching into the Thermaic Gulf, the Haliacmon, Lydias and Axius. The Macedonian people were semi-Hellenized, and its Argead royal house, presiding over an articulate nobility, claimed Greek origins. The coastland, from an early period, had been colonized by Greek city-states, seeking foodstuffs and metals (from Thracian Mount Pangaeum) and timber for shipbuilding. The Macedonian king Amyntas I became a vassal of Darius I of Persia (c.512), and his successor Alexander I accompanied Xerxes I against the Greeks (480), though he later welcomed Greek poets to his court. When the Peloponnesian War broke out, Perdiccas II refrained from committing himself. He was the father of King Archelaus, who established Pella as his capital, harboured Euripides and employed the painter Zeuxis. The defeat of his son Perdiccas III at the hands of his non-Greek (Illyrian) neighbours brought Perdiccas's younger brother Philip II into power (359).

Profiting from the military knowledge he had acquired – as a hostage – from Epaminondas, Philip defeated the Illyrians, seized Amphipolis (imperilling Athens's Black Sea grain route) and captured Crenides (henceforward known as Philippi) so as to control the Pangaean mines (356). Their resources enabled him to develop agriculture, engage in large-scale bribery, and create a professional, national army, based on an improved infantry phalanx (carrying long pikes) which coordinated its operations with impressive cavalry. He soon captured further Athenian dependencies, around the Thermaic Gulf (356–4); and the Third Sacred War (356–346), caused by the seizure of Delphi by Phocian separatists hostile to Thebes, brought him far south of his own land. Next he moved against northern targets again, attacking Thrace and the Chalcidian League, centred upon the city of Olynthus.

At this point Athens felt constrained to accept the Peace of Philocrates (346), which confirmed Philip's predominant position in central Greece. Invited by the Athenian rhetorician and educationalist Isocrates to lead a Panhellenic force against the Persian empire, he made overtures to other leading Athenians as well. The orator Demosthenes objected, but Philip pressed his point home by trying to capture Perinthus (Marmaraereğlisi) and Byzantium (Constantinople, Istanbul) on the Thracian Bosphorus, which controlled Athens's grain lifeline from the Black Sea. Demosthenes now found it possible to whip up an alliance against him, including even Athens's traditional enemy Thebes. But the coalition was decisively defeated at Chaeronea in Boeotia (338).

Thereupon Philip summoned Panhellenic Congresses at Corinth, with a view to invading the Persian empire, as Isocrates had suggested – an operation designed to endear him to all Greeks, which his generals Parmenio and Attalus then proceeded to launch. But in 336 Philip was murdered. Perhaps his assassin was one of his wives, Olympias (mother of Alexander the Great), who was angered by a new marriage he had contracted – his sixth or seventh.

Despite personal failings (including tendencies to drink and brawl), Philip possessed a variety of gifts, and was described by the historian Theopompus as the greatest man (man of action, that is to say) whom the continent had ever produced.[10] But what he had achieved by his manifold enterprises, in the end, was to terminate the classical age of the independent city-states. Some of these states, it is true, continued to survive and prosper. But, on the whole, their epoch had come to an end, since their armies could not match Philip's, and their perpetual disunity made it impossible for them to confront him effectively.

His second great achievement, though he did not intend or welcome it, had been to provoke and create the oratory of the infuriated Athenian Demosthenes (384–322). Demosthenes wrote and delivered many other speeches, but his warnings against Philip were what earned him his fame. The *First Philippic* (352 or 349) attempted to rouse his fellow-citizens' consciousness of the peril the king presented, and his *Olynthiacs* (349) urged them to prevent Philip from capturing Olynthus, the headquarters of the Chalcidian League. The *Second Philippic* (344) asserted that Macedonia's apparent friendship with certain Greek states was just a fraudulent device to line them up against Athens. Then, subsequently, a *Third Philippic* (341) appealed for Greek unity to confront the common threat that Philip posed.

The Athenians, not wanting war, had been slow to respond. But at last, in 340, they did so, and Demosthenes found himself in full charge of his city's war effort. To strengthen this, in his *Fourth Philippic*, he proposed that Persia should be asked to provide help: even that had to be done if it would help the Greeks stop Philip. But Demosthenes's rallying of the Greek city-states only led to the catastrophe of Chaeronea (338), which resulted in the collapse of all resistance to Macedonia. The orator's policies had failed: though much later, in his speech *On the Crown* (330), he eloquently, in retrospect, vindicated his intentions at that earlier time, before finally getting into fatal trouble with Alexander's successor Antipater (323–2), amid whiffs of corruption.

Had he been right to regard Philip as a mortal threat to Athens and to Hellenic civilization? The king only became an immediate menace after Demosthenes made him one. Nevertheless, it also remains true that, from the very outset of his reign, Philip had begun to work against the interests of Athens, by encroaching upon its vital northern grain route. We, with hindsight, can see, first, that Demosthenes was right to see Philip as a perilous threat, but also, secondly, that his struggle against the king was doomed to failure. Yet the alternative was to give in, and submit to the downfall of the entire institution of the city-state, which to Demosthenes (like Plato and Aristotle) was the only imaginable kind of political unit.

But in any case, whatever doubts we may have about the orator's realism – or about his personal character, which was not very agreeable – Demosthenes's unique greatness lay in his oratory. His language was superb, and he knew and practised every trick of the trade with supreme skill, in an epoch when this ranked as one of the highest arts. There was never a better speaker than Demosthenes in the entire ancient world. And perhaps there has never been a better one in later times either.

2 Poetry and Drama

In 476 Pindar of Cynoscephalae in Boeotia (*c.*581–*c.*438) had gone to Sicily at the invitation of Hiero I, tyrant-dictator of Syracuse, and stayed there for about two years. Thereafter, he was commissioned by patrons in many parts of the Greek world, on a lavish scale that had never been seen before. Aegina and Athens (despite the latter's disapproval of his homeland Boeotia's neutrality during the Persian Wars) gained his special devotion.

After his death his poems were collected into seventeen books. They dealt with many different subjects, but the only works to have come down to us more or less intact are four books of his Epinician Odes – choral songs composed in honour of athletic and musical victors in the principal Games of Greece (Appendix III). These Odes are between twenty-five and two hundred lines long. Each tells of the winner of a contest, and allusions to his relatives' earlier athletic achievements, or praises of his trainer, are sometimes added. The athletic victory itself, however, is never described in any straightforward fashion, since Pindar is more concerned to celebrate the whole way of life lying around and behind the moment of triumph. Mythical narratives are inserted and recast, often in order to point a moral. Oracles, proverbs and maxims also receive attention. The whole effect is oblique and enigmatic and involuted, as Pindar's verses project dazzling images amid disjointed, abrupt changes of topic and mood.

What emerges, however, is that he sees the victors as mortals elevated and illuminated, at their climactic moment, by a divinely inspired force. For, despite what at first sight seems a somewhat non-spiritual choice of subject, he is one of the most religious of all Greek poets. Although a gulf, he feels, usually separates gods and humans, the successful men whom he commemorates seem to achieve, in a flash, glory almost comparable to that of the deities themselves – thus justifying their own existence on earth. And to capture these awesome, beautiful moments for ever, Pindar displays a soaring, imaginative, emotional vigour, ranging from deft, sensuous delicacy to the sublime grandeur for which he is famous. His medium is an intricately patterned diction which builds up cumulative masses of poetic rhythm, reinforced, no doubt, by musical accompaniments at which we can only guess.

In later epochs, Pindar came to be regarded as the greatest of Greek lyric poets. In his lifetime, however, he seemed a nostalgic figure, out of sympathy with many aspects of his age. Despite his admiration of Athens, for example, he remained untouched by the democratic effervescence that the city was experiencing. For he himself believed, instead, in a conservative, hierarchical oligarchic system which revered hereditary nobility and tradition; and he admired the magnificent self-expression made possible by inherited wealth. These are the elements, he declared, that constitute god-given 'virtue' (*areta*), an excellence that is not only physical but embraces a large range of virtues as well: courage, moderation, hospitality and friendship – qualities redolent of the old-fashioned *eunomia*, good order reflecting the universal order that is the work of Zeus himself.

Athenian tragedy had emerged, in a primitive form, during the sixth century, under Pisistratus, when Thespis presented what passed for the first tragic play (*c.*534; Chapter 2, section 1). In due course, it became customary for dramatists to produce four plays, a tetralogy, at each annual competition, comprising three tragedies and a more light-hearted piece about satyrs. Although the music and dancing which formed an integral part of its performance are lost (like the music accompanying Pindar's *Odes*), this tragic poetry, even without such features, remains one of the decisive theatrical and literary achievements of all time.

Tightly packed and concise, it was designed to frame the profoundest thoughts of which human beings are capable. In particular, its task was to examine and assess, generally against a mythological background, the relationships of mortals with the divine powers, and to expose and analyse the self-estimates of its Athenian citizen audiences. Spoken, recited speeches or dialogues, portraying the plot, alternate with lyrics sung and danced by choruses (granted to competitors by the city), which set the action against a more timeless background. Characterization, though broadly effective, is restricted to the requirements of the plays themselves.

The only tragic dramatists whose work has, in part, come down to us are Aeschylus, Sophocles and Euripides. The real foundation of Greek tragedy is generally attributed to Aeschylus (525/4–456). It was he, apparently, who introduced a second actor – thus making dialogue possible. The son of an aristocratic landowner, Aeschylus was born at Eleusis in Attica, and fought in the battle of Marathon (490), and probably at Salamis too. He visited the court of Syracuse on three occasions, and died at Gela on the same island. But his spectacular successes were at Athens, where he won thirteen festival victories. His plays, like those of later tragedians, were staged in the new stone Theatre of Dionysus beside the Acropolis.

Seven of his approximately eighty plays have survived. *The Persians* (472), unusually, deals with a recent historical event, the invasion of Greece by Xerxes I eight years earlier. In this play, the king's mother Atossa learns of his defeat at Salamis, which the ghost of Xerxes's father Darius I ascribes to his presumptuous vengefulness. The *Seven Against Thebes* (467) is about the mythical Polynices and the six Argives whom he enlisted to win the Theban throne from his brother Eteocles, after their self-blinded father Oedipus had gone into exile. The brothers perish at each other's hands, but their sister Antigone proposes to disobey the order forbidding Polynices honourable burial (a theme subsequently worked out by Sophocles). Aeschylus's *Suppliant Women* (462–1) are the fifty daughters of Danaus, the Danaids, whom the fifty sons of his brother Aegyptus want to coerce into marriage. To avoid this, they take refuge with their father at Argos, whose people refuse to give the women up to their suitors.

The only completely surviving trilogy written by a Greek tragic poet is Aeschylus's *Oresteia*, about the mythical Argive house of Atreus, in which one crime led to another, over many generations. In the *Agamemnon*, the end of the Trojan War has come: and at his royal palace at Argos, where his alienated wife Clytemnestra awaits that monarch with her lover Aegisthus, there is sinister suspense. For, before he first set out for Troy, Agamemnon had offered up their daughter Iphigenia as a human sacrifice, in order that the gods should grant him a favourable wind for the expedition. Moreover, he is now bringing his captive mistress Cassandra back to his home. Clytemnestra murders them both.

In the *Libation-Bearers* (*Choephori*), however, their son Orestes returns to avenge his father's death, and kills Aegisthus and then Clytemnestra as well. But the Furies (Erinyes) come to haunt him, and, driven to insanity, he takes flight to Apollo's temple at Delphi. In the *Eumenides* the Furies are seen sleeping around him. But Apollo orders Orestes to submit to judgment at Athens, where Athena, who has created the homicide court of the Areopagus to hear the case, acquits him by her casting vote. She also persuades the Furies to relent, and at their new shrine beneath the Areopagus they will henceforward be known as the Kindly Ones (Eumenides).

Prometheus Bound (whose Aeschylean authorship has been disputed) is about the result of Prometheus's gift of fire to the human race, in order to save them from extermination planned by the tyrannical Zeus. We find Prometheus chained to a rock upon the Caucasus for evermore, as a divine punishment for what he has given to humanity. Addressing Io, Zeus's mistress condemned to wander the world, he prophesies that in the distant future a descendant of hers will free him. And the rest of the trilogy, which is lost, apparently led to his liberation, after thirty thousand years.

As Aeschylus's plots move remorselessly forward, they usually embody some austere, overriding passion or principle, illustrating a religious and moral problem or law. The dramatist stresses the fulfilment of providential evolution, in which human and divine purposes are ultimately reconciled, and cosmic justice, however late-coming and incomprehensible, is satisfied at the end, so that even the most disastrous pattern of evil and suffering finally takes shape as part of an exalted, beneficent design.

It was not a tragedian's function to comment directly upon contemporary events. And yet, all the same, what Aeschylus wrote, however universalized, must have harboured some contemporary underlying reference to his public and their concerns. He lived in an epoch when the contrast between tyranny and freedom was in every Athenian mind. And so *The Persians* indicated arrogant over-confidence, *hubris*, as the cause of Xerxes's failure; while reflections of Aeschylus's experiences of Sicilian tyrannies, too, have likewise been detected. The *Eumenides* exalts Athens as a place of reconciliation, under the auspices of the divine powers. But otherwise Aeschylus does not greatly help us to identify his political attitudes – which seem to endorse the values of the developing democracy, while at the same time he wonders, without complete assurance, how such values can best be implemented without destructive results.

However, the matters about which he is primarily concerned are different. They are antique inherited pollutions, punitive curses undermining families, and the dangers of too great prosperity. Yet much remains dark and ambiguous. For fate – and this seems to have been a novel exploration – does not entirely override human free will, since a victim will not be struck down unless he has already infected himself with *hubris*. Aeschylus still follows Homeric traditions, as he himself declares.[11] Yet he infuses them with his own ways of thinking. These ways are complex and deep, and the gorgeous, intricate grandeur of his language enables him to communicate what is almost incommunicable. After he died, the Athenian Assembly decreed that any citizen proposing to revive one of his plays should be granted a chorus for the purpose. He was the creator of the entire tragic drama of western Europe.

Sophocles (c.496–406), the son of a rich weapon manufacturer from Colonus outside Athens, became a friend of Pericles, and held official posts. In dramatic competitions twenty-four of his tetralogies won first prizes. These were groups of four plays – three tragedies and a satyr-play – like the productions of Aeschylus. Unlike him, however, Sophocles did not form the three tragedies into a single unit, making each, instead, an independent piece. Seven of these tragic dramas have survived.

Ajax (440s) is about the insanity of that hero of the Trojan War. For after failing in his claim to be given the weapons and armour of the dead Achilles, he went mad and mistook cattle for his enemies and attacked them, subsequently slaying himself out of shame. His strength, flawed by limitations and ignorance, has destroyed him: his grandeur is unmistakable, but the presumptuous self-assertion that prompted his disappointment and madness cuts off all possible escape from the fatal outcome. Sophocles is tracing the transition from an archaic code towards the *polis* ethic of his own day, in which heroes of this antique stamp no longer had any place to occupy.

Antigone (441) reverts to Aeschylus's theme of the *Seven Against Thebes*. After Oedipus's sons Eteocles and Polynices (who has attacked the city with Argive support) have killed each other in single combat, their sister Antigone defies the new king Creon's order forbidding Polynices funeral rites, and is consequently condemned to death. Warned by the blind seer Tiresias not to contravene divine law, the king relents, but too late, for Antigone has already killed herself, and so has her betrothed, Creon's son Haemon, and so too has Eurydice, Creon's wife. Here is an ever-memorable clash between the requirements of the state and the superior demands of universal morality, or, as the sophists put it (section 3), between law (*nomos*) and nature (*physis*). Creon displays a sinister reasonableness, tainted by *hubris*; Antigone is harshly impetuous and obstinate, yet not (Athenians probably felt) unconventional or independent, but doing what her family would have expected of her. And Sophocles was composing this play at a time when issues of legitimacy – what is right and what is wrong – were raised year after year, as the Athenian imperial democracy went on its headstrong way.

Oedipus the King (early 420s), in an intricate, succinct plot, goes back to an earlier phase of the same Theban family's mythological history. In his youth, Oedipus had left his original home at Corinth, where everyone believed him to be King Polybus's son, in order to avoid the fulfilment of an oracle pronouncing that he was destined to kill his father and marry his mother. He moved to Thebes, and (after triumphantly solving the riddle of the Sphinx) became the king of that city. But pestilence struck Thebes, and Oedipus became convinced that the plague was divinely prompted because of the unsolved murder of his predecessor Laius at a crossroads. In accordance with a warning from Tiresias (which Oedipus at first furiously rejects), it gradually dawns on him that he himself had been the murderer of Laius, that Laius – and not as he believed Polybus – was his father, and that by marrying Laius's widow Jocasta he had indeed married his mother: all of which the oracle had foretold. Jocasta hangs herself, and Oedipus puts out his own eyes and is led away out of the city. Such was the man who had fearlessly sought after the truth: it was his destiny to move, with harrowing inevitability, towards recognition and final catastrophe. He is courageous and resolute, but misplaced assurance (*hubris* once again) brings about his calamitous reversal, which so sharply underlines the fragility of the human condition.

The *Women of Trachis* (early 420s) is named after the play's chorus, who come from that region of central Greece. The queen of Trachis, Deianira, distressed by the prolonged absence of her husband Heracles, learns that Iole, one of the captive women he will be bringing home, is his mistress. Deianira sends him a robe smeared with what she thought was an aphrodisiac, but is really a poison, which kills him: whereupon she commits suicide. Their son Hyllus blames the gods, who load even the greatest men with miseries, while themselves remaining unconcerned. In the case of Heracles, they have made his downfall unavoidable: and Deianira had been wrong to believe that her magic could alter that result.

In the excellently constructed *Electra* (between 418 and 410), Orestes, accompanied by Pylades, is approaching his native city of Mycenae (Argos), by order of Apollo's Delphic oracle, in order to avenge his father Agamemnon's murder by his mother Clytemnestra (the theme of Aeschylus's *Oresteia*). Her daughter Electra reviles her, and Orestes and Pylades strike her down, together with her lover Aegisthus: whereupon the women of Mycenae, who are the chorus, welcome her murder, and hope it will bring the curse bedevilling the family, the house of Atreus, to an end. The play is full of cruelty, suffering, courage and violent love and hate.

Philoctetes (409) is named after a hero who had been left behind on the Aegean island of Lemnos by the Greek army on its way to Troy, because he was disabled by a snake-bite. During the nine years that followed, his possession of Heracles's bow and arrows had just saved him from starvation. But a seer foretold that Troy would fall only when Philoctetes, with the bow, was able to make his way there and rejoin the besieging army. The wily Odysseus, therefore, was sent by the other Greek commanders to Lemnos, accompanied by Achilles' son Neoptolemus: who then obtained the weapons by a trick – but afterwards, remorsefully, declared that he would take Philoctetes back to Greece. However Heracles, now a god, appears with orders from Zeus that all three of them should duly proceed to Troy instead: whereupon Philoctetes's wound would be healed. This psychologically perceptive drama shows how human beings make their inadequate plans, amid an atmosphere of deceit and violence that must have reminded Athenians of the degradations of their own war-torn world.

Oedipus at Colonus, performed in 401 after Sophocles's death, is the sequel to *Oedipus the King*. The self-blinded Oedipus, after years of wandering, comes to Colonus near Athens, led by his daughter Antigone. Despite the unwillingness of the Athenian elders (who form the chorus), their monarch Theseus, declaring that Oedipus has 'come to a *polis* that cultivates justice and sanctions nothing without law',[12] upholds his plea to be allowed to stay in Athenian territory, and frustrates Creon, the king of Thebes, who has come to seize him and take him back home. But Oedipus, cursing both his sons for their grasping eagerness to occupy his Theban throne, leads the way, attended by his daughters and by Theseus, to a place where he then vanishes off the face of the earth, taken by the gods. This is a mysterious play. Oedipus is still no saint, but his ordeal has ennobled him, and he has moved out of desperate isolation to ultimate acceptance by the gods.

Sophocles had introduced a third actor onto the stage, enabling him to present situations of increased complexity. His plots are taut, concise and economical, developing rapidly from point to point with the aid of a flexible style. His audiences were not ignorant of the myths he was handling and could forecast the progress of events, in contrast to the personages on the stage, who had no such foreknowledge, thus leaving room for Sophocles's famous 'tragic irony', stressing this difference in perceptions. The lyrical, imaginative, questioning odes of his choruses are employed to explore feelings and deepen perspectives, and to provide frameworks for the human endeavours and confrontations described in the narrative passages. The characters of the plays present stark contrasts designed to display the moral issues that lie behind their dilemmas. Disaster comes when the divine order has been flouted, by the *hubris* of these human personages, or even by their involuntary but unwise actions. The will of the gods is often inscrutable or even seemingly unjust, but it has to be accepted, all the same. Sufferings, like those of Oedipus, can bring tragic dignity, and, in his case, a solemn reconciliation follows. But in Sophocles' earlier plays, all too often, sorrow is left unconsoled and unredeemed. The traditional picture of the dramatist as tranquil and serene was misleading. His universe was full of pain, and tormented by bleak, agonized conflicts.

Euripides (485/480–406) belonged to a family of hereditary priests which owned a property on the island of Salamis. Unlike Sophocles, he played little part in Athenian public life. He wrote about ninety plays, of which seventeen or eighteen tragedies and one satyr-play survive. But he only won four dramatic victories during the whole course of his lifetime, and that may have been partly why in 408, not long before he died, he went to live at the court of King Archelaus of Macedonia. He won another prize at Athens after his death.

In *Alcestis* (438) Apollo, serving King Admetus of Pherae in Thessaly as a shepherd, has persuaded the Moirai (Fates) to agree that Admetus, when the time comes for his death, may escape this doom provided that a substitute volunteers to die in his place. His wife Alcestis offers herself, and Death comes to claim her. But Heracles, visiting Pherae, goes off to rescue her from his clutches, and she and Admetus are reunited. Heracles is exploited both for tragic and comic material. The brave and devoted Alcestis points the way to many of Euripides's strong-minded women, good or bad. Admetus seems shamefully unheroic.

Medea (431) takes its name from the daughter of King Aeetes of Colchis in the Caucasus, who in order to help Jason of Thessalian Iolcus, leader of the Argonauts, to seize the Golden Fleece, left her father and murdered her brother Absyrtus. Then she went back to Iolcus with Jason, and bore him two sons. He, however, now proposed to abandon her, and marry Creusa, daughter of Creon, king of Corinth, instead. So Medea, in revenge, committed four murders, assassinating not only Creusa and Creon but her own two sons as well. At the end of the play, however, a miraculous epiphany brings her back above the stage, in a fiery chariot sent by her grandfather the sun-god Helios. Jason, who has been swearing that she shall pay for her crimes, is left to his vain lamentations. He is an ungrateful snob, worse than Admetus in *Alcestis*. As for Medea, her fury, under the spur of unendurable wrong, has transformed her into a bloodthirsty demon. And we are introduced to a novel literary theme, the harrowing internal conflict that racks her heart.

Heraclidae (c.429/427) takes its name from the children of Heracles who are persecuted, as their father had been, by King Eurystheus of

Mycenae and Argos. The play is notable for its patriotic praises of Athens, in these early days of the Peloponnesian War. *Hippolytus* (428) is named after the son of King Theseus of Athens and the Amazon Hippolyte. He has rejected the overtures of the goddess of love, Aphrodite, and admires only Artemis, virgin goddess of the chase. But Aphrodite, to take her revenge, causes his stepmother Phaedra to fall in love with him. Phaedra duly becomes infatuated, but when her passion is not returned she hangs herself, leaving a statement that Hippolytus had raped her. This was not true, but he is banished by his too credulous father, whereupon the young man's horses, frightened by Poseidon, cause him to fall out of his chariot and be dragged along behind it. His injuries prove fatal, but before he dies he is reconciled with his father, who has learnt of his innocence. Here is a play in which two virtuous people have perished largely because of their virtue – and because of mis-information. Euripides refrains from openly censuring Phaedra's love. What he does, instead, is to provide a record of its grim results.

In *Andromache* (430/424) Hermione and her father Menelaus, king of Sparta, plan to murder Molossus, the child of her absent husband Neoptolemus (Achilles's son) by the captured Trojan princess Andromache. The play is a triptych deficient in unity, but its strongest idea, popular during the Peloponnesian War, is the nastiness of the Spartan king Menelaus. *Hecuba* (*Hecabe, c.*425/4) bears the name of the Trojan monarch Priam's wife, now a captive of the Greeks, who blinds King Polymestor of the Thracian Chersonese (Gallipoli peninsula), the killer of her son Polydorus. Once again, dramatic unity is weak. But we see the character of Hecabe deteriorating into murderous fury, under the pressure of wartime catastrophe that destroys the habits of decent behaviour. *The Trojan Women*, ten years later, reverted to these prisoners and the sorrows of war, with sharp and despairing emotional and lyrical force.

Meanwhile *The Suppliant Women* (*c.*422–1) had turned back to the Theban cycle. The women, mothers of the dead, beg Theseus, king of Athens, to induce the government of Thebes to relent and allow burial to Polynices and his Argive fellow-assailants of the city. But the refusal of Theseus to expel their surviving leader, Adrastus, from Athenian territory causes Thebes to declare war on Athens. In the hostilities that follow, however, the Athenians prove victorious: whereupon Adrastus swears that Argos will never fight against them again – a topical message at a time, in Greek fifth-century history, when the Argives were going to become, briefly, the allies of Athens.

Heracles or *Mad Heracles* (*Hercules Furens, c.*420) tells how the Theban

83

king Lycus plans to massacre the absent hero's family. Heracles returns in time to save them, and slays Lycus. But he is then driven insane by the goddess Hera – who has hated him ever since his birth – and in this shocking reversal of his greatness he puts his own wife and children to death. When he recovers, he is persuaded not to commit suicide by Theseus, who offers him an Athenian home.

Euripides's *Electra* tells the story of this daughter of Agamemnon and Clytemnestra that Sophocles had told – or was going to tell, for the relative chronology of the two versions is not certain – but diminishes the narrative into the seediness of an unglamorous down-to-earth situation, played out by warped and vicious minds. Clytemnestra, it was believed, had murdered her husband because he sacrificed their daughter Iphigenia at Aulis so that the divine powers might allow the Greek fleet to sail to Troy. But Euripides's *Iphigenia in Tauris* (414/412) pronounces that this had never happened at all, but that the goddess Artemis, instead, had magically whisked her off to the Tauric Chersonese (Crimea). This play, describing her rescue from the Chersonese by her brother Orestes and his friend Pylades, is crammed with suspense and dramatic irony. Euripides has entered a new phase of intricate, romantic stories of sentiment-laden intrigue and surprise, which seem closer to Menander's New Comedy of the next century than to the classical tragedy of the past. We are away in an exotic land, where the hero and heroine overcome every manner of obstacle to arrive at a happy ending. Life is never quite what it had appeared to be, and perhaps Euripides is telling his audience, amid wartime anxieties, that things need not always be as bad as they look.

In another fairytale, *Helen* (412), the heroine, once again, had really never left for Troy with Paris after all (as in Stesichorus's *Recantation*): it was only a phantom that went, whereas she herself had been conjured away to Egypt by the god Hermes. But her shipwrecked husband Menelaus arrives, and totters onto the stage: whereupon she tricks the barbarian king and gets away. *Ion* (c.411?) is the son of Apollo and the Athenian princess Creusa, who had given birth to him secretly in a cave; but Hermes takes the baby to Apollo's temple at Delphi. Many years later, Creusa, with her husband Xuthus, comes to Delphi and they gradually come to realize that Ion is her son. Here is another complicated drama, with a recognition theme that was, once again, to recur in the New Comedy.

Phoenician Women (c.410) takes us back to *Seven Against Thebes*, and belongs to a period in Euripides's career when he packs abundant subject matter into vigorous, speedily moving plots. *Orestes* (408) returns to the house of Atreus, which had figured in *Electra*, but here the brother and sister plan to kill Helen (who is visiting Argos with her husband Menelaus), and to kidnap their daughter Hermione. Helen is rescued, however, by Apollo, who predicts that Orestes will marry Hermione and become king of Argos. This is Euripides's most theatrical and violent melodrama, in which traditional mythology is, not for the first time, turned upside down to become an all too human world of squalor, venality and malice. *Iphigenia in Aulis* (performed posthumously in 406–5) cancels out *Iphigenia in Tauris* by declaring that the maiden did go to Aulis after all, and was sacrificed there in accordance with tradition. Pathos and entertainment march hand in hand, amid a bewildering series of muddles and doubts and reversals.

The terrifying *Bacchants* (*Bacchae*) was once again performed after Euripides's death (405). The Bacchants are attendants of the god Dionysus (Bacchus), who has returned to his native Thebes from Asia. King Pentheus's mother Agave and her sisters have become the god's devotees (Maenads) and departed for Mount Cithaeron, where he proposes to join them. One of Pentheus's servants comes to him with a captive, who is Dionysus himself, although no one realizes this. But the whole palace crumbles to the ground, and the king becomes fuddled, and allows himself to be persuaded by Dionysus to go and spy on the women upon the mountain. But when Pentheus reaches them they seize him and tear him to pieces. Their leader is Agave, who has gone mad, and arrives on the stage brandishing her son's head, which she believes to be a lion's. But her sanity comes back to her, and Dionysus reappears and justifies his vengeance on non-believers. What are we to think of him? He is an incomprehensible god, holy and diabolical, beyond all standards of good and evil. He presents a warning that we ignore the irrational orgiastic forces within ourselves at our own peril, even if they shatter the bonds of society and the *polis*. They are forces with which Pentheus, an ordinary man, is disastrously unable to cope.

The struggles of human beings to escape from such menaces often inspired Euripides to analytical, clinical observation, not unmixed with compassion. His legendary heroes may turn out to be unattractive and inferior, and love is all too often not a pleasure but a torment. War is full of horrors, and women are among its worst sufferers. They can be heroic, but sometimes too they are murderous, earning Euripides the reputation of misogyny; though his male characters are equally flawed. As for his gods and goddesses, it is clear what Dionysus is like: a demonic psychological power. But other divinities are sometimes mere sordid seducers, or figures of fun. Yet the playwright was not so much an atheist as a questioning agnostic, who distrusted too easy answers, especially in difficult times.

His plays often start with an explanatory prologue or introduction. A strange feature, too, is his *deus ex machina*, the divinity who appears and intervenes at the end of a drama, learnedly clearing up outstanding points or loose ends. And these epiphanies must also have displayed the spectacular theatrical stagecraft which was one of this playwright's specialities. His characters' clear diction abounds in quotable epigrams, and is interspersed by sparkling choral lyrics, enhanced, it was said, by original and excitable music. Despite the lack of official Athenian recognition in his lifetime, Aristotle later described Euripides as 'the most tragic of poets'.[13]

Such are the plays of Aeschylus, Sophocles and Euripides, which have implanted in us the classical, humane conviction that, for all their faults and failures, men and women are capable of magnificent exertions, and self-sacrifices as well.

The ancient origins of Attic Old Comedy are as mixed as those of tragedy. But the provision of comic plays at the annual Athenian festival of the City Dionysia did not begin until 488/7 or 487/6, and they were first included in another Dionysiac festival, in the Lenaea, during the 440s.

The only Old Comedy dramatist to have left us entire works is Aristophanes (457/445–before 385), from whom we have not only a list of forty-three titles, but eleven complete plays. *Acharnians* (from Acharnae near Athens; 425) shows Amphitheus being sent by Dicaeopolis ('just government') to Sparta in order to make a private peace for himself and his family. *Knights* (*Hippeis*, 424) obliquely reviles the Athenian statesman Cleon – who had brought a prosecution against Aristophanes – for 'attacks on the magistrates (state officials)'. Cleon is thinly disguised as a slave of Demos ('the people') from Paphlagonia (northern Asia Minor): Demos declares his intention of rejecting all fraudulent, innovative politicians and reviving traditional customs. *The Clouds* (*Nephelai*; 423) makes fun of Socrates (section 3, below) and his tricky Think School, which is burnt to the ground. *The Wasps* (*Sphekes*, 422) satirizes the legal system that was creating an epidemic of litigation in Athenian democratic society. *The Peace* (*Eirene*; 421) displays an unusually optimistic spirit because Athens and Sparta were, at this time, planning the Peace of Nicias, which temporarily called a halt to the Peloponnesian War.

The Birds (*Ornithes*) are a chorus which guides the hero Euelpides and his friend Peisthetaerus away from Attica – in the tense year 414, when the Sicilian expedition had been launched. They are hoping to found a community based on fashionable Utopianism (*Nephel-*

ococcygia, Cloudcuckooland), in the middle of the sky. *Lysistrata* (*'Demobilize the Army'*, 411) is a woman who summons other members of her sex, from all over Greece, who want an end to the Peloponnesian War, since she has formed a plan to restore peace to the country, urgently needed when the armies of its traditional foe (Persia) are supposedly close at hand. Her plan is that they should refuse sexual relations to their husbands until the fighting stops, and in pursuance of this aim the women occupy the Athenian Acropolis. The *Thesmophoriazusae* (411 or 410), once again, are women, attending their autumn festival of the Thesmophoria in honour of Demeter. They are devising vengeance against Euripides for his alleged anti-feminism, and the main purpose of the play is to make fun of the playwright.

The Frogs (*Batrachoi*; 405) has a somewhat similar aim, for the god Dionysus is proceeding to the underworld to bring Euripides back to the earth. In Hades, a poetical contest is held between Euripides and Aeschylus, and finally it is Aeschylus whom Dionysus decides to take back to the upper world. Aristophanes admired both dramatists, but evidently felt that Euripides's influence had been, on the whole, harmful, at this critical moment near the end of the Peloponnesian War. *Ecclesiazusae* (*Assemblywomen*, 392) returns to the feminist theme, represented by Praxagora who successfully proposes that the Athenian government should be handed over to women. Finally, in *Plutus* (388), Aristophanes has turned from political preoccupations to social concerns, describing Chremylus's consultation of Apollo's oracle at Delphi about how he can convert his son into a crook, so that the youth can make a success of his life at Athens.

These comedies are crammed with burlesque and fantasy, displaying inexhaustible powers of invention. The dramatist's attacks on prominent contemporaries, such as Cleon, are startlingly free, and so are his pleas for peace in times of war. His solid, old-fashioned convictions are a blend of commonsense, humaneness and moderation, mobilized in favour of ordinary Athenians and plain country people. His attitude to the gods seems, to us, curiously ambiguous: the community must offer them due worship, and yet they all too often seem ridiculous and dishonest. Women – although their parts are acted by men, as in tragedy – are astonishingly prominent.

Aristophanes's actors, usually four in number, wore ludicrous masks and padded clothes, and the performers of male roles displayed exaggerated penises. The choral songs, though important in the development of the plots, are often lyrical and light. The structures of the plays are more or less fixed and conventional. With the New Comedy of Menander (Chapter 7) and its Latin adapters Plautus and Terence

(Chapter 9) as intermediaries, the entire comic drama of Europe can be traced back to the exuberant art of Aristophanes.

3 Philosophy

The first half of Pre-Socratic philosophy, which sought to identify the basic materials constituting reality and the universe (Chapter 3, section 1), was brought to an abrupt end by Parmenides of Elea (Velia), whose short poem *On Nature*, of which about 160 lines have survived, probably belongs to the period soon after the Persian Wars. Parmenides tells us that these earlier thinkers had been labouring under a delusion. In particular, when our senses seem to demonstrate to us the plurality and multiplicity of the universe and world, they are wrong, he declares, since reality ('what is') is one, unchanging, continuous and permanent – occupying the whole of space, in which there can be no void, and no such thing as 'becoming' is possible. That being so, it is out of the question that such an indivisible unity could generate plurality. Heraclitus of Ephesus, therefore, in seeing change and flux as the essence of the world, had just been mistaken.

Parmenides was offering the first sustained discussion of philosophical method in European thought. That is to say, he was the first Greek thinker to base his findings exclusively on rational, logical, stringent argumentation – pointing the way to the formal logic of the future, and earning him comparisons with Descartes. In the process, however, while contradicting his forerunners, he had abandoned the evidence of the senses altogether. This was a conclusion that no one could believe. Yet he had reached it by arguments that no one could refute. And his bracing, cold-water paradoxes, explaining nature by shutting our eyes to its complexity, made a devastating impact.

In the hope of closing this alarming gap between reality and appearances, the Greek thinkers who came next attempted to find ways of retaining his intellectual method, but avoiding its outrageous deductions. Thus Empedocles of Acragas (Agrigento) in Sicily (*c*.493–422) – philosopher-poet, statesman, magician, pioneer in rhetoric and medicine – while accepting Parmenides's assertion that real being is permanent and everlasting, differed from him by admitting the existence, also, of material things and elements, as the second layer of a two-tier system. In other words, Empedocles conceded the reality of the sense perceptions: which, however, he interpreted as the mixture and separation of things or elements that already existed and are *undying*, within a unified, Parmenidean framework. But he saw Parmenides's unified reality not as single but as dual, falling back, here, on Heraclitus's opposites, and calling them Love and Strife. And whereas earlier Ionian philosophers had arbitrarily stressed one, basic primary element, Empedocles found no less than four – fire, air, water and earth.

Anaxagoras of Clazomenae in Ionia (c.500–c.428), who settled in Athens and became one of Pericles's friends, took Empedocles's compromise further. He agreed with Parmenides that there is a permanent reality in relation to which 'becoming' is unthinkable, and yet, against Parmenides's paradoxical insistence to the contrary, and in common with Empedocles, he was also prepared to accept the validity of sense perceptions. But he moved beyond Empedocles by asserting that the plural elements are not four but innumerable, and infinitely divisible – a firm denial of Parmenides's indivisibility – change, as Anaxagoras believed, being accounted for by the constant rearrangement of these innumerable, permanent element or particles. Moreover, he contradicted Empedocles once again by pronouncing that the universal governance is conducted not by opposites, Love and Strife, but by a single directive authority: which he called Mind (*nous*). He was building on both Parmenides and Empedocles, but altering them both, in the hope of finding out how the universe is run.

Another attempt to escape from the Parmenidean *impasse* was made by the atomists, Leucippus of Miletus and Democritus of Abdera (Avdira) in Thrace (born 460–457); we cannot easily distinguish between their two contributions. They conceded Parmenides's view that reality is homogeneous and unchanging, and yet saw it as composed of innumerable atoms, not unlike the elements postulated by Anaxagoras. But Leucippus and Democritus stressed that each of these atoms possessed the indestructible character of Parmenides's unity. However (as he would never have done), they also ascribed movement to them, since (again unlike Parmenides) they allowed the existence of a void, within which such movement was able to take place.

The next aspect of their views presented a departure from Empedocles and Anaxagoras as well. For they saw no need for universal controllers, Love, Strife or Mind. On the contrary, the universe seemed to them to be ruled by blindly mechanical, 'necessary' laws. So they were the first explicit, thoroughgoing materialists. Yet this did not remove their desire to allow human beings the power to manipulate mechanical necessity – up to a certain point at least – though the details of how this was to be done seem to have been left to a later philosopher, Epicurus (Chapter 7, section 2).

Philosophy next took a specialized turn, in the hands of the sophists.

The term *sophistes*, when it first came into use, meant simply a wise man (*sophos*) or expert or sage. Gradually, however, the word was applied to a new profession in Greek life: that of higher education.

By directing their endeavours towards this sort of activity, the sophists did something that had never been done before, and transformed Greek society in the process. Although they did not form a single group, and indeed differed greatly one from another, most of them had one thing in common: they were paid, itinerant lecturers. They taught all manner of subjects, but what they did most of all was to examine the meaning of words, and how to use them. For their object, although ostensibly defined as the teaching of virtue or excellence (*arete*), was primarily to help their pupils to get on in life – and at a Greek city nothing could serve this aim more effectively than a mastery of the art of speech and persuasion.

As time went on, the sharper kind of sophist became proud of his capacity to argue in favour of any point of view whatever, whether truthful or not. The contrast between *physis*, nature, and *nomos*, city-state law and custom, was constantly emphasized: often with the suggestion that the latter is inevitably arbitrary. So, to old-fashioned people, the word 'sophist' assumed a derogatory significance, whereas, on the other hand, such teachings excited those members of the younger generation who, in difficult times, felt that the establishment was letting them down, and had nothing honest to offer.

The earliest and most famous of the sophists, and the first, apparently, to describe himself by such a term, was Protagoras of Abdera (Avdira) in Thrace. After travelling about for many years, he went to Sicily, but also spent much time at Athens. His lectures sometimes formed parts of verbal, literary competitions between rival speakers; but he spent most of his time conducting private courses. 'Young man,' he is supposed to have said to a prospective client, 'if you come to me you will go home a better man.'[14] He became a friend of Pericles, who chose him to draw up the code of laws for the colony of Thurii (Sybaris) in south Italy, a joint venture by various cities which was mainly sponsored by Athens. And Protagoras underwent serious attacks by Pericles's political enemies.

One of his statements, in particular, seemed open to shocked criticism: 'I know nothing about the gods, either that they are or they are not or what are their shapes' – it is too uncertain a subject, and life is too short. This was not exactly atheistic, but it was enough to earn him a charge of impiety. But Protagoras's most famous assertion was that 'the human being is the measure of all things: of things that are, that they are; and of things that are not, that they are not.'[15] This did more than point to the central position of humankind in the universe: for it also suggested that all judgments and perceptions whatever, emanating from individual persons, are subjective and relative. The pronouncement hinted, that is to say, at scepticism about the claims of any and every belief to possess universal validity. Protagoras himself may not have gone quite as far as that, but in his *Antilogiae* (*Contradictions*) he was said to have indicated that on every subject there are two possible arguments, one for and one against: a suggestion which was potentially subversive. Nevertheless, as regards standards of practical conduct, he seems to have been a traditionalist, believing that we have an ingrained moral sense – and that morality means conformity with the laws and customs (*nomoi*) of one's state.

Other sophists, developing various aspects of Protagoras's work, found some of these assumptions too conservative. Thus the ency-clopaedic educationalist Hippias of Elis (*c*.485–415) gave the *physis-nomos* controversy the twist that was mentioned above, by declaring that, whereas *physis* binds human beings together by its natural bond, *nomos* often exercises a coercion that is contrary to nature and tyrannical. Gorgias of Leontini (Carlentini) in Sicily (*c*.483–376), specializing in words and style, displayed how arguments could be pursued to out-rageous conclusions – of which his exploitation of the *physis-nomos* antithesis in support of nascent ideas of Panhellenism (*physis*), con-trasted with city patriotism (*nomos*), appeared to many listeners, devoted to the city-state concept, to be a distressing example. Prodicus of Ceos, another expert on language, caused dismay by suggesting that religion is not natural, the gods being nothing more than man-made inventions expressing gratitude for nature's gifts. And Antiphon of Athens seemed more alarming still, since he would have nothing of Protagoras's moral restraints, regarding them as arbitrary impositions, which one should ignore if one gets a chance, acting with the egotism which is what one's nature (*physis*) demands. Callicles, a pupil of Gorgias, drew the logical conclusion that the stronger man should prevail over the weaker, and Thrasymachus of Calchedon (Kadıköy) saw 'justice' as meaning the same thing: that might is right.

Although empirical observation, on the whole, fell behind theory in Greek scientific research, medicine proved an exception, and during the sixth century several medical schools came into being (encouraged by the popularity of athletics, which demanded their services). Alcma-eon of Croton (*c*.500) laid stress on surgical practice, thus beginning the conversion of medicine into a scientific discipline. Yet at the same time he also relied upon undemonstrable theory, insisting that health depends on the balanced 'equal rights' (*isonomia*) of opposites – a concept borrowed from Ionian thinkers such as Heraclitus – in contrast to the *monarchia*, or 'tyranny', of disease.

But the marathon step forward, tradition maintained, was taken by Hippocrates of Cos, in the later fifth century. Son of a physician of the medico-religious Asclepiad guild associated with the healing god Asclepius – though he himself possessed no close links with the cult – Hippocrates was another heir of the rationalist Ionians, since Democritus of Abdera was said to have been among his teachers. Hippocrates, according to tradition, interpreted the human frame as an interrelated, single, unified organism. However, the fifty-eight works (in seventy-three books) known as the *Corpus Hippocraticum*, and constituting, all in all, a determined series of attacks on non-rational ways of thinking, do not all come from Cos and are mostly much later than Hippocrates (including the Hippocratic Oath, enjoining high standards of medical ethics).

Half a dozen of the writings in the *Corpus*, however, are at least attributable to his lifetime, though probably not to his personal authorship. One such work is *Airs, Waters and Places* (*On Environment*), which considers how differing environmental situations affect the human body, and notes the contrasting conditions of Europe and Asia. *On the Sacred Disease* shows that the ailment to which it refers (epilepsy) is no more 'sacred' and magical than any other illness. *On Diet, Epidemics* and *On Ancient Medicine* display empirical, systematic observation, and the *Prognosticum* elevates prognosis over diagnosis in a manner characteristic of Cos (which also stressed humanity, it was said, while a rival school at Cnidus emphasized science).

Socrates (*c*.470–399), a contemporary of Hippocrates, wrote nothing himself, and it is very hard to disentangle his true opinions from what Aristophanes, Xenophon and Plato wrote about him. He was on close terms, it appears, with Pericles's friends, and in his youth listened to Archelaus, an Athenian pupil of the philosopher-scientist Anaxagoras. But then Socrates turned away from cosmology, and spent the rest of his life enquiring into a matter which had begun to interest some of his predecessors, namely human behaviour: and what he particularly tried to do was to define what makes it right or wrong.

The most important of his beliefs was the conviction that there is an eternal and unchanging *absolute standard* of right and wrong – in conformity with which we must try to make our souls as good as possible. To do this, however, we must listen to our consciences, and use our brains to work out what is, indeed, right and wrong. For *virtue is knowledge*: know yourself, for no one does wrong willingly. This was a striking, if logically dubious, conclusion, and so was the 'teleological' belief (probably attributable to Socrates, as his followers maintained) that all nature works towards a purpose.

He himself, he ironically declared, knew nothing, but – with the exception of the two dogmas that have just been mentioned – he tried to arrive at the truth through rational enquiry, pursued by the 'Socratic method' of cross-questioning. Although scrupulous in observing his city's religious observances, he deplored immoral myths, and claimed, on occasion, to be guided by a divine sign or voice (*daimonion*).

His physical stamina was remarkable, and despite his love of irony, which could cause offence, he was genial and charming and kind, and possessed a varied and devoted circle of friends. Many of them came from the younger members of the upper class; Socrates never thought highly of the democratic form of government practised at Athens, and said so. When, therefore, this democracy was revived, after the end of the Peloponnesian War, he found himself brought to trial on a capital charge (399). The real, underlying accusation, however – his un-democratic political views – could not be admitted, since an amnesty was by this time in force. It was therefore declared, instead, 'that he does not believe in the gods in whom the city believes, but introduces other and new deities; also that he corrupts the young.' He was found guilty by 281 votes to 220. At that juncture, as earlier, he could have got away from Athens, but did not avail himself of this opportunity, since he regarded it as his civic obligation to remain in the city. Instead of escaping, therefore, he made a speech in court, suggesting that he should be maintained for life as a public benefactor. The jury felt insulted by what sounded like flippancy, and he was condemned to death. And so he drank the poisonous hemlock, and died. Eternally significant because he perished in the cause of freedom of conscience, he created the gigantic and potent Socratic legend.

One of his pupils was Plato (*c*.429–347), who, disgusted by his teacher's condemnation and execution, fled, after Socrates' death, to join other philosophical leaders elsewhere, Euclides of Megara and Archytas of Taras (Taranto) in south Italy.

Archytas, who successfully ruled his powerful city from *c*.380 to *c*.345, revived and rejuvenated the philosophical school of Pythagoras (Chapter 3, section 3), and was himself virtually the founder of mathematical mechanics: mathematical calculation alone, he observed, is able to breed confidence among men and prevent strife. Plato absorbed

93

Archytas's writings in this field, appreciating their application to ethics and the social order, and other Pythagorean features perceptible in Platonic dialogues bear witness once again to the same man's influence. Plato also paid three visits to Sicily, hoping to purify and philosophize the political life of Syracuse, under Dionysius I (405–367) and his nephew Dionysius II (367–357/6). These expeditions, however, were humiliating failures, especially on the last occasion, in 361, when he was detained and had to appeal to Archytas to secure his release.

After the first of the three Sicilian visits Plato had founded his Academy at Athens, where he taught, when not travelling, from that time onwards. Several of his works are related to the trial of Socrates, in an imaginative fashion which does not invite too keen a search for strict historical truth. *The Apology* is an idealized account of Socrates' trial, and a moving defence, in effect, of his entire life work. *Crito* discusses why Socrates, by his behaviour in court, threw his life away, and raises the whole question of what is right and wrong in relation to the state. In *Euthyphro*, Socrates is made to declare that true religion is not subservience to arbitrary demands but cooperation in the noble tending of the soul. In *Phaedo*, on the last day of his life, he is credited with the hypothesis that the immortality of the soul is a reasonable doctrine. Here, once again, is a doctrine Plato had probably learnt from Archytas.

Other Platonic dialogues, which do not deal directly with Socrates's trial and death, nevertheless present him, imaginatively, as the principal interlocutor, devoting himself to questionings that are 'aporetic' (full of puzzles). The *Charmides* shows him talking to a young man of that name, Plato's purpose, indirectly, being to clear him of the accusation that he corrupted Athenian youth. *Charmides* seeks to define temperance or self-control (*sophrosyne*), and *Laches* likewise attempts to reach a definition of courage. *Menexenus* (385) is amusingly scathing about the epoch of Pericles, whose mistress Aspasia talks with Socrates about the Corinthian War (Chapter 5). But that war had taken place in 395–387, long after both Aspasia and Socrates were dead – which is a warning against attempts to regard Plato's dialogues as historically authentic.

Meno asks us to consider whether virtue is teachable or not. This is, of course, relevant to the sophists – discussed above – about whom Plato has a lot of interesting, and often rather unfair, things to say, since he disapproves of their amoral attitudes and their frivolous logic-chopping (rebuked in *Euthydemus*), not to speak of their acceptance of fees. True, *Protagoras* offers a not wholly unjust picture of the teacher of that name. But one of his colleagues is less respectfully treated in

Greater and *Lesser Hippias*, and in *Gorgias* Socrates is made to maintain that the rhetoric taught by the eminent sophist of that name was no more than an expedient knack, far removed from the absolute standard our conscience ought to enjoin upon us.

Amid a homosexual aura (though that, we are told, had not been Socrates's personal taste), the dramatic, subtle and witty *Symposium* professes to record the various speeches in praise of Love (Eros) deliv-ered – in accordance with the oratorical tradition of such gatherings – at a banquet in honour of the tragic playwright Agathon. But the main purpose of the work is to show – as Socrates does, inspired, he declares, by the priestess Diotima of Mantinea – how love, at first excited by a beautiful body, can finally and rapturously rise to a super-sensuous, transcendental passion for abstract beauty itself, which only the intellect can apprehend. *Cratylus*, though roughly of the same date, turns to an entirely different subject. It amounts to our first etymological treatise, concluding that language, if we can get away from subjectivities, is a genuine instrument of thought, capable of expressing even the most ideal kinds of thinking with accuracy, and therefore of vital assistance in enabling us to get at the truth.

For now it was time for Plato, still ostensibly under the guidance of Socrates, to discuss what knowledge consists of. *Theaetetus*, on this topic, remains one of the best existing introductions to the science of epis-temology concerned with that subject. Relativism is refuted, and so is the equation of knowledge with sense-perception. But nothing much, at this stage, is put in their place. Was Plato, perhaps, beginning to feel that the truth, ultimately, defies definition altogether? This is a matter about which *Parmenides* makes us wonder. It is a disconcerting dialogue, because in some ways the philosopher of that name comes out of the debate better than Socrates himself – although we are left, it is true, with the impression that Parmenides' rejection of all material things, experienced by the senses, cannot be valid. Indeed, on the contrary, Plato's *Phaedrus* grants these sense perceptions substantial reality, pro-vided that they are examined according to legitimate logical procedures. And rhetoric, too, which is the main theme of the same work, can likewise be given a sounder foundation than the trickery, say, of Gorgias, once logic is properly applied.

And then there are dialogues in which Socrates is no longer the central figure. In the abstruse, polymathic *Timaeus* his place is taken by an astronomer of that name, from Locri Epizephyrii in south-east Italy, who returns to the Parmenidean attitude, treating the mutable temporal world as only a pale imitation of unchanging eternal being. A monotheistic god is introduced as the intelligent, effective director of

95

this whole providential, moral order, although he, or it, sometimes operates in incomprehensible and apparently aberrant fashions. In *Sophist* the principal spokesman is an unnamed follower of Parmenides (from his home town, Elea): yet, in spite of the *Timaeus*, the Parmenidean theory that the material world is a mere illusion is rejected after all. And then, *Philebus* – in which Socrates reappears as principal speaker – sums up Plato's final thoughts on ethics and the good life, which is a matter, he concludes, of both intelligence and pleasure, with intelligence occupying the major role.

Plato was impressed by Socrates's insistence on absolute standards, which he himself linked with the belief, adumbrated by earlier philosophers and variously discussed in his own works, that even if our senses are not a mere illusion there is a divine and unchanging reality transcending them. This was the doctrine that lay behind the Theory of Forms (*ideai*) which appeared again and again in Plato's thinking, though in his later dialogues it assumed a modified and less clear-cut shape. These Forms, apprehended by the intellect and crowned by the highest Form of all, the Form of the Good, are permanent, unvarying, eternal realities – which have given Plato his renown as the archetypal idealistic philosopher – in contrast to the shifting, imperfect, material phenomena (perceived by the senses) which 'participate' in the Forms, or, as Plato later said, 'imitate' them.

One can see why he is so fascinated by Parmenides's rejection of these material phenomena as unreal, in contrast to the eternal realities. But Plato himself, for all his insistence on those immutable realities, does not himself join in any such rejection, for he finds a bridge between them and the material world: and that bridge is the soul, as envisaged by Socrates as present in all individual persons, in whom it reflects the whole macrocosm of the universe and enables its possessors to reach upwards and grasp the unchanging principles by which the universe is governed. Moreover, like Socrates once again, he adopts the teleological view that everything has its purpose, seeing the well-being of the individual soul, at its greatest and best, as the natural end (*telos*) of all movement and endeavour.

Such were the various motivations that prompted Plato not only to intervene himself, disastrously, in the political affairs of Sicily, but also to earn the lasting interest of the western world by conceiving and offering theoretical views on political matters, and particularly on what might be the nature of a state's ideal constitution.

His major statements on such themes, widely separated in date, were the *Republic* (*Politeia*), *Statesman* (*Politicus*) and *Laws*. The ten books of the *Republic* (380s or 370s BC), blending politics, ethics and metaphysics in a complex, intoxicating spirit of crusading passion, are concerned with the nature of justice. It is shown, in a series of discussions led by Socrates, to be beneficial to all concerned, rationally defensible, and morally imperative: so that Thrasymachus's counter-definition of the concept as the advantage of the stronger is refuted.

Plato's imaginary ideal state is governed by guardians, who are presided over by a 'philosophical king' (for whom Archytas served as a model), and possess their wives, children and property in common. There will be three classes of citizens, each performing its proper function, and persuaded to do so, if necessary, by 'noble lies'. All political change is an illness (assuming its most virulent form in tyranny), and educational innovation is wrong, too, since it leads to cultural licence – of which poetry is an extreme example, being an imitation alien from truth, whereas mathematics, on the other hand, provides the ideal subject of instruction.

Plato's *Statesman* (360s), bringing back the *Sophist*'s Eleatic interlocutor, reaffirms the evils of tyranny, but, as an alternative, considers democracy inferior to elective monarchy. The *Laws* settles, in what some have seen as a disillusioned afterthought, for a second-best state. Communism is, in practice, abandoned, and a mixed constitution seems a suitable compromise. A hierarchy of functionaries, directed by a meticulous system of checks and balance, culminates in thirty-seven Guardians of the Law. But there is also to be a Nocturnal Council, presiding over a House of Corrections where delinquents are argued with or, if that proves useless, put to death. For citizens must maintain unwavering obedience to the rules. And these, incidentally – in the true spirit of the Greek *polis* – take for granted a continual state of undeclared war between one state and another, so that peace is a meaningless term.

Utilitarianism, the theory that action is right if it achieves the greatest good of the greatest number, has claimed Plato as its founder, owing to his desire to secure the welfare of the whole community. Yet as his *Statesman* and other writings showed, he was no friend of the democrats, any more than his master Socrates had been. Furthermore, his desire that people should be governed by Reason – and that they should be induced, if necessary, to accept this government by coercive means, since reasoning is not their natural inclination – prompted him to recommend the enforcement of authoritarian regulations: including, for example, rigorous controls of the teaching of music, art, and (as we have seen) poetry, so as to leave no room for emotional licence.

Our own minds, however, are easily distracted from the distaste that we may feel for such views, owing to Plato's superlative mastery of Greek prose, displayed by a potent, graceful, versatile style, ringing all the changes from humorous lightness to heartfelt solemnity. Plato employs the dialogue form with alluring skill, unpacks a wealth of sparkling, poetical metaphors, and shows himself a master of mythical and allegorical narrative, which he utilizes to convey otherwise scarcely expressible profundities.

Aristotle (384–322) was born at the Ionian colony of Stagirus in Chalcidice (Macedonia), son of the court physician of the Macedonian king Amyntas III. At the age of seventeen, he went to study at Plato's Academy at Athens, where he remained for twenty years. After Plato's death, however, he and a fellow-Academician, Xenocrates, migrated to Atarneus (near Dikili) in Mysia N.W. Asia Minor (ruled over by Hermias, a friend of Philip). Then he moved again to Mieza in Macedonia, where he allegedly supervised the education of Philip's son Alexander III the Great. In 335, however, back in Athens, he founded the school of the Lyceum, its members known as Peripatetics (from *peripatos*, covered court). After Alexander's death (323) he went to Chalcis in Euboea, where he died.

Aristotle's writings were of unparalleled size and range, and out of a huge number of treatises forty-seven have survived. Their foundation was the logical reasoning that Plato had so greatly admired, and which Aristotle located – under the name of 'analytics', the art of discourse – in the forecourt of the sciences, as a necessary preliminary to each and every one of them. His *Organon* (Instrument, Tool) consists of six studies on the theme. The most important of these essays are the *Prior* and *Posterior Analytics*, of which the former reviews the principles of inductive inference, and the latter indicates how the methods of proof and definition that emerge from that review can assess the validity of knowledge. For Aristotle was the first man to inspect, closely, the differing forms of linguistic statements, and the formal relations they bear to each other, and his *Organon* was the most important ancient collection of writings concerned with this matter.

Such was the tool with which he then proceeded to tackle the entire field of knowledge. His *Metaphysics*, examining the nature of reality, discern a hierarchy of existences, at the apex of which stands the 'Unmoved First Mover', identified with God, an eternal activity of thought, free from any material admixture, imparting motion to the universe. This was a concept which had already been suggested by Plato, and formed a fundamental feature of Aristotle's thought. The *Physics* are lectures on nature, in which he redefined Plato's Forms, which did not altogether meet with his approval. What he did not like was any supposition that the Forms enjoy a separate existence of their own, since he himself preferred to regard them as *immanent* in perceived material objects. For Aristotle, although he cherished a deep affection and reverence for Plato, felt an aversion from his idealistic, transcendental approach (and he refused to accept the preeminence of mathematics as well). On the other hand, like Plato and even more so, he was a teleologist, convinced that everything exists for an end, and a good end at that.

As for the sciences, Aristotle divided them into three groups, theoretical, practical and productive (that is to say, devoted to the creation of something over and above the activity involved). And he is the earliest author whose writings on these scientific subjects can be adequately studied in their original condition.

It was while undertaking the analysis of living things that he felt most at home. Biology was his key science, and it was a science (a 'theoretical' science) that he intended to present in its entirety – assigning the vegetable kingdom to his pupil Theophrastus, while he undertook most of the zoological part of the vast project himself. His several investigations of animals, which emerged from this decision, display originality, acumen and patience – although the Unmoved Mover and teleology do not fail to make their appearance once again. The treatise *On the Soul* interprets the soul as the internal principle which holds the body together and endows it with life, the human soul ranking above those of animals and plants, because it alone has the power of thought.

Aristotle's *Nicomachean Ethics*, named after his son, is the most famous of all studies of morality. It deals with the 'practical' human science of being good and behaving well, which is equated with well-being or happiness (*eudaimonia*). Here, the absoluteness of Plato's moral values is abandoned in favour of a more realistic and pragmatic diversity, allowing for the aspects of character that can be displayed in daily life. Pleasure, honour and wealth, however, are rejected as the bases of this *eudaimonia*, and at its apex stands Wisdom (*sophia*), finding its highest expression in the burning, indefatigable vision of philosophical truth. In the *Eudemian Ethics* Aristotle objects (rightly) to Socrates's dictum that 'no man is willingly bad', and excellence is seen to come as a result of deliberately selecting the Mean, the middle course (an idea much admired by the Greeks, so prone to extremes): which means the particular proportion of qualities that is suitable to one's own self.

Aristotle's *Politics* remains our most ample and searching investigation into the political conditions of ancient Greece. The city-state, despite Philip II of Macedonia and his son Alexander, is still treated as the norm, even though it is also taken for granted that every such state is riven by faction, based on the economic differences between one class and another. A painstaking examination of various 'model' constitutions leads to an enquiry into what the best sort of state may be. In Aristotle's view, it will be, once again, an expression of the Mean, an aristocracy of intellect and virtue, comprising, basically, people of moderate prosperity: for Aristotle, agreeing with Plato in this regards education (under state control) as the first essential, but, unlike him, he wants not only the intellectual capacities of pupils to be trained, but their emotions and bodies as well.

Education is pursued further in the *Rhetoric*, which considers the methods of persuasion open to the orator, and how they can be reduced to rule – a matter of keen interest to the Greeks, and to the Athenians most of all. The influential *Poetics* is a study of poetry, which is more 'philosophical' than history, Aristotle believes, because it tells general truths – and he does not, like Plato, regard its creation and existence as necessarily undesirable. Originally, the complete work dealt with epic, tragedy and comedy, but as it has come down to us tragedy is the principal theme. The components of a tragic drama are analysed, and so are some of its characteristic features – reversal, recognition, flaw (*hamartia*) – and the purpose of such a play is defined as 'effecting the proper purgation (or purification) of the emotions through terror and pity'.[16] A tragedy seeks to offer, that is to say, a cathartic and pleasurable outlet for the audience's emotions.

The writings that have survived, out of Aristotle's enormous output, are, clearly, not his most brilliant stylistic achievements – which are referred to by Cicero[17] but cannot now be located – but they are probably the most important works he wrote. He always remained, at heart, a speculative questioner, willing to consider new data whenever they appeared and to handle a matter again and again. And yet, at the same time, he was the orderly, responsive systematizer of vast tracts of knowledge and method. In the process, he established the major divisions of philosophy – which are still accepted as such today. And it was he, moreover, who endowed thinkers of the future with their philosophical terminology, which has entered into our inherited vocabulary, so that we employ his words continually without any longer recalling that he was their source.

4 Art

In the evolution of Greek sculpture, a large part was played by the adornment of temple pediments, of which the narrow tapering-off at their extremities made special demands upon the sculptors' skill. The well-preserved pediments, in two successive styles, from the Temple of Aphaea at Aegina (c.500–480), illustrating battle scenes of Troy, reflect a subtle move in the direction of naturalism, and show an awareness of the third dimension.

The 480s witnessed the origins of a new, post-archaic style which is known as Early Classical or Severe. The Doric temple of Zeus at Olympia (470–457), designed by a local architect named Libon, was larger than any shrine previously erected in mainland Greece. Its substantially surviving sculptures reveal novel, harmonious groupings of two and three figures, and mark further, gradual advances towards naturalistic representation.

The mythological scenes on the two Olympian pediments differ sharply from one another. The reliefs at the western end are violent, depicting the fight between the Lapiths of Thessaly and their half-horse neighbours the Centaurs, who had drunkenly tried to abduct the women at the wedding of the Lapith king: while the static figure of the god Apollo at the centre, calming the interlocked combatants with outstretched arms, displays a tranquillity which offers a dramatic contrast. The east pediment, on the other hand, offers no fighting or action at all. Its subject is the mythical chariot-race between the invading Pelops (after whom the Peloponnese was named) and King Oenomaus of Pisa, which would decide if Pelops's demand for the hand of Oenomaus's daughter Hippodamia should be granted (after earlier suitors, having lost similar contests, had been killed). Here we see the frozen, tensely immobile, expectant scene just before the race began. Oenomaus and Pelops, with the Pisan queen and Hippodamia by their respective sides, are at the altar of Zeus, swearing to abide by the outcome, with their chariot teams on either flank.

A visitor, passing through the outer columns of the temple, could also see six sculptured panels or metopes above the inner side porches, at either end of the *cella*. The Labours of Heracles are depicted, with Athena playing a prominent role. The identity of the sculptor, or two sculptors, who designed and executed these metopes, and the pediments as well – or presided over their design and execution by skilled assistants – has not been agreed upon with any degree of certainty. Nor has the place of his, or their, origin.

101

The rendering of free-standing statues too, independent of the adorn-ment of temples, had already had a long history in Greece, exemplified, in particular, by the nude male (*kouros*) and the draped female (*kore*).

Early in the fifth century, both these branches of statuary progressed. In marble the full-length 'Critian Boy' and the head of the 'Fair-Haired Boy' (490–480) illustrate the tentative, partial, current amendment of idealism by observed physical fact. The bronze Delphi Charioteer is also outstanding, although, from this naturalistic point of view, slightly regressive. Dedicated at the Delphic sanctuary of Apollo by Polyzalus, brother of Hiero I of Syracuse, as part of a bronze group of a parade celebrating a Pythian chariot-race victory (478 or 474), it moves back to an entirely impersonal and idealistic manner. It is all the more remarkable, then, that shortly afterwards a more or less completely realistic portrait appeared elsewhere. Labelled by the name of Them-istocles, it seems to have been made in the 460s, after the exiled statesman had been granted a governorship at Magnesia on the Mae-ander in the Persian empire, where the Greeks' objections to repre-senting individuals were lacking.

A bronze Zeus or Poseidon from the sea off Artemisium in north-western Euboea returns, with differences due to the passage of time, to the earlier delicate blend of anatomical sophistication and imper-sonality. Who made this particular statue is not known. The out-standing mid-century sculptor was Myron of Eleutherae. While he did not bring the Early Classical (Severe) style entirely to an end, he foreshadowed its termination by experimenting in novel bodily postures and the movements of men engaged, or about to engage, in vigorous action – falling, about to run, drawing a bow. Myron worked entirely in bronze, but his Discus-Thrower (Discobolus) – which probably formed part of a group – has only survived in Roman marble copies. The athlete is about to wheel round and make his throw. The moment before activity is caught, in a momentary suspension of time.

The climax of sculpture at this epoch, however, is presented by the two bronze statues discovered in 1972 in the sea off Riace in Calabria. The statues are about six feet in height. Their faces are bearded, and each figure, apparently, carried a shield and short sword. That is to say, the men are warriors. Statue A, the more youthful and theatrical of the two, his features decked out with copper, silver inlay and vitreous paste (for the corneas of the eyes – the eyeballs are missing), displays a strong, confident turn of head, and a far-off but resolute gaze. One of Statue B's eyeballs survives, made of a mixture of ivory and a calcareous substance. His right arm, and lower left arm, are additions, soldered on during some later period of antiquity.

Despite arguments against this, the two bronzes appear to have come from the same workshop, and the same hand. They were made in c.450, at the moment of transition from the Early Classical (Severe) to the High Classical Style, when poses were becoming less stiff. Their sculptor may have worked at Athens, since Statue B's beard recalls a statue of Pericles by Cresilas, of which we have copies. But we have no idea who this artist was. And how or why or when his statues came into the sea at that particular place is likewise unknown.

The sculptor Polyclitus, who was active for more than forty years (c.464–420), was born at Sicyon but lived and worked at Argos. Two of his most famous bronze statues are known from marble copies. The Doryphorus (Youth Holding a Spear) is stockier and heavier than earlier figures. But its pose, contrasting taut and slack muscles in a harmonious balance of tense arm and relaxed leg on one side and the reverse formula on the other, marks a liberation from former rigidities. This statue was known as the Canon or Model, because it embodied Polyclitus's view of what ideal human proportions should be. And indeed the sculptor himself wrote a book called the *Canon*, showing that the Doryphorus was a deliberate proclamation and illustration of this very ideal. Beauty, to him, was a matter of ratio and proportion (*symmetria*), and the figure demonstrated the corporeal proportions which he regarded as perfect.

Yet the *Canon* was flexible enough to accommodate variety, for Polyclitus's later Diadumenus (Youth Binding a Fillet Round his Head), although clearly akin to the Doryphorus, is a more youthful sort of athlete, with less conspicuous muscles (c.420). The same sculptor also designed a colossal seated image of Hera for the Heraeum at Argos. The statue can only be partially reconstructed from sketches of much later coins of that city, but was evidently 'chryselephantine', that is to say made of wood veneered with gold for the drapery and with ivory for the features.

It was Polyclitus's depictions of men, however, and not of deities, that stamped themselves on the generation that followed him, and was perpetuated by the school which he himself had founded at Argos. The learned Roman Varro later complained that his figures had been too square, and too like one another. Nevertheless, his *Canon* exercised a persistent effect on later sculptors, and served to steady their endeavours. For what he had done was to impose a meaningful, definable pattern on the chaos of nature.

103

When Phidias the Athenian competed with Polyclitus for the statue of an Amazon for the Artemisium at Ephesus, it was Polyclitus who won. Yet Phidias, too, had already gained an early reputation, for two memorials that he composed to celebrate the battle of Marathon. And then Pericles placed him in charge of his construction programme for Athens, thus granting him a status that no architect or sculptor had ever attained before.

On the Athenian Acropolis, the Temple of Athena Parthenos (the Maiden), the Parthenon – paid for largely by Athens' allies – was not only the shrine of a goddess but one of the principal monuments to Athenian piety and power. Designed by the architect Ictinus, and made by the master-builder Callicrates, it was the largest Doric temple on the Greek mainland, measuring 228 feet in length, and 101 in breadth. Eight columns instead of the usual six appeared at front and rear, and almost subliminal 'refinements' were introduced into the design to soften the unresilient Doric impact. These sophistications included *entasis*, a swelling of the columns (not new, but now assuming a subtler form); and the columns leant gently inwards as well, while the temple's platform, too, curved down from the centre to the corners.

The reliefs that adorned the Parthenon are the most substantial body of first-class sculpture that any Greek temple has bequeathed to us. Under the direction of Phidias, numerous sculptors evidently took part. The metopes of the shrine (446–440) were unprecedentedly numerous, adding up to a total of ninety-two. The subjects that they represented included the struggle between Lapiths and Centaurs (already depicted at Olympia), and battles between gods and giants, and probably fights between Greeks and Amazons as well. The common theme binding these topics together was the victory of Hellenism over barbarism, of reason over irrationality – the same sort of victory which had been won by the Greeks in the Persian Wars, with Athens, so it was claimed (with some measure of justice), playing the preeminent part.

These metopes vary in artistic quality, but by the time the Parthenon's frieze was undertaken (from c.440), sculptors of uniform excellence had been brought together. Located above the exterior walls of the building's inner porches (as at Olympia), but in this case at their ends as well as their sides, the frieze, originally 520 feet long, was a continuous relief, depicting a single, unified scene. This was the procession of the Great Panathenaic festival, which was held at Athens every year, and every four years with special pomp. Despite modern arguments to the contrary, the frieze seems to depict such a procession not with reference to an actual celebration performed at any specific date, but in generalized terms. The Panathenaea and its procession

104

were religious occasions, and deities appear on the frieze. And yet, nonetheless – as some pious Athenians may have noted without total approval – it strikes a basically secular and human note.

The Parthenon's frieze was high up, and not very easy to see, but it must have exhibited an interesting interplay of light and shade, enhanced by the tinting which, as usual, was added. Here the High Classical Style shows a technical advance. Yet, although the sculptors of these reliefs understood the human anatomy, they still prefer to elevate its rendering onto an impersonal plane, and do not join those contemporary painters who, as we shall see, were attempting to represent emotion and mood. On the Parthenon frieze, faces remain aloof, and these Athenians rise, disengaged, above passions and disturbances, in a timeless state of being which sought to give ideal, symbolic expression to the Periclean vision of the city.

The two broad pediments of the Parthenon (c.438–432), on the other hand, have only come down to us in fragmentary form, owing to severe damage that was inflicted on them during the seventeenth century. The west pediment showed the mythical conflict between Athena and Poseidon for dominion over Athens and its territory. Although Poseidon continued to be honoured, it was Athena who became the city's principal patron, and the east pediment offered a picture of her birth from the head of Zeus, cloven by the axe of Hephaestus. Lateral figures of divinities, recumbent, seated and standing, have partially survived from these two pedimental groups, but without their heads. The goddesses wear a newly fashionable type of clinging, shape-revealing drapery, with deeply cut, razor-edge folds that catch the shadows and achieve a novel visual impact.

The principal sacred statue on the Athenian Acropolis had long been the Athena Promachos (Champion in Battle), outside the Parthenon. Phidias produced a new version of the venerable image, and in c.447–439 he also created a further figure for the interior of the building. This was the Athena Parthenos, forty feet high, chryselephantine, that is to say with the gold and ivory veneers already seen in Polyclitus's Hera at Argos. Like the Athena Promachos, the Parthenos no longer exists, but we can recapture its appearance from literary descriptions, copies and coins. The goddess was armed, and wore her miracle-working goatskin cloak (aegis). The three crests of her helmet possessed the shapes of a sphinx and two winged horses. Her shield was engraved with reliefs repeating the metopes' theme of the struggle between Greeks and Amazons.

Phidias was accused of insinuating his own portrait into these reliefs, and this enabled critics to denounce him, in the hope, indirectly, of

105

discrediting his political patron Pericles. That may well have been why Phidias moved to Olympia, where he executed, for Zeus's temple, a huge chryselephantine image of the god. The expression of Zeus, both sublime and gentle, it was said, could console the deepest of sorrows: and the statue was numbered among the Seven Wonders of the World.

It seems probable, though it cannot be proved, that the whole general configuration of the Acropolis, including three further, later buildings as well as the Parthenon, was a result of the planning by Phidias.

This is likely, in particular, of Mnesicles's Propylaea, the entrance structure leading into the whole complex, which seems to have been erected before Phidias left Athens (457–2). The Propylaea was a large, square, three-aisled hall, pierced by five gateways. It blends the traditional, solid, Doric architectural Order with its more delicate Ionic counterpart, somewhat new to the mainland but echoing Athens's claim to be the colonizer and leader of the Ionian Greeks. Mnesicles also added asymmetrical wings, including, on the north side, a picture-gallery (*pinakotheke*), its walls decorated by Polygnotus and other painters.

The elegant little Ionic shrine of Athena Nike (Victory), up on the bastion of the hill, may well likewise have formed part of Phidias's original plan, but was not constructed until the 420s, after his departure from Athens and his death. Its balustrade, added in *c.*410–407, included reliefs by at least half a dozen sculptors, depicting seated figures of Athena and winged Victories, who wore the wind-blown draperies already foreshadowed by the Parthenon pediments.

Work on the Erechtheum, once again, even if planned earlier, was not initiated until *c.*420, and continued in 409–408. Designed to replace a sixth-century temple of Athena Polias (Patron of the City) and to house her revered olive-wood image, it was also intended to enshrine a number of other sacred objects and locations, as its complex, irregular, tripartite layout recalls – the antithesis of the tautly unified, rectangular Parthenon nearby. The Erechtheum was embellished by gilt, inlay and polychrome decoration, and its east and north sides were fronted by graceful Ionic porticos, while to the south projected the 'Porch of the Maidens' (Caryatids), elaborately draped female figures which served as columns and supported the architrave.

Wall-painting was one of the greatest Greek arts. And yet, because of its almost total non-survival from the classical period, we are forced back into the position of trying to reconstruct it from various sources: Etruscan adaptations (which deviate, in any case, from their Greek models), Greek vases (which only copy wall-paintings to a limited extent), and descriptions by ancient writers.

It is upon this last source that we have to rely for our information about Polygnotus of Thasos (*c*.500–440). He was, it appears, not only the supreme master, in this medium, of the Early Classical (Severe) style, already mentioned in connection with sculpture, but also the most innovative and revolutionary of all the wall-painters of his age – and the earliest painter, anywhere in the world, to achieve a contemporary social position in his own right, and upon his own merits. From about the 470s he painted major mythological pictures for various cities, but most of all for Athens, where he gained citizenship and became a friend of the statesman Cimon. Polygnotus, we are told, explored spatial depth, dispensing with a single base-line and allowing his figures to move freely up and down the field, so that groupings might become more elaborate, and psychological relationships could be more subtly conveyed. He also abandoned his predecessors' exclusive concentration on profiles. A master of nuances of poses and gestures and facial expressions (not to speak of diaphanous draperies), Polygnotus, in his depiction of human beings, was reputed to have achieved a novel combination of *ethos* (character, moral purpose) and *pathos* (feeling).

Yet despite the advance towards mimetic naturalism which such assessments imply, Polygnotus (in very Greek fashion) wanted to represent human beings not as they are but as 'better than they are'.[18] Intent, moreover, upon 'atmosphere', he resembled the sculptor of the Olympia east pediment in his liking for quiet, intense, contemplative scenes, just before or after the instantaneous moment of action. Furthermore, his battle-pieces, such as the *Sack of Troy*, are likely to have shown an emotional awareness of the misery of defeat, like literary descriptions by Athenian tragic poets of the same epoch.

The Athenian red-figure vase painters, whose continued activity (in sharp contrast to wall-paintings) is illustrated by huge surviving numbers of their works, came, in due course, to echo the innovations of Polygnotus. This they did, particularly, by simple but intelligible portrayals of spatial depth. Their endeavours in this direction can be seen in the work of the Niobid painter (during the second quarter of the fifth century), who sometimes placed his figures not upon a single base-line but at different levels – in the manner attributed to Polygnotus, whose influence is once again detectable in the Niobid artist's pictures of silent concentration (in contrast to the violent scenes favoured by some of his predecessors, notably the Brygos painter, *c*.490–480).

The Achilles painter, too, working after 450, once again created calm, serene, balanced compositions, suggestive of models such as the Parthenon sculptures. He also adopted, on occasion, a delicate 'white-figure' technique, which meant placing the designs on a white instead of a black ground. This form of painting, especially employed for *lekythoi*, oil-flasks offered to the dead, had been evolved towards the end of the previous century, but reached its climax in the Achilles painter's work.

For the second revolution in fifth-century mural- and panel-painting we are once again dependent on what we read. In the latter half of the fifth century, it was recorded, Agatharchus of Samos became the earliest artist to employ a sort of perspective, which denoted spatial depth, and was probably prompted by the requirements of theatrical scene-painting. And then Apollodorus of Athens, the first man to gain a reputation for easel- as well as wall-painting, developed shading of a more or less realistic character.

Next came Zeuxis and Parrhasius, who were said to be the leading figures of the 'Asiatic school', although, whereas Parrhasius was indeed an Ephesian, his contemporary Zeuxis came from Heraclea (Policoro) in Lucania (south-east Italy), and both lived at Athens; while Zeuxis also worked for King Archelaus of Macedonia (413–399). He employed highlights to express three-dimensional volume, while Parrhasius was said to have been an outstanding draughtsman, famous for his subtle outlines and contours. Nor was he conspicuous for his modesty, describing himself as the perfect prince of painters, of divine lineage.

The innovations introduced by these men may well be indirectly reflected in the theatrically mannered, idyllic, sensuous vases decorated by the Meidias painter towards the end of the century.

The work of such artists has been described as the last phase of High Classical Art, and the Later Classical style which followed began in the earlier decades of the fourth century. It found little expression, however, in Athenian painting, which, as far as originality was concerned, had come to the end of the road. But the new phase, on the other hand, produced outstanding sculptors. They were still intent upon idealism, which was now combined, however, with a closer and more analytical observation of nature. This Later Classical epoch was also an increasingly individualistic age as far as these sculptors were concerned, since in more and more cases they were mentioned not only corporately, as members of schools, but as individuals in their own right.

Outstanding among them was the Athenian Praxiteles, who remained active between 370 and 330 BC. His masterpiece was the nude

Aphrodite which he made for Cnidus in c.364/361. Only a fragment of the original has survived, but copies make it clear that the sculptor was adopting a novel approach to the female form, displaying it naked and meaning it to be seen from the back and sides as well as from the front. The buttocks and hips of Praxitelean women swelled, beneath drooping upper torsos with unemphatic breasts. Aphrodite's expression, grave and calm, was said to convey a hint of invitation, and her gesture concealing the genital area drew erotic attention to it all the same.

A surviving figure of Hermes, carrying the infant Dionysus, may be an original work of Praxiteles; or at least, if not, it is an early copy of unusual distinction. The statue was found in the temple of Hera at Olympia, the very place where the travel-writer Pausanias saw and described it.[19] The god leans upon one leg in a pronouncedly double-curved attitude that was characteristic of Praxiteles's work. Hermes gazes dreamily into the distance, with a hint of a remote smile. Here is a new ideal, based on a fascination for physical beauty that had never received such open expression before.

The material favoured by Praxiteles – unlike so many earlier sculptors – was not bronze but marble, of which the smooth, fluid, receptive planes, enhanced by delicate colouring, seemed to him best suited for the representation of skin. The more austere Phidian and Polyclitean styles, already modified in the later fifth century, had now been finally transformed by Praxiteles's sinuous poses, soft contours and pensive expressions. That was what people meant when they said that he represented the emotions of the soul with particular poignancy.

Praxiteles was also believed, by some authorities, to have participated in the adornment of the most notable of all fourth-century buildings, the Mausoleum of Halicarnassus (Bodrum). The son of a local hereditary prince Hecatomnus, whom the Persians had made satrap of Caria (c.392/391), Mausolus (c.377–353) transferred his capital from Mylasa (Milas) to Halicarnassus, which he converted, by massive building operations and population transfers, into a spectacular city, equipped with a royal palace and Greek temples.

At the centre of its waterfront he planned his own burial place, the Mausoleum, constructed after his death by his widow and successor Artemisia II. The Mausoleum has now disappeared. But it appears to have been a huge rectangular structure, a hundred and forty feet high and sixty-three feet wide, surrounded by an Ionic colonnade of thirty-six columns. Its podium soared upwards from the ground to the foot of this colonnade in three huge receding steps, and its roof, too, was another stepped cone, or perhaps a pyramid. Upon the apex of the monument stood a gigantic marble four-horse chariot, driven by Apollo as the sun-god Helios, who symbolized the passing of the dead. The chariot was the work of Pythius, who also designed the whole building – and was the writer of books on architectural theory. Moreover, Vitruvius, who wrote on these subjects in Roman times, mentions a second architect of the Mausoleum as well, the co-author of Pythius's book, who was Satyrus of Paros.[20]

The conception of the building, as befitted the mixed origins of Mausolus, was multi-racial, blending Greek motifs and styles with non-Greek forms, since the lofty podium was inspired by Persian prototypes from Lycia (southern Asia Minor), whereas the roof, whatever its exact configuration, appears to have echoed Egyptian models. The Mausoleum also broke new ground by the novel and sophisticated manner in which it integrated architecture and sculpture. For altogether it housed something like three hundred statues, nine or ten feet high. But from all these, only fragmentary parts of the figures have survived – and a single face, that of Mausolus or one of his ancestors.

Substantial portions of the sculptural friezes of the Mausoleum, however, have also been unearthed, depicting a chariot-race, a battle between Lapiths and Centaurs, and another battle between male Greeks and Amazons (which is the best preserved). Pliny the elder lists four sculptors whose work appeared in the building, Scopas, Bryaxis, Timotheus and Leochares.[21] Vitruvius is uncertain about Timotheus, but adds the name of Praxiteles.[22] Apart from this possible participation of Praxiteles, the outstandingly distinguished figure on the list is Scopas of Paros. And indeed, although it remains uncertain which of these various artists designed which part of these sculptures, the unrestrained movements which are such a conspicuous feature of some of the Mausoleum friezes, foreshadowing Hellenistic compositions of the future, may reflect the known activity of Scopas, and so may the restlessly emotional expressions and poses of heads that have survived from a further group of figures from the same building's pediment. It is understandable that, with all this wealth of artistic and architectural originality, the Mausoleum ranked as one of the Seven Wonders of the World.

5 The Classical Achievement

The classical Greeks, then, produced an unprecedented, unparalleled abundance of outstanding practitioners in a great variety of different fields of human activity, many of them during the span of only a few lifetimes. What was the cause of this astonishing, almost incredibly varied outburst?

Certainly, it did not occur because the Greeks belonged to a superior race, since their ethnic components had been inextricably mixed and 'impure' from the very beginning: and the Athenian rhetorician Isocrates was right to point out that the only way to define a Greek was by culture, not race.[23] What was more important was the fact that they lived in the Mediterranean area. For not only was this region accessible to the ancient near-eastern kingdoms and empires, which had contributed so greatly to the rise of Greek culture, but the Mediterranean zone itself, too, provided a uniquely inviting blend of natural wealth and frugal austerity, which presented – at one and the same time – not only obstacles needing to be overcome but the encouragements that made it possible to overcome them.

Yet even that cannot be the whole story. Granted the allurements of the Mediterranean area – and granted also the essential early contributions from the near east – one must still ask why the Greeks, during this relatively short period, developed and gave expression to their talents in such an exceptional and many-sided fashion.

One principal explanation must be their city-states. And here again the Mediterranean environment is far from irrelevant. The Greeks liked talking, and their climate (in which much of daily life could take place out-of-doors) supplied sufficient and suitable space to talk: that is to say, to exchange and test thoughts and plans and ideas. They had leisure to engage in these activities – and leisure was a thing that they prized – because they owned slaves, and could hire other, 'free' men as well, to perform routine labour, and because their own personal lifestyle was so simple that its mechanics did not take up much of the day. All this offered individuals the time and opportunity to give of their best – outstanding individuals, that is to say. Here is something of the paradox. For if the collective, corporate city-state provided the framework and background for this lavish array of feats, they were actually undertaken and performed by a relatively few persons. Some forty of fifty of them created the classical Greek achievement. Without them, it would only have been a shadow.

Even so, however, the city-states did not provide *all* the prominent personages of the age: most notably in the political field, where Philip II of Macedonia, for instance, was not one of their products.

And if we return to the city-state itself, it is too often, and with too great ease, implicitly identified with democracy. The term democracy is ambiguous today, because it is subjected to a variety of conflicting

111

interpretations and definitions in different countries of the world. The classical Athenian democracy, the earliest and most thoroughgoing ancient constitution that could be described by such a term, was typical of the others of its time in so far as it excluded women, metics and slaves. In those respects it should be distinguished from what we understand as democracy today. And it differed from modern patterns, once again, in that it was not representative (operating through parliamentary or congressional organs) but direct (functioning through an Assembly and judicial institutions of which every citizen could become a member).

This democracy was the seedbed in which the geniuses who created Athenian tragedy, comedy, philosophy and art found it possible to flourish. In the political field, on the other hand, the democratic system, of this particular kind, had both good and bad results. The good result was that an extraordinarily large proportion of the citizen population was able to participate, personally, in public affairs. The bad result was that the government of Athens, thus guided, made appallingly unwise decisions, some of which, for example, lost it the Peloponnesian War.

Another misapprehension that sometimes arises in connection with the ancient Athenians comes from the modern idea that democracy is 'good' but that imperialism is 'bad'. That contrast cannot be applied to the classical world, in which Athens was a democracy *and* an imperial power, which could not have built the Parthenon (or allowed its writers and thinkers and artists the time to produce their works) without the revenue from its imperial subjects. Still, when even all that has been said, Athenian democracy remains the ancestor or forerunner, or even the founder, of the different types of democratic government that prevail in the west today.

Many of the disastrous decisions made by this Athenian democracy relate to a wider political question – the relations between Greek city-states. These were all too often catastrophic. There was a failure, at all epochs, of almost all attempts at collaboration between one city-state and another, so that Plato's grim observation that the natural inter-state relationship was one of war cannot truthfully be contradicted. However, these bickerings between city-states did not, clearly, impede or stifle the makers of classical Greek literature or art. On the contrary, the rivalries that such strife created supplied these men's endeavours, in some cases, with a stimulus that they would not, in different circumstances, have possessed. In the political field, on the other hand, this inability to unite with one another, which characterized the Greek city-states, led to Philip II: that is to say, to the virtual destruction of the city-state as an independent, leading political entity and form.

Part III

THE
HELLENISTIC
GREEKS

6

Alexander and his Successors

When Philip II was, murdered in 336, his nineteen-year-old son Alexander III (the Great) enthusiastically inherited his plan to invade the Persian empire. Two years later, at the head of 40,000 Macedonian and Greek troops, he crossed the Hellespont (Dardanelles) and won a victory over the Persian advanced forces on the River Granicus (Çan Çayı), which made it possible for him to conquer western and southern Asia Minor. In the following year, upon the plain of Issus at the borders of Cilicia (south-east Asia Minor) and Syria, he defeated the Persian king Darius III Codomannus himself, whose wife, children and mother fell into his hands. Rejecting peace offers, Alexander then, after a long siege, captured Tyre (Sur) in Phoenicia, and occupied Egypt in 331. Next he overran Mesopotamia, and overwhelmed Darius at Gaugamela (Gomal). This enabled him to capture Babylon, Susa and Persepolis (which was burnt to the ground), and Darius fled to Media where he was murdered. Thereupon Alexander assumed the Persian monarchical title in his place.

During the next three years he extended his frontier as far as the Punjab, before turning homewards because his army refused to go any further. Arriving back in Susa, after an arduous journey, he executed governors and officers charged with misconduct during his absence, and dealt with alleged plots involving his own intimate friends. A mutiny among the Macedonian soldiers was caused by his project for a mixed army of which Persians should form part – in accordance with a plan, announced at Opis on the Tigris in 324, to govern his empire in some sort of collaboration with the conquered peoples: a policy which he led and symbolized by marrying Barsine Statira, a daughter of Darius III (while retaining, also, his wife Roxane, daughter of an eastern Iranian chieftain).

However, in the summer of 323 Alexander fell ill of a fever, aggravated by a wound suffered in India and by drink, and then died. He

114

was only thirty-two at the time of his death. But he bequeathed an empire extending from the Adriatic to Soviet Central Asia and Pakistan and India, leaving the world transformed.

His motives for these enterprises was mixed. The Macedonians were regarded as barbarians by the Greeks, and he was eager to show the Greeks they were wrong. He wanted also to carry out his father's plan – and outdo him in the process. And he felt what he described as an imperative yearning (*pothos*) to achieve the almost impossible, and reach the uttermost confines of the world. Moreover, he possessed the frightening ability to give practical effect to his yearning. He and his helpers explored immeasurably numerous and distant lands. He inspired a longlived religious cult of rulers. He founded (mainly for military purposes) perhaps twenty new Greek cities. And he issued a fine currency for the entire world that he had conquered. He became an enormous, eternal legend. Yet his empire did not survive his death.

For there followed four decades of hostilities between his former generals and would-be successors. From these struggles, the three major, warring kingdoms of the new Hellenistic epoch emerged: Macedonia, Ptolemaic Egypt and the dominion of the Seleucids.

Macedonia was still the old state of the past, although the events following Alexander's death left its four million inhabitants weakened and impoverished. However, the Macedonian Cassander (son of Alexander's general Antipater) founded Cassandrea (316, on the site of Potidaea) and Thessalonica (which replaced Pella as the country's capital). Furthermore, Demetrius I the Besieger (son of the briefly dominant Antigonus I the One-Eyed) established a fortress at Demetrias on the Gulf of Pagasae (c.293), to preside over the control of Greece. But it was Antigonus II Gonatas (284–239) who decisively revived the Macedonian kingdom's fortunes, with the help of a success against invading Celts (Gauls). Thus began a new and tenacious line of monarchs, pursuing the Hellenization of their country and drawing the bulk of their revenue from their personal estates, without the need to impose oppressive taxation upon their subjects.

The Egyptian kingdom of the Ptolemies was quite different. The way had been prepared for its establishment by Alexander's foundation, on the site of a fishing village, of an urban centre which was given the name of Alexandria, and soon became the largest of all Greek cities. On arrival in Egypt, Alexander had at once set about the foundation of this new township and port, of which he saw some of the immense potentialities. To its north, Alexandria had two fine harbours opening onto the Mediterranean Sea. With the Pharos lighthouse (one of the

Seven Wonders of the World) to regulate their traffic, these harbours were capable of accommodating the large ships which became a feature of the Hellenistic age, and enabled Alexandria to export the surpluses of Egypt, and conduct trading far and wide, becoming the most important maritime base in the entire Mediterranean area.

Centring upon a main avenue of unprecedented width, Alexandria extended over a rectangular territory measuring four miles in length and three-quarters of a mile in width, and its inhabitants, by 200 BC, had reached a total of half a million. They included the largest Greek (and Macedonian) population of any colonial foundation, and these people enjoyed their own exceptional privileges and organization. The large Jewish community, too, possessed an administration of its own (Appendix VI). But the city also housed tens of thousands of Egyptians and people of many other races. For it was a truly cosmopolitan centre, to a greater extent even than Syracuse had ever been: the supreme Hellenistic melting-pot.

Many of Alexandria's finely constructed buildings became renowned – for example the Museum and Library, which ranked with older Athenian institutions as the most important cultural centres of the age. There were also the palaces of the Ptolemies, and the temple of Sarapis, the god they had invented to satisfy their national needs, whose cult and festivals spread rapidly (with those of Isis) throughout the Hellenistic world. And yet Alexandria remained a peculiar sort of city, because it was scarcely part of Egyptian territory. Despite canals linking it with Lake Mareotis and the south, it seemed like a kind of superstructure added to the country from outside, and people spoke of travelling from Alexandria to Egypt.

It was to Alexandria, however, that Ptolemy I Soter (304–283) moved his capital from Memphis – Lower Egypt's ancient, traditional centre. He found a country devastated by recent wars, but his brilliant and original administrative talents brought it into working order, lodging it at the very centre of international affairs.

Efforts were made to control adjacent territories, in order to protect Egypt and bring in commercial profit, needed to finance military expenditure. Ptolemy I Soter began the task of multiplying industrial and agricultural productivity, and his son Ptolemy II Philadelphus (283–246) elaborated the system. In the process, he created the most complex and far-reaching civil service the world had ever known. It was a bureaucracy which subordinated the entire economy to state power, so that every conceivable form of enrichment could be extracted for the benefit of the king, at minimum expense. Spurred on by Egypt's natural resources, and by their own possession of enormous royal estates, these two monarchs exploited their opportunities to the utmost extent.

The results of this command economy included a spectacular increase in the production of cereals, especially wheat, which converted the rulers into grain merchants and exporters such as the world had never seen. Taxation, too, reached unparalleled dimensions, and its revenue helped the Ptolemies to encourage the development of banking. The temples had been, for millennia, the basic institutions of Egyptian society, and banks were sometimes attached to them.

The Greco-Macedonian governing class stood apart from the seven million Egyptians whom they ruled. But Ptolemy III Euergetes (246–221) tried to gain favour with the native priesthood, wanting himself to be seen not merely as a Greek king but as an Egyptian pharaoh as well. Moreover, it was only by the extensive mobilization of native soldiers that Ptolemy IV Philopator (221–205) defeated the Seleucid monarch Antiochus III the Great at Raphia (Tell Rafah, 217); and then Ptolemy V Epiphanes (205–180) was crowned at Memphis according to Egyptian rites. But now nationalist rebellions began inside the country, and proved impossible to stop, while the welfare of the population, especially throughout the countryside, fell into a catastrophic decline.

The Seleucids ruled over the middle east. Seleucus I Nicator (304–281) ceded Alexander's easternmost territories to the Indian emperor Chandragupta Maurya in exchange for war elephants (c.303). But even after that, he still ruled over an empire of a million and a half square miles, extending from the Aegean Sea to Afghanistan and Turkestan, and containing some thirty million people. It took the early Seleucids all their time to keep a grip over these huge and cumbrous territories.

They possessed two capitals, Antioch (Antakya) in Syria, and Seleucia on the Tigris (Tell Umar) in Babylonia. These were both new cities, two of the many Greek foundations, perhaps totalling as many as seventy, which Seleucus I Nicator and Antiochus I Soter (281–261) and other members of their line, following and outdoing Alexander, established throughout their territories. This Seleucid colonization, attracting many impoverished Greeks from their home country, exceeded even the archaic age of Greek settlements in its dimensions.

The Seleucid colonies at first, like Alexander's, possessed a military purpose. Before long, however, some of them – notably the two capitals – became large-scale commercial centres as well. Moreover, Asians too, as well as Greeks and Macedonians, arrived in the new cities, and even became partially Hellenized, but rarely took on the Greek spirit in its entirety: particularly as the settlers, for the most part, still arrogantly and condescendingly practised linguistic and cultural Hellenic apartheid.

However, the revolt of Diodotus I Soter, satrap of Bactria-Sogdiana (Afghanistan), against the Seleucid monarch Antiochus II Theos (c.256–5) meant that the eastern territories of the empire, and what had remained of the Indian borderlands, were lost to the Seleucids for ever. Next, Parthia broke away under Arsaces I (247), whose non-Greek dynasty soon ruled over the whole of Iran. And during the same period Eumenes I of Pergamum (Bergama, 263–241), assisted by Ptolemy III Euergetes of Egypt, threw off Seleucid suzerainty in western Asia Minor, thus adding another to the various secondary Hellenistic kingdoms of the epoch. Moreover, it soon gained widespread prestige, when, before 230, Eumenes's cousin Attalus I Soter halted the Celtic (Gaulish) invaders of Asia Minor.

But kingdoms by no means form the whole of the Hellenistic picture. There were also, both within the royal dominions and outside them, hundreds of more or less independent city-states, whose mode of government, indeed, still constituted the normal, basic form of Greek existence.

The first and foremost of all such independent city-states, in almost everyone's view, was still Athens. After their defeat by Philip II of Macedonia at Chaeronea (Chapter 5, section 1), and the subsequent death of his son Alexander III the Great, their failure to resist the kings' former right-hand man Antipater in the Lamian War (323–2) forced the Athenians to accept a Macedonian garrison. Subsequently, too, another Macedonian warlord, Cassander, made the cultured but authoritarian Demetrius of Phaleron his agent in the city (317–307). Later, the Athenians revolted once more, but were defeated again by the Macedonian monarch Antigonus II Gonatas in the Chremonidean War (267–2). With the help, however, of increased silver from the Laurium mines, Athens temporarily recovered its former preeminence as a commercial state, and in 229 was able to buy the Macedonian garrison out.

Another outstanding city-state of the Hellenistic epoch was Rhodes. After Alexander's death its leaders expelled the garrison which he had planted in the city, and in 305–304 they gained further renown by repelling a siege by one of his would-be successors, Demetrius I the Besieger (Poliorcetes).

Rhodes was ruled by a limited democracy – with an aristocratic tinge – which earned it the name of the best governed city in the Hellenistic world. It was also one of the first places to feed its poor systematically, at the expense of the community and its wealthiest members. Public education, too, was highly developed. All Rhodians

118

had to serve for a time in the fleet, which was built for the most part at the expense of the richer citizens.

Clearing the eastern Mediterranean of pirates (before and after 200), Rhodes rivalled Athens as the principal Aegean commercial state, profiting mainly from its carrying trade, which undertook the lucrative transportation of grain. The city also became a headquarters of international finance and banking and exchange, forming a business partnership with Ptolemaic Egypt. Moreover, Rhodes was one of the leading cultural centres of the Greek world, producing eminent philosophers and sculptors, of whom something will be said in the next Chapter.

There were also other important Hellenistic city-states as well, which possessed not republican but monarchic forms of government. One was Sparta, where the ancient forms of kingship (Chapter 2, section 2) persisted even into these changed times. The Spartans had not joined the Greek movement broken by Philip II at Chaeronea (338), and when they did decide, belatedly, to stand up to Macedonia – during Alexander's absence in Asia – they were crushed by his regent Antipater. Subsequently it was the Spartan king Areus (309/8–265) who took the lead in creating the Greek coalition that was defeated by the Macedonians in the Chremonidean War.

The most noteworthy developments in the subsequent history of the city were reformist drives sponsored by three later kings. Spartan territory had become divided into large estates, and Agis IV (244–241), supposedly inspired by the traditions of the legendary Lycurgus, endeavoured to redistribute the land into 4,500 equal lots. The Spartan ephors, suspecting revolution, objected, and put Agis to death. Cleomenes III (235–219) was another reformer or reactionary militarist, claiming to revive the glorious past. Believing that military success would assist him, he moved against the Aetolian and Achaean Leagues (see below), while the impoverished elements in many cities flocked to his support. Then he returned home, declared that the ephorate was abolished, redistributed Spartan land, and sold some thousands of serf-like Helots their freedom. After defeat, however, at Sellasia (222) by the Macedonian monarch Antigonus III Doson and his allies – who captured Sparta itself – Cleomenes III fled to Egypt and committed suicide. The Spartan crown was later seized by Nabis (207–192), who revived the same programme with even greater determination, but succumbed to assassination.

Syracuse in Sicily was another state which retained power in Hellenistic times under mainly autocratic domination. After a revival of prosperity (extended over the whole of the island) under Timoleon

(345–337), the city came under the dictatorship of Agathocles (317–289), who mobilized the unprivileged classes as his supporters and terrorized the aristocracy. Despite an unproductive attack upon Carthage (310–307), he succeeded in imposing his rule over most of Sicily itself, and then went on to intervene on the Italian peninsula and even across the Adriatic, where he captured Corcyra (Corfu). Agathocles became the outstanding figure in the western Mediterranean world – which he claimed to have pacified. After he was dead, however, a period of chaos and Carthaginian peril followed. Subsequently Hiero II, commander of the Syracusan army, seized power in the city, and reigned there for no less than fifty-four years (c.269–215).

But perhaps the most important constitutional development of the Hellenistic age was the evolution of leagues or confederacies of cities as political units and powers. Leagues were not new; those in the Peloponnese and Boeotia, for example, had been ancient foundations. But they had each come under the domination of one preeminent city, Sparta and Thebes respectively, whereas now, in Hellenistic times, two leagues came into being in which the member cities were more or less equal. The confederacies of this new type arose in Aetolia and Achaea, north and south of the Gulf of Corinth: both regions where the local communities were weak and backward, and in isolation easily overrun, so that it was useful or essential for them to work together.

By 367 BC, at latest, the little towns of Aetolia had formed themselves into a federal League, which evolved an ingenious and flexible constitution. At the head of the League was an annually elected general or president. There was also an Assembly, which met twice a year, at Thermum. Apparently all adult males had votes, although those of the richer elements tended to prevail. The federal Council consisted of a thousand delegates, drawn from the Aetolian towns in numbers corresponding with their population. It could delegate business to a steering committee of thirty or forty members (*apokletoi*).

After capturing Naupactus on the Gulf of Corinth, and repelling attacks by Alexander's successors, the Aetolians won possession of Delphi (c.300), and gained renown by protecting the sanctuary from invading Celts (Gauls, 279). Then, by defeating the Boeotians (245), they completed their control over central Greece. Moreover, they intervened successfully in the Peloponnese as well, though an unsavoury reputation for piracy continued to haunt their endeavours.

The second important confederation was that of the Achaeans, on the opposite, southern side of the Gulf of Corinth. Quite early on, the people of Achaea had formed an insignificant association among themselves which, in 280 BC, they recast on a larger scale, so as to include not only towns and villages in Achaea itself but a number of non-Achaean communities as well. This League's Assembly, presided over by ten deputies (*demiourgoi*), was open to all male citizens of the member communities. As in Aetolia, the upper-class vote was decisive. But voting was not counted, as there, by individual heads but collectively by cities, hinting at the sort of representative government with which we are familiar today. Moreover, from the later third century onwards, however, this Assembly (and the League's Council as well) were virtually supplanted by a new Representative Council, which seems to have been elected by the member towns on a proportional basis.

From 245 onwards the Achaean League's most notable leader Aratus held the presidency or generalship in alternate years (continuous reelection not being permitted). An incorruptible guerrilla leader, he seized Corinth from the Macedonians (243) and succeeded in incorporating Arcadian Megalopolis in his confederacy (235). But later he came to regard Sparta as a worse danger than Macedonia, whose king Antigonus III Doson, in consequence, he helped to defeat the Spartan monarch Cleomenes III at Sellasia (222). When Aratus died in 213, he had been one of the few Greek leaders of the time, outside the monarchies, to make a substantial mark on his age.

Hellenistic Man and Woman

1 Reality and the Individual

A common form of education is one of the phenomena of the Hellenistic epoch. It was dominated by the rhetorical type of instruction advocated by the Athenian Isocrates (*d*.338), who had become the chief creator of rhetoric as a distinct science. For him, education above all meant developing the ability *to speak*, which distinguishes human beings from animals – and was, in any case, the favourite occupation of the Greeks. Yet he was also at pains to propose a broader and more liberal programme than the mere rules and techniques of the professional rhetorician. In fact, he wanted to reduce theory to a minimum; whereas Aristotle on the other hand (Chapter 5, section 3), although he saw the dangers of the rhetorical art, elaborated it by introducing a variety of new definitions. And it was under the influence of Aristotle's *Rhetoric* that Greek education assumed its typical Hellenistic form, characterized by a multitude of rhetorical textbooks.

In most parts of the Greek world the primary stages of teaching were left to private enterprise, although some cities appointed official supervisors of primary education (*paidonomoi*). Children were usually taught reading, writing, gymnastics and music, and sometimes painting, too. In secondary schools, physical and musical training proceeded further, and a certain amount of mathematics and science was taught as well. But literary subjects also played an extremely prominent part: Homer, Euripides and others were studied with care and in detail.

Athens, where this type of work was especially well developed, also became the model for the form of training known as the ephebate, organized in *c*.335 and 322, and copied at numerous other centres. It started as a sort of upper-class militia for eighteen-year-olds, but came to concentrate on character development and instruction in social behaviour. The ephebes congregated, and were taught, in their city's gymnasium, which increasingly superseded family life as the principal training ground of the young, and became, indeed, the focus and hallmark of Hellenism.

Directors of gymnasia, the gymnasiarchs, were appointed by their governments. But the extent of civic intervention varied widely from place to place. Rhodes and Miletus were among cities which believed that education should be the business of the state, as Plato and Aristotle had urged. Royal Pergamum had no less than five gymnasia. Like Rhodes and Athens, too, Pergamum was a place which provided a higher education, in rhetoric and philosophy. And in Alexandria was another centre where one could learn a variety of subjects at this more elevated level.

Aristotle's share of responsibility for the rhetorical, word-orientated bias of Hellenistic education was counterbalanced by the stimulus that he also offered to Greek science. The scientific developments that continued to occur after his lifetime formed part of a new, general drive towards seeing things as they are: a drive, that is to say, towards greater reality and realism, accompanied by a conscious or unconscious jettisoning of some of the more idealistic, unreal conceptions that had characterized the classical past.

At the outset of this Hellenistic epoch, Aristotle's successor Theophrastus of Eresus on the island of Lesbos (d.288), while understandably dubious about the purposefulness (*telos*) of the universe envisaged by his master, nevertheless inherited his flair for classification, undertaking for botany what Aristotle had achieved for human beings and animals. After Theophrastus, the Greek study of biology did not advance much further. Other scientific studies, however, liberated at last from *a priori* speculations, showed greater progress than in any comparable period until the birth of modern science.

The same applied to mathematics, and one of the first men of learning to reside at Alexandria (*c*.300), where the Ptolemies lavishly stimulated such studies, was the mathematician Euclid. His summing up of the current condition of his subject was the culmination of all that had gone before, for the benefit of the future. His *Elements* demonstrated how knowledge can be attained by rational methods alone: and no book except the Bible has enjoyed such a long subsequent reign. Another Alexandrian, Ctesibius, who flourished in the 270s, was a versatile mechanical inventor. Then Strato of Lampsacus (*d.c*.269) confirmed the growing opinion that science had a right to exist independently of philosophy, and converted the Lyceum – of which he succeeded Theophrastus as head – from the latter to the former.

Archimedes of Syracuse (d.212) was a legendary mathematical genius who expanded the frontiers of knowledge. In solid geometry, he broke entirely new ground. He also prepared the way for the integral calculus, devised a new system for expressing large numbers, virtually invented hydrostatics, and excelled as an engineer. The polymath Eratosthenes of Cyrene (c.275–194), who lived at Athens and Alexandria, was the author of a *Geographica*, which was inspired by the conquests of Alexander the Great, and contributed to an accurate delineation of the surface of the earth. Greek mathematical geography was largely based on astronomy, which fascinated Hellenistic scholars. Aristarchus of Samos, a pupil of Strato, discovered that the earth revolves round the sun. Hipparchus of Nicaea (c.190–after 126) regarded this as unproven, but nevertheless transformed observational techniques, gaining recognition as the outstanding astronomer of antiquity.

Medicine, too, benefited from notable improvements. Most of the Hippocratic Corpus was of Hellenistic date (Chapter 5, section 3), and the various advances that its contents registered meant that the Greeks could now increasingly employ methods based not only on theory but on accumulated case studies as well. The dissections conducted by Herophilus of Calchedon, in the first half of the third century, enhanced knowledge of the brain, eye, duodenum, liver and reproductive organs. His younger colleague Erasistratus, who like him worked at Alexandria, made discoveries relating to digestion and the vascular (circulatory) system. Herophilus has been called the founder of anatomy, and Erasistratus of physiology. Moreover, Erasistratus also turned his attention to the nervous system, and led the way towards psychiatry (which was also practised, after a fashion, in the sanctuaries of Asclepius at Epidaurus and Cos, where 'miraculous' cures owed much to autosuggestion).

The science of the Hellenistic age terminated with Posidonius of Syrian Apamea (c.135–50), who summed up human knowledge in a wide variety of fields, for the benefit of the generations that lay ahead (Chapter 7, section 2).

The impulse towards finding out about reality which had set science and medicine, for a time, on such a prominent course was paralleled in literature, and particularly in writings related to the operations of the human personality.

The thoughts of the Greeks had already been working in that direction when Euripides produced his harrowingly true-to-life personality studies, and when Aristotle amassed evidence about differing patterns of human behaviour. Then his pupil Theophrastus wrote his *Characters*, thirty satirical, razor-sharp sketches of persons suffering from various psychological flaws. One of his pupils was the Athenian practitioner of the New Comedy, Menander (*c*.342–292), who was also keenly interested in human emotions, at a down-to-earth level. Substantial passages or fragments of ten of his more than a hundred plays are now available, including a more or less complete text of the *Epitrepontes* (Arbitrators). These works show that Menander prefers to avoid the politics dear to the Old Comedy of Aristophanes (Chapter 5, section 2), whose stock figures he replaces by more three-dimensional people. Their portrayal displays an unfamiliar realism, tempered only by a preference for traditional plots, although Menander papers over their hackneyed character by presenting ingeniously convincing situations in up-to-date, colloquial language, including a good deal of quotable epigram.

In the next generation, the literary mimes of Theocritus (*c*.300–260?) – who came from Syracuse, but lived at Cos and then worked mainly at Alexandria – introduced a new sort of realism. Mimetic dances had been popular since early times, and mime had now become the most favoured Greek theatrical form. For it was a popular medium among people who wanted a humorous, but direct and unencumbered, picture of the world around them. Theocritus, famous for his pastoral idylls – of which more will be said in the next section – endowed this sort of composition with a new life, adapting the mime-form to elegant allusive verse, and employing his strong sense of the ridiculous to make fun of a vast section of contemporary life – the sort of men and women whom the poet's own fastidious circle despised. He brings to life their platitudinous sentiments with an unerring light touch, and the joke is enhanced by the inappropriately unnatural literary diction that he puts into the mouths of these trivial low-brow characters.

Not long afterwards Herodas, perhaps from Cos, evolved another type of literary mime, the *mimiambus*, comprising brief, pithy, versified sketches of relentless pungency. Once again part of the joke lies in the piquant contrast between his treatment of his themes, which is naturalistic and realistic, and the artificial, elevated, erudite style in which it is paradoxically framed.

The visual art of the Hellenistic period, while following on with direct continuity from the achievements of the previous epoch (Chapter 5, section 4), nevertheless also rivalled contemporary literature in its increasedly determined move towards various forms of realism. The figure of the Apoxyomenus (Man Scraping Himself), made in the later years of the fourth century by Lysippus of Sicyon, shows not only a new and more natural, or at least more fashionable, set of anatomical proportions (smaller head, more slender body), but also a new sense of spiral movement, and a new three-dimensional method of composition. The Tyche (Fortune) of Antioch by his pupil Eutychides developed this three-dimensional concept further, presenting a cunning structure of lines and folds set obliquely in different planes.

The climax of these techniques, however, was to be seen in the no longer surviving bronze Helios or sun-god (Colossus) of Rhodes by another of Lysippus's pupils, the Rhodian Chares (292–280), and in the still extant Victory (Nike) of Samothrace, by an unknown sculptor of early second-century BC. Originally tinted, the Victory is seen alighting exultantly upon a ship's prow – and a calculated counter-twist of her swirling, windswept robes shows how she is leaning forward to meet the rush of the wind.

Yet, somewhat paradoxically, this very time when drapery was receiving such sensitive attention also witnessed an intensification of the interest in the naked feminine form, which Praxiteles had stimulated. Thus the bodily planes of the Venus of Milo (Melos), of the second-century date, move and turn in multiple, contrasting directions, which reveal how, although classical purity and austerity have not been abandoned, they are modified by novel ideas and methods that have been mobilized to exploit the Hellenistic taste for realistic interpretation.

And meanwhile another sort of sculptural realism was developing too, with theatrical emphasis upon the emotions, which the sculptors of the time, echoing Aristotle, regarded as an essential element in human character. Major achievements in this field took place at Pergamum, the only royal capital where sculptors undertook extensive and important work with the backing of ample official patronage. Thus the bronze groups of statuary dedicated by the Pergamene king Attalus I Soter to the goddess Athena (c.200), in order to celebrate his victories over the Celtic Gauls (Galatians) who had invaded Asia Minor, was one of the most ambitious sculptural complexes ever attempted. The bronze originals have vanished, but a marble copy of the centrepiece still survives. It is the 'Ludovisi Group', consisting of the figure of a defeated, desperate Gaul stabbing himself to avoid capture while supporting the body of his wife whom he has just killed. Her limp, inanimate form contrasts with the tension of the man's contorted pose, as he plunges the dagger into his own neck. This central composition was originally surrounded by a series of half-recumbent figures, of which one, the 'Dying Gaul', is preserved, in the form of a fine copy, perhaps of the first century BC. Although set in a calculatedly complex and histrionic pose, the figure makes an exceptionally poignant impression.

126

For the 'Dying Gaul' once again combines the traditional simplifying pattern of Greek classicism with the emotional impact, and freshly direct observation of nature, which were features of contemporary Hellenistic art. There is emphasis upon the vanquished in this monument: they appear not as embodiments of evil, but in all the defiant agony of their defeat. And their portrayal is realistic. The same taste for realism, too, inspired other sculptors belonging to what has been called the 'miserabilistic' school, who depict hunchback dwarfs, and battered fishermen, and maudlin female alcoholics. And yet another facet of realism can be seen in the intimate, amusing terracotta statuettes which take their name from Tanagra in Boeotia, although they were first produced at Taras (Taranto, c.350) and then at Athens.

Wall-painting evidently reflected similar tendencies, represented above all by Apelles of Colophon (Değirmendere) in Ionia, who enjoyed the patronage of Alexander the Great and Ptolemy I Soter. His exploitation of illusionistic *trompe l'oeil* and foreshortening effects was especially notable, and the men and women whom he painted were shown exhibiting a whole range of different emotions. He specialized in easel-paintings, none of which have survived.

But his style may well be reflected in some of the large pebble-mosaics of the period. One such mosaic at Pella, the capital of Macedonia, is a picture of a stag-hunt signed by Gnosis (c.320–300), whose fore-shortened figures and shaded, wind-blown draperies convey an illusion of depth and of real life, as it appears to the eye.

This realism was a keynote of contemporary art, because it mirrored what Hellenistic man was thinking and feeling. And, by the same token, he was individualistic. Despite all the troubles of the time, he was liberated from many earlier conventions and restraints, and more and more conscious of his own capacities and needs and rights. City-state life had weakened, and the royal centres were too remote to occupy its place. To fill the vacuum, people belonged to clubs, lived in better houses, read more – and read about other individuals.

Theophrastus's *Characters* had described what individuals were like, without naming anybody in particular. But people also wanted to read about real, important, picturesque men – in an age which indulged, freely, in personality cult. They were catered for by Aristoxenus of Taras (b.375/360), who did much to develop, out of earlier precedents, the art of biography – including lives not only of men of action, but of philosophers as well. In the third century, Satyrus of Callatis Pontica (Mangalia) composed further biographies, writing attractively but inserting much legendary material. But the *Lives of Philosophers* by

Antigonus of Carystus (*c.*240) showed an unprecedentedly high standard of accurate description. So biography, by now, had been launched; and autobiography, too, was foreshadowed by the *Memoirs* of the Achaean League statesman Aratus of Sicyon (271–213; Chapter 6).

Sculptural portraiture, the visual counterpart of the biographer's art, was likewise virtually an original creation of the Hellenistic world. Men who sought to depict Alexander the Great set the tone. The king's own favourite sculptor, as far as portraits of himself were concerned, was Lysippus of Sicyon, who alone, Alexander believed, could truly capture the leonine aspect of his appearance. Such portraits, like other forms of art, retained a delicate balance between the old idealism and the new realistic trends: as Lysippus himself remarked, 'While others made men as they were, I make them as they appeared to be'[1] – or as they wanted to be, for heads of early Hellenistic monarchs tend not only to reproduce their actual features, but also to hint at the providential foresight and care for his subjects that a king ought to display, and wished to seem to be displaying.

So realism, of a sort, was a characteristic of 'Hellenistic man'. But this was also an age when Greek women came to the fore. As we saw, Hellenistic sculptors, for the first time, were exploring the naked bodies of women: and this was only one aspect of a whole phenomenon of female emergence that was typical of the age.

The tendency was stimulated by the careers of queens of terrifying ability and force, enjoying unlimited freedom of action and power: women such as Arsinoe II Philadelphus, sister and wife of Ptolemy II of Egypt. The reverence accorded to these Ptolemaic queens was related to the worship of the mother-goddess Isis, with whom, indeed, it seemed natural that such formidable human women should be identified.

But, in addition, the prestige and activities of such personages could not fail to contribute to the emancipation of women in general – which in consequence proceeded on a substantial scale, though sometimes patchily. Liberation had at least gone far enough for two ladies whom Theocritus brings to the festival of Adonis to grumble about their husbands in a highly unsubservient fashion. Moreover, although homosexuality by no means ceased, Menander was clear (as Euripides, too, had been) that it is heterosexual love which causes life to continue. The development of private houses made women's lives more agreeable, and eminent women of the time included a portrait-painter, an architect, harpists and at least three poets.

And male poets, too, wrote elegies and epigrams reflecting a new kind of literary interest in the analysis of heterosexual love. The best epigrams of Asclepiades of Samos (*c.*290), for example, deal with this kind of erotic theme, employing his original, dramatic talent to explore the neurotic obsessions which accompanied it. But love, to him, meant sex more than romance. The women he wrote about were mostly attractive prostitutes (*hetairai*), and he commented on them in satirical and scandalous language – himself being weary of living, to use his own words, at the age of scarcely twenty-two. Theocritus, too, agrees with him in failing to envisage love as an ennobling or purifying passion, but stresses it for a different reason: because he knows all about the misery of amorous frustration, the agony of the heart.

In the next generation Apollonius Rhodius, librarian at Alexandria from *c.*260 to *c.*247, by depicting Medea's passion for Jason in his poem the *Argonautica*, became the first poet to use love, romantic love, as the central theme of a whole epic. And meanwhile the same passion, too, of a more middle-brow and saccharine nature, was the main feature of a series of Greek novels that were being launched on the world, perhaps under Egyptian influence, and were supplemented, subsequently, by spicier short stories, the *Milesian Tales*.

2 The Search for Peace of Mind

So the Hellenistic epoch devoted a new, sympathetic interest to the individual man and woman who inhabited its Greek world. Much of the best thought of the time, therefore, was devoted to analysing his and her predicaments.

The outcome of such analyses, in many instances, was despair: never had Chance (Tyche, Fortune) been so assiduously venerated. Or, alternatively, many people talked about Fate – and how, despite its apparent inevitability, it might be possible to circumvent it, for example by magic, or by the equally fallacious but popular methods of the astrologers, who could advise their clients how to evade or outwit the oppressive dictations of the sun and moon and stars. But pagan religion, too, was still very active, in certain of its forms. In particular, the mystery cults of Dionysus, Demeter, Cybele and Isis not only claimed to confer upon their devotees the strength and holiness to endure their present life upon earth, but also proposed to lighten its woes and anxieties by the promise of invulnerable immortality and happiness after death.

More thoughtful people had recourse to the traditional Greek medium of philosophy. The various schools that succeeded to the heritage of Aristotle (Chapter 5, section 3) converged in their pursuit of an imperturbable, invulnerable freedom from disturbance (*ataraxia*) that would enable people to face the buffets of fortune and circumstances and survive: 'The reason for discovering philosophy', said Xenocrates, head of the Platonic Academy, 'is to allay what causes disturbance in life.'[2]

This was not altogether a new idea. During the fifth century BC Democritus of Abdera, the atomist, had put forward a similar concept, and Antisthenes of Taras (*c.*445–360), founder or forerunner of the Cynic school, dwelt on a comparable goal, which he defined as *to apathes*, absence of suffering or (unpleasant) feeling. But it was during the Hellenistic age that this purpose became all-important – with the result that the philosophers, who professed to explain how such an aim could be fulfilled, became famous men, surrounded by crowds of admirers. And people wanted this impregnable self-sufficiency *instantly*, so that schools claiming total knowledge on the subject – almost as if they were religious cults or sects – had to be run up as an emergency measure to satisfy this widespread need.

The most influential of these schools proved to be Stoicism, named after the Painted Portico (Stoa Poikile) at Athens. The founder of the school, Zeno of Citium in Cyprus (335–263), was a master of vivid oratory which relied on the impact of brief, unqualified, vehement assertions. His successor Chrysippus became the scholar and dialectician of Stoicism, which he turned into a technical philosophy. The Stoics insisted that all human beings share a spark of divinity – making us a Brotherhood of Man – so that, as earlier philosophers had suggested, mortal and cosmic events belong to one single, indissoluble process; and it is therefore incumbent upon us to live 'according to nature', of which the formative and guiding principle is Reason (*Logos*), identifiable with God and Fate.

It is *right* to do this, for to the Stoic school ethics come first and foremost, and we find the moral law of Socrates and Plato expressed with a new imperative urgency. Moreover, it is by thus submitting to nature, which is the same as submitting to Fate, that we will find and achieve *apatheia*, or *ataraxia*, that inner tranquillity or peace of mind, which is our armour against all manner of fear or suffering or discomfort. Thus armoured, even a beggar, the Stoics maintained, can become triumphantly independent of Fortune and anxiety. And thousands of people, over a period of many centuries, found this dramatic ideal of the imperturbable Stoic sage an inspiration.

The principal rival of the Stoics, Epicurus (341–270), was born on Samos but became a citizen at Athens, where he formed his school in what was known as the Garden, its membership based on mutual ties of friendship and affection. He was a pragmatist, impatient of all knowledge that seemed irrelevant to the overriding purpose of securing well-being, which he saw, once again, as *ataraxia*. But this, he maintained, could only be achieved by the recognition that the universe is material – consisting wholly, in his view, of the atoms believed in by the philosopher-scientists Leucippus and Democritus (Chapter 5, section 3). This understanding that everything is material seemed to Epicurus to remove, automatically, the two greatest hindrances to peace of mind, which he saw as fear of death and fear of the gods. But is there a logical hitch or snag? For if we human beings, as he believed, like everything else, consist of mechanically moving atoms, how can we have any freedom of will or action at all? However, the atoms, he pronounced, do sometimes make a swerve (*parenklisis*). This swerve does the same job as Aristotle's Unmoved Mover (Chapter 5, section 3), an ultimate, uncaused cause of movement: and it does allow us free will. So it is, after all, up to us to do the best we can, and strive for what we want, and aim at what we believe to be right. Epicurus has gone down to history as the apostle of pleasure, but misleadingly, because the ultimate pleasure he aimed at was freedom from disturbance.

Diogenes of Sinope (*c.*400–325), who developed the Cynic way of thinking, sought the same *ataraxia* by advocating the total overthrow of conventions (*nomoi*). Rules are a bondage, he declared: pay no attention to them at all, and live precisely as nature prescribes – which means, like a dog (*kuon*), his enemies said, and that is how the name Cynic originated. The most important things in life, Diogenes believed, are complete, uninhibited freedom of speech and freedom of action, and the people who truly achieve an undisturbed peace of mind are those who use these freedoms to make their own decisions about how they shall live, without hindrance from anyone else.

All this was stuff of future legend, and Diogenes's followers, building on the picturesque possibilities of such doctrines, invented a method of serio-comic popular preaching, which consisted of accosting and haranguing bystanders and subjecting them to abusive challenges and exchanges of repartee. The hunchback Crates of Thebes (*c.*365–285) was one of these anti-bourgeois practitioners, and Bion of Borysthenes (Olbia, *c.*325–235), son of a former slave and prostitute, wrote 'diatribes', stingingly vituperative, fictional conversations or dialogues denouncing other people's ambitions and prejudices. Then Menippus of Gadara, in the first half of the third century, evolved a new sort of serio-comic, philosophically humorous cross-talk (*spoudogeloion*), which gained the name of 'Menippean satire'.

There was a compelling attraction in this Cynic counter-culture which told men and women there was nothing they need or should fear, desire or possess. But it was a negative movement. And so indeed, many felt, were all these Hellenistic schools. One refuge from them was Scepticism. The sophist Protagoras had led the way (Chapter 5, section 3), but a firm formulation was the work of Pyrrho of Elis (*c*.365/360–275/270), who taught that, in practice, nothing at all can be known, so that speculation is merely waste of time. And that, deliberately, was *his* preferred path to avoid disturbance and anxiety. The man who thus suspends his judgment, Pyrrho maintained, preserving total unconcern and indifference about everything in the world, achieves the imperturbability that is everyone's goal.

The Sceptics, once again, seem to be striking an attitude which is as unpositive as those of any other school, though in a different way. Yet many of them possessed powerful intellectual gifts, and their critical onslaught did at least enable them to jettison many fatuous doctrines of the past. The man who principally saved their standpoint for future generations was Timon of Phlius (*c*.320–230), whose *Silloi* or 'squinteyed' pieces were mockeries and lampoons, full of ridicule and invective – assailing, in particular, the credulity of all dogmatic philosophers, living and dead. Once again, the purpose of attacking all these dogmas was to put their disturbing influences out of the way, by which means it ought to be possible to achieve freedom from care.

Another, more subtle and oblique approach to the same aim was undertaken by the poet Theocritus (*c*.300–260?). The realism of his literary mimes has already been mentioned (section 1 above). But in his bucolic pieces (from *boukolos*, cowherd), he got away from realism altogether, seeking his own version of *ataraxia* in a wholly unreal pastoral world. The outstanding writer of the Hellenistic age – although Callimachus of Cyrene (*c*.305–240), who contested his pupil Apollonius Rhodius' preference for long poems, was often, instead, regarded as the supreme Alexandrian – Theocritus is composing pastoral verse for the townsmen of an urban civilization, in artificial, superbly ordered poetry of a delicate, concentrated precision.

His scene is the limited world of the rustic bower, magically sealed off from ordinary human life. Yet Theocritus, when we look beyond his piquant ironies, is also searching after an entire human community which will realize its potential amid this healing environment – or amid its symbolic equivalent, wherein the unrealized individual can awaken, as he calls it, *hasuchia*, true tranquillity: 'On *hasuchia* be our minds set,' sings a shepherd to his friend.[3]

3 Epilogue

The political failure of the Hellenistic world was due to the military superiority of the Romans, aided and accentuated by the usual, fatal disunion between Greek states. And so it was that, during the second century BC, one Hellenistic country after another, failing to form anything approaching an effective coalition, collapsed after unsuccessful attempts to confront Rome.

Thus, in the First Macedonian War, the Romans defeated King Philip v of Macedonia (200–197). Then in 191–188 they pushed the Seleucid monarch Antiochus III the Great out of Asia Minor. A Second Macedonian War waged by Rome against King Perseus (171–168) brought about the end of his kingdom. Next, in 146, the Romans dissolved the Achaean League, and annexed Macedonia and Greece. In 133 King Attalus III of Pergamum bequeathed them his state. In 63 they finally defeated Mithridates VI of Pontus, and abolished the Seleucid kingdom. In 30 Octavian annexed the Egypt of Cleopatra VII, and made it into a Roman province, under his personal control.

However, this gradual, ineluctable, political decline of Hellenism, brought about by Roman military might and accelerated by internal disunity, was not accompanied by decline in other, cultural, fields.

For example, the Hellenistic world produced Polybius of Megalopolis (c.200–after 118 BC), who was one of the outstanding Greek historians of all time. His original purpose had been to narrate the history of the fifty-three years (220–168) which left Rome mistress of the world. Subsequently, he revised this plan, in order to analyse the methods by which the Romans exercised this supremacy; and the work was extended down to 146. Polybius wrote history with a twofold purpose, in order to train statesmen, and to teach the general reader how to avoid disaster. His theory of historical motivation is characteristic of the Hellenistic age, since he placed Chance (Tyche) at the very centre of the world he portrayed, indicating that the total conquest of that world by the Romans cannot be explained by any other means. Yet there is also a touch of ambivalence in this insistence on a fortuitously operating power, since Polybius, at the same time, saw Rome's conquest of the Hellenistic world as *destined* to happen, so that Chance is, to this extent, helping to work towards a providential goal – in which human beings can control the sub-plots, but not the Grand Design, which is planned by Fate: a comfort to his fellow-Greeks, who could by this doctrine shift the blame for their humiliations and failures, at the hands of the Romans, onto historical inevitability.

A second Greek adjustment to the new world dominated by Rome was made by the Stoic Panaetius of Rhodes (c.185–109). As a start he brought Stoicism, of which we saw the beginnings in the last section, into focus as a guide to Roman careers. As befitted a man who, himself, was an upper-class property owner – the first leader of his school to possess material resources of his own – he laid stress on the virtues which were appropriate to a ruling class, such as justice and courage and generosity. Moreover, after living for a time in Athens, he himself transferred his residence to Rome (c.144), where he took his place among the most enlightened circles of metropolitan society.

He was eager (as Polybius, too, had been) to encourage these power-ful, sympathetic Romans, in whose company he spent his time, to use their authority well, and his creation of a Stoic gentleman's code exercised a major influence on Roman moral and political thinking. So did Panaetius's interpretation of the Stoic law of 'living according to nature', which he presented as a universally valid set of precepts that could be adjusted to become the philosophical justification of Roman supremacy and imperial rule.

Then, in the hands of the polymath Posidonius of Rhodes (c.135–c.51/50 BC), Stoicism was watered down once again, with the aid of the Platonic view that the soul contains both rational and irrational elements, so that Romans need not worry too much if they are not perfect – they must do the best they can: and as the unifiers of the earthly world state, reflecting the heavenly cosmopolis, they fulfil a beneficent and necessary role.

Meanwhile Hellenistic art had continued to proceed on its distinguished way.

The climax of the contemporary drive towards realism was the frieze of the Gigantomachy, the battle of the Gods against the Giants, upon the Altar of Zeus and Athena commissioned at Pergamum by Eumenes II Soter (197–160/159). This was the largest Greek sculptural work in existence, designed to outdo the Parthenon frieze. Its reliefs ran onwards in one continuous band, more than four hundred feet long and seven feet high. This massive array of pictures displayed twelve hundred divinities and part-human, part-animal giants. The work was inscribed with the signatures of its artists, although only one of their names, that of Orestes of Pergamum, has survived.

The effect is of unrestrained emotion and turmoil, accentuated by wildly contorted limbs, disordered hair, and facial expressions con-veying extreme exultation, distress, terror and pain. What is portrayed is chaos: for it was out of chaos that the gods asserted the victory of civilization – like the victory that Attalus I Soter, the father of Eumenes II, had won over contemporary Celtic (Gaulish) invaders of Asia Minor.

This kind of excitable art reached its climax in a statuary group by three second-century Rhodian sculptors (unless what we have is a first-century copy), which represents Laocoon and his two sons struggling in the grip of a monstrous snake. The scene is from the mythological cycle of Troy. Laocoon, the son of King Priam of that city, and a priest of Apollo, had been suspicious of the wooden horse introduced by the Greeks within the walls, and secretly containing a body of combatants. But Athena, wishing the stratagem to succeed, dispatched this serpent which crushed him and his sons to death. The elaborate cross-rhythms of the composition depict violent expressions of physical tension and anguish, displayed with skilled anatomical virtuosity, for the artists seem to be exploiting the clinical interest in the human physique that was aroused by the current anatomical researches of Hellenistic scientists.

By the same token, portraiture, too, had moved a long way, by this time, in the direction of thoroughgoing realism, especially in peripheral territories where the power of the idealistic Greek traditions was not so strong. Thus an idiosyncratic portrait of the Bactrian monarch Euthydemus I Theos (*d.c.*190), wearing a sun-hat, presents him humorously, but surely also as he must have been. Moreover, outstanding advances towards lifelike portraiture are likewise to be seen on the coinage of the period. Once again the eastern territories are well to the fore, notably in a portrait of the Indo-Greek ruler Antimachus I Theos Nicephorus of the Punjab and eastern Gandhara (from *c.*171), in whose features are strength of personality blended with sophistication.

Moreover, as it was with human beings, so it was with nature. It received, that is to say, a closer and more realistic look. After various preliminaries, landscape painting emerged as an autonomous artistic theme in the second century BC – perhaps in the first instance at the hugest of urban conglomerations, Alexandria, where most people saw little of nature, and in some cases wished they could see more.

The landscape movement is associated with the name of a painter of that period, Demetrius of Alexandria, known as the *topographos* or landscapist. He went to Rome and may well have been the artist of excellent pictures of the Wanderings of Odysseus, copies of which, from a villa on Rome's Esquiline Hill, displays the hero's adventures against romantic natural settings of land and sea. In an unknown painter's *Lost Ram*, too, a man and the ram he has recaptured are only diminutive objects against a varied background of land and sky, illuminated by dramatic lighting effects.

Thus the art of the epoch maintained its own course well enough, uninfluenced by the Romans, except that it profited from the wealth of their patrons (whose craggy features, too, some Greek portraitists appreciatively reproduced), and taught Roman artists a great deal, just as the Roman writers, too, had lessons to learn (Chapter 9, section 1).

This Hellenistic age was an age of autocrats. There had been autocrats before, and in Sicily, for example, there had been little else. In most parts of the Greek world, however, the dominant political form had hitherto been the republican city-state. However, these states, with a few exceptions – and except, too, when they were occasionally grouped together in federations – had now been demoted from their independent dignity. In the past, such city-states had produced political personages, and the Greek world still produced them, but now they were mostly absolute rulers or, sometimes, heads of confederacies.

Nevertheless, the makers of this Hellenistic world, as we have seen, were not only politicians but, as before, writers, philosophers and artists, many of them of the utmost distinction. These were the people who made the age an epoch of contradiction, characterized, on the one hand, by a new or intensified urge to see things as they really were and are, and on the other by a counter-urge to get away from this unsatisfactory reality into the peace of mind (*ataraxia*) that is impregnable against the world's blows: a contrast between, on the one hand, buoyant realism, and on the other a healing retreat into undisturbed inaction, which seemed the only means of keeping life's pressures at bay.

The contradiction is apparent over the entire field of Hellenistic life. Scientists sought to see things as they are, and many authors and artists, too, tried increasingly to depict men and women in a more realistic manner than had ever been seen before. Meanwhile, however, a different set of writers preferred the search for *ataraxia*, and so did the mystery religions which set up their own fantasy worlds, enabling people to hope that they could be rescued from having to suffer from their lives as they are. And the philosophers, too, who are so important in this epoch, almost all regarded it as their function to satisfy this pressing, universal hankering after *ataraxia*, invulnerable liberation from the troubles of this world; a world in which there was such a glaring contrast between the remote grandeur of the dominating governments and the helpless smallness of the men and women who lived in their dominions.

These people were forced back into individualism. Deprived of the cosy protection of their now much less meaningful local communities, and stimulated by philosophical, religious and poetical advice, each individual man fended for himself and developed and fostered his own personality and potential, feeling that these things were all he possessed. And women developed similar habits of thought.

Although much of this was largely new, nevertheless – and this is one of the most elusive contradictions of the age – tradition still loomed quite as large as novelty, or larger. Hellenistic Greeks never ceased to be conscious of the portentous classical past. And yet, while admiringly and inextricably attached to that past, they were at the same time eager to reshape it and improve upon it, and it was to fulfil that aim that their innovations were designed.

With this grand past behind it and Rome's empire lying ahead, the Hellenistic age has sometimes been rated dismissively as a merely transitional, characterless phenomenon. Yet this is a misguided conclusion. For while the Hellenistic states and societies lasted they constituted a civilization in their own right, one of those that rank high in the history of the world – the western world, that is, for despite the non-Greek populations of the enormous Hellenistic kingdoms their important creations, and those of the city-states, remained Greek in almost every field, with only modest infusions from the other eastern cultures that they temporarily overran.

When Rome conquered the Hellenistic world, we come to another and perhaps even more paradoxical contradictory feature. For military defeat and political subjection to the Romans came to mean not the end of the Greek society, but, on the contrary, its maintenance and perpetuation. For quite apart from the effects which this Greek culture had on the Romans, the Greek world, although politically subjected to Rome, had not been Romanized at all – and was never going to be either, to any marked degree. Extended rather than diminished in size, it was going to remain Greek. And, eventually, the Greeks got their revenge, when Constantine I the Great (AD 306–337) created his new capital Constantinople, on the site of the Greek city of Byzantium: with the logical result that some centuries later the language and culture of the surviving Byzantine, east Rome empire became, officially, Greek, so that Hellenistic art and thought had once again taken over the western world.

THE ROMANS

Part IV

EARLY ROME
AND THE REPUBLIC

8

The Etruscans and the Rise of Rome

Italy's central position in the Mediterranean is a call to self-assertion, promising opportunities when its population is capable of grasping them. For the country links the eastern and western reaches of the sea. Moreover, its elongated peninsula provides, next only to Greece, the most extensive coastline in Europe. At least three-quarters of Italy's territory, however, consists of hills, rising up into the central heights of the Apennines. Yet there are also plains overlooked by this mountainous mass. They supply convenient inland corridors, and for the most part enjoy a relatively temperate and humid climate, which, in early times, invited possibilities of agriculture on a scale that no other Mediterranean country had ever before been able to attempt.

It was in the southern part of the country that the most fertile districts were to be found, and it was here and in Sicily that the Greeks undertook their early, adventurous colonizing drive. It was initiated in Campania (Chapter 3, section 3). But the Greek colonists there looked northwards, through Latium and across the River Tiber, to the city-states of Etruria.

Etruria, the land of the Etruscans or Tyrrhenians, comprised what is now Tuscany, in western Italy, together with the northern part of Lazio. Their language, which has been partly elucidated, was non-Indo-European. But the tradition that they originally came from Lydia in Asia Minor, reported from that country by Herodotus,[1] is based, like many similar ancient interpretations, on false etymologies. The Etruscans must be regarded as an Italian people, whose origins, however, were complicated by numerous population movements which cannot now be traced.

Greek culture impinged on their territory from the eighth century onwards, when merchants and settlers on the island of Pithecusae and at Cumae on the adjoining mainland traded gold and other precious objects – imported from Greek markets in Syria operated by Chalcis in Euboea (Appendix II) – with the Etruscans, who had outposts of their own in the same part of Campania, at Capua (S. Maria Capua Vetere), Cales (Calvi) and elsewhere. Through these channels the Greek businessmen and colonists also transmitted the Greek alphabet of Chalcis to the Etruscans, who adapted it for their own use.

In exchange, the Etruscans provided the iron of which they possessed an abundance unparalleled in other Mediterranean lands. The riches that they acquired by these commercial exchanges are reflected in lavish tombs, decorated by paintings in which the dominant influence of Chalcis yielded, in due course, to that of the Corinthians, whose fantastic orientalizing art (followed by that of the Ionians) created the blend of Greek and native styles characteristic of the Etruscan art of the sixth century BC.

Under the stimulus of this wealth, the habitation centres of Etruria had become city-states. Tarquinii (Tarquinia), which was already exploiting the metals of Mount Tolfa as early as c.900 BC, provides the largest range of wall paintings in its graves, demonstrating how successive Greek artistic influences were grafted onto Etruscan motifs and methods. A Greek, Demaratus, was believed to have come from Corinth and settled at Tarquinii, from which one of his sons, Tarquinius Priscus, reputedly emigrated to Rome and became one of its kings. From c.600–580, one of the ports of Tarquinii, Graviscae (Porto San Clementino), included a residential quarter occupied by Greek merchants, who built shrines of their own.

Caere (Cerveteri), notable for its huge mound graves, in due course challenged the political and economic supremacy of Tarquinii, from which it took over most of the Tolfa mines. Caere joined Carthage in trying to repel the Greeks (from Phocaea and Massalia) at the battle of Alalia (Aleria, c.540/535), and inscriptions on gold leaf from the Caeretan port of Pyrgi (Santa Severa) reflect the Carthaginian connections of Caere's ruler Thefarie Velianas.[2] However, Pyrgi also possessed a shrine of the Greek goddess Hera, while the Caeretans imported quantities of Corinthian pottery, and reliefs and sculptures found in the area reflect blends of Ionian and native motifs and treatments.

Excavations at Vulci have likewise disclosed an influx of Corinthian vases, acquired, no doubt, in exchange for metals from Mount Tuniae (Amiata). Men from Vulci also seem to have played a large part in the southward Etruscan expansion into Campania. North of Vulci, Vetulonia and Rusellae (Roselle) were rival maritime cities on Lake Prilius, which is now dry land. Moreover, Vetulonia was also apparently served by the harbour of Populonia, which became the largest importer of Greek artefacts into the area.

Another Etruscan centre, however, namely Volaterrae (Volterra), must have been the main starting-point for the Etruscanization of north Italy, based on Felsina (Bologna). Clusium, too, was a prominent leader of this movement, and acquired powerful influence in the south as well, not only in Campania but in the intermediate territory of Latium, now the southern part of Lazio. For there the outstanding Clusian monarch, Lars Porsenna, probably captured Rome itself for a time, after the expulsion of its last king Tarquinius Superbus (?) towards the end of the sixth century. Veii (Veio), also, played a major intermediate part between north and south, and derived its revenue not only from agriculture but from salt at the mouth of the Tiber. But Veii was far too close to Rome for coexistence to continue for long, and in c.396 the historic clash between the two cities took place, which resulted in the destruction of Veii. This heralded the eclipse of the other city-states of Etruria as well – which had not given Veii the help that they might have.

Already before then, however, the Etruscans' position in their outlying territories, too, had been weakening. Towards the end of the fifth century their power was broken in the north, while Aristodemus of Cumae undermined it in Campania and Latium. Next, in 474 the Campanian Greeks and Hiero I of Syracuse finally checked their naval expansion in a battle off Cumae; and then Etruscan Capua, like Greek Cumae itself, succumbed to the Samnites (c.430–423).

The future of Italy, then, lay not with Etruria – though its people's sense of identity and cultural pride did not disappear – but with Rome and Latium.

Some thirty miles deep and sixty miles long, Latium was a well-watered territory, extending from the Tiber down to the borders of Campania, and consisting of rolling plains which furrowed into gullies and undulating folds. Before 1000 BC, populations that had earlier established themselves in the region were joined by immigrants of mixed origins coming from the Balkans in small, isolated groups, and speaking Latin. These people became increasingly familiar with the use of iron, a knowledge they had acquired along the sea-routes from the Aegean. In contrast with their pastoral forerunners in Latium, they cultivated the soil with light ploughs and cremated their dead; another people who joined them, perhaps from south Italy, practised inhumation instead. One of the nuclei of these Latin communities, based upon their common religious sanctuary dedicated to the sky-divinity Jupiter, was the Alban Mount (Monte Cavo), thirteen miles south-east of Rome. Earlier volcanic activity of the mountain (which was by this time extinct) had covered the plain for miles around with fertile new soil impregnated with phosphates and potash.

In the tenth century BC the settlement of Latium was approaching completion, and it was at this juncture that some of its inhabitants moved up to the country's northern border, the River Tiber, and established themselves at Rome. Leaving aside the much more northerly Padus (Eridanus, Po) – which long remained outside the confines of Italy – the Tiber is the peninsula's largest river, and dominates its most substantial drainage area. Descending from the central mountains, it becomes navigable in its lower reaches. And fifteen miles from the Mediterranean, or twenty for those travelling on the river – far enough to give advance warning of sea raiders, but near enough to provide access to the sea – was the lowest of the Tiber's practicable crossing points: at Rome.

At the final point where the stream turns and breaks through low hills to the marshy coastal plain, before entering the sea beside the only possible harbour for many miles in either direction, this crossing, adjacent to an island in the river, linked pieces of firm ground on either bank. The crossing was also particularly significant because it served one of the few longitudinal, north-south routes of Italy, a route which provided the principal passage along the western and more thickly populated flank of the peninsula. Moreover, the site commanded a passage not only across the Tiber, but up and down the course of its waters as well. The road down the river, that is, supplied access to precious, rare salt-pans on the shore; whereas in the opposite direction the continuation of the same road led upstream into the central regions of the country. Once the inhabitants of Rome became strong enough, they would be able to control all these vital communications. However, this possibility was a challenge and danger as well as an allurement. For people at such a strategic junction are likely to be attacked, and the immigrants who came to live at Rome were liable to aggression from every side, from which they would have to defend themselves.

Their defence came from the hills of Rome, upon which they planted their settlements. For the river lay, here, in a deep trough, and the settlers made their homes upon the elevations overlooking its southern bank. Between a hundred and three hundred feet above sea-level, these eminences formed a group of flat-topped spurs projecting (more abruptly than now) towards the Tiber, and safely elevated above the floods with which from time to time it inundated its valley. The hills were divided, one from another, by ravines which had formerly contained tributaries of the river. Water supply remained good at all seasons, and fertile soil was within easy reach.

The first new arrivals at Rome settled on the level summit of the isolated and well-protected Palatine Hill, and in the marshy valley (later the Forum) which lay between the Palatine and three other hills. These were the Quirinal, the Esquiline and the precipitous Capitoline, which were likewise settled, like the Caelian, during the times that followed. As for the Forum valley, it was first not only inhabited but also employed for burials, both of the cremation and inhumation type, indicating that the two groups which practised these different customs lived together and gradually amalgamated on the site.

The traditional date for Rome's foundation, 753 BC, is fictitious. But from the early seventh century BC the communities upon the Palatine and Esquiline Hills had joined together, at least for religious purposes and perhaps in some sort of political amalgamation as well. The unit they now formed was the Septimontium or Seven Mounts, which was the number of spurs on those two main hills and the Caelian. Then in c.625–600 the Forum valley was drained, and thus started its long career as Rome's meeting-place. Next, the area was paved, and the Forum Boarium (cattle-market) beside the river, too, was laid out. And then the Quirinal and Viminal Hills joined the growing community, which the Capitoline served as a common acropolis and citadel.

The appearance of such changes, accompanied, as excavations show, by the establishment of professional handicrafts, indicates that these developments were prompted by Etruscan influences. Close contacts between Iron Age Latium and the city-states of southern Etruria had been taking place from the mid-eighth century onwards, and the Romans participated in them almost from the beginning, gradually assimilating their material culture to that of the Etruscan world. For at just about the time when the Forum was drained the first pottery and metalwork from the nearest Etruscan cities, Caere (Cerveteri) and Veii, began to be seen at Rome. The place was evidently on the way to becoming an Etruscan town.

And from that time onwards the myths and legends with which the earliest Roman history was inextricably encrusted begin to take more palpable shape. The tradition that Rome, like Etruscan and Greek cities, was originally governed by monarchs may be accepted: and the last three of these rulers, at least, seem to have been Etruscan, or under Etruscan influence.

The first was Tarquinius Priscus, who reigned, according to tradition, from 616 to 579 BC, and supposedly (as we saw) originated from Etruscan Tarquinii – though that could merely be a supposition based on his name, and he may instead have come from Caere, which was closer.

Next ruled Servius Tullius (578–535?), who was believed, later, to have been Latin, although some contradicted this assertion, believing instead that he was an Etruscan – and he does appear to have developed Rome on Etruscan lines. Then, finally, came Priscus's son Tarquinius Superbus (if indeed there was a second Tarquin at all; he may have been invented to allot the 'bad' deeds, and the fall of the monarchy, to a scapegoat, distinct from Priscus, who was regarded as 'good').

The Roman state, it was subsequently maintained, had been originally divided into three tribes – which bear Etruscan names. Each tribe was subdivided into ten *curiae* or wards, and the earliest known senate contained thirty members from each *curia*, while the *curiae* also met together to form an Assembly, which was therefore known as the *comitia curiata*. This crucial, tribal system also formed the basis of Rome's first army, consisting of 3,000 men. Next, supposedly by Servius Tullius, the three original tribes were superseded by twenty-two new ones, four in the urban area (corresponding with the Four Regions into which the town was divided) and seventeen in the country. As happened when comparable changes were introduced in Greek towns, the new tribes were established on a geographical, territorial basis, in order to diminish traditional family groupings (though the portrayal of Servius as an early democratic reformer was anachronistic). In perhaps the same period, too, the Roman army – doubled in size – lost its links with the *curiae* and tribes and was reorganized in 'centuries', that is to say in units of 100 men each, which owed much to the hoplite revolution that had been taking place in Greece. The *comitia curiata*, accordingly, was supplemented (and for most purposes superseded) by a *comitia centuriata*, which was based on these military 'centuries' – but dominated by property owners, so that it served to strengthen the monarchy, which they supported.

This was about the time when Rome emerged as the leading power of north-western Latium, capturing the key town of Alba Longa (Castelgandolfo), on the slopes of the Alban Mount, whereupon certain of Alba's leading families came to settle in Rome. This capture conferred religious advantages, owing to the mountain's association with the worship of Jupiter. In the same epoch, too, one of the Roman kings – reputedly Servius Tullius – built a temple of Diana ('the bright one', like Jupiter or Diou-piter) upon the Aventine Hill, just outside the boundaries of the Four Regions of this early Rome. The new shrine was intended to increase the city's prestige in Latium. But it also looked further afield, deriving inspiration from the Greek cities whose federal worships it echoed. In particular, the models were Massalia (Massilia,

Marseille, Chapter 3, section 3) and its cult of Ephesian Artemis, with whom Diana was identified.

Thus the Romans took a decisive step away from their own earlier conceptions of deity, which were impersonal and alien from Greek ideas, towards the anthropomorphic religion of Hellenism. Moreover, the Aventine temple of Diana (Artemis) stood guard over the river-wharves of the Tiber, which provided a centre for Greek traders from an early date. Below the hill, too, lay the altar known as the Ara Maxima, dedicated to Hercules, who was Heracles, Greek god of commercial enterprises.

Another new Roman shrine, however, was more Etruscan than Greek. This was the triple temple shared by Jupiter the Best and Greatest with Juno and Minerva, the 'Capitoline Triad', on the hill of the same name. Jupiter's statue was made by Vulca of Veii. Even if, as was later said, both the Tarquins, Priscus and Superbus, played a part in the foundation of the temple, it was in the main (if indeed there were two Tarquins) the latter's work. Although the temple's rows of free-standing columns down each side were Hellenic in character, the sixteen-foot-high platform on which the building stood, and the shape of the wooden superstructure (decorated, probably, by the colourful paintwork) reproduced Etruscan traditions.

But then, almost immediately afterwards, probably between 510 and 506 BC, the Roman monarchy, represented, according to tradition, by the 'bad' Tarquinius Superbus, was swept away. It was a time when, in Etruria itself as well, monarchic governments were losing their grip and collapsing. It was also a time when the Etruscans both in Latium and in Campania were generally in retreat, hard pressed by the Greeks. In particular, the second victory of Aristodemus, of the Greek city of Cumae, against the Etruscans took place at Latin Aricia (Ariccia) shortly after the downfall of Rome's Etruscan monarchy – and Aristodemus's success was one of the reasons why attempts to reestablish the Roman kingship failed.

The Republic which replaced it was presided over by a pair of annually elected officials who were known, at least later, as consuls. But their task was difficult, since the collapse of Rome's royal government left the city weak and vulnerable, menaced by Italian enemies on all sides who were eager to take advantage of its diminished position. In consequence, the greater part of the two centuries that followed witnessed continual, grimly fought battles against each one or another of these Italian foes in turn.

Sometimes they were struggles on which the very survival of Rome depended. A dangerous threat, for example, came from Aricia. For that town, after it had helped Aristodemus to win the victory at its gates, became the leader of a religious and probably also political Latin League – such as Alba Longa had headed in earlier years – and exploited its own cult of Diana in order to eclipse her sanctuary at Rome. Nor was this the only Latin town that became recalcitrant. For it was at about the same period that legend-encrusted Lavinium (Pratica del Mare), near the sea sixteen miles from Rome, threw off its allegiance to the Romans and asserted its claims, not unlike those of Aricia, to provide the common sanctuary of a group of townships in Latium.

Tusculum, too, resisted the Romans, and led a Latin army against them at Lake Regillus (*c*.496). The Romans remembered the engagement as a victory. Yet this may not have been entirely true, since soon afterwards we learn that they made a treaty with the Latins *on a basis of equality*. However, it was not long before the political balance did, in fact, tilt over in favour of the Romans. In *c*.415 they were entrusted with the organization of the Latin Festival on the Alban Mount. And then we find them concluding a treaty with Aricia, and with Lavinium too, in each case separately – on a bilateral basis: actions which showed a Roman capacity to disregard those towns' corporate membership of the Latin League.

Nevertheless Rome, on the whole, maintained a close association with the Latins, since such an alliance was essential to all the parties involved, who were equally menaced by neighbouring Italian tribes. And proof that the Latin League, corporatively, recognized this danger was its invention in the 490s, with Roman support, of *federal Latin colonies* – towns intended to provide defensive bases against external threats. Much later on, the romans were to borrow, and adapt to their own purposes, this fruitful idea of urban colonization, which was thereafter to play a dominant part in their development of Italy, and eventually of the empire.

Prominent among the enemies against whom the Latins and Romans felt obliged to join forces were the Sabines, whose tribal units lived in independent Apennine hill-top villages north-north-east of Rome. They were eager to have a share of Roman amenities, and in *c*.460 even succeeded in briefly occupying the Capitoline Hill itself, before suffering a severe defeat at the hands of the Romans some eleven years later. Thereafter hostilities came to an end, and from that time onwards the association of Romans and Sabines proceeded apace, until in the end they virtually amalgamated.

During this whole period, too, Romans and Latins had been menaced by other tribes from the valleys and glens of the Apennines. Foremost among them were the Volsci, who had come down and established themselves beside the River Liris (Garigliano) in south-eastern Latium. From c.494 the Volsci raided Latin and Roman territory almost every year, capturing the port of Antium (Anzio), from which, however, their final ejection in 338 marked the end of their power. The Aequi, also, had descended from their unfertile hills, and in c.484 captured the strategic pass of Mount Algidus (Algido) on the Alban Mount. But they lost it again in c.431, whereupon they too fell into gradual decline, leading, almost, to extermination. It had been a piece of good fortune for Latium and Rome that these hostile Sabine, Volscian and Aequian neighbours had been too poorly led and organized to combine forces and mount coordinated attacks. So, in the end, they ceased to constitute a serious menace.

This was all the more fortunate for Rome, since at the same time the gravest of all the threats to its existence came from quite another source – Etruria, just across the Tiber. The enemy was Veii. As we saw earlier, the place was intolerably close to Rome, only twelve miles away, and the two cities' competing demands for markets and land and coastal salt had probably lead, from an early date, to serious clashes – which became exacerbated by the fall of Rome's Etruscan monarchy. A semi-feudal Roman force provided by the clan of the Fabii was defeated by the Veientines on the River Cremera (Fosso Valchetta, c.476/5). But in c.396, after a long and legendary siege, Veii was captured and almost obliterated by the Romans, under the leadership of Marcus Furius Camillus, who has a claim to be regarded as his city's earliest historical figure. The success almost doubled Roman territory, and meant that the other Etruscan states could, during the following decades and centuries, be picked off one by one.

However, this Roman success was immediately followed by a grave setback, at the hands of the Celtic Gauls whose hordes were spreading throughout Europe. In c.387/6, under their monarch Brennus, 30,000 of these Gallic migrants drove southwards from the River Padus (Eridanus, Po) into the Italian peninsula, hoping for land and for plunder. After calling off a drive against Etruscan Clusium (Chiusi), the Gauls moved down against Rome itself, and eleven miles from the city, beside a Tiber tributary, the Allia (Fosso della Bettina), they put a Roman force to rout. Next they marched on, and captured and burnt the city itself. But then, on hearing of threats to their territories in the north, they allowed themselves to be bought off, and departed from central Italy altogether.

The Romans never forgot this humiliating event. But useful results emerged all the same. Etruscan Caere (Cerveteri) – which had always liked them more than it liked its compatriots at Veii – had helped to get Brennus away, and was now rewarded by a novel, privileged status, the *hospitium publicum* (386). This entitled its people to come to Rome on terms of legal equality with Roman citizens, and stipulated mutual tax privileges, thus establishing a formula which the Romans, during the centuries to come, would extend, with adaptations, to other cities. And a second result of the Gallic onslaught was the erection of a defensive rampart round the habitation centre of Rome itself, of which the portions that still remain standing bear the erroneous, anachronistic name of the 'Wall of Servius Tullius'. The circumference of the fortification, enclosing an area of more than 1,000 acres, shows that Rome, by this time, already possessed by far the largest perimeter of any town in Italy.

Under the shock of the Gallic invasion Rome displayed tact to the Latins by giving them a share in the settlement and defence of the lands that it had recently taken from Veii. Moreover, when, in 381, the Latin town of Tusculum showed signs of hostility to the Romans, they not only incorporated it into their own state, but conferred full Roman citizenship on the Tusculans. This concept that citizenship could be enlarged in such a way was a fruitful new doctrine which later became a source of Rome's numerical superiority and strength.

Nevertheless, certain other Latin communities, dominating important roads, were now beginning, more and more, to resent Roman predominance. One of them was Praeneste (Palestrina), home of a shrine of Fors Fortuna: it chose to side with the Volscians against Rome. Another hostile Latin town was Tibur (Tivoli) – where the River Anio (Aniene) leaves the Sabine mountains – which skirmished frequently with the Romans. They showed their refusal, however, to feel overawed by extending their tentacles down beyond Latium altogether and into Campania; and when the League of Campanian cities appealed to them for protection from invading Samnite mountaineers (*c.*343) they duly responded. Latin cities interpreted this intervention as a menacing attempt to encircle them, and became involved in a bitter war against Rome. But finally the Latin confederates were forced to submit, and their League was broken up (338).

At this juncture Rome showed a gift for conciliation which the Greeks had never displayed. Its technique was to make piecemeal arrangements with each individual Latin city, on a practical basis, without venge-fulness. Aricia and three other places were given full Roman citizenship, (such as had been earlier granted to Tusculum). Tibur and Praeneste were allowed to retain formal independence, with the status of allies. Other Latin cities, too, were permitted to make bilateral treaties with Rome (but not with each other), and were awarded a sort of half-way citizenship (*civitas sine suffragio*), which carried legal privileges, but also involved an obligation to contribute troops for mutual defence. This Roman device was one-sided, but it was also astute, since it offered a sufficient degree of satisfaction to the towns that were treated in this way.

Latin colonies continued to be founded, but an innovation, now, was the purely *Roman* colony, manned by 300 Roman families, at selected geographical points. Among the first of such settlements were Ostia, Antium (Anzio) and Tarracina (Terracina). Altogether, 60,000 hold-ings were established at Roman colonies between 343 and 264 BC, multiplying the city's territory to 50,000 square miles, which was three times its previous size.

Thus strengthened, the Romans next had to fight three wars against the Samnites, the group of Italian peoples who occupied the centre of the peninsula – and possessed twice as much land and population as Rome. In the Second (Great) Samnite War the battle of the Caudine Forks (321) was a terrible setback for the Romans, but their subsequent construction of the Appian Way (Via Appia) traversing the 132 miles from Rome to Capua proved a powerful political and military instru-ment, and victory finally followed (304). The grimly fought Third War (298–290), including a military triumph at Sentinum (Sassoferrato), ended in total success, which resulted in the annihilation of Samnite independence.

During these struggles, the Roman army had become a good deal larger. It was now divided into two legions, modelled, originally, on the Greek phalanx, but more mobile, and equipped with standard weapons, which included a six-foot-long throwing javelin in the place of its thrusting forerunner.

The Romans were dourly persevering, and always convinced that they were right. They could also be cruel. Yet, as we have seen, they showed an unprecedented political reasonableness, and this they now demonstrated once again in dealing with the defeated Samnites, to whom they granted treaties – 'unequal' and not 'equal' treaties it is true, but treaties all the same.

Moreover, in whatever parts of Italy it had conquered, Rome always took trouble to establish a friendly relationship with local governing classes. Although it is true that its complex, empirical multiplication of differing treaties with the various towns and tribes exemplified an imperialistic principle of 'divide and rule', yet the instinctive Roman genius for commonsense statecraft made sure that the relationships worked – and they continued to work for centuries to come. Their first major achievement was the unification of Italy – which had now, except in the Greek south, been completed.

However, during these 170 years of almost incessant fighting, the Roman community had also found itself racked by the most serious internal disturbances it was ever to experience. Its republican system of government was complex, and did not at once achieve maturity. The Greek historian Polybius admired the mutual automatic balances which created an equilibrium between its legislative, executive and judicial institutions.[3] Yet much depended also on a cluster of impalpable customs and conventions which took pragmatic effect in accordance with each successive situation as it arose.

The power of the two annually elected consuls was checked by the Senate, which, although it possessed no executive powers, advised them on policy, finance, law and religion. The body, however, which elected the consuls, enacted laws and declared war and peace was the Assembly (*comitia*). But at this point Polybius's 'balance' and 'equilibrium' became illusory, because the Assembly's decisions were decisively influenced by individual senators and the groups that supported them. For Roman society was a structure composed of rich, influential men and their dependent clients, who were in duty bound to vote for their patrons at the annual elections, and to serve them in other ways as well – receiving protection in return. In consequence, Rome never became a democracy, in any of the ancient or modern senses of the word.

This cliental relationship reflected, to some extent, a basic division between patricians and plebeians, which could not always be solved in a cooperative manner. Excluded from the consulships and, at first, from membership of the senate, the plebeians, after a time, began to resent this exclusion – or, at least, that was how the more prosperous and articulate plebeians felt. As for their less prosperous fellows, what they wanted to be rescued from was oppressive abuse of power, and the misery of poverty. For in the early days of the Republic, before its conquests began, there had not been enough land to go round, so that famines were a familiar occurrence. To ward them off, and calm the public, the government built a temple of the grain goddess Ceres (the Greek Demeter) on the Aventine (*c*.496/3) – a centre for Greek traders.

And then, to counteract the epidemics which came in the wake of the famines, they constructed another shrine dedicated to the Greek healing god Apollo (c.431).

Meanwhile, however, many plebeians fell into debt (as had happened at Athens), and blamed the authorities for unjust enforcement of the relevant laws. As early as 494, it appears, a body of plebeians 'seceded' by marching up to the top of the Aventine Hill, which because of its links with Greek commerce became a hotbed of democratic ideas. These secessionists demanded the creation of tribunes (tribuni plebis) – functionaries to represent plebeian interests – and the government felt constrained to agree. Then, later, the protesters demanded (once again like their earlier counterparts in Greece) that the laws, hitherto orally transmitted, should be written down, so that people could know how they stood – and the result, in 451, was the temporary replacement of the consuls by a board of ten (decemviri), led by Appius Claudius, who drew up the Twelve Tables of the Law. Their terse, gnomic sentences already displayed, at this early date, Rome's unparalleled gift for legal definition and equity. At first, however, they were ill received, because plebeians, though not always organized on a formal basis, did not like the look of the regulations that they were now, at last, able to see, and further discontent followed.

After a prolonged struggle, two tribunes, Gaius Licinius Stolo and Lucius Sextius Lateranus, continually reelected for ten years, carried a proposal (the Lex Licinia Sextia) that, henceforward, one of the consuls could always be a plebeian (367). The same two men also established limits upon the amount of land that might be owned by any single person. Moreover, in the year of their measures a temple was vowed to Concord (the Greek Homonoia), in the hope that internal disharmonies would be ended.

In the following year, too, a new office of state, the praetorship (next below the consulship in rank) was created, and its annually elected occupants issued legal edicts every year. These edicts included numerous remedies against unfairness and oppression. And yet, all the same, they were not altogether lacking in a certain class bias, so that during the Second Samnite War new measures of social appeasement still seemed necessary, in order to persuade Rome's plebeian soldiers to continue the fight. So in 326 the consul Gaius Poetelius Libo Visolus took various new steps to mitigate the laws against debtors, and in 312 Appius Claudius Caecus employed his censorship (an office filled every five years, originally for maintaining the official list of citizens) to increase the part played by the plebeians in public life, through the creation of a council of their own, the concilium plebis. Then in 298

Quintus Hortensius, appointed dictator (a temporary extraordinary magistracy to provide leadership in times of emergency), arranged by his Lex Hortensia that the resolution of this council (*plebiscita*) should henceforward have the force of law, so that from now on the decisions of the plebeians, at least theoretically, were just as valid as those of the executive.

Yet democracy had not triumphed, all the same. For example, the debt problem was still almost as intractable as ever. Moreover, since the system binding patrons to their clients, and vice versa, remained very much in evidence, the plebeian council was usually controlled by its richest members, just like the Assembly (the poor were only interested in obtaining a fair share of public land). And, most important of all, the tribunes were, in successive stages, 'nobbled' by the Senate, and (with later exceptions, as we shall see) became its agents instead of serving the plebeians as they had been intended to. Nevertheless, the balance and equilibrium referred to by Polybius had, by a complex series of compromises, been more or less achieved – to an extent, certainly, that no Greek city-state had ever equalled. Moreover, despite phases of friction, the Roman class struggle had, by ancient and modern standards alike, been conducted in an unusually peaceable fashion. And the result – like Rome's arrangements with Italian cities – proved effective. Indeed, it remained effective, with relatively little change, for as long as any politico-social arrangements have ever existed in the history of the western world. Furthermore, soon after this Roman system had attained something like its final form, it underwent and survived its first acid test, by enabling Rome to face mortal external enemies with an imposingly united front: as we shall now see.

9

The Imperial Republic

1 Rome as a Mediterranean Power

The end of the Samnite Wars brought Rome's sphere of influence, including the territory of its subject allies, far down to the south of Italy, within easy range of the Greek city-states which abounded there.

The most important of them, at this time, was Tarentum (Taras, Taranto; Chapter 3, section 3), which possessed the largest fleet in the country and an army of 15,000 men, supplemented by mercenaries hired to ward off its Italian (Lucanian) neighbours. The city had an old agreement with the Romans, but this was subjected to a severe strain when in 291 a substantial Latin colony was established at Venusia (Venosa), near the extremity of defeated Samnium. Venusia was less than ninety miles from Tarentum, which felt that it was provoked and threatened by the new foundation: and it felt threatened again when nearby Thurii (the former Sybaris), attacked by the Lucanians, appealed to Rome – which responded by sending a garrison (282).

The Tarentines, however, drove the Roman garrison out of Thurii, sinking a Roman fleet and killing its admiral. And they begged for help from King Pyrrhus of Epirus just across the Adriatic, one of the foremost of the adventurers who had proliferated since Alexander the Great's death half a century earlier. Pyrrhus responded to the appeal, and sailed for Italy, bringing a phalanx of 20,000 men, a mercenary force, and twenty Indian war elephants.

After a costly military success at Heraclea in Lucania (Policoro), he marched right up into Latium. Then, in the absence of defections to his cause, he felt obliged to fall back. Before long, however, he won another battle against the Romans, near Ausculum (Ascoli Satriano, 279 BC). But this engagement, too, was expensive, even for its victor (hence the term 'Pyrrhic victory'), so that the king – after the Romans had refused an offer of peace – withdrew to the island of Sicily. Three years later, however, he returned to the Italian mainland, in a further attempt to defeat Rome. Yet, once again, the enterprise came to nothing, and after two more years had passed he went back home to Epirus.

In consequence the Tarentines, abandoned, no longer had any alternative to accepting a Roman 'alliance'. It lost them their territorial suzerainty, so that the Romans had also now added the Greek region of Italy to their expansion across the rest of the country. That is to say, the whole of the peninsula was now under their control.

Their war against Pyrrhus had brought them into closer contact with the leading Mediterranean power, Carthage, which lay only 130 miles across the sea from Sicily; while the Carthaginian settlement at Pyrgi, the port of Etruscan Caere (Cerveteri), was scarcely thirty miles from Rome. Carthage had renewed earlier treaties with the Romans in 279, because it shared their hostility to Pyrrhus. After he had left Italy for good, however, relations between the Romans and Carthaginians deteriorated. The final break was caused by the Greek leaders of Messana (the former Zancle, now Messina) on the Sicilian Strait, who, faced with a threat from Hiero II the king of Syracuse, first appealed to Carthage and then, reversing their position, appealed to Rome instead – which duly undertook to help them, thus irrevocably upsetting the Carthaginians: and so the First Punic War began (264).

Hiero II went over to the Romans, thus becoming their first foreign 'client-king', and encouraged by this move they challenged the Carthaginians at sea, creating their earliest navy for the purpose. In 246 a naval success off Cape Ecnomus (near Licata) enabled their fleet to invade north 'Africa, but to no avail. Finally, however, the Romans won a conclusive victory off the Aegates (Egadi) islands, and Carthage was forced to make peace. Polybius called this the longest, most continuous and greatest war that had ever been fought.[4] Its main result was to give Rome its first overseas province, Sicily (with the exception of Hiero's kingdom, which retained its independent, though client, status). And the Romans went on to annex a second province as well, comprising Sardinia and Corsica.

The First Punic War had witnessed the introduction to Rome of brutal gladiatorial combat. But Greek humanizing influences had arrived as well, exemplified by the first Latin literature, consisting of the poems and plays of the Greek or half-Greek Livius Andronicus of Tarentum.

The same period also witnessed advances in Roman law, including the *responsa prudentium*, answers to questions provided by lay lawyers.

Moreover, a second praetor was appointed from *c.*242 onwards, the *praetor peregrinus* whose task it was to deal with lawsuits in which at least one of the contestants was a non-Roman; so that the Roman viewpoint had become more ecumenical. This new post also stimulated the evolution of one of Rome's most effective ideas, the *ius gentium*, 'law of nations', which, despite various changes of meaning over the years, displayed systematically how a body of law could apply to the members of different peoples and races. But this was only one feature of the development of Rome's law throughout the whole millennium of antiquity – upon which, since then, the very survival of civilization itself has often seemed to depend.

However, the underprivileged had still not benefited as much as they might have from Rome's constitutional reforms described in the last chapter; and in 230 the tribune Gaius Flaminius (showing that not every tribune became a henchman of the Senate) supported their claims to be given allotments on the territory of the Ager Gallicus south of the Padus (Eridanus, Po), thus named because it had been conquered from the Gauls. Leading Romans, who held leaseholds in the region, objected, and efforts were made to keep land confiscated by the state (*ager publicus*) intact, whereupon Flaminius unprecedentedly carried his proposal through the plebeian Council (*concilium plebis*) over the heads of the protesting Senate.

However, Gauls in north Italy objected to this provocative introduction of Roman manpower so close to the lands they still held just beyond the Ager Gallicus, and sent a hostile army which penetrated deep down into the peninsula, until, in 225, it was destroyed at Telamon (Talamone). Two years later Flaminius, although a 'new man' (not of noble origin), was elected to a consulship, and led the first Roman army ever to have crossed the Padus, thus foreshadowing the future flourishing Roman possession of Cisalpine Gaul, as northern Italy came to be called.

It was not the Gauls, however, but once again the Carthaginians, who offered the gravest threat to Rome and Italy during the 220s. This time the menace came from the armies they maintained in Spain, where Hamilcar Barca had revived their earlier coastal empire, with his capital at Acra Leuce (Alicante). After he was drowned in 229, his son-in-law Hasdrubal established a new capital beside the harbour of Carthago Nova (Cartagena), and advanced his Spanish frontiers northwards to the River Iberus (Ebro).

Then Hasdrubal was murdered (221), and Hannibal (Hamilcar Barca's son) expanded the Carthaginian dominions further still. But one city south of the Iberus, Saguntum (Sagunto), decided to stand in his way, and asked Rome to help it to do so. Rome was willing to assist, but Hannibal besieged and captured the town (219). So in the next year the prolonged Second Punic War began – the most exacting of all Rome's struggles, and the most far-reaching in its results.

Hannibal decided to invade Italy by land, and on arrival won military victories beside the River Trebia (Trebbia) and Lake Trasimene (218, 217). Then he marched southwards, but, disappointed by the lack of defections, swerved aside from Rome in order to move further south still. At Cannae he gained another crushing military success (216). But the Romans still did not give in. True, during the next three years, Capua, Syracuse and Tarentum did decide to abandon their cause, but Rome won them all back again (211–209), and as this process of recovery began, Hannibal, who had approached the actual outskirts of the city, turned away.

During these campaigns in Italy there was a second field of operations in Spain, where Publius Cornelius Scipio Africanus the elder, taking over in 210 from his father and uncle Publius and Cnaeus Cornelius Scipio (who had both been killed), defeated Hasdrubal Barca at Baecula (Bailen) two years later, and then won a decisive victory at Ilipa (Alcalá del Rio) in 206. And so now the most valuable parts of the Iberian peninsula were in the hands of the Romans; and they created two new provinces, Nearer and Further Spain.

After the battle of Baecula, Hasdrubal Barca had succeeded in extricating himself, whereupon he evacuated the Spanish peninsula, and moved by land into Italy. His purpose was to reinforce his brother Hannibal, who now felt encouraged by the progress of his invasion of the country, since twelve Latin colonies had warned Rome that they were exhausted, and could not support its war effort any longer. But at the Umbrian river Metaurus (Metauro) Hasdrubal was intercepted by the Romans and killed, together with most of his army (207). Then in 205 Scipio Africanus, fresh from his Spanish exploits, became consul and gained the Senate's (reluctant) permission to invade north Africa and attack Carthage itself. In 203 Hannibal returned from Italy to Africa, his prolonged expedition at an unsuccessful end; only to find that Scipio, upon landing in the country, had been joined by King Masinissa of Numidia (eastern Algeria). So Hannibal lost the final battle of the war, named after his encampment at Zama.

Carthage had ceased, for ever, to be a major power, and Rome's long future domination of the western Mediterranean world was assured. But the triumph of Scipio, against the equally talented Hannibal, had introduced a new and disturbing element into Roman affairs. His technical innovations in soldiering had created a virtually professional army, and his personal success raised him to the most powerful position any individual Roman general had ever enjoyed – pointing to the eventual emergence of war-lords, with autocratic powers and ambitions.

Hannibal's polygot Carthaginian armies had failed to equal his foes in tenacious oneness of purpose and action, and during the decades that followed a similar lack of unity between the three Greek kingdoms of the near east, the Antigonids, Seleucids and Ptolemies, likewise brought about their subjection to the Romans.

Thus Philip v lost the Second Macedonian War at Cynoscephalae in Thessaly (197). The Seleucid Antiochus III the Great was defeated at Magnesia beside Sipylus (Manisa) in Lydia (190) and pushed out of Asia Minor. The Third Macedonian War ended with the fall of King Perseus at Pydna in his homeland (168), followed by the abolition and dismemberment of the Macedonian kingdom – the first Hellenistic power to be completely annihilated by Rome. Then Rome destroyed the Achaean League and Corinth, and finally Carthage itself, all in the single year 146. Next, Attalus III Philometor left his kingdom of Pergamum to the Romans (133), who had also, in the meantime, reduced Ptolemaic Egypt to a virtually subordinate status.

During this period, too, there had been big changes in Roman life. For one thing Latin literature, already initiated by the compositions of Livius Andronicus, had come into its own. Cnaeus Naevius (c.270–201), from near Capua in Campania, wrote tragedies and comedies and an epic about the First Punic War, but incurred the hostility of the ruling class. Plautus (c.254–184) from the Umbrian town of Sarsina (Mercato Saraceno) brought Latin comic drama to its precocious zenith. His models came from the Athenian New Comedy of Menander, familiar to many educated Romans now that contracts had developed with Greek south Italy and Sicily. But Plautus rewrote and totally changed these Greek plays, discarding their subtleties in favour of his own explosive, quick-firing buffoonery, and at the same time contriving to impose Greek metres on the still cumbrous and graceless Latin language.

Romans were ready to abandon boxing matches, chariot races and dancing in order to come and laugh at what they heard and saw on Plautus's temporary stages. Yet they also received from him, at the same time, some indirect social criticism. It assumed the form of a carnevalesque inversion of traditional moral standards: reverence for parents and matrimonial respectability were stood on their heads, as well as the traditional contempt for women and clients and slaves. However, unlike Naevius, Plautus escaped upper-class retaliation, because he did not call his characters Roman, but made them foreign and Greek, so that if they were ludicrous or subversive it did not matter.

Ennius (234–169) came from Rudiae (near Lecce in south-eastern Italy), a place where Greek and Latin and Italian cultures came together, giving him, he said, three hearts. His rough, vigorous *Annals* were an epic poem chronicling the entire course of Roman history from its start, and earning him the title of Father of Latin Poetry. Ennius also rationalized the traditional mythology, without even sparing Jupiter himself.

Ennius had been brought back from Sardinia in 204 by Marcus Porcius Cato the elder (234–149), who did not, however, approve of the new Hellenism – or of the personal reverence accorded to Scipio Africanus the elder – as he showed upon gaining election to the censorship in 184, an achievement for a 'new man' whose family did not belong to the charmed circle. As censor he introduced conservative, puritanical measures, taxing luxury and restricting the emancipation of women. The disappearance, however, of his seven-book *Origines*, a history of Rome, is one of our gravest literary losses.

Publius Cornelius Scipio Africanus the younger (Scipio Aemilianus, 185/4–129) was likewise a man of integrity (in short supply at this epoch), who remained Rome's key personality for two decades, and went even further than his adoptive grandfather the elder Africanus in the direction of Renaissance-type individualism. Unlike the elder Cato, however, Scipio Aemilianus admired Hellenic and Hellenistic culture. His 'circle' of men who felt as he did included the comic dramatist Terence (*c.*190–159), a former slave from north Africa. Terence's six, surviving, well-constructed plays are far more gentle and contemplative than those of Plautus, although their philosophical humaneness ensures that, once again, social criticism is not lacking. Nor was it lacking in the poet Lucilius (*c.*180–102) of Suessa Aurunca (Sessa), in northern Campania, whose incisive, irreverent humour made him the virtual founder of satire as a Roman literary form.

During these years an ever-increasing stream of coin and bullion and plunder flowed from overseas into Rome's treasury, and into the hands of its senators.

The city was already the largest in the western world, and began to assume a monumental appearance. The revolutionary discovery of concrete, enabling arches and arcades and vaults to be constructed, can be noted in Rome's Porticus Aemilia (193, restored 174); and the

Basilica Porcia, built by the elder Cato in 184, led the way to a series of these large, internally colonnaded halls. Then in 179 the old wooden bridge (Pons Sublicius) across the Tiber was replaced by the Aemilian bridge resting on stone piers, and in the year 144 witnessed the erection of Rome's first high-level aqueduct, the Aqua Marcia. Moreover, houses with wall facings of dressed stone were making their appearance, for example at the Campanian town of Pompeii.

At the lower end of the social spectrum, the elder Cato's surviving work *On Farming* (*De Agricultura*) casts light on the institution of slavery. The way to run the large, mixed ranches that were coming into being, Cato explained, was by making good use of slaves, of whom many had become available from Rome's wars of conquest. Household slavery could be relatively humane, and, indeed, provided one of the principal channels through which Greek culture came to the city. In the country-side, on the other hand, slaves fared a good deal worse. Cato, for example, advised that when they were old and sick they should be sold like superfluous tools.[5] However, he also maintained that slaves, in general, should be looked after at least as well as farm animals, so they would not become too useless to work. Other landowners, however, subjected their slave workers to appalling ill-treatment. Consequently, in 135 the slaves in Sicily broke into revolt, under Eunus, a Syrian, who called himself King Antiochus and held out for three years. Then, after Attalus III of Pergamum had left his kingdom to Rome (133), Aristonicus led a popular rebellion in that region, which attracted many slaves before it was finally put down.

2 The Fall of the Republic

The slave-plantations had a disastrous effect on the 'free' but indebted rural poor, for they could not get work on the large estates which had absorbed and suppressed their small-holdings; and the *ager publicus* (land acquired by the government since the Second Punic War) had done the same. For some time past these impoverished people had been migrating to the capital, where they lived badly and could be mobilized as rioters. Moreover, this situation had a military aspect as well, since recruits for the legions were required to possess certain property quali-fications, which this extensive section of Roman manpower inevitably lacked.

So something had to be done to improve its lot. The task was attempted by two young brothers, Tiberius and Gaius Sempronius Gracchus, brothers-in-law of Scipio Aemilianus. Elected to the tribunate in 133, Tiberius brought forward a measure providing for the creation of individual private allotments on the government's public land. Tiberius may have been moved by urban impoverishment, but his main preoccupation was with the military problem – the need to increase the number of men eligible for legionary service. Yet the plan seemed unduly radical, to Scipio Aemilianus and others, and so Tiberius Gracchus (like Flaminius a century earlier) decided to short-circuit such obstruction to his bill by presenting it direct to the Assembly, without prior reference to the Senate. A fellow-tribune, his relative Marcus Octavius, vetoed the measure, and Tiberius, unprecedentedly, had him deposed. The bill was passed, and Tiberius and his brother Gaius and their father-in-law Appius Claudius Pulcher were made commissioners to supervise its implementation. Then Tiberius by-passed the Senate once again, in order to divert some of the funds left by Attalus III of Pergamum, so as to finance his projected creation of private allotments.

Next, in order to safeguard these measures against possible annulment, he offered himself for immediate reelection to the tribunate. This may not have been illegal, but it was a departure from custom: and in consequence a crowd of senators and their clients marched on the Assembly, and clubbed Tiberius and 300 of his supporters to death. Such violence was an ominous model for the future. Indeed Tiberius, although this was not what he wanted, had contributed to the eventual disintegration of the Republican system.

In the face of continued opposition, the surviving land commissioners persevered with their work. Moreover, one of them, Tiberius's brother Gaius, was elected tribune for 123 – and elected once again (unlike Tiberius) for the immediately following year. Gaius was more able, more active and more radical than his brother, whose agrarian measure he supplemented by proposing Roman colonies at Tarentum, Capua and Carthage – this last suggestion involving what seemed the shocking novelty of overseas colonization.

Furthermore, Gaius sought to undermine the Senate by favouring, as its rival, the rising body of knights (*equites*) – the men whose property qualifications, although considerable, were beneath those of senators. This he did by providing that all the judges, or jurymen, of the *quaestio de repetundis* (a lawcourt set up in 149 to investigate abuses by provincial governors) should henceforward be knights. This action might be said to mark the true beginning of the knightly (Equestrian) Order as a separate class, whose interests must clash with the Senate's. And then Gaius promoted the knights' interests again by putting tax collection of the new province of Asia (the former kingdom of Pergamum) up to auction at the capital; which meant that the powerful equestrian group consisting of tax-farmers (*publicani*) would control this lucrative activity.

Finally, Gaius tackled the status of Rome's Latin and Italian associates or subject allies. This had been, for some time, a burning problem, since the allies felt aggrieved because, after helping to win the Second Punic War, they had still been shut out of full Roman citizenship and partnership; and they did not like the Gracchan land-law, by which many of them would be dispossessed. So in 122 (modifying an earlier proposal by Marcus Fulvius Flaccus, who was now his fellow-tribune) Gaius proposed not only that the Roman franchise should be conferred on all Latins, but that other Italian communities should be promoted as well, by the gift of the half-way Latin right (providing that locally elected civic officials should become Roman citizens). However, a conservative opponent cunningly outbid and discredited him, by proposing an even more ambitious policy, on his own account: whereupon Graius Gracchus, considering it advisable to absent himself from the scene for a time, withdrew to Carthage to supervise his new foundation there.

But rumours went round that the enterprise was ill-omened and doomed, and when Gaius stood for a third tribunate he found himself rejected. Skirmishing broke out, and the consul Lucius Opimius persuaded the Senate to declare a public emergency (*senatusconsultum ultimum*). Fortified by this decree, Opimius led a crowd in a physical attack upon Gaius and Fulvius Flaccus, who were both killed. Then, after perfunctory trials, 3,000 of their supporters were executed as well.

The *senatusconsultum ultimum* continued to be prominent during the decades that ensued, and divided Roman society. The lines of battle, in regard to this issue, remained fluid, but in general the conservatives supported such measures as needful repressive instruments of state – calling themselves the *optimates*, or best men – whereas their opponents, the *populares*, not only deplored *senatusconsulta ultima* as tyrannical, but followed the Gracchi in displaying willingness to work through the Assembly and bypass the Senate. Faced with this division, the Republican constitution was even more ready to fall apart than it had been before.

Yet, meanwhile, there were still gains. In southern Gaul, after Massilia (Massalia, Marseille) had appealed to Rome for help against Ligurian tribesmen, the Romans seized the opportunity to annex the whole region and form the province of Narbonese (Transalpine) Gaul (*c.*121?), in which Massilia was left as an independent enclave, while a road (the

164

Via Domitia) was built from the River Rhodanus (Rhône) right on into Spain. Then hostilities broke out between Rome and King Jugurtha of Numidia. This struggle brought about the rise of Gaius Marius of Arpinum (Arpino), who, although a 'new man', gained the consulship for 107 and the supreme command in the war. On arrival in north Africa, he won successes, and his lieutenant, Lucius Cornelius Sulla, organized the capture of Jugurtha, who was put to death (104).

Meanwhile, however, the new province of Narbonese Gaul had become imperilled by the massive invasions of two German tribes, the Cimbri and Teutones, who had earlier migrated from Jutland. In 105 they defeated a Roman army at Arausio (Orange), but three and four years later Marius overwhelmed the Teutones at Aquae Sextiae (Aix-en-Provence) and the Cimbri at Campi Raudii (near Rovigo?).

Marius had transformed the effectiveness of the Roman army. But he had also, in the process, achieved personal power for himself, which he exploited by mobilizing a demagogic tribune Lucius Appuleius Saturninus to secure (after the example of Gaius Gracchus) the settlement of his veterans on colonial land (103, 100). Subsequently, however, Marius concluded that his protégé's methods were unacceptable after all, and raised a force to suppress him – a demonstration, for the future, of how generals could raise private armies. Yet now followed a period, the opening decade of the first century BC, when Marius, his tactlessness having caused general offence, took a back seat in Roman political life.

It was a time, however, when the claims of the Italian allies, which had been so prominent in the time of the Gracchi, began to be pressingly revived. They had played a full part in defeating the Numidians and Germans, and had, once again, not been given the rewards and lands that they hoped for, so that many of them now flocked to Rome prepared to make trouble. In 91 the tribune Marcus Livius Drusus proposed that they should be given full Roman citizenship. But he was murdered, whereupon the Italians, outraged by his death, revolted in the unparalleled Social War (90–87 BC), which took its name from their formal status as allies (socii).

The insurgents established their capital at Corfinium (Corfinio), in the centre of Italy, where they issued coins labelled ITALIA. Their basic aim was Roman citizen status, but the Samnites and others who joined them went further, and demanded independence. The Romans made concessions, first conferring the franchise on everyone who had remained loyal or would lay down his aims, and then extending the offer to all men south of the Padus (Po), while communities between that river and the Alps, if at present unprivileged, would be admitted to the intermediate Latin right. And so the Social War faded away, but not before it had devastated Italy and its countryside. Moreover, it had taught Italians to fight against their compatriots.

The Hellenistic east was the next region to witness an uprising against Roman rule. This was organized by King Mithridates vi the Great of Pontus in northern Asia Minor, who expanded his kingdom, encouraged the cities of Rome's province of Asia (the former kingdom of Pergamum) to massacre local Italian businessmen, and launched an invasion of Greece. The Romans appointed a patrician officer, Lucius Cornelius Sulla, to take the command against him, rejecting the rival candidature of Marius, whose name had been proposed by the tribune Publius Sulpicius Rufus. Sulpicius was hunted down and killed, Marius fled, and Sulla proceeded to Asia Minor, where, however, in 85 BC he ceased fighting, and negotiated a treaty with Mithridates at Dardanus (Maltepe) in the Troad. This he did because Rome had fallen into the hands of his political enemy Lucius Cornelius Cinna. Cinna became engaged in attempts to solve a revived debt problem. But his efforts were cut short because in early 84 he was killed.

At this juncture Sulla, who had been outlawed in Rome, rebelled against its government and invaded Italy. The troops of the disintegrating Roman administration, joined by the Samnites, were annihilated by his army outside the city's Colline Gate (82). Sulla massacred the prisoners and, after publishing a proscription (list of outlaws), slew many more people as well, including forty senators and 1,600 knights.

Then he felt free to put into effect his vision of how the nation should be reconstructed. For himself he revived the obsolete position of dictator. This emergency office (limited originally to a six months' duration) had been abolished in 216/202 BC, owing to the fear that it might encourage would-be autocrats. But now Sulla resuscitated the dictatorship, for the novel purpose of 'making laws and setting up the state' – and with the equally novel absence of any declared time-limit restricting the length of its tenure.

He still chose, however, to pass his laws in proper form, and they proved conservative in character, since his solution for Rome's troubles was to restore the flagging powers of the Senate. To this end, he created many additional senators, eliminated the power of the tribunes – who had in recent years so conspicuously escaped from senatorial control – and reserved the lawcourts completely for members of the Senate, excluding the knights altogether. The rules regarding the Senate's membership were also overhauled, to prevent the rapid rise of dangerous young careerists; and provincial governors were brought more closely under senatorial direction.

It was strange to see these measures produced by an unprecedented autocrat – who had marched on Rome, was not averse to a personality cult devoted to himself, and sponsored a building programme worthy of a Hellenistic monarch. Despite, however, the absence of restrictions on his tenure, Sulla had no desire to retain the dictatorship that he had resuscitated. For he resigned from the office, becoming consul in 80 BC and then retiring to private life, until he died shortly afterwards (78). Nevertheless, his career had shown that the Republic could come under the control of one man. He had been ruthless – but recollections of his cruelty had the good effect, at least, of deterring later Romans from a repetition of large-scale civil war for three decades to come, although, thereafter, it appeared once again.

However, Sulla's national reconstruction failed; and its failure was immediately demonstrated, when one of his former officers, Marcus Aemilius Lepidus, tried to restore the tribunate, leading a force in a dash to the capital (77). But an emergency decree was passed, and he was defeated at the Milvian Bridge, and died soon afterwards.

Much more able was another anti-Sullan, the Sabine Quintus Sertorius, who won over the whole eastern seaboard of Spain, and set up an independent Roman government throughout the area he controlled. Reinforcements sent out by the Senate to suppress him were commanded by a young officer Cnaeus Pompeius (Pompey), who had built up a personal following in central and eastern Italy. After Pompey arrived in Spain, Sertorius was murdered by one of his own officers, whom Pompey then suppressed, thus somewhat undeservedly increasing his military reputation.

And he did the same again when the Thracian Spartacus led a slave rebellion at Capua – the first such revolt in the Italian peninsula. The millionaire Marcus Licinius Crassus defeated and killed Spartacus in Lucania (south-west Italy), crucifying 6,000 of his slave followers. But Pompey arrived back from Spain in time to take part in the man-hunt, so that he was able to credit himself with yet another major military success, eclipsing the more substantial victory of Crassus.

At this juncture Crassus and Pompey might have come to blows. Instead, however, they decided to cooperate, and hold the consulship jointly, overriding the Senate's objections. They devoted their year of office (70 BC) to the overthrow of Sulla's constitution, reducing the senatorial jury membership to one-third, and rehabilitating the position of the tribunes. Pompey's desire to increase his military renown received a further opportunity when pirates in the eastern Mediterranean (a longstanding scourge) were seen to be directly menacing the grain-supply of Rome. In 67 therefore, ignoring the Senate, a tribune put through a bill entrusting Pompey with the pirates' destruction, and he obliterated them within the space of three months.

In the next year he was entrusted with the conduct of the revived war against Mithridates VI of Pontus, which his predecessor Lucullus – whose troops did not appreciate his aristocratic, disciplinarian ideas – had failed to finish off. Pompey, on the other hand, successfully put an end to Mithridates. Then, after doing so, he directed a sweeping, detailed settlement of the affairs of western Asia, which was the most durable achievement of his life, and gave him quasi-imperial prestige, not to speak of wealth exceeding even that of Crassus, which resulted in a vast enrichment not only of the Roman treasury, but of himself as well.

Catiline (Lucius Sergius Catilina), an impoverished and unscrupulous patrician who failed to secure a consulship, sought to attract the poor to his cause by a revolutionary programme (including the cancellation of debts), which caused an emergency decree to be directed against him (63). After the First Catilinarian Oration of the consul Marcus Tullius Cicero (106–43 BC), he departed from Rome to command his supporters in Etruria, whereupon Cicero arrested five of his leading fellow-conspirators in the city and with the Senate's agreement put them to death: an action of dubious legality, and contrary to the wishes of Julius Caesar – a thirty-seven-year-old rising luminary, member of a patrician but impoverished family. Shortly afterwards (January, 62 BC), Catiline himself and his followers were defeated and killed at Pistoria (Pistoia) in northern Etruria.

And so Cicero was now, for a brief moment, the hero of the hour, and he never, subsequently, let the Roman people forget it. Cicero had come, like Marius, from Arpinum (Arpino). He had not been born to grandeur, and did not possess, on his own account, the means to pursue a successful political career – although he owned eight houses – but was fortunate to have the staunch support of a wealthy knight and banker, Titus Pomponius Atticus. As regards Cicero's own personal talents, he owed his rise to his oratory, for he was one of the most persuasive public speakers who have ever lived, in an age when public speaking was still, as it had been in classical Athens, the core of political life. Fifty-eight out of his hundred speeches survive, reflecting all the stresses and strains of the crumbling Republic; and his 800 extant letters, written to Atticus and other friends, offer further revelations.

But Cicero did not have the right temperament to become a successful politician, overestimating his own position and showing a tendency to vacillate, except on two or three occasions in his life when he screwed up his courage to oppose the tyrannies that he genuinely hated. For Cicero, like Socrates and the Stoics, was convinced that, as a matter of objective fact, right is right and wrong is wrong, and that no laws or arguments can make them otherwise. That is one of the principal and most noble features of the *humanitas* which he insisted upon and bequeathed to the world of the future, in a series of attractive treatises on political philosophy and questions of morality.

Fired by such ideals, and encouraged by his success against Catiline, Cicero proclaimed a conciliatory political programme, the Concord of the Orders, requiring unity between the senators and the order of the knights, of which he had originally been a member himself. But it was Cicero who made his own proposal stillborn, by reiterating his own glorious achievement to the returned Pompey, at a time when the latter wanted only his own triumphs, and not the successes of others, to receive adulation. At this juncture, however, the Senate decided to snub the pretensions of Pompey and Crassus alike, and of Caesar too, back from a governorship of Further Spain during which he had invaded territories outside the provincial boundaries. So the three men secretly made common cause, in a dictatorial coalition later known as the First Triumvirate (60). According to this agreement, they would jointly rule the Roman world, refrain from impeding each other's ambitions, and join forces against those who insulted or opposed any one of them. It was another large step towards the downfall of the Republic.

One of the projects arranged by the First Triumvirate was the election of Caesar to a consulship in 59. Once appointed, despite opposition from Marcus Porcius Cato the younger – a determined Republican – he pleased Pompey (who married his daughter Julia) by passing a land-bill for his veterans, and arranged that Pompey and he himself should share an enormous bribe from the king of Egypt, and contented Crassus by securing a concession for his friends the tax-collecting knights. It was now, in return, up to the two other triumvirs to satisfy Caesar's own military ambitions, stimulated by his successes in Spain. After holding consulships, men were customarily made provincial governors, but the Senate had voted Caesar – an insultingly inferior post. Now, however, his position in the triumvirate secured him the much more important province of Cisalpine Gaul (northern Italy) together with

Illyricum (Dalmatia), to which, on the death of its governor, Narbonese (Transalpine) Gaul was added.

Thereupon Caesar decided to press northwards into the remaining, hitherto unconquered parts of Gaul. His masterly, though egotistical, *Gallic War* describes the successive stages of what happened during these campaigns. First of all, the immigrant Helvetii were annihilated near Bibracte (Mont-Beuvray, near Autun), and then the German Ariovistus (invited to Gaul by one of its major tribes) was put to flight on the plain of Alsace. Next, the more powerful tribe of the northern Belgic group, the Nervii, were destroyed on the River Sabis (Sambre, 57).

Pompey proposed a thanksgiving of unprecedented duration for these victories won by his colleague. And yet, for various reasons, tensions arose between the three triumvirs. So they met in 56 at Luca (Lucca) – just outside what was then the frontier of Italy, so that Caesar could not be prosecuted for irregularities which he had committed during his consulship. At Luca, the future activities of the three men were decided. Pompey was to become governor of Spain, but could stay in Rome, Caesar was free to exploit and extend his new conquests, and Crassus, too, would have the opportunity to win distinction in war by confronting the Parthians beyond the Euphrates, the only major power bordering on Roman territory.

So, while Pompey controlled the capital, Caesar made a brief reconnaissance of Britain, impeded by tides (55), and followed this up by a second invasion in the following year. This expedition, although again hampered by storms at sea, terminated in the surrender of King Cassivellaunus of the Catuvellauni (Hertfordshire), which amounted however, as it turned out, to nothing: so that here, for once, was an enterprise in which Caesar did not prove successful. Next, in Gaul, after a revolt among the Carnutes (round Cenabum [Orléans]), he had to confront a national resistance movement led by Vercingetorix, the king of the Arverni, and joined by many other Gallic peoples. At Alesia (Alise-Ste.-Reine), however, Caesar finished Vercingetorix off, and then the total subjugation of Gaul was only a matter of time.

In the preceeding year, however, Crassus had met his death at Carrhae (Harran), after defeat by the Parthians. This meant that Pompey and Caesar now confronted each other directly, without any third party to mediate between them, and all the more irreconcilably since Julia, Pompey's wife and Caesar's daughter, had died in 54. Moreover, Pompey now proceeded to marry Cornelia, daughter of the noble Quintus Caecilius Metellus Pius (Scipio), thus implicitly announcing that, in any future struggle between the aristocracy and Caesar, he would take the nobles' side. Friction arose over the termination date of Caesar's command, and, after prolonged disputes, civil war between himself and Pompey became inevitable.

But the fifties BC had not been all war and politics. For this was also a period in which two of the world's outstanding poets completed much or most of their work.

Catullus (c.84–54 BC), from whom 2,300 verses survive, came from Verona, so that like other, slightly earlier or contemporary, writers of Latin poetry he was a product of Cisalpine Gaul. For their formal inspiration, these men went back to the elaborate, refined, individualistic Hellenistic poetry of Alexandria. However, this new Latin, Alexandrian movement, known as 'Neoteric' (novel or modern), had at first differed from its Greek forerunners in purpose. For, Roman poetry, when their influences became apparent, had still been relatively raw and crude, far from the refinement of the Hellenistic Greeks. But Catullus put an end to this situation, since his technical perfection equalled any product of Greece.

This mastery is displayed in his miniature epics. Yet it was not by such poems that he placed the future in his debt, but by the shorter pieces that he also composed. In particular, his love for the unfaithful 'Lesbia' (Clodia, sister of an erratic politician Publius Clodius Pulcher) inspired verses of heartbroken intensity, conveyed in precise and lucid language which heightens the force of their impact. Catullus's tormented emotion, oscillating between ecstasy and desperation, is communicated with a total intimacy intended for an élite circle of like-minded friends. To Caesar and Pompey, however, he only alludes briefly and contemptuously, while expressing fastidious distaste for their upstart supporters.

Catullus's older contemporary Lucretius (c.94–55 BC), in his poem *About Reality* or *How Things Are* (*De Rerum Natura*), does not mention the two great men by name at all, but takes the lowest view, in general terms, of the politicians whose rat-race was dragging the Roman Republic down towards its final extinction. Yet his adverse comment on this theme is a mere digression, for the poem is about philosophy: the only philosophical poem of antiquity that has come down to us intact. Lucretius was an adherent of Epicurus (Chapter 7, section 2), who had sought to show that the universe is wholly material, consisting of nothing but atoms. But Lucretius transmuted his master's humdrum Greek prose into impassioned Latin poetry, offering a flashing profusion of visual images which display him as one of the most adventurous, imaginative and dedicated Latin intellectuals of all time. Epicurus's assertions that our purpose of life should be happiness (that is to say

171

freedom from disturbance), and that fear of the gods, and of death, is unwarranted are taken up and restated. And so is the Greek philosopher's view that a certain independence of movement, an unpredictable swerve, sometimes displayed by the atoms, means that individual men and women are not slaves to destiny but free agents. In this vein, Lucretius goes on to picture the triumphs of the human brain and will – which have created civilization.

Early in 49, by crossing the River Rubicon (Pisciatello?), which formed the northern border of Italy, Caesar committed the first act of war. Then he rapidly gained control of the peninsula, overcoming last-ditch resistance by Pompey's adherent Lucius Domitius Ahenobarbus at Corfinium (Corfinio). Thereupon Pompey and the consuls evacuated Italy and made their way across the Adriatic Sea. Caesar did not follow them at once, but first proceeded to Spain, where he crushed a Pompeian army at Ilerda (Lerida). Next Massilia (Marseille), which had sided against him and entrusted its defences to Ahenobarbus, was compelled to surrender, bringing its long career of independence and influence to an end.

Only at that juncture did Caesar pursue the principal enemy force, commanded by Pompey himself, to the Balkans, where he put it to flight at Pharsalus in Thessaly (48). Pompey escaped to Egypt, of which the Ptolemaic government killed him, and soon afterwards Caesar, too, arrived in the country – and was captivated by the youthful Queen Cleopatra VII. In the following year, however, after destroying her Greco-Egyptian opponents in Alexandria, and then overwhelming Pharnaces II (son of Mithridates VI) of Pontus at Zela (Zile), Caesar at last returned to Italy and the capital. But after quelling a mutiny there, he did not stay long, but moved south and west, where he defeated Pompey's two sons in turn: Cnaeus at Thapsus (Ed-Dimas) in north Africa (46), and Sextus at Munda in southern Spain (45). Cnaeus fell at Thapsus, but Sextus escaped to Sicily. Nevertheless, with this exception, Caesar was now master of the entire Roman world.

During the brief interval between these campaigns, and then, after they were finished, in the single year of life that remained to him, he began, only began, the huge, overdue task of overhauling and reorganizing the administration of Rome and its provinces. But first he had to provide for his own soldiers, which he did by settling them in colonies in the Italian peninsula, and initiating the establishment, also, of at least forty additional colonies overseas, including Corinth and Carthage. Nor were these foundations for veterans only, since his plans provided, too, for the inclusion of civilians, among them were 80,000 of Rome's destitute unemployed.

But Caesar also had to deal with the problem of debt throughout Italy, which the disturbances of recent decades had made more acute and widespread than ever. Here prevailed a dilemma: for, on the one hand, something had to be done for the debtors, and on the other, any cancellation of debts was anathema to established opinion, and would cause a widespread panic among creditors. After severe tensions and disturbances, Caesar's solution was to cancel all interest due since the beginning of the civil war – thus wiping out a quarter of all indebtedness. Those who had been owed the money were shaken, but had to admit, all the same, that Caesar was not the destroyer of private property which his opponents had made him out to be. He had broken the back of the Republic's most intractable social problem, and financial confidence began to return.

But Caesar also wanted to appear in a more spectacular light, and showed a taste for magnificent shows and programmes of construction. The more brilliant heir to a series of recent Roman war-lords, he was moving in the direction of autocracy, as can be deduced from his portrait-busts – symbol of a rising personality cult. And he was pushed in the same direction by Cleopatra, who had come to join him at Rome. After his victories Caesar had assumed the title *Imperator* (the traditional reward for military successes) as a special, personal, permanent appellation, to show that as a commander he was peerless. *Imperator* did not, however, yet mean emperor or monarchic ruler, and Caesar had no intention of resuscitating the ancient Roman kingship, which people equated, censoriously, with tyranny.

Instead the constitutional status he chose for himself was the dictatorship, like Sulla before him. From 49 onwards Caesar was reappointed to this post on a number of occasions, and in 46, by an innovation, for as long as ten years. But then, in February 44 BC, he was appointed dictator for the rest of his life – as his coins unequivocally confirm.[6] If he continued to hold the office until he died, as, unlike Sulla, he evidently intended to do, this was the total negation of the Republic (in which dictatorships had, originally, been emergency, temporary appointments), and was bound to arouse disgusted opposition, especially among the former governing class.

The opposition came to a head when it was learnt that Caesar proposed, immediately, to go to the east to become an oriental conqueror, greater than Alexander. For, if it was bad for the senators to be ruled by a dictator, they would find it even worse, in his absence, to be under the thumbs of his henchmen. So on March 15th two former praetors, Brutus (Quintus Caepio Brutus) and Cassius (Marcus Cassius Longinus), joined by other conspirators, attacked him at a meeting of the Senate in Pompey's Theatre, and put him to death.

Part V

ROME
UNDER THE
EMPERORS

10

The Augustan Age

1 Augustus

Following Julius Caesar's murder, his right-hand man Marcus Antonius (Antony), consul in 44 BC, sought to take control, and aroused the people against the assassins, Brutus and Cassius. But Cicero, true to his distaste for autocracy, attacked Antony in the *Philippics*, and with the orator's encouragement the young Gaius Octavius, Caesar's grand-nephew and testamentary heir (so that his name was henceforward Gaius Julius Caesar [Octavianus]), emerged as a rival to Antony, joining a senatorial coalition which defeated him at Mutina (Modena) and compelled him to withdraw to Narbonese Gaul (43).

There, however, Antony was joined by another of Caesar's hench-men, Marcus Aemilius Lepidus – the dictator's successor as chief priest. Moreover, Octavian, too (who had been snubbed by the Senate), proved willing to meet the two men at Bononia (Bologna), where they formed the Second Triumvirate. Unlike the First, this was an official creation, granting the three men joint five-year dictatorial appoint-ments with the task of reconstituting the government, of which the usual organs, including the consulships, continued to exist, but only under the overlordship and orders of the triumvirs: so that the Republic had not been restored.

Antony and Octavian organized a massacre of their political enemies, including two thousand knights and three hundred senators. One of the victims was Cicero. His fame remained eternal, although, almost immediately after his death, it received a dampener from a historian of outstanding literary gifts, Sallust (86–35 BC). For in writing his monograph *The Catilinarian War*, about the suppression of the 'con-spiracy' of 66–63 BC (Chapter 9, section 2), which Cicero had regarded as his own outstanding political achievement, Sallust says little about the part that the orator had played, preferring instead to highlight

176

the roles of the 'popular' Caesar and the ultra-conservative Cato the younger, whom he contrasts with one another as phenomena of these last years of the dying Republic.

Sallust had been forced out of political life in Caesar's time, for extracting illegal gains as a provincial governor, and now, all the more disillusioned because he had never been recalled, he possessed ample opportunity to reflect on the causes and persons behind the downfall of the Republican régime, illustrating the theme in a series of trenchantly described incidents and dramas. In the same spirit he shortly afterwards composed his *War against Jugurtha* (the campaigns of 111–105), which had involved the earliest challenge by a Roman general, Marius, to the supremacy of the governing class. Sallust subsequently wrote his *Histories*, giving an account of Roman affairs down to the early 60s BC. But the work is lost, and its loss has handicapped our endeavours to reconstruct the course of events throughout the Republic's final decades.

Antony and Octavian crossed the Adriatic and won two battles at Philippi in Macedonia against Brutus and Cassius, who both committed suicide (42). Antony was the main victor, but Octavian's prestige became enhanced by the recognition of Julius Caesar as a divinity of the Roman state (*divus*); which made his adoptive child Octavian the son of a god.

While Antony now took over the eastern provinces, Octavian assumed control of most of the west, encountering serious opposition, however, both from Pompey's second son Sextus, who was launching piratical raids from Sicily, and then from a brother of Antony, Lucius Antonius, in Italy itself. Nevertheless, Antony and Octavian came to a fresh agreement at Brundusium (Brindisi), confirming the division of the empire between them, and arranging that Antony should marry Octavian's sister Octavia (40 BC). But the relations between the two men continued, all the same, to show increasing strain. One cause of this deterioration was Antony's virtual abandonment of Octavia in order to live with Caesar's former mistress Cleopatra VII of Egypt, in a liaison of which Octavian was able to exploit the xenophobic propaganda value.

In 37, however, yet another partial reconciliation between the two men, arranged at Tarentum (Taranto), provided for a five-year renewal of the Second Triumvirate. But this understanding, too, proved short-lived, since henceforward Antony, deserting Octavia altogether, lived openly with Cleopatra in her palace at Alexandria. An expedition he launched against the Parthians, in the hope of annexing Armenia, did not prove successful, though he subsequently rectified the setback. Octavian's fleet, on the other hand, under Marcus Vipsanius Agrippa – who although unpopular with the nobles was a commander of genius – defeated Sextus Pompeius off Cape Naulochus (Venetico) in Sicily (36). At this juncture Lepidus tried to contest Octavian's western supremacy, but was disarmed and forced into retirement, although his tenure of the chief priesthood was not terminated.

Octavian now advanced into Pannonia (Yugoslavia) and captured Siscia (Sisak, 35). But his relations with Antony became increasingly hostile and in 32 each of the two leaders induced the populations under his control to swear allegiance to his own cause and person. Having raised as much money as he could, Octavian declared war – not indeed against his compatriot Antony, but against the foreign woman and temptress Cleopatra. With her help, Antony brought up his fleet and army to guard the western coast of Greece. But early in 31, when it was still mid-winter, Agrippa sailed across from Italy and captured decisive strong-points, and, after Octavian too had arrived, Antony found himself cornered and economically blockaded within the Gulf of Ambracia (Arta). In the naval battle of Actium (31), just outside the gulf, he tried to save what he could. But although he and Cleopatra succeeded in breaking out of the blockade, only a quarter of their fleet managed to follow them.

With these ships, the two defeated leaders fled to Egypt, but when the country fell to Octavian in the following year both he and she committed suicide. The victor annexed the country – thus eliminating the last of the three historic Hellenistic monarchies – and made it a province of an exceptional kind, under his own direct control. The huge wealth that had been at the disposal of the Egyptian kingdom (despite the temporary financial embarrassment of Cleopatra's father) enabled him to pay off his soldiers, for whom in due course he founded seventy-five colonies in Italy and many other parts of the empire, particularly in the west.

Although the battle of Actium had not been a spectacular naval engagement, it was hailed as one of the world's decisive battles, because its outcome confirmed that the Greco-Roman world was going to be ruled from the Latin west, that is to say from Rome.

Actium also established Octavian as master of that world. Remembering, however, that Caesar had been murdered because of his recourse to naked power, he understood that, although everyone longed for the stable conditions that he alone could bring, the governing class would only tolerate this ascendancy if he concealed it behind acceptable

Republican façades and traditions. So in 28/27 BC he announced 'the transfer of the state from his own control to the will of the Senate and Roman people',[1] thereby claiming that he had restored the *res publica*, the traditional, ancestral system – a fantastic claim from an autocrat, it would seem, and one which, from time to time in the future, prompted senatorial conspiracies, though without, apparently, incurring general incredulity or opposition.

At the same juncture he was granted, for an initial period of ten years, the rulership of a 'province,' or rather a group of provinces, which included all the military concentrations of the empire; and he was authorized to administer these regions *in absentia* – as Pompey had governed Spain – through his own subordinates (*legati*) at the various centres. The principal remaining provinces, however – headed by Asia and Africa – continued to be governed by proconsuls nominated by the Senate (although a reserve power was vested in himself, to override these senatorial nominees in an emergency): and the proconsuls were expected to be more honest and efficient than in the past. Meanwhile, he also kept a close eye on Rome's 'client-states', internally autonomous but externally dependent on himself, which continued to line the frontiers of the empire.

He believed that the supreme prestige (*auctoritas*) which his public offices and career and sonship of the deified Julius conferred upon him would be sufficient to guarantee the carrying out of his wishes in all important matters; and for the most part his supposition was justified. Moreover, to ram the point home, four days after the new political arrangements were announced in 27 BC, his name Gaius Julius Caesar was supplemented by the new appellation 'Augustus', by which he came subsequently to be known. It was a term that carried reverential religious overtones, setting him apart from everyone else. And yet it avoided dictatorial implications, that would offend conservative opinion.

Then, in 23 BC, he made one more major adjustment to his constitutional position, by assuming the powers of a tribune of the people (*tribunicia potestas*). This designation, unaccompanied by office – a novel conception – enveloped him in a popular aura, because of the tribunes' antique role as protectors of the people. And he subsequently endowed the conferment with the maximum significance by employing the tribunician power to date the years of his rule. His preeminence was coming to be known as the 'principate', based on his unofficial position as *princeps civitatis*, 'leading man in the state'. Later, in 2 BC, he also agreed to be called *pater patriae*, 'father of the country', which, during the centuries to come, like his other designations, became a characteristic feature of the imperial titles of subsequent rulers.

Armed with these propagandist strengths, Augustus belied his 'handing over of the state to the Senate and people' by arranging a thorough overhaul of the Senate's personnel. Reducing its membership from 900 to 600, he ensured that it should comprise a judicious mix of nobles and 'new men', including, in both categories, those who had supported him during the civil war. Yet he did not diminish the Senate's functions but enlarged them, so that it came to possess, for example, its own high court of justice, alongside another new 'imperial' court, over which he himself presided. Moreover, he facilitated the conduct of the Senate's business by equipping it with an executive committee which could draft its agenda and guide its discussions.

As for his own vast burden of work, it was lightened by the expansion of his own personal staff, pointing the way to the gradual development of a civil service, which the Republic had lacked. Some of his senior assistants were knights, and their Order was also drawn upon to provide members of important commissions, as well as his financial agents (*procuratores*) in every province, and the governors (*praefecti*) of small provinces and even of one important and special one, Egypt.

Thus over a considerable period, by patient trial and error, he reconstructed the administrative structures of Rome and Italy and the empire, veiling his transformations, whenever he could, under the guise of traditionalism. He also arranged for measures designed to revive morality and family life. This social legislation did not meet with lasting success, but in other respects Augustus proved one of the most energetic and skilful administrators that history has ever known. The far-reaching work of reorganizing and rehabilitation which he undertook in every branch of the vast Roman world created a new Augustan Peace, in which all but the humblest – an unprecedented large proportion of the empire's inhabitants – benefited from improved communications and flourishing commerce, facilitated by a reformed, complex, durable monetary system.

And this Augustan achievement was destined to have a long life, bringing security and prosperity for well over two hundred years. Indeed, what Augustus had done was to ensure the previously imperilled survival of the whole political, social, economic and cultural heritage of the classical world, Greek and Roman alike, and its eventual transmission to the future.

In one respect, however, Augustus ran into a series of setbacks, which caused him grave and recurrent worries. What produced these difficulties was the problem centred around his principal helpers, from his own family: which meant, also, the problem of the succession to his position. For although the 'principate' was not a formal office to which a successor could be appointed, the attention of other leading Romans, and of the public as a whole, was unceasingly fastened upon his plans for what would happen after his death.

For a long time, these plans were not openly formulated. It was at first thought, however, that his nephew Marcus Claudius Marcellus, husband of his daughter Julia, might become his successor. But Marcellus died in 23 BC. Later in the same year, Agrippa was dispatched to the east as Augustus's deputy, and four years later he went to Spain, where he suppressed rebels who were objecting to the Roman conquest of the country. But although the widowed Julia had been given to Agrippa in marriage, the nobility would never have accepted such a 'new man' as *princeps*. In 17 BC, therefore, Augustus adopted the sons of Agrippa and Julia, Gaius and Lucius, as his own sons, so that they both assumed the name of Caesar.

At the time, however, they were only aged three and one respectively, so that Augustus gave the principal military jobs to his adult stepsons Tiberius and Nero Drusus (Drusus the elder) – the sons of his wife Livia by a former husband. It was they who annexed Raetia, north of Italy (16–15 BC); so that this was the time when the imperial frontier was extended to the Danube. After Agrippa's death in 12 BC, Augustus obliged the dead man's widow Julia to enter into yet another marriage, this time to Tiberius. Both Tiberius and Nero Drusus, however, spent the next few years fighting, once again, in the north. Nero Drusus, after he had advanced as far as the River Albis (Elbe), died in 9 BC. Three years later Tiberius was elevated to a share in his stepfather's tribunician power, but then, unexpectedly, retired from public life altogether, withdrawing to the east. No doubt he detected, with some resentment, that the hopes of Augustus were pinned not on himself but on Gaius and Lucius. But both those two young men died, in AD 4 and 2 respectively, and their deaths were the outstanding disappointments of Augustus's career.

Tiberius now returned as his adoptive son, and during the last ten years of the latter's life played a dominant part. First he was sent to Boiohaemum (Bohemia) to conquer the west German (Suebic) tribe of the Marcomanni, whereby the imperial frontier would be shortened. But this task was cut short when rebellions broke out in Pannonia and Illyricum (Yugoslavia) in AD 6 and, next, in Germany as well, where Arminius, chief of the Cherusci, destroyed Publius Quinctilius Varus and his three legions in AD 9: with the result that Germany never

181

became Roman, either then or in any subsequent reign.

In 13 Tiberius was made Augustus's constitutional equal in every respect, and then the *princeps* lodged with the Vestal Virgins his will and the *Acts of the Divine Augustus* (*Res Gestae Divi Augusti*), a subtle, never inaccurate but tendentious document which has survived. In the following year Tiberius went on his way to Illyricum again. But he was recalled when his stepfather fell seriously ill. And soon afterwards Augustus died.

2 Architects, Sculptors, Writers

Although Augustus himself lived in a modest style, he boasted that he found Rome a city of brick and left it of marble. Of his public buildings he left record in his *Res Gestae*:[2]

I built the Senate House and the Chalcidicum which adjoins it, the temple of Apollo on the Palatine with its colonnades, the temple of the deified Julius, the Lupercal, the Porticus Octavia near the Circus Flaminius, the temples of Jupiter Feretrius and Jupiter Tonans on the Capitol, the temple of Quirinus, the temples of Minerva, Juno Regina and Jupiter Libertatis on the Aventine, the temple of the Lares at the summit of the Sacred Way, the temple of the Penates on the Velia, the temple of Juventas, the temple of the Magna Mater (Great Mother) on the Palatine. I repaired the Capitol and the Theatre of Pompey, both at great expense, without any inscription bearing my name. I repaired the water conduits which in very many places were collapsing through age. I doubled the flow of the Marcian aqueduct by connecting it to a new source. I completed the Forum of Caesar (Forum Julium) and the Basilica Julia, which was between the temple of Castor and the temple of Saturn, and had been begun and partially built by my father. When the Basilica Julia was destroyed by fire, I began to rebuild it on a larger site under the names of my sons, and ordered my heirs to complete it if I did not live to do so. In my sixth consulship [28 BC] I repaired, on the instigation of the Senate, eighty-two temples of the gods within the city and passed over none that needed repairing at that time. In my seventh consulship [27 BC] I repaired the Via Flaminia from Rome to Ariminum [Rimini] and all the bridges except the Milvian and the Minucian. On land which I personally owned I built the temple of Mars the Avenger and the Forum of Augustus from the spoils of war. I built the theatre near the temple of Apollo on land mostly purchased from private citizens, which should bear the name of my son-in-law Marcus Claudius Marcellus.

These buildings rejected the architectural innovations made possible by the discovery of concrete in favour of a classicizing revival, based on Athenian and Hellenistic models. Some of the edifices, however, deserve special mention. The temple of Apollo on the Palatine had ivory doors, and was faced with Luna (Carrara) marble – employed for the first time at Rome – of which the brilliant whiteness contrasted with the coloured African marbles of the colonnades. As for the immense Forum of Augustus, which sealed the Forum Romanum off from the quarter known as the Subura and contained the new temple of Mars the Avenger (avenger of the murder of Julius Caesar), Suetonius observed that Augustus's purpose in building this complex was to provide for the increase in the city's population and the consequent number of its lawsuits, which required a third Forum, since the Roman Forum and Forum of Caesar were no longer adequate for the purpose.[3]

In addition, Augustus could have added to this list of his buildings his own mausoleum in the Campus Martius. Its shell remains today, but Strabo saw it complete:[4]

On a high base of white marble near the river is a lofty mound, densely covered with evergreen trees to the summit. On the top is a bronze statue of Caesar Augustus; within the mound are the tombs of himself and his relations and his friends. Behind is an enclosed precinct with wonderful colonnades.

Furthermore, over and above his own construction programme, Augustus urged his friends and other prominent persons to embark on similar activity. Outstanding among them was Agrippa, who not only transformed Rome's water supply, and equipped the city with a warehouse (the Horrea Agrippiana), but erected a group of buildings in the Campus Martius. Monuments were also voted and brought into existence by the Senate, including the Altar of the Augustan Peace (Arca Pacis Augustae), once again in the Campus Martius. Its friezes are the most typical examples of the kind of sculpture favoured by Augustus, which was, once again, of a classicizing character: technically impeccable, and rather cold and solemn, though relieved (in this frieze) by lighter touches.

The most notable creation of Augustus's style of sculpture, however, was the portraiture of himself. These portrait busts, distributed all over the empire, skilfully depict himself in a variety of guises, as simple citizen, philosophical thinker, man of religion, Hellenistic monarch and military conqueror.

His *Res Gestae*, although so ingenious, was scarcely a work of art. But Augustus was also fortunate, or clever, enough to be able to encourage a historian who could write artistic history on lines that he found acceptable. This was Livy (Titus Livius) of Patavium (Padua, *c.*59 BC–AD 17). His *History of Rome*, from its first beginnings, was an unequalled achievement which took nearly forty years to complete. It consisted of 142 books, of which 35 survive.

Writing in fluent, rich language, and making imaginative use of a variety of sources, he presents colourful evocations of the past ages of Rome. The traditional Roman heroes and their actions, as he depicts them, are revelations of what the human, Roman spirit could achieve. To many readers, his first ten books, which are not history in any real sense of the word but myth, form the best part of his work, because his gifts are essentially romantic and poetical; he is an epic poet in prose. And he is always eager to draw moral lessons from the past to serve the present – lessons, above all, which would contribute to the greater glory of Rome, and of Italy, too, from the frontiers of which he himself came (hence the charge of *Patavinitas*, provincialism, launched against him by a contemporary historian Gaius Asinius Pollio).

Livy's books concerning his own contemporary epoch are lost, but we can detect from his earlier allusions and foreshadowings that, although he remained a dedicated Republican, this did not prevent him from admiring Augustus as the climactic personage in his gallery of heroes, the man who had brought back peace and order. Yet the historian persisted in a certain self-withdrawal, revealed, for instance, by his doubts whether Julius Caesar's career had really been beneficial; and he also glossed over the youthful brutalities of Pompey, so that Augustus could even jokingly call him a 'Pompeian'.[5] But to interpret this as meaning that Livy was anti-Augustan would miss the point, because all his nostalgic reverence for the Republic and its protagonists was permissible and even praiseworthy under the new order, seeing that Augustus himself claimed not to be an autocrat, but the restorer of venerable Republican institutions.

Augustus also had the excellent fortune to be a contemporary of some of the greatest poets the ancient world ever produced: men, who like Livy, admired him and his gift of peace – and who expressed their admiration and accepted his patronage, and that of his talented Etruscan adviser Gaius Maecenas, without allowing it to damp down or deflect their genius.

Publius Vergilius Maro, Virgil (70–90 BC), was born near Mantua (Mantova), of a family which was partly of Etruscan origin. Later, he moved to Neapolis (Naples), where his father, expropriated by the Second Triumvirate (41 BC), came to join him. Virgil first astonished literary circles by his *Eclogues* (*Bucolics*, 42–37). These ten short poems

transposed into melodious, evocative Latin the bucolic themes introduced to Alexandrian Greeks by Theocritus more than two centuries
earlier (Chapter 7, section 2). Virgil's *Eclogues*, unpretentious and
unheroic, exercise an enigmatic fascination, derived from the apparent
simplicity of their rural subject and the artistry with which, by way of
contrast, it is treated. The scenery of the poems is a composite blend of
Arcadia, Sicily and the north Italian countryside, but remains, above
all, an imaginative creation – nowhere in the real world. The sensuous,
enchanted light in which he bathes this ideal landscape established
Virgil as an outstanding poet of nature, the model of much subsequent
European poetry. The fourth *Eclogue*, written at a time of temporary
reconciliation between Octavian (the future Augustus) and Antony
(40 BC), reflects the widespread 'Messianic' belief that a saviour was
about to appear and rescue the world from its ever-continuing troubles
(the belief that also accompanied the career of Jesus, who was born in
Augustus's reign, Appendix VI). The saviour remains unnamed by
Virgil, but elsewhere in the *Eclogues* this task of cosmic rescue is ascribed
explicitly to Octavian.

The longer *Georgics* that followed (36–29 BC), dedicated to Maecenas,
celebrated the beauties and labours and rewards of rustic life. The first
of the work's four books discusses the cultivation of crops, with a
digression on weather signs. The second book is concerned with the
growing of trees, and the third with the rearing of cattle. The theme of
Book Four is the keeping of bees. Thus the ostensible aim of the *Georgics*
is to provide agricultural advice and instruction. Yet this is infinitely
more than a pedestrian agricultural textbook. For one thing, the four
poems, composed in verse of a new flexible delicacy and strength, are
also tributes to the glorious antiquarian, legendary past of the Italian
countryside. As such, they reflect that emotional love for Roman Italy
which was a feature of the times and became a keynote of Augustus's
policy and peace: the peace for which these poems offer him heartfelt
praise.

Next, Virgil turned to heroic epic, in the tradition that went back to
Homer (Chapter 3, section 1). But although Homer's sonorous majesty
reappears in the twelve books of Virgil's *Aeneid*, their sensitive subtleties
are far removed from the ballad-like extroversion of his distant predecessor. And so is the intricate complexity of Virgil's poetry, extracting
from the Latin language its ultimate potentialities of significance and
emotion.

The mythical hero of the *Aeneid*, the Trojan Aeneas, escaping
from the Greek sack of his city foreshadowed in Homer's *Iliad*,
undergoes numerous wanderings and adventures. In north Africa, he

encounters Queen Dido of Carthage, and their doomed romance owes less to Homeric epic than to the more recent Greek poetry of Alexandria, magically transmuted. Finally, Aeneas succeeds in reaching Italy. As he lands on its shores, he is conducted by the Sibyl of Cumae to the underworld, where the spirit of his father Anchises grants him a revelation of the glorious future of Rome. Then, after a visit to the place where that city would later be founded, he receives, from the god Vulcan (Hephaestus), a divine shield, engraved with designs conveying a further forecast of Rome's destiny. In the centre of the shield is depicted the sea-battle of Actium, in which Antony and Cleopatra had been put to flight. The last four books are devoted to the hostilities of Aeneas and his Trojans against the peoples of Italy. Through Olympian intervention, the wars end in a peaceful settlement. Aeneas marries a Latin bride Lavinia, and Rome's foundation will follow.

The theme of the *Aeneid* is very often war – it is an *Odyssey* followed by an *Iliad*, this warlike section mirroring an earlier tradition of national Roman epic poetry. War leads to peace, and it is once again the Augustan peace of which Virgil is thinking. For his age, following decades of war, was one of those epochs in which order looked even more desirable than liberty, and Augustus's achievement in pacifying the world seemed to Virgil (as to many others) the most welcome of all possible gifts.

However, Aeneas is only permitted to win his war, and personify the virtues, after he has suffered many troubles. One of his most painful ordeals in his parting from Dido, fated by Jupiter himself. Dido stands for Rome's most dangerous past enemy, Carthage. But she also brings to mind the recent challenge presented by another foreign woman, Cleopatra. And yet, all the same, the Carthaginian queen is portrayed with moving sympathy – Aeneas has done right to leave her, but the parting is tragic. By the same token, his later enemy, Turnus, too, sometimes seems to be nobler than he need be, or would be expected to be. For despite Rome's radiant future Virgil is telling us (even more pointedly than Homer) that wars, even victorious wars, turn to dust and ashes and sorrow. True, the Pax Augusta must inspire gratitude. And yet, even so, military conquest, in the end, is a sad affair – ranking lower than the human spirit's conquest of itself.

Virgil was, in fact, a divided personality, and it was probably because of this unsolved dilemma in his heart that, before he died in 19 BC, he had made his literary executor promise to burn the *Aeneid* (not yet quite completed) after he died. But Augustus disregarded his wish, and arranged for the publication of the poem: of which Maurice Bowra observed, 'the unparalleled variety of appeal has helped many generations to formulate their views on the chief problems of existence'.[6]

Horace (Quintus Horatius Flaccus, 65–8 BC) was born at Venusia (Venosa) in Apulia. But his father, a collector of auction payments, managed to give him the best education of the day, in Rome and Athens. At the battle of Philippi (42) he served as an officer on the side of Brutus and Cassius, but after their defeat and death at the hands of Antony and Octavian (who with Lepidus formed the Second Triumvirate) he returned to Italy. There his family farm, like Virgil's, had been confiscated by the triumvirs. Yet Horace obtained work at Rome, and gained the friendship and patronage of Augustus's counsellor Maecenas.

His *Satires* (35, 30 BC) are hexameter poems expressing rejection of public life and – in terms familiar from Hellenistic philosophy – the need to achieve imperturbable serenity, which will bring wisdom. The poet deplores ambitious races for position and wealth, and deprecates the folly of extremes, and urges tolerance. His *Epistles* (20–15 BC) strike a similar note, praising the excellence of the simple life, and warning against the dangers of avarice. Yet these poems also reveal a new maturity. Latin letters in verse had been written before (notably by Lucilius), but Horace gave them inimitable form as a framework for informal and conversational yet serious discussion. Literary criticism finds a place (and Horace's observations, notably in the *Epistle* known as the *Ars Poetica*, have remained unforgotten). Autobiographical touches, too, seem to appear. Such ostensible self-revelations are a conventional and cunning device: not necessarily factual descriptions of what had happened to Horace himself. Nevertheless, the personality of Horace emerges from his *Epistles*. He is kindly, tolerant and humane, capable of an astringent, detached realism that enables him to make fun of himself as well as of others.

But it is as a lyric poet that he particularly excelled. After his *Epodes* (40–30 BC) – which attack social abuses – came the historic *Odes* (23, 13). Horace asserts that Alcaeus and Sappho (Chapter 3, section 1) are his models, but his debts to Hellenistic Alexandrian polish are also great. Yet these Horatian *Odes* are not derivative but entirely original. Their epigrammatical succinctness, too is extraordinary: 'Jewels five words long,' said Tennyson, 'that on the stretched forefinger of all time sparkle forever.'[7] The dominant, formal theme of more than a third of the poems is friendship, and indeed their addressee is usually a friend, to whom Horace offers advice, encouragement, or philosophical comment.

Nearly another third of the pieces deal with love, a topic which the poet handles with pathos and charm, a considerable degree of detachment, and, at times, some measure of ironic flippancy. Another of his specialities is the *recusatio*, a polite refusal to tackle this or that sort of poem that someone has requested – in particular, the grand sort of national epic: although, despite this ostensible reluctance, a group of the *Odes* do in fact devote themselves to patriotic themes, and glorify the Augustan régime.

After Virgil's death, Horace became virtually the poet laureate in his place, and was commissioned to write the *Carmen Saeculare* for the antique Secular Games which Augustus revived in 17 BC in order to endow his new imperial system with religious solemnity. Nevertheless, when the ruler offered him the post of his private secretary, he declined, preferring to remain his own master, and thus to remain one step short of obsequious adulation.

Employing elegiac couplets, Sextus Propertius of Asisium (Assisi, *c.*50–*c.*16 BC) wrote love poems of a far greater intensity than those of Horace, and, in his own idiosyncratic way, proved unequalled in his poetic treatment of erotic passion. Pale, thin, delicate and obsessively over-emotional, he devoted his elegies to depicting the ups and downs of his love affair with 'Cynthia' (who was really a woman called Hostia). Spanning the shifting border between classicism and romanticism, Propertius veered rapidly, in accordance with her whims, from high ecstasy to wild, self-pitying depression. This self-abasement (mitigated by flashes of rueful wit) owes something to the Hellenistic, Alexandrian convention, which also stood behind his self-conscious artistry and taste for learning. It was a taste which prompted him, in his fourth and last book, to write a group of poems on that blend of mythology and patriotic antiquarianism which had been the mainspring of Virgil's inspiration – and doubtless gave pleasure to Maecenas, whose patron-age Propertius shared with Virgil and Horace. But in his earlier poetry he had remained aloof from the régime.

Another elegiac poet, however, whose aloofness veered over into catastrophe, was Ovid (Publius Ovidius Naso) of Sulmo (Sulmona; 43 BC–AD 17). Member of a smart new sophisticated social group, he was younger than Horace and Propertius, and long outlived them. His light, speedy, scintillating verse belonged to a different era and atmosphere, for he was born too late to experience emotional com-mitment to the new order, or to feel gratitude for its peaceful contrast with the turbulent past.

His *Amores* (*Loves*, 20 BC and two decades later), presenting a girl called Corinna, display various kinds of male lover, ranging from the simple, faithful type to the seducer. This is love poetry as flippant as Horace's, but adds a Hellenistic, Alexandrian interest in female psychology, looking at women with a gaze which, although not altogether untender, can sometimes seem cold-blooded. Another of Ovid's collections was the *Heroides* (*Heroines*), or, more precisely, their letters, twenty in number, purporting to have been addressed (often complainingly) by mythological females to their absent lovers or husbands and including, in three cases, equally imaginary replies from the addressees.

The *Ars Amatoria* (*Art of Love*), produced not before I BC, advises how to set about amorous seduction and intrigue. While pretending to treat love poetry as a serious science, Ovid succeeds in making fun of it, and makes a joke of the whole literature of moral uplift as well. The poem also exemplifies his talent for vivid description and narrative, illustrated by a series of pictures of contemporary society. It appears, however, that the *Ars Amatoria* caused shock in imperial circles, since Ovid next wrote a recantation, called the *Remedia Amoris* (*Cures of Love*). But these second thoughts did not altogether ring true, and the sort of self-indulgent, smart poetry to which Ovid had been devoting himself still remained too immoral and cynical to appeal to Augustus, the leader of moral reform. So in AD 8 Ovid suddenly found himself exiled to remote Tomis on the Black Sea (Constanţa in Rumania). The causes of his banishment were described by himself as *carmen* (a poem, which could be the *Ars Amatoria*) and *error*[8] (a mistake, perhaps complicity in the loose behaviour of the emperor's granddaughter Julia – daughter of Julia, also disgraced – who was banished at the same time). For the nine years that remained to him Ovid did not cease to bemoan his banishment, notably in the *Tristia* (*Lamentations*) and *Epistulae ex Ponto* (*Letters from the Black Sea*).

When he was sent into exile, however, he had already completed the most substantial and influential of his works, the *Metamorphoses*, composed not in the elegiac couplets that he otherwise wrote, but wholly in hexameters. This long poem, in fifteen books, tells of miraculous changes of shape, and presents a succession of Greek mythological themes. Although this is, formally, an epic (of which the hexameter was the traditional metre), it resembles, rather, the Arabian Nights, comprising every sort of legend and folk-tale and anecdote, and offering inexhaustible opportunities for Ovid's narrative gifts. He is erudite, but carries his erudition lightly, and infuses the myths with new life, irreverently clothing their characters, and those of the gods and goddesses, in lifelike modern personalities.

At the time of his expulsion, too, Ovid had half finished a new elegiac work, his *Fasti*. This is a study of the Roman calendar in the light of old stories and records, including a mass of antiquarian, religious and historical lore. Propertius had made a similar attempt to write poetry of a national character, but Ovid utilizes such material as a medium for his own peculiar gifts and ingenuities. The *Fasti*, extended to please Augustus yet published after Ovid's death, made him a patriotic poet, but too late. For during his lifetime (which extended for three years beyond that of Augustus) he was never called back to Rome. He was the reverse face of Augustan society, the poet who was not equipped to live in that bracing climate, and prevail against the ruler's seriousness.

11

Rome After Augustus

1 The Empire and its Transformation

The emperors who followed Augustus were all plagued by terror of conspiracies, some of which were authentic.

The reign of Tiberius (AD 14–37), whose unfair depiction is the most brilliant achievement of the historian Tacitus, was noteworthy – apart from the mission of Jesus (Appendix VI) – for two things, both arising from this very fear: which was exacerbated by his personal inability to get on well, as Augustus had, with senators.

First, Tiberius found it necessary, for this reason, to hand over a great deal of business to an adviser, choosing for this purpose Lucius Aelius Sejanus of Volsinii (Orvieto) in Etruria, prefect of the praetorian guard. In AD 23 Sejanus concentrated his guardsmen, previously dispersed by Augustus round Italian towns, within a single new barracks in Rome itself, with ominous consequences in the ensuing centuries. Secondly, finding life in the capital increasingly distasteful, Tiberius retired permanently, for the last eleven years of his life, to Capreae (Capri), where he arranged, at a distance, for Sejanus, now suspected of plotting, to be struck down (31). His eccentric, brutal young successor Gaius (Caligula) became the first *princeps* to show aversion to the long hours of work required by his job, devoting himself to amusement instead, until he was murdered by a group of praetorian officers.

An incident from the reign of Gaius has made its way into history, because of the man who recorded it. He was Philo Judaeus (*c*.30 BC– early 40s AD), a Greek writer on Hebrew religion and philosophy. One of his numerous works was *On the Delegation to Gaius*, which describes his participation in a mission to Rome (AD 39–40) on behalf of the large section of the Jewish Diaspora which resided in Alexandria. The mission was sent to try to persuade the ruler to withdraw his insistence that the Jews must worship him as a god. Gaius showed no sign of doing so, and

191

a lost, final part of Philo's work apparently dealt with the emperor's subsequent assassination, representing it as an act of retribution from heaven.

However, Philo was by no means an enemy of the Roman system or of Hellenistic civilization. On the contrary, his philosophical works made a determined attempt to show that Greek and Jewish doctrines were by no means dissimilar, thus influencing many branches of future thinking.

Gaius's uncle Claudius (41–54) annexed southern Britain, allowed ex-slaves to attain great power as his advisers and ministers, and in his last years became the first emperor to lose control of affairs to a woman, his niece and wife Agrippina the younger.

Her son Nero, when he became emperor (54–68), provided the new phenomenon of aesthete and would-be poet on the throne. He built himself a palace of unprecedented dimensions, the Domus Aurea (Golden House). Nero had at first delegated political authority to the tragic poet and Stoic philosopher Seneca the younger (Lucius Annaeus Seneca, c.4 BC–AD 65), son of a rhetorician of the same name from Corduba (Cordova) in Further Spain (Baetica). In contrast to earlier Roman tragic drama, which is almost entirely lost, eight or nine tragedies attributable to Seneca have come down to us. These plays, which influenced later Europe, convey the enlightened tolerance and humanity of men who, like Seneca, were heirs to the Hellenistic phil-osophy of Stoicism. And the same spirit, too, more explicitly, pervades Seneca's ethical treatises and literary, philosophical letters (*Epistulae Morales*). He also wrote a lengthy scientific work (*Naturales Quaestiones*), and a satire, the *Apocolocyntosis*, in which the previous emperor, Claudius, was treated as a bad joke.

One of Seneca's specialities was a sparkling, oratorical, 'Silver Latin' style, which, once again combined with a Stoic viewpoint, was adapted, for poetical purposes, by his own nephew Lucan (Marcus Annaeus Lucanus), in his *Civil War*. This epic described, in philosophical terms, the struggle between Pompey and Caesar (culminating in the battle of Pharsalus [48 BC], hence the poem's alternative title, the *Pharsalia*). But Lucan, as time went on, veered towards anti-monarchistic views, which eventually caused his death at the hands of Nero. His friend the young poet Persius (Aulus Persius Flaccus) likewise succumbed to suspicions of seditious activity, and so did Seneca himself; and the 'arbiter' of court fashions, Petronius (Titus Petronius Niger) underwent a similar fate.

Petronius was the author of the earliest extant Latin novel, the scandalous *Satyricon*. This narrates, with needle-sharp liveliness, the wanderings of three shady but well-educated young men around the Greek towns of southern Italy. Fashionable writings are obliquely criticized by Petronius, and the anti-heroes' renunciation of women for boys is a burlesque of middle-brow heterosexual Greek romances. The *Satyricon* also contains set pieces or short stories, of which the longest and most famous is the 'Dinner of Trimalchio', a coarse, self-made industrial millionaire of slave origin living in Campania. Poems, too, find their way into the work.

After Nero, who had already murdered his mother, chose to sacrifice, in addition, his more reliable friends and advisers, he fell into sinister hands. Finally, while he was engaged upon a prolonged artistic and dramatic tour of Greece, Gaius Julius Vindex, the governor of Lugdunese Gaul, launched a military insurrection (68). He was put down, but Galba, his colleague in Tarraconese (Nearer) Spain, likewise rebelled, and his success, bringing someone outside the Julio-Claudian house to the throne, initiated the Year of the Four Emperors, in which various contenders fought it out.

The eventual victor was Vespasian, whose principal achievement, as governor of Syria, had been the suppression, with the help of his son Titus, of the First Jewish Revolt (First Jewish War, AD 66–73). This rebellion was notable, first, as a decisive event in Jewish history (Appendix VI), involving the destruction of the temple at Jerusalem (70) and the dramatic siege and capture of the rebels' last stronghold at Masada (73), and, secondly, because it was recorded by the outstanding ancient Jewish historian, Josephus (37/38–after 94/95).

Josephus's account was the *History of the Jewish War*, originally written in an Aramaic version although only the Greek translation has survived. A priest at Jerusalem, Josephus had gone over to the Romans and collaborated in their suppression of the Jewish revolt, and his pro-Roman bias is apparent not only in his adulation of the Roman leaders but also in the conviction that their empire's might was too unassailable to be resisted. Except when engaged in self-justification, he is a reliable historian, on whom we have to depend for a significant chapter of history.

In Vespasian, Rome for the first time had an emperor of undistinguished Italian connections and origins – which he liked to stress, by permitting determinedly bourgeois looking portrait busts of himself to be made and distributed. His major achievement, after coming to the throne, was the reconstruction of the imperial administration, finances and defences, all of which had been damaged by the civil wars. He also openly declared his intention of founding a new dynasty (known as Flavian after his family name), since he was the earliest ruler to have a son of his own blood, whose maturity and distinction already fitted him to succeed to the throne.

This was Titus, who duly took his father's place in 79. His rule was brief, however, and little happened except the eruption of Mount Vesuvius and the dedication of the Colosseum. Vesuvius's eruption in 79, of which one of the casualties was the learned historian and scientist Pliny the elder, left, for disinterment by later excavators, remarkably intact, innumerable aspects of Roman private life – including a lavish supply of mural paintings – at Pompeii, Herculaneum (Ercolano), and country villas outside those two towns and at Stabiae (Castellamare di Stabia) and Oplontis (Torre Annunziata). At Rome, the four-tiered Colosseum or Flavian Amphitheatre, begun by Vespasian and completed and dedicated by Titus, is a huge, majestic, dramatic building designed for 45,000 seated spectators, and a further 5,000 standing who assembled there to watch gladiatorial combats and the slaughter of wild animals. Furthermore, the arena could be flooded, in order to stage imitation sea-fights.

Titus' brother Domitian (81–96) broke new ground by assuming a more or less undisguised autocracy, without the surface Republicanism maintained by Augustus. Domitian also wanted military glory, at which he aimed by sending his generals to conquer king Decebalus of Dacia (Rumania). The attempt was interrupted, however, by a military plot in Upper Germany (89), which Domitian blamed not on the legionaries, who liked him, but on the senators, who did not; and seven years later some of them arranged to have him struck down.

It is a curious coincidence that this authoritarian and menacing reign witnessed a large part of the poetical activity of Martial (Marcus Valerius Martialis, c.40–104) of Bilbilis (Calatyud) in Spain. The outstanding satirical epigrammatist of the ancient world, it was he who introduced to this type of literature the point and wit that have endowed the term 'epigram' with its permanent meaning. Martial left Spain to come to Rome, where he fulsomely flattered Domitian (changing course, however, after that emperor's death). Yet his keen eye for the ridiculous enabled him to puncture a variety of Roman social shams, and made him a potent witness to his age, depicting a wide range of its characters and types. He writes with polish and with pungent ingenuity, and his favourite effect is surprise: a stimulating confrontation with the unexpected.

Domitian's successor, the sixty-six-year-old lawyer Nerva (96–98), in order to save his precarious throne and his life, adopted a son and heir from outside his own family, namely Trajan (98–117), the governor of Upper Germany. Trajan's accession set a precedent because he was not wholly Italian but half Spanish, born at Italica (near Seville) in Baetica (Further Spain). Furthermore, his elevation inaugurated a period of over sixty years in which successions to the throne were determined by adoption rather than birth.

Attractive and affable, Trajan possessed the rare qualification of gaining affectionate support from Senate and army alike. Moreover, his popularity was confirmed by two wars in Dacia (101–6), which ended in the downfall of its ruler Decebalus and the influx of enormous plunder into Rome. The victory was celebrated by the reliefs on Trajan's Column, which include no less than 2,500 human figures and depict the manifold activities involved in the campaigns. The Column formed the central feature of a building complex at Rome, designed by the architect Apollodorus of Damascus to comprise the Forum, Basilica and Market named after the emperor.

Trajan also coveted Alexander the Great's renown as a conqueror in eastern lands. But his attempt to destroy the Parthian kingdom and extend Rome's frontier down to the Persian Gulf proved one of the most glaring failures of imperial history – which was destined never to be attempted again. On his way home, Trajan died at Selinus (Selindi) in Cilicia (south-eastern Asia Minor).

The reign of Trajan had witnessed the most important work of Rome's foremost historical writer, Tacitus (Cornelius Tacitus, c.AD 55–c.116?). Perhaps the son of an imperial representative (*procurator*) on the Rhine, he had become a well-known advocate, although, as he pointed out in his *Dialogue on Orators*, forensic pleading could not flourish under the emperors as it had in the Republic; so that Tacitus moved over to an official career. But the perils and shames which he and other senators had undergone under Domitian continued, even after that emperor's death, to disturb the thoughts of Tacitus, who criticized Domitian in the *Agricola* (98), while eulogizing his own father-in-law Cnaeus Julius Agricola who had been governor of Britain. The *Germania*, of the same year, is an ethnological study which shows foresight in describing the Germans as a potential menace to Rome.

Next Tacitus turned to his *Histories* and *Annals*, narrating Rome's history from the accession of Tiberius to the death of Domitian (AD 14–96). From the *Histories*, which dealt with the later part of this period, only the initial section, dealing with the Year of the Four Emperors (68–69), has survived. But the subsequently published *Annals*, covering the earlier period from Tiberius to Nero, are still extant. These haunting, abrupt, tortured analyses of the men who held such monstrous power represent our most searching account of the imperial phenomenon.

Yet despite Tacitus's meticulous evaluation of facts and events, his claim to impartiality remains unjustified, since his hatred of Domitian, for example, spills over into unfair bias against an earlier ruler who seemed to foreshadow that tyrannical emperor, namely Tiberius. Tragic drama is recalled by the historian's insistence upon the malevolence of destiny and, again, by his emphasis on the grimmer aspects of the imperial régime. Nonetheless, the relative advantages and disadvantages of this absolutism and the old Republic are objectively weighed. For if Tacitus's heart was romantically Republican, his brain told him that Rome could not avoid one-man rule. In consequence his heroes tend to be people who (like himself) had just quietly got on with their jobs even under emperors as menacing as Domitian. What he wrote about the current ruler Trajan has unfortunately not survived; it must have been hard for a man of Tacitus's temperament to employ favourable terms about any autocrat at all.

A large proportion of the Greek biographical writings of Plutarch (before AD 50–after 120) likewise belong to the principate of Trajan. Most of these *Lives* of soldiers and statesmen are grouped in pairs, one Greek and one Roman, linked by a comparison between the two. His initial intention in launching the series was to show that Greece, in the past, had produced men as great as the greatest Romans. Yet his work, like his public career, epitomizes the coming together of the Greek and Roman cultures within the imperial world of the day. In that world, while remaining thoroughly Greek, he is also loyal to Roman rule, recognizing and urging that it would be useless to attempt anything else.

As the title of the *Moralia*, the collective designation of Plutarch's sixty ethical, religious, physical, political and literary treatises, suggests, his interpretation of life and history is determinedly linked to ethical standards: we must study the past, and particularly its great heroes, in order to derive moral uplift. This means that Plutarch's historical sense remains defective. Yet he possessed a unique talent for the selection of anecdotes, capable of catching and keeping his reader's interest.

Trajan's reign – apart from his mania for conquest – looks to us in retrospect like a pretty satisfactory affair (which seemed to justify his novel title 'the best of emperors', *optimus princeps*). And that is also the impression created by contemporary writers such as Pliny the younger, who offer a picture of imperial enlightenment.

To a poor and embittered man, however, like the satirist Juvenal (Decimus Junius Juvenalis) of Aquinum (Aquino; 50/70–after 127), that is not how the scene appeared at all. Juvenal's hexameters offer a series of forcible hammer-blows. Imbued with a fierce sense of unfairness and failure, he fills his poems with crushing vituperation, stormy mockeries, and relentless caricatures.

In his first satire he explains that no poet, when he looks at what was going on at Rome, can restrain himself from writing about its lamentable condition: although he adds that, for safety's sake, he himself will not attack the living but the dead. In the third satire his friend Umbricius declares that he, for his part, is going to shake the dust of the city from his feet, because honest people cannot make a living there, and to suffer from poverty at Rome involves continual degradation. Other pieces by Juvenal bemoan the fate of writers who lack generous patrons; and, in Stoic vein, noblemen who rank their aristocratic blood above virtue are rebuked. Another poem denounces women, launching a relentless attack on the entire sex, and subjecting immoral and tiresome wives to particularly venomous treatment.

Trajan was succeeded by his general Hadrian (117–138), a distant relative who, although born in Rome, was a member of a family from the same Spanish town as his predecessor. However, Hadrian immediately abandoned what was left of Trajan's eastern conquests, and withdrew the Roman frontier to the Euphrates again, no doubt deciding (probably with some justice) that its permanent extension to the Persian Gulf would have been beyond the Roman army's capacity. In his initial absence from the capital however – since he had been with Trajan in the east when the latter died – four of the most eminent senators found themselves accused of plotting against Hadrian's life and were put to death (118), to the lasting detriment of his relations with the Senate, although his responsibility for their execution remains doubtful.

The outstanding feature of his reign was the fact that he spent more than half of it outside Italy, travelling throughout the provinces of the empire. Like other people of his time, he was a fanatical sightseer. But in addition, as the designs on his coinage confirm, he had formed an unfamiliar and unprecedentedly progressive conception of what the imperial territories signified. He envisaged them no longer as a collection of conquered provinces, but as a commonwealth in which each individual region and nation possessed a separate and proud identity of its own. Yet another purpose of his journeys was something else again, namely the inspection, maintenance and improvement of the Roman army. A witness to this military determination is Hadrian's Wall in Britain, extending from the mouth of the River Tinea (Tyne) to the Ituna (Solway Firth), and manned by 15,000 auxiliary troops.

The Second Jewish Revolt (Second Roman War) in 132–5, led by Simeon Bar Kosiba (Bar Kochba), was put down by the emperor's initiative. He felt no sympathy with its intentions at all. For he was a determined classicist and Hellenist, who saw no reason why people should fail to fit into the Greco-Roman tradition. His Hellenism is displayed by his country palace, or complex of palaces, at Tibur (Tivoli), echoing a variegated array of Greek models. Another building which owes its design to Hadrian was Rome's Pantheon, a temple in the Campus Martius (adapted from a shrine built by Agrippa), of which the soaring concrete rotunda stands as his monument today.

The earlier part of Hadrian's reign witnessed the completion of the *Lives of the Caesars* by Suetonius (Gaius Suetonius Tranquillus) of Hippo Regius (Annaba in Algeria). Following upon an earlier collection of *Lives of Illustrious Men*, by the same hand, these *Lives* are biographies of the rulers known as the Twelve Caesars, starting with Julius Caesar and ending with Domitian. Well aware of the overpowering contemporary historical work of Tacitus, Suetonius realized that he must strike out in a different direction, and in consequence abandoned the chronological method of historians in favour of classification according to subject matter, listing the different characteristics and idiosyncracies displayed by the personages he depicted. This sometimes looks like scandal-mongering, but Suetonius's contribution was his relatively high degree of objectivity, which was, indeed, rare. His viewpoint, reinforced by a command of rapid narrative – occasionally set off by dramatic set-pieces – has moved away from eulogistic and moralizing methods into a more astringent atmosphere, through which the subjects of his investigation are discerned by a cool and disenchanted eye.

Hadrian was a many-sided personality, abounding with ideas and devoted to administrative efficiency and judicial reform, exemplified by his north African jurist Salvius Julianus. Yet his reign continued to be flawed by the unhappy relationship with the senators which had dogged his early years: and it culminated in a conspiracy against his life (136). After that, Hadrian adopted an heir, who soon, however, died, whereupon he appointed his second choice, Antoninus Pius. Antoninus's family were Romans from Nemausus (Nîmes) in southern (Narbonese) Gaul.

He ruled from 138 to 161, with impeccable excellence, deferring to the Senate's prestige while quietly continuing to follow a policy of more efficient coordination and taking steps to cut down unnecessary public expenditure. The greater part of the empire enjoyed peace during the long years of his principate.

The population of Rome at this epoch cannot be estimated with any certainty, but it was probably over a million, of whom between one-third and one-quarter were slaves. We cannot see much of the imperial city today, but still available for our inspection are the remains of its port at Ostia. Claudius had provided Ostia with a new harbour, connected by canals to the Tiber, and subsequently Trajan added a land-locked hexagonal inner basin as well; whereupon the port began to handle the largest volume of goods of any Mediterranean city apart from Alexandria.

Ostia's population grew rapidly, to a total of about 100,000. This expansion dictated changes in housing, during the course of which the widely outstretched sort of dwelling that had been seen, for example, at Pompeii was supplemented, and largely replaced, by lofty apartment blocks housing far greater numbers of occupants. Constructed of brick which was no longer covered, as in the past, by stone or stucco facings, these high buildings relied for their architectural effect upon the scale and spacing of their windows, which had panes of selenite and were framed by external balconies. The interiors of the apartments often contained seven rooms or more, and sometimes as many as twelve.

This Ostian type of house was the empire's most significant contribution to urban living. And, indeed, this was an epoch when cities prospered and flourished. The towns of the provinces, as well as those of Italy, abounded in rich, public-spirited benefactors competing with one another in their contributions to local amenities. The consequent outburst of construction produced many achievements, among which Thamugadi (Timgad), and Lepcis Magna and other cities in north Africa are particularly available for study because they have never been built over in subsequent epochs and have therefore survived on a substantial scale. Such cities frequently had their origin in military camps. But these camps rapidly developed civilian appendages, engaging in extensive industry and commerce.

As the resources of the provinces developed, the glass and bronze wares of Italian Capua were superseded by products made in Gaul, and during the first century AD the pottery industry of Arretium (Arezzo) was displaced to the same country, becoming established first at Condatomagus (La Graufesenque) and then at Ledosus (Lezoux). Next, in the following century, the principal output of pottery was from the Rhineland, which became before long the chief industrial region of Europe.

The zone bordering the Danube, too, along its entire length, was developing an east-west trading axis of future significance. Nor was this commercial expansion a purely European phenomenon. Reference has already been made to the north African cities, but in Asia Minor as well, and in Syria – where habitation zones extended almost uninter-ruptedly – export businesses in textiles and other materials continued to prosper and multiply. Commerce was assisted by the efficient monetary system established by Augustus, which was made possible by elaborate mining facilities and augmented by local small change.

Yet the fundamental features of Roman trading retained the same limitations that had always been present in the ancient world, due to the lack of any solid capitalistic infrastructural basis. Indeed, the foundation of the entire imperial economy was still not trade at all, but agriculture. This latter activity, therefore, developed on a far-reaching scale. The empire still depended primarily on the growth of grain. Fruit trees, too, were planted in many regions, and south-eastern Spain became the principal centre of the conversion of olives into oil. Wine drunk in many countries, too, was of Spanish origin, though production extended far and wide in numerous lands. Wool, leather and meat also played a part. The wealthy farming landowners lived in elaborate residential and agricultural complexes. Their slaves, as ever, were excluded from political and social privilege. But excluded as well – and this, once again, was no novelty – were the 'free' agricultural workers who formed an even larger proportion of the population than slaves.

Nevertheless, in the eighteenth century, the historian Edward Gibbon believed that the Antonine Age witnessed more widespread happiness and prosperity than the world had ever seen before. This prosperity did not, it is true, extend to the poor cultivators of the land, and did not extend either to the impoverished majority in the capital itself, whose discomforts (despite pampering by free 'bread and circuses', *panem et circenses*) are feelingly communicated by Juvenal. These exten-sive sections of the population did not prosper: and yet, at a time of flourishing, peaceful trade and intercommunications, the number of people enjoying favourable conditions had been remarkably enlarged.

So Gibbon may have been right, and what he said perhaps still applies today: for although so many were still excluded from privilege and although the lives of the privileged may have seemed, at times, a little sluggish, it is difficult to think of any subsequent epoch when the inhabitants of the same areas have included a larger proportion of more or less contented and fortunate people.

When Antoninus Pius died in 161, he bequeathed the imperial throne to Marcus Aurelius, his adopted son and the husband of his daughter, Faustina the younger. Aurelius's most intimate thoughts have come down to us in his *Meditations*, written in Greek, the most famous book ever written by a monarch. Framed in literary form, although not intended for publication, these essays in self-scrutiny and self-admonition present an austere doctrine, offering barely a minimum of comfort. Our brief lives, Aurelius declares, are merely temporary visits to an alien country, in which we must just enduringly struggle on as best as we can, drawing upon our own inner resources for courage and strength. Much of this was traditional Stoicism, but none of its recent exponents, not even Seneca or another eloquent Stoic, the ex-slave Epictetus from Phrygia in Asia Minor (*c.*AD 55–135), had ever communicated the gospel of self-reliant moral and social effort with such poignancy. Many things, Aurelius believed, are predestined. But many others, too, he added, *can* be changed and improved – if we summon up the self-discipline to try hard enough.

Aurelius himself, occupying the burdensome office of emperor, worked incessantly and idealistically, according to his principles. They required him, at first, to fall in with Antoninus's wishes, and elevate another of that emperor's adoptive sons, Lucius Verus, to become co-ruler with himself. Verus was presentable enough, but a light-weight. Nevertheless, he was sent east to deal with a Parthian crisis, which his generals handled effectively. But in 169 he died.

While he had been away in the east, however, events were occurring, on another imperial frontier, which permanently transformed the world scene. For German tribesmen were pouring across the Danube. Their migrations, or invasions, were prompted by 'Third World' eagerness to leave their marshy forest clearings behind for ever, in favour of the richer territories within the Roman provinces. But this attempted influx brought about more serious fighting than had ever been seen on the frontiers before; and it engaged the personal attention of Marcus Aurelius during the last fourteen years of his life. The land-hungry Germans penetrated as far as the Alps, and even across the Alps into Italy itself, where they besieged Aquileia, while another group surged down into the Balkan peninsula, penetrating as far south as Eleusis, which they devastated.

Faced with this military emergency, Aurelius formed two plans. One was to accept unprecedented numbers of Germans into the empire as cultivators. The other was to annex the territory of the Marcomanni (Boiohaemum, now Bohemia), and a further region, Sarmatia, to its east, so that the empire would thereafter have a much shorter northern boundary, and one which depended on mountains rather than on the line of the Danube.

Aurelius's successor Commodus (180–192), however – who was also his son, for Aurelius departed from the adoptive principle – abandoned the idea altogether. Because he was eccentric, and enjoyed performing as a gladiator, his decision was sure to incur criticism. But (like Hadrian when he withdrew from the Persian Gulf) he may have been wise not to aim at even greater expansion of the empire. His principate was a time of serious plots, which made him hostile to the Senate; and he delegated too much power to his praetorian prefects, until the last of them, Quintus Aemilius Laetus, had him murdered.

The reign of Commodus witnessed the best work of Apuleius (c.123/5–190?), the second Latin novelist to emerge after Petronius. Born at Madaurus (Mdaourouch in Algeria), he was a lawyer who became one of the leading lecturers in popular philosophy. They were known as sophists after their Greek predecessors more than half a millennium earlier (Chapter 5, section 3), and had become, once again, characteristic of this second century AD.

The astute manipulator of a lush Latin style, archaic and florid, Apuleius's *Apologia* is an outrageous sort of defence against charges of magic. But this extravagant manner reaches its climax in his *Metamorphoses* or *Golden Ass (c.*180–190). Adapting an earlier Greek narrative, the writer tells of a certain Lucius, who is transformed into a donkey and undergoes other macabre experiences, interwoven with numerous tales including the story of *Cupid and Psyche*, whose fantastic, romantic adventures have attracted age-long admiration.

When Apuleius goes on to describe how his hero is initiated into the Mysteries of the Egyptian goddess Isis, he seems to be recording a vividly, profoundly felt experience of his own, echoing his passionate belief – which was widespread at this time – in a saviour who would endow devotees with a life of blessedness after they were dead.

Of such a kind, going back to the ancient worships of Demeter and Dionysus, were the cults revering Isis, and the Great Mother Cybele, and Mithras (a development of the ever more popular Sun-worship):

forms of religion which in this Roman imperial age helped thousands to reject current astrological doctrines (declaring that everything was fixed by the stars, whose purpose must somehow be circumvented), and prompted them to turn their longing, panic-stricken attention to these more comforting and reassuring faiths instead.

AD 193 and the immediately ensuing period were a repetition of the Year of the Four Emperors, with four brief, contested imperial reigns – two in Rome, and one each in the east and in Gaul. The victor who emerged was Septimius Severus (193–211), the first north African to obtain the throne.

Severus was a purposeful realist who appreciated that the new, worsened frontier situation, combined with the ever-present, recently experienced dangers of internal strife, required a much larger Roman army. And so he made sure that this was provided, even if it meant the imposition of severely increased taxation upon the middle class – although this was also, by way of contrast, an epoch of enlightened legislation. Severus's chief advisers, in this conduct of what is sometimes known as the Military Monarchy, were his Syrian wife Julia Domna and his praetorian prefect Gaius Fulvius Plautianus, whose death, however, was brought about by the emperor's elder son Caracalla in 208. As to the frontiers, Severus decided to jettison Hadrian's and Antoninus's Walls in Britain, both of which had been breached by tribesmen, and to annex Caledonia (Scotland) so that the whole main British island would come under Roman rule. But he still was a long way short of that aim when he died at Eburacum (York).

Caracalla and his younger brother Geta had been nominated as his joint successors, but they hated each other and raced back to Rome, where Caracalla had Geta murdered (212), and thenceforward ruled alone. He was temperamental and violent, and yet, maintaining a powerful legal tradition inherited from his father, passed the most famous measure of antiquity, known as the Constitutio Antoniniana, which bestowed upon virtually the entire male population of the empire (except slaves) the status of Roman citizens – not so much from motives of liberalism, but in order to increase the number of those who had to pay the indirect taxes on inheritance and slave-emancipation for which citizens of Rome were liable. He also built the magnificent Baths of Caracalla at Rome, again displaying a 'democratic' tendency characteristic of the times, which saw the people, however, not as individuals but as a mass. Caracalla was murdered by the Mauretanian Macrinus (217–218), who was noteworthy as the first Roman emperor who had not been a member of the Senate but a knight.

Then the young Elagabalus (218–222) of Emesa (Homs) became the first sexual invert to occupy the throne, and the first ruler to confer open, official status upon the fashionable eastern religious tendencies to which he, personally, possessed a family attachment, and also the first to be wholly directed by a woman, his grandmother Julia Maesa, the sister-in-law of Septimius Severus. But when Elagabalus alienated the senatorial class Maesa had him assassinated, switching her allegiance to his cousin Severus Alexander (222–235), whose policies then came under the control of his mother Julia Mamaea (the daughter of Maesa [d.226]).

In 231 Alexander and Mamaea left Rome for the east to repel an invasion of Mesopotamia by the Persians (Sassanians). Their leaders had overthrown the Parthian kingdom and replaced it by their own superior power, which brought about a permanent readjustment of the world situation to the disadvantage of the Romans. The subsequent attempt by Alexander and Mamaea, however, to buy off German aggressors on the River Rhenus (Rhine) proved unpopular with their own officers, who put them to death.

The Military Monarchy had now been replaced by the Military Anarchy. The new soldier-emperor Maximinus I, a giant Danubian officer and former peasant, displayed such savagery towards his subjects that he was killed in 238, which was a re-run, like 193, of the Year of the Four Emperors, except that now there were seven. The survivor among them, Gordianus III (238–244), was a youth aged thirteen, whose praetorian prefect Timesitheus governed the empire effectively until he died; and his emperor followed him to the grave shortly afterwards.

Then came a fresh batch of soldier-rulers. Philip the Arabian (244–249) sought to distract attention from the empire's woes by celebrating the thousandth anniversary of Rome. He was overthrown, however, by Trajanus Decius (249–251), who came from the same region as Maximinus. But Decius created an unheard-of precedent by his defeat and death at the hands of a foreign enemy, the Gothic invader Kniva, at Abrittus (Razgrad in north-west Bulgaria). His successor Trebonianus Gallus (251–253) had to deal not only with renewed Gothic attacks but also with a prolonged pestilence – perhaps bubonic plague – which ravaged the empire. Valerian (253–260) inflicted on himself and Rome a new kind of disaster by being taken prisoner at Edessa (Urfa in south-eastern Turkey) by the Sassanian Persians, whose King Shapur (Sapor) I gained enormous successes against the Romans. Valerian's son, co-ruler and successor Gallienus (253–268) found himself confronted with internal and external difficulties of every kind. The worst of these problems, throughout the whole of this period, was the proliferation of military usurpers, placed on the throne by one or the other of the armies – especially the Danubian army, which was the most powerful force of all – but nearly all succumbing to violence: as, indeed, did most 'regular' emperors as well. Rome failed, perpetually, to solve its succession problem, with catastrophic effects, since as a result of this continued failure repeated and costly civil wars shattered the Roman world. In particular, two dissident states, in Gaul and Palmyra (Tadmor in Syria), dismembered the empire: and this was at a time when unity had never been more greatly needed, in the face of intensified Gothic and Persian threats.

Meanwhile, too, the collapse of the imperial finances, due to this widespread disintegration, had caused Rome's coinage to become diminished in weight and cheapened in content, so that, when the people would no longer accept this poor money, inflation reached precipitous heights, multiplying the miseries already caused by wars and epidemics. Indeed, the wages of soldiers, as of other state employees, had been practically wiped out, so that they had to be kept quiet by special bonuses, which could only be contrived by inflicting even larger taxes upon the rest of the population, raised from them in kind, that is to say by levying supplies of foodstuffs and other goods (*annona militaris*).

2 Recovery and Fall

Rome's situation appeared desperate: by all the 'rules' of history and destiny, it would have seemed that the empire had been fatally dislocated and was almost at an end. But that did not, at this time, happen. By what looked like a miracle, brought about, in fact, by a series of competent military rulers, the Roman world recovered, and entered a new and powerful phase.

The emperor Gallienus was condemned by some of his contemporaries as a Hellenizing dilettante, but it was he who paved the way for this revival. Above all, his solution was military: for he set up, with its headquarters at Mediolanum (Milan), a new mobile, strategic force, largely consisting of cavalry – which now for the first time became a primary element in the imperial army. In the last year of his reign (268), his new army won a major victory over the Goths, at Naïssus (Niş in Yugoslavia), where 50,000 enemy soldiers were slain.

Next, his Danubian successor Claudius II (268–270), after the west German Alamanni had penetrated into Italy itself, overwhelmed them beside Lake Benacus (Garda), and then inflicted a series of defeats on the Goths as well, which earned him his title Gothicus. Their expulsion was completed by Aurelian (270–275), one of the ablest commanders ever to occupy the throne, who proceeded to overwhelm further masses of invading Germans, in battles at Fanum Fortunae (Fano) and Ticinum (Pavia). Next Aurelian destroyed the separatist states of Palmyra (Zenobia, 271) and Gaul (Tetricus, 273). He had restored the unity of the Roman world. However, he also decided that its frontiers could only be made defensible by a diminution of its size, and with this aim, in 274, he carried out the permanent evacuation of Dacia (Rumania). Tacitus (275–6) and his brother Florian repelled Gothic invaders in Asia Minor, Probus (276–282), a Danubian, defeated additional German hordes, and then Carus (282–283) did the same, and subsequently turned east to conduct a victorious campaign against the Persians.

By the talents of these successive rulers, commanding troops as good as any that the army had ever produced, the entire military position had unexpectedly been reversed and transformed in Rome's favour, within the space of only fifteen years.

Nevertheless, as we saw, this revival had taken place against economic dislocation: which exacted an enormous human price.

But that was not all, for it was clear that, if the recovery was to be backed up and maintained by efficient imperial organization, all-pervasive constitutional changes were required. They were duly introduced by a Dalmatian emperor of humble origin, Diocletian (284–305). Concluding that no single man could any longer control the affairs of the entire empire, Diocletian established a tetrarchy of rulers, comprising two senior emperors (Augusti), himself and Maximian, and two junior colleagues (Caesars), Constantius I Chlorus and Galerius. These tetrarchs had four separate, splendid capitals: Nicomedia (Izmit), Mediolanum (Milan), Treviri (the former Augusta Trevirorum, now Trier) and Thessalonica (Salonica). Rome was not included among these imperial headquarters, since it lay too far away from the critical frontier regions, over which the rulers had to keep watch. But the Senate was still at Rome, and it was at Rome that Maximian constructed the massive Baths of Diocletian.

With the help of his colleagues, Diocletian became the most comprehensive imperial organizer since Augustus. He increased the number of provinces from fifty to a hundred, and grouped them into thirteen major units, named dioceses. He and his fellow-rulers also overhauled the structure of the Roman army, dividing it into two branches, the *comitatenses* or mobile field force, and *limitanei* or static frontier units. The military strength of the empire was now half a million or more, much larger even than the expanded army of Septimius Severus a century earlier – larger, in fact, that it had ever been in the course of Roman history.

In consequence Diocletian did not, could not, lessen the tax burden imposed upon the civilian population. Indeed, he increased it. But at least he tried to see that the taxes were levied fairly. This he attempted to do by eliminating the irregularity and suddenness of tax demands – which had been one of the population's major hardships and grievances – for instead he required that a new and revised announcement giving full information about the taxes that were going to be demanded should be made afresh every year.

Moreover, as had also not been done in the past, agricultural land was divided into units of measurement deliberately calculated to take the differences between various crops and qualities and regions into account. This meant, once again, that taxes could be assessed with greater fairness, that is to say in a less mechanical and arbitrary fashion. And Diocletian sought also to mitigate the hardships of the empire's inhabitants in another way as well, by issuing an edict fixing maximum prices,[9] which has come down to us (and is the most valuable of all ancient economic documents that have survived). The edict did not, however, prove effective, since goods merely disappeared from the market, and inflation continued to shoot up. Another grave hardship, too, was Diocletian's insistence, in order to collect taxes, that the whole population should stay at work, on a hereditary basis, in the towns and villages where they were registered. And this remained a disagreeable feature of the later empire.

The tetrarchs fought wars, and their publicity agents laid ever-increasing emphasis on their role as triumphant defenders against the numerous external enemies by whom the empire was beset.

As a further stimulus to patriotism, too, enormous stress was placed upon the pagan religion, the faith, it was said, that had made Roman great and was still seen as the mainspring of its continued survival and power. This revival of paganism, on a more emphatically national basis than ever before, was accompanied, from 303 onwards, by violent persecutions of the faith that had become its principal competitor, Christianity. There had been persecutions of Christians half a century earlier, from similar motives. But the aim of Diocletian and his fellow arch-regimenters was nothing less than the total extirpation of the

207

Christian religion. It was a struggle to the death, between the old order and the new, in which 3,000 people lost their lives.

But then in 305 Diocletian, whose health had become precarious, did an unprecedented thing. For he abdicated from the throne – and, with difficulty, induced his colleague Maximian to do the same. Constantius I Chlorus and Galerius duly succeeded them, until their deaths in 306 and 311 respectively. During this period, however, the regular, planned successions to the tetrarchy broke down in confusion, amid a welter of mutually hostile contestants. In 312 Constantine I, son of Constantius I, emerged to defeat Maxentius (son of Maximian) at the Milvian Bridge, thus becoming sole emperor of the west; and in the following year another potentate, Licinius, gained unchallenged control of the east. Then in 323–4 Constantine destroyed Licinius, and became the ruler of all Roman territories, until his death in 337.

Constantine was a man of impetuous, versatile drive who knew it was his duty to recast the world, and to this end plunged ahead with many of the policies of Diocletian, augmenting taxation, bureaucracy and regimentation, and further enlarging and reorganizing the army.

He also found it necessary to equip the empire with a new capital. His tetrarchic predecessors had bequeathed him four such cities, and Constantine himself experimented with a number of other centres as well. But he finally decided that the ideal location was the ancient Greek city of Byzantium on the Bosphorus strait. For it possessed an excellent harbour, and enjoyed a strategic location from which wars could be simultaneously directed on the Danube and Euphrates fronts. So he founded Constantinople, where Istanbul stands today. Like Rome which formed its model, the reconstituted city was given a Forum and Senate of its own, and its inhabitants received free distributions from the grain-fleet that had served the ancient western capital. At first Constantinople and its senators still ranted beneath that capital, but Constantine intended that it should become the new metropolis in its stead. And by this decision the scene was set for the Middle Ages.

Constantine also carried through a second and even more far-reaching revolution, the conversion of the Roman world from paganism to Christianity. Galerius, before he died, had recognized that the persecutions directed against the Christians were proving counter-productive, and had called them off. Next, in 312, Constantine and Licinius, jointly, in the Edict of Mediolanum (Milan), gave official and practical effect to this tolerance. Constantine was a man who felt impulsive need for a divine companion and sponsor. For a time the Sun-god, whose worship was ancestral in his family, had been the object of his veneration. But from the time of the Edict onwards he was already revealing his adherence to Christianity, since this faith, unlike the Sun-cult, offered the attraction of a personal saviour who had actually come to live in our own world. The literature and inscriptions of the time often refer, somewhat vaguely, to the One Supreme Power. But the Power was henceforward identified, more and more explicitly, with Jesus.

In pursuance of this attitude, Constantine also brought forward, over a period of years, a series of measures favouring the adherents of Christianity (provided that they did not belong to dissident sects). Its priests were exempted from municipal obligations, its churches drew subsidies from imperial funds, and the Church was granted its own independent jurisdiction – though it remained subordinated to the emperor's will. He himself attended the ecclesiastical Council of Nicaea (Iznik, 325), and stimulated the construction of magnificent churches: the Basilica of St Peter and Basilica Constantiniana (St John Lateran) at Rome, the Holy Apostles at Constantinople (where work on the Church of the Holy Wisdom [Aya Sofya] was also begun), the Golden Octagon at Antioch, the Holy Sepulchre at Jerusalem. These were buildings in which the old form of the basilica was boldly adapted from pagan to Christian purposes.

Constantine's later years, before his death in 337, were marred by suspicions and executions within his own family, and he made the classic mistake of bequeathing the empire jointly to no less than five members of his house. By 350, after various wars, his son Constantius II (337–361) was their sole survivor. He devoted much of his long reign to attempting to transform Constantine's Christian revolution into a permanent reality. He himself, however, belonged to the Arian sect which held Jesus to be inferior in status to his Father, but was destined to be overtaken by orthodox Catholicism; and his attempts to grapple with the theological disputes that were splitting the Church did not prove effective.

His cousin and successor Julian 'the Apostate' (361–3) undertook a reversion to paganism, which proved too archaistic to prevail, however. He also sought to deal with the Persians, but this attempt, too, was never brought to a satisfactory conclusion. The Danubian officer who succeeded him on the throne, Jovian (364–4), reversed both these policies, negotiating an unpopular peace with the Persians, and restoring Christianity as the religion of the state.

The army next acclaimed Valentinian I (364–375), another Danubian, as emperor: and he was the last truly effective ruler to occupy the throne before the western empire fell. Although cruel and choleric by nature, Valentinian was an excellent commander and organizer. He felt no affection for the Roman nobility, but was unusually sympathetic to the plight of the poor. More unusually still, he was prepared to tolerate differences of religious opinion.

Like Diocletian before him, however, Valentinian I felt that more than one ruler was needed, and in consequence he handed over the eastern provinces to his brother Valens, who took up residence at Constantinople. Valentinian himself stayed in the west, retaining Mediolanum (Milan) as his own capital (while permitting the Senate to remain at Rome).

During his reign, he found himself confronted by a succession of external crises, which he handled with efficiency. First, Germans had broken across the River Rhenus (Rhine), capturing Moguntiacum (Mainz). But Valentinian defeated them on three different occasions, and then marched deep into the interior of their country. Staying in the north for seven years, he reconstructed the imperial defences, successfully set various German tribal groups at odds with one another, and agreed to admit many other Germans within the western provinces. Next, in 374–5, he repulsed further hordes that had penetrated across the middle and lower Danube. At that juncture, however, the offensive form of language employed by a party of German envoys so greatly angered him that he burst a blood vessel, with fatal results.

But he had left the western empire a good deal stronger than he found it eleven years earlier. No one could have believed that it only had a century of life ahead of it.

Three years later the other, eastern Roman empire experienced a catastrophic reverse. Beyond its frontiers, two German states had become established, the Ostrogoths ('bright Goths') in the Ukraine, and the Visigoths ('wise Goths') based in Rumania. The Ostrogothic group, however, crumbled before the cavalry onslaught of a non-German people, the Huns (c.370), who also drove the Visigoths across the Danube into the eastern Roman provinces, where they were permitted to settle. But there were not treated fairly by Roman governmental officials, and their chief Fritigern, in disgust, rebelled and took over large areas of the Balkans. Valens marched from Asia to deal with the emergency, but perished in 378, in a battle at Hadrianopolis (Adrianople, Edirne), and the greater part of his army died with him. His nephew Gratian, the son and successor of Valentinian I in the west, had failed to reach the scene of the disaster in time to rescue his uncle. And now he appointed, as the dead man's successor, Theodosius I (378–

395), an officer from Cauca (Coca) in Spain. Theodosius's personality veered abruptly between feverish activity and idleness. His rule, however, was notable in certain respects. First, he accepted a further, unprecedented mass of Visigothic settlers within his borders. And secondly, he insisted on strict Christian, Catholic orthodoxy, thus earning the title 'the Great'.

But the enforcement of this intention involved the rise of unmanageable churchmen. In particular, the reign of Theodosius witnessed the principal activity of Saint Ambrose (c.339–389). Ambrose was a new sort of Christian theologian, since he was not only a copious writer and preacher but also showed himself a man of political authority and action. As bishop of Mediolanum (Milan), his aim was the creation of a wholly orthodox, Catholic, Christian empire, from which heresy and paganism and Judaism should all be eradicated. This was entirely in keeping with the ideas of Theodosius. However, Ambrose's actions also began to display resistance to the Constantinian doctrine that the Church should be subordinate to the state.

He had already shown his power when he persuaded Gratian's colleague in the west, Valentinian II (375–392), to reject the Roman aristocracy's pleas for the reerection of the Altar of Victory in the Senate house, a decision which inflicted a decisive blow upon paganism (384). But then he stood up to the more important eastern emperor, Theodosius I, as well. For in 390 – when Theodosius was temporarily accessible to him in the west – Ambrose was bold enough to rebuke him publicly, and subject him to a penance, for having ordered a punitive massacre at Thessalonica (Salonica).

But not all the leading cultural figures of the time were Christians. For example, Ambrose's principal opponent in the Altar of Victory controversy was the scholar, statesman and orator Symmachus, a supporter of the ancient pagan religion.

Moreover, Ammianus Marcellinus of Antioch (325/330–c.395), one of the outstanding historians the empire ever produced, was also a pagan. After a military career, he wrote his *Roman History*, at Rome, during the later years of his life. The narrative, in Latin, covers the years from the accession of Nerva in AD 96 to the death of Valens in 378. Ammianus's account of the events of his own lifetime, in which he himself had participated, is particularly vivid. His determination to tell the truth is voiced with an insistence that is, on the whole, convincing. Yet, in the atmosphere of the later Roman spy state, it was impossible to write with candour about everybody – and the anti-Christian Ammianus stopped his history before the point when Theodosius I would

211

have been discussed. Yet his admiration for the pagan Julian emerges, as so does his approval of the tolerant, though Christian, policies of Valentinian I.

Displaying a gift not only for dramatic narrative but also for the depiction of character, Ammianus provides invaluable evidence for the declining years of the western empire: of which, over-optimistically, he did not foresee the imminent fall. He tends to under-estimate the Germans, but his treatment of the Persians is relatively unbiased.

After putting down two usurpers, Theodosius I succeeded in reuniting the eastern and western empires. But this reunification only proved momentary and transient, because after his death the two empires became divided once again, and this time division was permanent.

In the east ruled Theodosius's elder son Arcadius (395–408), and in the west his brother Honorius (395–423). Both were incompetent, and relied on their regents, Rufinus and Stilicho respectively. Stilicho, half-Roman and half-German, had Rufinus murdered, and then failed to act effectively against the Visigoth Alaric I, because of his own continuing plans, from the west, to subvert the eastern government.

On 31st December 406, however, a group of invaders belonging to various German tribes broke across the frozen River Rhenus (Rhine), and after plundering a number of frontier cities fanned out across the whole of Gaul, where they encountered little serious resistance. This proved a decisive breakthrough, because the Rhine border could never be established again, as it turned out. In 408, Honorius, at Ravenna which had replaced Mediolanum as the western imperial capital, had Stilicho put to death, on a charge of plotting against him. Two years later, annoyed by his friend Stilicho's removal and by the rejection of his own demands for money and land, Alaric briefly occupied and sacked Rome – which had not been captured by a foreign enemy for nearly eight hundred years.

Soon after his onslaught on the city, Alaric died, and his brother-in-law and successor Ataulf moved his people out of Italy into south-western Gaul, from which, however (despite his marriage to Honorius's half-sister Gallia Placidia) he was compelled, by the western general Constantius (III), to withdraw to Spain; and there he was killed (415). But the next Visigothic king, his brother Wallia, after returning Placidia to the Romans, was authorized to take his compatriots back to Gaul, where, establishing their capital at Tolosa (Toulouse) in 418, they were granted federal status – an important step towards the independent statehoods which were soon to obliterate the western Roman empire.

*

The reign of Honorius witnessed much of the activity of two Christian theologians, whose work dominated the future.

One was Saint Jerome (340/8–420), who came from Stridon on the borders of Dalmatia (Illyricum) and Pannonia, but after a period of residence at Rome spent most of the last three decades of his life at a monastery he had founded at Bethlehem (together with a convent for women). His works – which fill nine volumes of J.P. Migne's *Patrologia Latina* – included a new Latin translation of the Bible, known as the Vulgate. One hundred and fifty-four of his letters have also come down to us, written over a period of nearly half a century. They cover an enormous breadth of subject matter, and his satire flashes over a wide range of society.

Saint Augustine (354–430) of Thagaste (Soukh-Aras in Algeria) became a convert to Christianity (387), and was bishop of Hippo Regius (Annaba) for thirty-five years. His *Confessions* (*c*.397–400) present an intense account of the spiritual struggles of his early life, and conclude with passionate, philosophical reflections. The spread of asceticism in the Latin world ensured the work widespread readership. Augustine presents his sombre, neurasthenic self-criticisms with dedicated honesty and not a great many illusions.

His later achievement, the *De Civitate Dei* (*City of God*), lays down a philosophy of history, embodying God's design for the salvation of humankind. Prompted by the sack of Rome by the Visigoth Alaric in 410, the *City of God* was written to answer the widely asked question: why have things gone so disastrously wrong with the empire ever since it became Christian? Augustine attempts to answer this question in detail, pointing out, in particular, that earlier paganism, too, had failed to provide a defence against catastrophe. Then the last twelve of the twenty-two books in the work develop the concept of the Two Cities: a heavenly city comprising righteous people on earth and the saints in heaven, contrasted with the earthly city perverted by worldly and selfish considerations and ideas. Augustine also expresses his belief in predestination, based on his faith that every happening is a deliberate act of God, who grants mercy to the elect, and judgment to the damned.

For 'heretics' he displays a lack of sympathy, directing attacks against a wide range of those Christian (and Manichaean) groups that failed to conform with Catholic orthodoxy, and maintaining that the Church, in alliance with the imperial government, should employ every possible means, including coercive persecution, to shut these dissidents' mouths. In this cause, Augustine was willing to plunge into an endless series of controversies, developing his ideas with a fierceness that sometimes alarmed even his admirers. Introspective and intellectual, imaginative,

213

sensitive and emotional, he was also a man capable of action, imbued with a restless desire, at all times, to examine and improve his ardent religious faith. His articulate powers of self-expression have left us with knowledge about all that he thought and felt.

When Valentinian III (425–455), the son of Placidia, was brought back from Constantinople at the age of six, in order to succeed to the throne of Ravenna, the principal western general Aetius tried to block the return of the child's mother, but failed: and it was she, Placidia, who took charge when she and her son arrived. Subsequently Aetius led an army to north Africa – on which Rome depended for its grain – in order to put down its semi-independent governor Boniface, and Placidia seized the opportunity to back Boniface against him. But this proved no more successful than Aetius's earlier attempt to keep her out of Italy.

However, neither Aetius nor anyone else could check the perilous Vandal Gaiseric, who had moved from Gaul to Spain and then to north Africa (429). There, the federal status which he was granted in Mauretania and Numidia (Morocco and western Algeria) amounted, in fact, to independence from the western empire, as he demonstrated by capturing its second city, Carthage (439). Gaiseric had done more than any other single man to accelerate the fall of the Roman west.

The next threat was presented by the non-German Huns, who came from the east, and by exploiting their ability as horsemen, had built up an empire extending from the Baltic to the Danube. In 434 this dominion was ruled by the tireless Attila, the 'Scourge of God', in conjunction with his brother, whom he murdered eleven years later. For a time the two Roman empires held him at bay, but in 451 he marched on Gaul, where an army of Aetius's Roman troops, and federated Visigoths and other Germans, confronted him on the Catalaunian Plains (near Châlons-sur-Marne). The Visigothic monarch fell in the battle, but Attila was defeated, and evacuated Gaul. In the following year, however, he and his Huns crossed into Italy, sacking Mediolanum (Milan). But Pope Leo I came north from Rome, and, presumably by the offer of a subsidy, persuaded Attila to leave the peninsula: thus demonstrating the increasing importance of the papacy as a political force – in the absence of any imperial government in the ancient capital.

Two years later Attila died, and the Hun empire disintegrated. But Aetius too was dead, since Valentinian III, wrongly suspecting a conspiracy, cut him down. For two decades and more Aetius had laboured to repel the western empire's destroyers. Now its terminal crisis had begun. The death of Valentinian III, six months later, was another turning point – despite his own personal inadequacy – since his imperial house, which had exceptionally lasted for nearly a century, ended with him, and thereafter no dynasty existed any more.

In the very year of Valentinian III's death Gaiseric the Vandal, whose fleet ruled the seas, landed at Ostia and captured Rome. He remained in the city for two weeks, outdoing Alaric's earlier depredations, and when he left he took thousands of captives with him, including Valentinian's widow and two daughters.

The dominant figure in the western empire was now the German commander-in-chief Ricimer, whose making and unmaking of successive western emperors added to the general instability. After his death (472), and the loss of most of what remained of Roman Gaul to the now independent Visigoths, a new military commander, Orestes, gave the Ravenna throne to his own son Romulus Augustus, known as Augustulus (475). At this stage, however, a Roman general, Odoacer, demanded lands for his men in Italy, and, when the request was turned down, killed Orestes and forced Romulus into retirement (476).

Odoacer became king of Italy (with the *de facto* agreement of the eastern ruler Zeno), and although the penultimate western emperor Julius Nepos still lived on for four more years in Dalmatia, to which he had fled, historians fastened on this year 476 as the date at which the western empire finally fell.

The causes of its fall were complex, and have been much debated. It had succumbed, in the first place, to its external enemies. But it had succumbed to them because of manifold internal disunities. For one thing, there were far too many civil wars, disputing the imperial succession. Secondly, the western imperial authorities increasingly failed to enforce conscription in the army: and even when they succeeded in doing so, it was of no avail, because the defenders of vital posts just melted away. So the emperors had to enrol (and pay for) German troops instead – sometimes whole tribes of them. There was a total lack of sympathy between the army, Roman or German, and the civilian populations, which resented and failed to hand over the gigantic taxes, in cash and kind, required to pay for these soldiers, and hated the mobilization of compulsory labour. Innumerable people went underground and joined travelling gangs of marauders and bandits.

Alternatively, they sought the protection of powerful landlords against the demands of the state. For the wealthy men, the senators, detested the emperor's ministers, and paid little attention to anything the court had to say. So, while vainly trying to keep its armies in the field, the imperial government had not only ruined the poor, but alienated the rich. And, in addition, its oppressions, conducted by a bureaucracy of vast size and deteriorating quality, virtually destroyed the huge numbers of people who came in between, the middle class that had formed the backbone of ancient society. But the western emperors, personally, had little to do with all this, because, living cloistered lives at Ravenna, they became out of touch with everyone except the members of their own entourage.

What was equally disastrous, too, was their repeated friction, and that of the administrations that served under them, with their colleagues at Constantinople. Nor did these rulers ever make even the smallest practical attempt to come to terms with the Germans who were playing a more and more significant part in their society, government and army. Besides, among the peoples who inhabited the empire there was a proliferation of human drop-outs, who refused to participate in communal and public life. For one thing, there were repeated risings by dispossessed, displaced persons known as the Badauae, especially in Gaul – often peasant farmers fighting for independence from land-owners, and encouraged by the weakness of the central government. And very prominent among the drop-outs, too, were an ever-increasing number of monks. Furthermore, the official Church itself contributed to the national downfall, first by persecuting pagans, secondly by insisting on equally forcible action against Christian 'heretics', and thirdly by refusing altogether (like Saint Ambrose) to work in harmony with the state – and, in consequence, even regarding its faith as incompatible with state service.

Augustine, for example, declared, in his *City of God*, that the earthly[1] city only looks for glory from men, carrying self-love to the point of contempt of God; whereas its heavenly counterpart, on the other hand, finds its glory in loving Him.[10] That cut human authorities firmly down to size, and if and when Augustine's view became a widespread attitude it was difficult to see how the western empire could survive.

3 The Roman Achievement

Roman civilization could not have begun to be what it was without the Greeks. True, Etruscan influence was also at work: and that, too, indirectly, brought in much additional Greek culture. But direct Greek influence, also, was a dominant force. Roman literature, art, architecture all started from Greek prototypes, and after the Greek world had been conquered by the Romans, the process continued. 'Greece,

216

the captive,' as Horace observed, 'made her savage victor captive.'[11] Thus the societies and cultures of Greece and Rome became intertwined and inseparable.

Yet while parts of a single whole, the Greek and Roman worlds form its parts with a difference. For while taking over Greek literature and art and architecture, and much else as well, the Romans made them all into something original – just as the Greeks had made something original out of the near-eastern cultural elements which they themselves had taken over. But there was a difference between the 'originality' of the Greeks and the Romans, all the same. For whereas the Greeks had been adapting features of external civilizations, the Romans were incorporating elements from a civilization in which they themselves participated – the classical world.

That makes it all the more difficult, but also all the more necessary, to assert and emphasize the degree of originality which can be authentically credited to the Romans. In this task, the Latin writers themselves do not always help: since they were sometimes unnecessarily humble or modest, allowing themselves, in comparison with the Greeks, less credit than they deserve. Take, for example, a famous assertion by Virgil. When, echoing the views of Augustus, he combines his belief that the Romans must remain the political masters with a reverent admiration for the superior cultural tradition of the Greeks,[12] he is inclining his hearers or readers to underestimate Roman culture. Certainly, the Greek literary and artistic masterpieces remain peerless. But to regard the Roman cultural achievement, because of its Greek roots, as merely a faint imitation of Greece – as is still occasionally suggested – betrays a misapprehension, since what Rome achieved, too, was of singular originality and distinction.

After first looking at the Greeks, we have seen how the Roman world came about. In so far as our sources, numerous but often unsatisfactory, permit us to find out what happened, it is possible to trace a rise from nothing to prolonged epochs of diverse and fertile efflorescence, followed by an initial, narrowly averted fall (in the mid-third century AD), a subsequent recovery involving massive changes, and then a second and more fatal collapse.

It is a very long story. Ancient Rome is unparalleled among the great communities of the western world (except for Byzantium, which grew out of it), because it lasted so long. With that same exception, no other occidental civilization or major political unit has ever rivalled its millennial duration. It is a story that extends from the establishment of insignificant Tiber villages to the creation and maintenance of a vast multi-racial society, which was then, many centuries later, fragmented, in the west, into units foreshadowing the nations of the modern world. And yet, despite this fragmentation, very much of Rome, in modified forms, continued to live on within these successor states: its language, government, law, Church, literature, oratory, art, business, and habits of thinking and living. And of these continuing Roman elements western civilization has remained aware ever since, recalling and cherishing them in one revival and renaissance after another.

What the whole immense story of the Romans shows, moreover, is not only what a tightly knit community can achieve by mutual cooperation, but also the possibilities of self-expression for single individuals within such a framework. For although the large, suppressed majority still failed to benefit, the other, and more formative, elements of Rome's society did enable it to achieve an unprecedented measure of personal self-realization and achievement. And it is that tradition which wins our admiration and requires us to be proud that we are among its inheritors.

The tradition, it should be repeated, was maintained despite and after the western empire's fifth-century fall, or transformation.

That fall is, in itself, such an enthralling event, or series of events, that any attempt to 'update' it, by comparisons with what may happen to ourselves, almost seems to spoil the grandeur and fascination of the undiluted ancient story. Nevertheless, the fall of the western empire has exerted such a fascination throughout the centuries that the search for possible modern analogies is almost forced on us by the determination, in many countries of the world, to undertake precisely this form of updating, and detect what analogies it can find to present times. Britain looks back on its own vanished empire. The United States of America think of their current leadership of the world, and of how it might be in danger of coming to an end. The Soviet Union seems to be showing, at this very moment, how smaller peoples can break away from empires. France is the country where, in Roman times, this first happened. Italy is the land where the western Roman empire ruled and fell. Germany is very conscious of its role as that empire's invaders and destroyers, and spans, moreover, today's no less controversial east-west border. Besides, some writers see an analogy between those ancient German invaders and the Third World today, which is, and will become increasingly, discontented with the economic gap which separates it from its more developed neighbours who inhabit our own lands.

And yet, as I have observed elsewhere,[13] although our own society's 'resemblances to the society of declining Rome are so numerous and

218

powerful, that does not mean it is inevitable for us to succumb to the same fate as the Romans did. It is not necessarily, in the words of Cyril Connolly, closing time in the gardens of the West. There is nothing inevitable about the process at all. As Maxim Gorki insisted, man has to understand that he is the creator, controller and master of civilization, and that the decision whether things turn out badly or not so badly rests with himself. The history of the Romans is what they made of it; what we make of our own history is likewise our own choice.'

However, the history of the Romans does raise awkward, and perhaps embarrassing, moral questions and dilemmas today. On the one hand, they employed brute force, and employed it lavishly. Yet, on the other hand, the solid and excellent results that they achieved by its employment have never been equalled. For Rome conferred, or imposed, upon the western world a desirable unity – largely force-free, once achieved – which these regions had never known before. And will they ever regain it? In these early 1990s, this is a question very much worth asking.

But what, in the second part of this book, we have had to deal with is how the Roman empire came about, and developed its fundamental characteristics, and then fell. It did not fall, however – it must be said again – for an extremely long time. Its greatness lies in its endurance and survival for no less than five hundred years. Indeed, this is one of the world's success stories: the story of an achievement whereby a heterogeneous mixture of races, customs and creeds was induced to settle down under the single rule of the Pax Romana for this immense passage of time, which the creators of modern empires and states can only look upon with respect and envy.

Certainly, long before the bad years at the end when the structure crumbled, Rome's subjects were sometimes restless. But when, for example, two Gallic tribes, the Treviri and Lingones, had joined a German rebellion in AD 69, the historian Tacitus places in the mouth of the Roman commander Quintus Petillius Cerialis a speech which sums up the whole situation. For it presents a contrast between Roman domination and what things had been like before – and, in the process, offers a skilful vindication of Roman rule, which is seen as less undesirable than any likely alternative:[14]

The occupation of your land and that of the other Gauls by Roman generals and emperors was not prompted by self-interest, but happened at the invitation of your forefathers, whose quarrels had exhausted them to the point of collapse, while the Germans summoned to the rescue had imposed their yoke on friend and foe alike. ... Do you imagine that [the rebels] Civilis, the Batavians and the tribes east of the Rhenus (Rhine) care any more for you than their ancestors did for your fathers and grandfathers? ... Liberty and other fine phrases serve as their pretexts – indeed, no one has ever aimed at enslaving others and making himself their master without using this very same language. Throughout the whole of Gaul there were always despots and wars until you passed under our control. We ourselves, despite many provocations, imposed upon you by right of conquest only such additional burdens as were necessary for preserving peace. Stability between nations cannot be maintained without armies, nor armies without pay, nor pay without taxation.

Everything else is shared equally between us. You often command our legions in person and in person govern these and other provinces. There is no question of segregation or exclusion. Again, those emperors who are well spoken of benefit you as much as they do us, though you live far away, whereas tyrants wreak their will upon such as are nearest to them. You adopt an attitude of resignation towards natural disasters like bad harvests or excessive rainfall: in the same way you must put up with spending and avarice on the part of your masters. There will be faults as long as there are men. But the picture is not one of uninterrupted gloom. From time to time there are intervals of relief by way of compensation.

You are surely not going to tell me that you expect a milder regime when [the rebels] Tutor and Classicus are your rulers, or that less taxation than now will be required to provide the armies to defend you from the Germans and Britons? For if the Romans are expelled – which heaven forbid! – what else will result but world-wide war in which each nation's hand will be turned against its neighbour? The good luck and good discipline of eight hundred years secured the erection of the imperial fabric, whose destruction must involve the destroyers in the same downfall. But yours will be the most dangerous situation, for you have the riches and resources which are the main causes of war. At present, victors and vanquished enjoy peace and imperial citizenship upon an equal footing, and it is upon these blessings that you must lavish your affection and respect. Learn from your experience of the two alternatives not to choose insorbordination and ruin in preference to obedience and security.

Except, perhaps, to the downtrodden lowest fringes of society, the commonsense arguments ascribed by Tacitus to Cerialis remained convincing enough for centuries, and deserve attention for that reason. Indeed, they only ceased to carry conviction when it became clear to the subject nations that the position had changed, and that Roman government was not giving them anything that was worth fighting for any longer: and then came the end of the western empire.

220

4 The Aftermath

When that empire ceased to exist, the Visigoths remained in control of southern Gaul and Spain, and the Burgundians ruled in south-eastern Gaul: until other Germans, the Franks, who had established themselves in the north of the country, obliterated both these Gallic régimes in 507. This was accomplished by Clovis (c.482–511), founder of the Merovingian dynasty, who had abandoned paganism in favour of the Catholic Christianity and the Church of Rome. Later, in the northern regions of Europe, the Carolingian ruler Charlemagne (772–814) broke with his dynasty's policy of peaceful missionary penetration by undertaking repeated military campaigns and forcible conversions. Finally, he declared himself Roman emperor, and in 800 had himself crowned at Rome by Pope Leo III.

Meanwhile, in Spain, where the Visigothic kingdom continued and prospered, Reccared (586–601) had, like Clovis, joined the Church of Rome – deserting his Arian faith in order to do so – and by this act founded Iberian Catholicism. But Islamic power, exploding across north Africa after the death of the Prophet Mohammed (632), impinged forcibly upon the Spanish peninsula which was invaded in 711 by the Islamic prince Tarik. His successors, of the same religion, asserted their control throughout the southern part of the country, relegating the Christian monarchy to its northern regions for centuries to come.

Meanwhile in Italy, after Odoacer became virtually independent of the eastern (Byzantine) empire, his Ostrogothic successor Theoderic (493–526) had brought back peace and prosperity to the country. Latin literature flourished under Boethius and Cassiodorus, who served as bridges between classical culture and the dawning Middle Ages, and, although the régime itself was still Arian, the papacy – the Roman Catholic Church – continued to gain in power, and increasingly came to be the means by which Roman culture and civic values were perpetuated.

In the sixth century, however, the Ostrogothic kingdom was wiped out by the troops of the Byzantine emperor Justinian I (527–565). And the same befell the Vandal state in north Africa. But Byzantine rule did not last in those countries for long, and thereafter the various other régimes of the Middle Ages took over.

Yet the Byzantine empire itself survived; and this raises a question. Why did this eastern, Byzantine dominion have such a different story from its western counterpart? Very far from collapsing in the fifth century, it continued to exist (with only a brief interval of Crusader rule from 1204 to 1261) until its capital fell to the Ottoman Turkish sultan Mohammed II in 1453. And throughout the greater part of the entire millennium preceding that date Constantinople had been the largest and most splendid and learned city in Europe, producing an art that distinctively blended Greek, Roman and eastern elements.

The reasons for the Byzantine empire's survival, in such marked contrast to the collapse of the western régime, were various. Its frontiers were not so vulnerable. It was supported by a sounder social and economic framework, embodying fewer disunities. It had preserved its middle class (and, in consequence, possessed a better administrative structure). Its provinces were more populous and better cultivated. And its internal political stability was greater, as the relative paucity of usurpers confirmed. True, Constantinople had its troubles, notably ferocious ecclesiastical divisions. But it could weather them, owing to its superior strength in the other respects that have been indicated. That was why it was the west that fell, or had to assume new political forms, whereas the eastern, Byzantine empire found it possible to survive for another thousand years. And in the process, despite its differences from the Roman world of the past, it was able to maintain many of the customs and traditions that it had inherited from that world.

We have now reached the point when the claims for classical civilization made in the introduction have been examined: and it can be seen that they are justified. We in the west have owed to the Greeks and Romans, throughout all the intervening centuries, an enormous proportion of our cultural property. That does not mean that we have always consciously imitated those peoples. But whether we know it or not, they have been our models. Even in this twentieth century, when deliberate attempts have been made to bring other legacies into play, what would any of the essential branches of our life consist of without the long, varied, preceding story of the Greeks and Romans, and the contributions that they handed down to us?

Moreover, we owe the Greeks and Romans warnings as well as gifts. There are various ways in which we do not want to be as they were. In government, for example, we hope not to make the disastrous decisions of the Greek city-states. Nor can we use imperialistic force like the Romans. Yet, once again, we are only able to heed these warnings if we know how it was that the Greeks and Romans acted. And, in any case, the negative warnings that we owe them are far less numerous and prominent than the positive debts for which we have reason to be grateful.

We are what we are, and we hope to be what we hope to be, because of what we learn from the classical civilization, and that remains true however much – like the Greeks and Romans themselves – we have adapted and modified what we learnt, for our own use. Let us not make the mistakes, then, of forgetting what they did and thought and wrote and made. For if we forget, we shall be saying that we do not want to know what we ourselves are. And if we do not know what we are we shall be helplessly adrift in our own world.

APPENDIX I

The Plots of Homer and Hesiod

The *Iliad* describes a brief and late stage in the siege of Troy, in north-western Asia Minor, by the combined forces of numerous states of the Achaeans (pre-Dorian Greeks) commanded by Agamemnon, king of Mycenae. The purpose of the expedition was to avenge the injury to his brother Menelaus, king of Sparta, whose wife Helen had been abducted by the Trojan prince Paris. For nine years the Greek army has been encamped beside its fleet outside the walls of Troy, which has not yet fallen.

As a result of a quarrel with Agamemnon the most formidable of his allies, Achilles, has furiously withdrawn from the fight, taking his Myrmidon followers with him. This is the wrath – the first word of the poem – which, as Homer declared, caused disaster to numberless other Achaeans. When Priam's son Hector storms the rampart protecting the Achaean ships, Hector allows his beloved friend Patroclus to lead the Myrmidons to the rescue. But Patroclus is killed by Hector, whereupon the grief-stricken Achilles returns to the battle and slays Hector, ferociously ill-treating his body. Prompted by Zeus, however, Priam visits Achilles in his camp by night, to appeal for the return of his son's corpse. Achilles grants his request, and the poem ends with Hector's funeral, amid an uneasy truce.

Achilles possesses to a superlative extent all the virtues and failings of the 'hero' constructed by Homer's nostalgic imagination, embodying the heroic honour code. Such a hero, aided by birth, wealth and prowess, dedicated his whole life to a violently competitive struggle to win acclamation – together with the material possessions by which it is measured – by excelling his peers, particularly in warfare, which formed his principal occupation. Yet this zest and lust for fighting is overshadowed by pathos, and by a sense of the fragility of all human endeavour. For although, at climactic moments, the heroes' achievements seem to bring them not far short of the gods, they still have no way of escaping the mortal destiny that inevitably awaits them. When, at the moving climax of the poem, Achilles comes face to face with old Priam, whose son Hector he has killed, the exultant din of war has faded into sadness and compassion.

The *Odyssey* narrates the return of another Greek hero, Odysseus, from the Trojan War to his home on the island of Ithaca. His wanderings went on for a decade, but the action of the *Odyssey* concentrates on the last few weeks, and what came after. He has arrived at the island of the nymph Calypso, who compelled him to stay there as her lover for nearly eight years. Meanwhile, at Ithaca, his home is filled with uninvited guests, the suitors of his wife Penelope. Feasting at the expense of their absent host, they urge her to choose one of themselves as her new husband. Odysseus has made an enemy of the god Poseidon, whose son the Cyclops Polyphemus he blinded. But he has a staunch divine patron in Athena, who directs his son Telemachus to seek information about him in Greek cities. And meanwhile Zeus orders Calypso to release him. His ship is wrecked, and he is cast up on the coast of Scheria, mythical land of the Phaeacians, whose princess Nausicaa encounters him and takes him to her father, King Alcinous. At a banquet, Odysseus describes his travels and adventures. He is given a ship, and arrives back at Ithaca disguised as a beggar. Reunited with his son, he slays the suitors, whereupon Penelope identifies him as her husband, and he rules his island kingdom once again.

Dozens of fantastic stories, of many origins, are incorporated in the poem, but its basic subject is that of a standard folktale: the theme of the man, long absent and believed to be dead, who after adventures returns home and rejoins his devoted wife. The *Odyssey* resembles the *Iliad* in its exaltation of courage, and it has its share of the same poem's bloodshed as well. Yet there has been a shift from passionate, doomed heroism towards calmer virtues such as patience and self-control and love of home. We are not told only of kings, but hear also of the social and family lives of noblemen dwelling on their estates, with emphasis on courtliness and hospitable guest-friendships and exchanges of gifts. Odysseus is the archetype of the complete man who has striven enduringly against all the perils of life and vanquished them, thus discovering many things, including himself. Calypso – and before her Circe, on the fabulous island of Aeaea – whose sexual conquest of him, for a time, reversed what seemed to the Greeks the natural superiority of the male – are vividly depicted witches. But other women, too, not witches but human beings, find themselves for the first time endowed with developed, potent personalities, notably Nausicaa and, above all, the ingenious and resolutely faithful Penelope.

Hesiod's *Works and Days* begins with an invocation to the Muses to sing the praises of Zeus, and continues with a conciliatory appeal to the poet's brother Perses (with whom he had quarrelled about the division of their father's property), declaring that strife, as opposed to mere rivalry, is evil.

And Hesiod goes on to explain how man's fall had been caused by the curiosity of the first woman Pandora, a bad though seductive creature whom Zeus had brought into existence to punish mankind for accepting the gift of fire from her father Prometheus. By stressing this theme Hesiod perpetuated the anti-feminist feeling that could so often be found among Greek males. Yet he was also, like the author of the *Book of Job*, grappling with the problem of evil, and trying to explain why we have to suffer in a world controlled by a supposedly benevolent supreme deity. But Zeus's envoy, Dike (Justice), helps his master to take note of everything; and so we should endeavour to behave decently, because heaven eventually rewards the righteous, and punishes the wicked. True, however, it does not look like this at present; since Hesiod enumerates the ever-deteriorating five stages of humanity, in the fifth and worst of which – the iron age – we ourselves are living. Next, the poem turns to the practical, un-mythological (and un-Homeric) details of the farmer's year, calling his hearers and readers not to Homeric glory but to a gospel of sober, thrifty labour as a defence against miseries and injustices.

226

The *Theogony* is quite a different kind of poem – apart from a renewed attack on women, and another invocation to the Muses. This invocation, however, is very personal: the first literary manifesto that has come down to us, confirming Hesiod's title as pioneer of didactic (instructive) poetry. As for the main part of the work, it sets out to expound the divine creation and organization of the universe and the world – an early attempt to combine a mass of mythological material together (much of it of non-Greek, eastern origin) to form a picture which is on the way towards the scientific attempts of future generations. Order is imposed by Zeus, and once again Dike (Justice) is his agent: she occupies the place that honour holds in Homer, as the central virtue of society. A new stage of civic consciousness, in which citizens have to live with one another respectably, is at hand – although whether Hesiod, chronologically, comes after Homer or not, remains a disputable point, as indicated in the text.

The East

A. Phoenicia and Syria

An essential feature of early Greek culture was its derivation from near-eastern models, elaborately absorbed and radically adapted.

The maritime city-states of the Phoenicians – speaking a north-western Semitic language – led by Sidon (Saida) and its colony Tyre (Sur) began from c.1000 BC to fill the vacuum left by the Mycenaean collapse, reestablishing trade in the Mediterranean area, and founding settlements in Cyprus, north Africa (first Carthage), western Sicily, Sardinia and Spain. Inland lay small north Syrian states, in which Aramaean influences were strong, and so were 'Neo-Hittite' cultural elements remaining from the Hittite civilization of Asia Minor, and from another second millennium people, the Hurrians. The Creation Myths in Hesiod's *Theogony* go back to those sources.

In the coastal regions adjoining these north Syrian states, Greeks took the initiative in establishing trading posts (*emporia*). These were among the principal centres which transmitted near-eastern cultures to the Hellenic world elsewhere. The harbour towns of the Greeks on this coast included Al Mina, Posidium and Paltus. Al Mina – its ancient name is unknown – stood beside the estuary of the River Orontes (Nahr-el-Asi, now in the Turkish province of Hatay). The place was a trading post established in c.825–800 BC. The leaders of the enterprise seem to have been the Euboean cities of Chalcis and Eretria. They acquired fabrics, ivory, metals and slaves at Al Mina, bringing Greek wine and oil in order to pay for them. Far to the west, too, the Euboeans possessed other trading stations in Campania (Pithecusae and Cumae), to which they conveyed some of the gold they had acquired at Al Mina, in exchange for Etruscan copper and iron.

Al Mina was destroyed in c.700–675, revived before and after 600 (under Babylonian suzerainty), lapsed into inactivity once again, and began a new life under the Persians (c.520). During most of its long existence, however, it had shared its role as a Greek outpost with two other north Syrian ports. One was Posidium (Ras el-Bassit), thirteen miles away south of the Orontes, providing access to an inland route. The other was Paltus (Tell Sukas, Bulda), thirty-two miles south of Posidium, which supplied contact with the ivory-working Syrian state of Hamath. Early pottery found at Paltus mostly comes, once again, from Euboea. But Paltus suffered destruction on several occasions (c.675, c.588 and c.552).

It appears likely that the alphabet, adapted by the Greeks from north Syrian and Phoenician scripts, first reached them at Chalcis and Eretria from these ports. They were also the main influences upon the 'orientalizing' artistic movement led by Corinth.

Subsequently, Assyrian, Babylonian and then Persian control eclipsed the Greeks in the area, until Alexander III the Great conquered Syria and Phoenicia from the Persians in 332: whereupon those countries passed into Greek (and later Roman) world, although they retained tenacious cultural and religious survivals from ancient times.

B. Egypt

When the Hittites and Mycenaean worlds were swept away, Egypt had to confront not only Libyan tribesmen but sea peoples from the north (in the later thirteenth and early twelfth centuries BC), and, although the invaders were repelled, the country suffered fragmentation, followed by periods of Libyan, Nubian and Assyrian control. Necho II (610–575), however, asserted his independence, based on Sais and Memphis, and his son Psammetichus (Psamtik) I declared himself pharaoh of all Egypt. Psammetichus employed Greek (Ionian) soldiers, and he and his successors established them at a number of settlements (Greeks from the Laconian colony of Thera [Santorini] had already colonized Cyrene in c.632).

The most notable of these Egyptian settlements was Naucratis (Kom Gieif), converted, probably by Amasis (570–526), into an important commercial *emporion*, in which nine east Greek city-states cooperated to build a joint shrine, the Hellenion, while two others, Miletus and Samos, founded sanctuaries of their own. But the town's greatest claim to fame – shared, presumably, by other settlements in Egypt – was to have acquainted or reacquainted the early Greeks with the achievements of Egyptian sculpture and architecture, which they assimilated and dramatically improved upon.

After the Persians had destroyed and taken over the Egyptian kingdom (525), Naucratis continued to prosper; and once Alexander's conquest (followed by the foundation of Alexandria) had given place to the Ptolemies the town produced authors and local histories. When the last Ptolemy, Cleopatra VII, committed suicide (30 BC), Egypt became a Roman province, of which the production and export of cereals required direct imperial control.

C. Persia and Parthia

Throughout the early part of the first millennium BC, Medes, Persians and other Iranian peoples, speaking versions of an Indo-European language, gradually moved into the western half of the Iranian plateau and became the dominant powers in the region. The Median monarch Cyaxares (c.625–585), allied to Nabopolassar of Babylon, sacked the Assyrian capital Nineveh (612). But Cyrus II the Great (559–530) substituted Persian for Median suzerainty throughout the region, and laid the foundations for the Achaemenid Persian empire, the most formidable political organization that the near and middle east had ever known.

He conquered the kingdom of Lydia in Asia Minor (546) – including the Greek,

Ionian cities on its coast – and overran Babylonia as well (539), and Cambyses II (530–522) reduced Egypt to subjection (525). Darius I (522–486), by his invasion of Thrace and Scythia in c.513–512, brought the Persian empire into Europe and dangerously close to the Greek homeland. The subsequent revolt of the Ionian cities against Persia (499) was stamped out after a naval battle off Lade (490).

Then followed Darius I's invasion of Greece, repelled at Marathon (490), and the invasions of Xerxes I, defeated at Salamis (480) and Plataea (479), which the Athenians followed up by the victory of the River Eurymedon in southern Asia Minor (c.469/8). Under Artaxerxes I Macrocheir (465–424), however, the situation in the empire remained stable, and Persian funds were able to exploit the dissensions between Greek city-states. Athens failed in its attempts to detach Egypt and Cyprus from Persia, and in c.448 it concluded the (perhaps not wholly official) Peace of Callias whereby it abandoned the war with Persia, which acknowledged the loss of its cities in Asia Minor, now under Athenian rule.

When Greece became involved in the Peloponnesian War, the collapse of the Athenian expedition to Syracuse (413) gave Darius II Ochus (423–404) an opportunity to intervene decisively. Through the agency of his son Cyrus the younger's friendship with Lysander, the Persians made an alliance with Sparta, and their subsidies brought about the overthrow of Athens in 405–404. Subsequently, however, Artaxerxes II Mnemon (404–359/8) supported the Greek enemies of the Spartans, whose power was crippled by a naval defeat off Cnidus (394). This gave Persia the mastery of the Aegean, and in 386 the exhausted Greeks accepted the Peace of Antalcidas which recognized Persian rule over the Greek cities of Asia Minor and Cyprus.

Artaxerxes III Ochus (359/8–338/7) reconquered Egypt (341) – which had been free since earlier in the century – but found himself challenged by Philip II of Macedonia, whose generals began the invasion of Asia Minor which was subsequently resumed by Alexander III the Great. By 333 he had won most of the peninsula, and defeated Darius III at Issus (333). The occupation of Persia's western provinces, including Egypt, was completed by the following year. In 331 Darius III was defeated at Gaugamela (Gomal), and fled to Bactria, where he was murdered. The Achaemenid empire was at an end.

Its successors, after the death of Alexander, were the Greek Seleucid monarchs, but in 247 BC the Parthians (based originally in Khurasan, south of the Caspian Sea) broke away. The rebellion was led by Arsaces I, founder of the Arsacid dynasty, and subsequently Mithridates I (c.171–138) achieved an enormous geographical expansion, including the conquest of Media and Babylonia.

Setbacks at the hands of Tigranes I the Great of Armenia (c.87) were reversed, and under Orodes II (c.57–37) a resounding victory was won at Carrhae against the Roman triumvir Crassus, who lost his life. The Second Triumvirate witnessed further wars between the Romans and Parthians, with whom Augustus, however, came to an agreement in 20 BC, recognizing Roman overlordship of Armenia (which could not, however, be enforced). Vologeses I (AD 51/52–79/80) fought a long war against Nero's general Cnaeus Domitius Corbulo, terminating in a peace which confirmed Rome's suzerainty but recognized the Parthian claimant to the Armenian throne (63).

Trajan made an attempt to conquer the whole Parthian empire, which failed (117). In 161 Vologeses III invaded Asia Minor, but four years later temporarily lost his capital Ctesiphon (Tayfasun) to Marcus Aurelius's and Lucius Verus's general Avidius Cassius. Septimius Severus occupied Seleucia on the Tigris and Babylon and Ctesiphon (198).

These events weakened the Parthians, who in 223/6 were overthrown by the Persian prince Ardashir (Artaxerxes), founder of the Sassanian empire which faced the Romans with a greatly increased threat.

After a series of wars Shapur (Sapor) I (239–70) proved, next to Hannibal, the most dangerous enemy Rome ever had, devastating Mesopotamia, Armenia, Syria and Asia Minor. Shapur I claimed to have captured thirty-seven towns, and made the emperor Valerian his prisoner (260). Carus (282–3) regained Mesopotamia, temporarily occupying the Persian capital Ctesiphon, and then Galerius's victory over king Narses (293–302), after a setback, resulted in a treaty in Persia's disfavour (296).

But the struggles over Armenia and Mesopotamia continued, and Jovian's treaty of 363 conceded much to the Persians. Bahram V Gor (420–438), unsuccessful in a war against the eastern emperor Theodosius II (421–2), made a peace granting freedom of worship to the Christians. The Nestorian branch of their religion was favoured by Firuz (457/459–484), who fell in battle against nomad marauders.

The Principal Greek Shrines

Delphi was in the central Greek territory of Phocis. Its site is spectacular, located on the steep lower slopes of Mount Parnassus, beneath the two Shining Cliffs (Phaedriades) above the Gulf of Corinth. The place was believed by the Greeks to be the central point of the whole earth. Inhabited from the Late Bronze Age, it later derived its holiness and renown from Apollo, a god of Anatolian origin who, absorbing northern elements, had been imported by Dorian invaders or immigrants. The seventh-century *Homeric Hymn to Apollo* and other poems present Apollo both as formidable archer and peaceful god of the lyre: glamorous, lustful, both remorseless and merciful, the most powerful of all gods next to his father Zeus, whose will he pronounced through his oracles.

He declared these oracles through a priestess, the Pythia, who sat in his sanctuary beside the rim of a chasm, from which rose an intoxicating vapour. A male functionary transmitted to her the questions put by those who consulted the oracle, whereupon she produced not always coherent utterances, which attendant priests then reworded in hexameter verse.

Attaining Panhellenic renown, Apollo's oracles played a prominent part in the plans of overseas Greek colonizers, who told the oracle where they proposed to go, and sought its approval. In other matters, its rulings were often cryptic and ambiguous, founded on reliable information but leaving room for adaptability to later circumstances. Sometimes, nevertheless, they went wrong – for example in taking a pessimistic view of the Persian Wars. But usually the oracle showed good political sense. And it often adopted a popular moralizing tone, exemplified by the injunction 'Know Thyself' and 'Nothing too much' inscribed on Apollo's temple.

After a rapid rise during the eighth century, Delphi, and its cult of Apollo, became revered throughout the Greek world, receiving rich dedications from many leading city-states. Nor could it escape involvement in the politics of the surrounding Greek states. Originally under Phocian control, it later joined a regional Amphictyony ('dwellers around'), of which the capital was Anthela. A quarrel between Delphi and its harbour-town of Cirrha, over the right to levy tolls on pilgrims, led to the First Sacred War (*c.*595–583). Athens and Sicyon sided with the Delphians, and Cirrha was crushed. It was probably at this juncture that the Amphictyonic Council moved its headquarters from Anthela to the more central location of Delphi.

Soon afterwards (582/1?), an ancient Delphic festival in honour of Apollo was reorganized in the form of the Pythian Games, held every four years. Musical competitions were preeminent (as before), but athletic and equestrian contests modelled on those of Olympia were added. The prizes were garlands of bay-leaves from the valley of Tempe. The Amphictyony proclaimed and endeavoured to enforce a truce between warring city-states for the duration of the festival.

These Pythian Games, which ranked second only to their Olympian counter-parts in Panhellenic importance, brought many rich gifts into Delphi, where Greek city-states, in the sixth century, established Treasuries to house them. After the temple of Apollo had been destroyed by fire in 548, a new shrine was erected, with the aid of funds provided from all over the Greek world, and even by foreigners beyond its frontiers.

Olympia was in the territory of Pisa (Pisatis), bordering upon Elis in the western Peloponnese. It lay seven miles from the Ionian Sea, at the foot of the low hills of Cronus, the father of Zeus, where the River Alpheus joins the Cladeus before they move into the coastal plain. After Bronze Age habitation, the place became, once the Dorians had arrived, the scene of an athletic festival founded, according to rival mythologies, by Heracles, or Pelops who gave the Peloponnese its name.

In continuity with earlier cults at the place, the Dorians introduced the worship of Olympian Zeus, Zeus of Mount Olympus, within his Altis precinct. Local athletic competitions were held before 900, and the Games, in their developed form, seem to have started in the eighth century, though the traditional date, 776, is fictitious. At first, construction on the site was negligible; even the altar of Zeus was merely an ever-renewed mound of ashes heaped up after sacrifices. The earliest architectural remains are those of a rebuilt temple of Hera of c.600, perhaps the most ancient monumental shrine on the Greek mainland, containing statues of Zeus and Hera herself.

After various struggles, the Games passed in c.572 under the control of Elis, and were recognized on a Panhellenic basis, reflected, as at Delphi, in Treasuries built by various cities to house their gifts, which exemplified the stimulus offered by the Olympic Games to sculptural and other artistic achievement. The Games were held in every fourth year. Although exceptionally giving no place to music and poetry, they excelled the other three major festivals (Pythian, Isthmian and Nemean) in prestige. Three heralds dispatched from Elis (like the envoys of the Delphic Amphictyony) declared a Sacred Truce for the duration of the festivals, and no war between Greek city-states ever prevented them from being held. In their eventual form the Olympic events continued for five days. For women, additional running races, outside the main schedule, were eventually introduced, in honour of Hera.

Despite discomfort, 40,000 or 50,000 people, from all over the Greek world, attended the Games. This did something to counterbalance the separatist frag-mentation of the Greek city-states. However, the entries were not made, as now, by states, but by individuals (who had to be free-born Greeks). The only prizes were wreaths woven from a sacred olive tree in the precinct of Zeus. Nevertheless, an Olympic winner received rich rewards, after he went back to his own city, and was honoured for the rest of his life. Associations of these contests with an amateur

233

spirit are wishful thinking, since a high degree of professionalism inevitably arose: *athlon* meant not play, but struggle, suffering and pain.

It was Delos, infertile, and only about three miles long and a mile and a half wide, which gave the Aegean archipelago its name, the Cyclades, because the other islands seemed to form a circle (*kuklos*) round holy Delos. Before 1000 BC Ionian colonists had arrived from the Greek mainland, inheriting a sacred grotto on Mount Cynthus from earlier inhabitants, and by the time of the *Odyssey* and the *Hymn to Apollo* Delos was already venerated as the birthplace of Apollo and Artemis.

The *Hymn* also tells how Delos became the seat of a festival to which the Ionian states, including Athens, sent an annual deputation to celebrate the birthday of Apollo, including not only men, but their wives and children too. The original date of the sanctuary of Apollo is uncertain, but as time went on it came to excel all other sacred places in the Greek world in fine sculpture and other splendour with the aim of exalting the Ionians, for whom Delos served as the centre of an Amphictyony, or religious league. During the sixth century, however, the island passed under the successive control of Lygdamis of Naxos (*d.c.*524), Pisistratus of Athens and Polycrates of Samos. Early in the fifth century, the island was chosen as the headquarters of the Delian League under Athenian direction.

Another famous sanctuary was Apollo's oracular shrine at Didyma, ten miles from Miletus in Ionia (which endeavoured to influence it).

A temple of sixth-century date – the second to be erected on the site – was burnt down by the Persian king Darius I after the collapse of the Ionian Revolt (494), and in 480 Xerxes I removed the priestly clan of the Branchidae to central Asia. A huge third temple was begun by Seleucus I Nicator in *c.*300, and its construction continued, at intervals, for 600 years. The precinct was approached by a Sacred Way from Ephesus, which was lined by statues of seated figures.

In *c.*675 the Athenians completed their control of Attica by reducing Eleusis to subjection. This gave them control of the local Mysteries (initiation rites) in honour of Demeter and her daughter Kore (Persephone), who had been seized by Hades (Pluto), the god of the underworld. The rites acted out the rape of Persephone and her mother's arrival at Eleusis to search for her; and these Mysteries were able to promise their devotees, as they passed through successive stages of initiation, unique benefits in the afterlife, which offered an irresistible appeal. Before long the Athenians had elevated the widely attended cult to Panhellenic status, which reflected glory upon their own city and state. Pisistratus rebuilt the Telesterion (Hall of Initiation) on a magnificent scale.

Corinth's Neighbours: Megara and Sicyon

A. Megara

Megara lay in the narrow but productive White Plain, the lowland portion of the Megarid which formed the northern part of the Isthmus of Corinth. Its total territory did not exceed 180 square miles, but it possessed two harbours, Pegae to the west on the Gulf of Corinth, and Nisaea to the east on the Saronic Gulf. The Dorian immigrants to Megara, made their city (established in c.750) into one of the leading military states of early Greece.

Impatient, however, with the smallness of their lands, the Megarians fulfilled a preeminent, pioneer role in Greek colonization away from the mainland. In Sicily they colonized Megara Hyblaea, and then, suffering from Corinthian encroachments at home, they turned east to the Thracian Bosphorus, a fishing region and the strategical channel through which Black Sea grain had to pass on its way to Greece. There they established Calchedon (Kadıköy) on the Asiatic shore of the Bosphorus (c.685), and Byzantium (later Constantinople and Istanbul) on a fine site beside the European shore (668/657).

Soon afterwards, however, quarrels among Megara's aristocratic leaders offered an opening for one of the dictatorial 'tyrants' who became so characteristic of its region. He was Theagenes (c.640–620?), who, tradition recounted, 'slaughtered the cattle of the rich', to make himself popular. Moreover, to offset losses of territory to Corinth, he seized the island of Salamis from Aegina. Later, however, he was expelled by oligarchs – men whose power was based on making and exporting woollen goods. Yet they, too, in their turn, were forced to give way to a more broadly based administration, displaying democratic, radical tendencies. These convulsive changes were a classic, disastrous early example of *stasis*, internal warfare between quarrelling classes and groups.

Light is thrown upon this epoch of civic strife by graceful verses attributed to Theognis of Megara. He emerges as an extreme conservative, who angrily backs the claims of aristocratic lineage and breeding, and in bold vivid metaphors deplores the upstart lower orders – but equally dislikes the new rich and the dubious values of the colonial world which gave them their wealth. For the worst of all sins, he feels, is *hubris*, in the form of arrogant greed for the possessions of others. Theognis also provides the largest offering of homosexual, pederastic poetry before the Hellenistic age; and he writes disagreeably about women, although conceding that the possession of a good wife is a source of satisfaction. There is

235

also reason to suppose that comic drama, in an embryonic form, existed at Megara and Megara Hyblaea before it took root at Athens.

During the sixth century, however, Megara suffered political setbacks. In 569/568 it lost its eastern port Nisaea to Athens. Then, some decades later, a long drawn-out struggle with the Athenians over the island of Salamis again resulted in defeat, after an unfavourable Spartan arbitration. In compensation for the first of these blows, the Megarians had extended their colonization, by establishing a settlement at Heraclea Pontica (Ereğli) in Bithynia, on the southern coast of the Black Sea (c.560/558).

At home, however, Megara no longer ranked as one of the principal powers in Greece, and in the later years of the century it became a member of the Peloponnesian League, under Spartan domination.

B. Sicyon

Sicyon, 'town of the cucumbers', one of the vegetables which flourished on its well-watered territory, stood upon a tongue of land beneath two plateaux (one of which was its acropolis), about eleven miles west of Corinth, near the point where the two deep gorges of the Rivers Asopus and Helisson (Lechova) met and merged. After a Mycenaean past the place was refounded as a dependency of Dorian Argos, from which, however, it broke away. In addition to the usual three Dorian tribes, it possessed a pre-Dorian serf class, resembling the Spartan Helots, and known as Club-Carriers or Weavers of Sheepskin Cloaks.

The local royal house was replaced, at some stage, by an aristocracy, and in c.655 this in turn was superseded by a dictatorial 'tyranny', which thereafter lasted for a century – a longer duration than any other similar régime in the area. The founder of this dynasty, Orthagoras, ruled mildly and by almost constitutional, non-tyrannical methods. Then his grand-nephew Cleisthenes (c.600–570), gaining influence both at Delphi and Olympia, invited suitors from all parts of the Greek world to compete for the hand of his daughter Agariste, who was awarded to Megacles of Athens (c.576); their son was the Athenian statesman Cleisthenes. The aim of Cleisthenes of Sicyon, throughout, was to set himself up against Argos. And with the same intention he transferred the principal religious entertainment of his city, the performance of 'tragic choruses', from the cult of the Argive hero Adrastus to the worship of Dionysus (thus leading the way to Athenian tragedy). At this time, too (c.580/577?), the Sicyonians seem to have pioneered or developed the art of sculpture, under Dipoenus and Scyllis, the sons or pupils of the Cretan Daedalus.

Fifteen years after Cleisthenes' death, however, his dynasty came to an end, like others elsewhere during the preceding decades. The oligarchic Sicyonian régime that followed could not achieve much in the political field, owing to the proximity of Corinth and its Acrocorinthian citadel. Sicyon at this period, however, excelled in bronzework, culminating in the masterpieces of Canachus (before 500). Moreover, fragmentary wooden panels (small easel pictures) of c.530, found in a cave at Pitsa nearby, recall the Greek tradition, recorded by Pliny the elder, that the 'discovery' of painting should be ascribed to Corinth or Sicyon, and that line-drawing was first undertaken by artists from one or the other of these states.[1] The

Pitsa panels do not solve this ambiguity, since although found on the territory of Sicyon they were dedicated to the nymphs by a Corinthian, and show an inscription in the Corinthian alphabet.

APPENDIX V

Solon and Cleisthenes of Athens

Solon, in the later 590s BC, annulled all debts for which land or personal freedom were the security, and abolished debt-bondage – borrowing on the security of the person. Those who had been sold into slavery were redeemed, and tenants' interest payments to their masters were pegged at a tolerable level. Solon had saved wealthy creditors from any wholesale, egalitarian distribution of land. Yet their rapacity had been curbed, and they must have denounced his legislation as revolutionary – on a long term view, not unjustly, since the measures led to the creation of a free peasantry which had a lot to say in Athens's future democratic system.

Solon also established the right of any citizen to initiate legal proceedings. And he made families go to law when one of their members had been murdered, rather than killing the murderers themselves. Yet, once again his domestic legislation was not solely concerned to break up the old order, because the purpose of his rules concerning the rights of women, recognizing their role as transmitters of property and the social order, were designed to ensure the survival of families that would otherwise have been extinguished.

Yet reform was in his mind, for his numerous laws, virtually amounting to a comprehensive codification, included a provision that every citizen should teach his sons how to write. And society was likewise nudged in the direction of change by an institution known as the Heliaea – comprising the members of the Assembly, or some of them – which listened to appeals from individuals against decisions and verdicts of state officials.

A merchant himself(?), Solon promoted an unusually active economic policy. He stimulated the production of olive oil, and encouraged trade and manufacture by fostering the training of sons in their fathers' skills. With the same purpose, too, he encouraged metics (*metoikoi*), resident aliens, whose commercial abilities could fulfil a useful role in the exportation programme which played a part in Solon's plans for industrial growth.

Solon also, perhaps in a second phase of activity, altered the structure of the Attic society by dividing the citizens into four new census classes. Although this classification was still conservative, requiring that everyone should know his place, it completed the setting up of wealth (timocracy) instead of birth as the framework of the community, and thus opened up a breach in the supremacy of the aristocratic Eupatrids. Moreover, although only the topmost class was eligible, at first, for the archonship and life membership of the Areopagus, even the fourth class, in due course, was enabled to attend the Assembly and Heliaea, and the third class was entitled, together with the two above it, to serve in an altogether new Council, the Boule. The ancients were probably right to credit Solon with the creation of this body, whose function was to serve as a partner to the Areopagus in keeping the city steady. Its four hundred members may have been elected by the Assembly, which Solon, although (like everyone else) not yet thinking in terms of popular sovereignty, recognized as a political force.[2]

Solon enjoyed his comforts, knew the value of sons and foreign guest-friends, horses and hunting dogs, and admired an attractive woman or boy. Before he died at the age of eighty, he declared that what satisfied him most was his refusal to become the dictator of Athens, although he had been pressed to accept such an office.[3] He wanted the people to be contented, but they must find out how to achieve this by themselves.

The ten new Athenian tribes of Cleisthenes (c.506–500) were deliberately disconnected from the old tribal past, and geographically scattered. The 140 demes (demoi) into which they were divided became the basic political, social and religious subdivisions of society; and every Athenian citizen was given a chance to understand, without dominance by a patron, how things were being run.

This new widening of opportunity was given expression by Cleisthenes's new Council of Five Hundred, which was more meaningful, in terms of popular self-expression, than the Four Hundred it supplanted. These Five Hundred comprised fifty men (over thirty years of age) from each of the ten new tribes, serving for a year, and later, after an interval, eligible for a second year of council membership. They were appointed by lot, and so were members of the Heliaea – a system that gave everyone an equal chance, although ignoring merit: which, however, crept in because the lot was taken from names chosen by a vote of the demes (prokrisis). In due course, too, and perhaps from the outset, the business of Cleisthenes's Council was prepared by committees of fifty of its members (prytaneis), each serving for one-tenth of the year.

Furthermore, the Assembly now enjoyed considerable powers which it had never possessed before. Inviting political oratory before wide, interested and critical audiences, it could amend or reject notions put before it by the Council, and it exercised essential functions, including the responsibility for declarations of war. Nevertheless, it was the Council that determined what business should be laid before the Assembly, just as it was the Council's task to see that the Assembly's decrees were carried out. And a second limitation of the Assembly's powers was the provision (some time during these years) that it should elect a board of ten generals (strategoi), one from each tribe, to command Athens' military forces. This meant that the polemarch (war archon) lost much of his importance, and so did the other archons, too, when under Cleisthenes, or a little later, they came to be appointed by lot. Cleisthenes may also have provided for the curious institution of ostracism, though it was not put into effect until 487. This was a method of exiling politicians who had become unpopular. Any Athenian who wished such a person out of the way wrote the man's name on a fragment of pottery (ostrakon), and if the total number of votes exceeded 6,000 the politician whose name headed the list was banished for ten years.

239

As Aristotle observed, Cleisthenes was evidently 'giving the people a share in public affairs'.[4] Though he can scarcely have foreseen how Athenian democracy would grow, his *isonomia*, equality under the law, replacing the old aristocratic, hierarchical orderliness (*eunomia*), was the most democratic form of government that human ingenuity had so far invented, giving the citizens of Athens a glimpse of what would be their eventual powers.

APPENDIX VI

Jews and Christians

The massive Diaspora (Dispersion) of the Jews had already been taking place from at least the eighth century BC. In Israel (Palestine) itself, although the Hebrew Torah (the Pentateuch, or first five books of the Old Testament) remained paramount, Greek influences were apparent at least by 600, and fourth-century silver coins from the Persian province of 'Yehud' imitate Greek issues for trading with the Greeks.[5]

But it was not until after Alexander the Great took the country from the Persians in 332 that it felt, for the first time, the direct impact of the Greek world and way of life, conflicting with the monotheistic beliefs, of the Hebrew population, in which the Sadducees and Pharisees were now the dominant groups. The Ptolemies of Egypt, who annexed Judaea after Alexander's death, saw it as a temple state (of which there were examples in other lands as well), and in consequence recognized the High Priests of the country as its rulers, under Ptolemaic suzerainty.

In 200 however, after a victory at Panion (Banyas), the Seleucid monarch Antiochus III the Great annexed Judaea from Egypt. His successor Antiochus IV Epiphanes, in exchange for larger tribute than usual, gave the High Priesthood to Jason (Joshua), who made Jerusalem into a city of the Greek type (175–172). But the arrangement did not last, and in 167 Antiochus IV rededicated the Temple of the Hebrew God Yahweh to Olympian Zeus. This prompted a Jewish insurrection led by Judas Maccabaeus of the House of Hasmon – with the support of the puritanical, xenophobe group of the Hasidim – and completed by his brother Simon (142). Then, for the next eighty years, the Jews, under the Hasmonaean house, were usually independent, adopting the institution of monarchy and increasing their military strength.

This régime reached its climax under Herod I the Great (37–4 BC), a client-king dependent on Augustus. From AD 6 onwards Judaea was annexed as a Roman province. Philo Judaeus is a mine of information about the centre of the Jewish Diaspora (Dispersion) at Alexandria, and suggests the variations of doctrine and attitude that existed in different Jewish communities and their subdivisions.

Tactless inefficiency, however – reaching, in Judaea, depths unusual among the Romans, and exacerbated by total religious incompatibility and incomprehension between the two races – brought about the First Jewish Revolt (First Roman War) in AD 66–73. It was crushed by Vespasian and his son Titus, who in 70 destroyed Jerusalem. Thenceforward, synagogues superseded the Temple as the focuses of Jewish religion, and rabbis increasingly replaced priests as leaders Jamnia

241

(Yavneh) became the centre of rabbinic learning and the seat of the Jewish council (Sanhedrin), which was authorized by the Romans. In AD 115–117 a widespread revolt of the far-flung Jewish Diaspora throughout the near and middle east radically upset Trajan's plans for eastern conquests. In Judaea itself, the Second Jewish Revolt (Second Roman War, 132–5), led by Simeon Bar Kosiba (Bar Kochba), broke out because Hadrian had decreed the refoundation of Jerusalem as a Roman colony, under the name of Aelia Capitolina. This Second Revolt, like the First, ended in failure, accompanied by huge loss of life and property.

The principal centre of Jewish habitation in the country was henceforward Galilee, to which the Jamnia Academy moved. The Romans authorized a reconstituted Jewish Council of which the most notable chairman (patriarch) was Judah I ha-Nasi (135–219), regarded as the principal editor of the Mishnah. Meanwhile in Babylonia, which passed from Parthian to Persian (Sassanian) rule, the Jewish communities enjoyed an efflorescence, under directors (*geonim*) of centres of learning who presided over the creation of the Babylonian Talmud.

Within the Roman world, however, the conversion of Constantine I the Great (306–337) to Christianity initiated a period of difficulties for the Jews in the Roman and then the Byzantine empire.

After Judaea became a Roman province in AD 6, Galilee and Peraea (across the River Jordan) continued to constitute the princedom of Herod Antipas (4 BC– AD 6), who like his father Herod the Great ruled as a client of Rome. Upon the desert fringes of this dominion, in c.AD 28–29, John the Baptist, hailed as the successor of the prophets Elijah and Elisha, proclaimed to his fellow-Jews the imminence of the Kingdom of Yahweh, following the apocalyptic tradition that awaited the Day of the Lord. John insisted on repentance, a change of heart, after which, he maintained, all Jews would be forgiven their sins. But Herod Antipas saw his emphasis upon an imminent change of régime as treasonable, and put him to death.

Jesus, who probably came not from Bethlehem but from Nazareth in Galilee, was baptized by John, but amended his preaching: the Kingdom of God was not merely imminent, he declared, but had already begun to arrive, by his own Godsent agency, which also empowered him to forgive sins, himself, on his own account. Jesus's adherents saw him as a member of the House of David, born of a virgin, and as the heir to the prophetic succession – and the Son of God. The Jews, however, believed that this last claim was a blasphemy against Yahweh's uniqueness, and that the same applied to his claim to forgive sins – which they regarded as the prerogative of Yahweh alone. And his injunction to love your enemy as yourself, they believed, was mistaken, because it could not be done.

For such reasons, Jesus's mission to the Galilean Jews encountered opposition, and in consequence he moved gradually to Jerusalem (c.AD 30 or 33). There, as a result of collaboration between the Roman governor Pontius Pilatus (Pilate) and the Jewish High Priest Caiaphas and the council of his people (the Sanhedrin), he was crucified. Three days later, his followers declared that they had witnessed his bodily resurrection and ascent to heaven, as Enoch, Moses and Elijah were also believed to have ascended.

The conversion of this story into a posthumous triumph was the work of Saul –

a Greek-speaking Jew of the Dispersion, belonging to a Pharisee family of Tarsus in Cilicia (south-eastern Asia Minor), which had obtained Roman citizenship, whereupon his name was changed to Paul. As his *Epistles*, our earliest Christian documents, reveal, he became converted to Christianity because he could no longer accept the Jewish Torah as the director of life, declaring that its unrealistic perfectionist legalism had failed to rescue the Hebrews from their miseries. Paul came to feel that the history of the world had been set on an entirely new and revolutionary course by Jesus, the second Adam, who, cancelling and obliterating the original sin of the first, redeemed the whole of humankind through his crucifixion and resurrection, beside which events all traditional wisdom, he asserted, was insignificant and useless.

Yet the Jews of Asia Minor mostly rejected Paul, because they regarded his insistence upon Jesus's divinity as a blasphemous betrayal of monotheism. So he turned to the Gentiles, non-Jews, instead. But it was only after the First Jewish Revolt had discredited the Jews in Roman eyes that Christianity truly took root among the Gentiles: and it was in their hands that the future of the faith in later centuries was to remain.

Soon after the revolt, it was they who began to produce the Four Gospels – preaching sharp dissociation from the Jews, and displaying the Jewish Christians also (exemplified by Jesus's apostles) in a critical light. By the second century AD, belief in Jesus had been found to be incompatible with Judaism, and Christianity went its own way. Amid sectarian divisions, a decisive factor was the enrolment of powerful intellects in its cause: those of the Latin writer Tertullian (died *c*.220), who wished to divorce the Church from classical culture, and the Greek theologians Saint Clement (*c*.150–211/216) and Origen (*c*.185/186–254/5), both of Alexandria, who instead, saw their faith as the answer to the quest of the philosophers.

The Roman government, whose earlier balanced attitude is exemplified by Trajan's letters to his governor of Bithynia, Pliny the younger (*c*.110–112), gradually formed the impression that this alternative loyalty was a seditious danger, especially in times of national emergency, and the third-century persecutions were the result. They reached their climax under Diocletian (284–305), whose hostile attitude, however, was reversed shortly afterwards when Constantine I the Great (306–337) identified himself with the Christian movement. The extent to which Christianity later shared responsibility for the fall of the western Roman empire has been discussed elsewhere (Chapter 11, section 2).

List of Roman Emperors

Augustus	31 BC–AD 14
Tiberius	AD 14–37
Gaius (Caligula)	37–41
Claudius	41–54
Nero	54–68
Galba	68–69
Otho	69
Vitellius	69
Vespasian	69–79
Titus	79–81
Domitian	81–96
Nerva	96–98
Trajan	98–117
Hadrian	117–138
Antoninus Pius	138–161
⌠ Marcus Aurelius	161–180
⌡ Lucius Verus	161–169
Commodus	180–192
Pertinax	193
Didius Julianus	193
Septimius Severus	193–211
⌠ Caracalla	211–217
⌡ Geta	211–212
Macrinus	217–218
Elagabalus	218–222
Severus Alexander	222–235
Maximinus I	235–238
⌠ Gordianus I Africanus	238
⌡ Gordianus II Africanus	238
⌠ Balbinus	238
⌡ Pupienus	238
Gordianus III	238–244
Philip I	244–249
Trajanus Decius	249–251
Trebonianus Gallus	251–253
Aemilian	253
⌠ Valerian	253–260
⌡ Gallienus	253–268
Claudius II Gothicus	268–270

Quintillus	270
Aurelian	270–275
Tacitus	275–276
Florian	276
Probus	276–282
Carus	282–283
⌠ Carinus	283–285
⌡ Numerian	283–284
⌠ Diocletian	284–305
⌡ Maximian	286–305
⌠ Constantius I Chlorus	305–306
⌡ Galerius	305–311
⌠ Constantine I the Great	306–337
⌡ Licinius	308–324
⌠ Constantine II	337–340
⌡ Constantius II	337–361
⌡ Constans	337–350
Julian the Apostate	361–363
Jovian	363–364
⌠ Valentinian I (W.)	364–375
⌡ Valens (E.)	364–378
⌠ Gratian (W.)	367–383
⌡ Valentinian II (W.)	375–392
⌡ Theodosius I the Great (E.)	379–395
⌠ Arcadius (E.)	395–408
⌡ Honorius (W.)	395–423
⌠ Theodosius II (E.)	408–450
⌡ Johannes (W.)	423–425
⌡ Valentinian III (W.)	425–455
Marcian (E.)	450–457
Petronius Maximus (W.)	455
Avitus (W.)	455–456
Leo I (E.)	457–474
Majorian (W.)	457–461
Libius Severus (W.)	461–465
Anthemius (W.)	467–472
Olybrius (W.)	472
Glycerius (W.)	473–474
Julius Nepos (W.)	474–480
Zeno (E.)	474–491
Romulus Augustulus (W.)	475–476

References

Part I: The Rise of the Greeks

1 Aristotle, *Politics*, II, 9, 7, 1285b.
2 Pseudo-Plato, *Epinomis*, 987d.
3 Plato, *Laws*, 626a.
4 Herodotus, v, 97.
5 Homer, *Iliad*, II, 570.
6 Thucydides, I, 13, 2.
7 *Ibid*, I, 10, 2.
8 *Homeric Hymns*, III, 172.
9 Asius, fragment 13.
10 Theophrastus in Simplicius, *On Aristotle's Physics*, 149, 32.
11 Heraclitus, fragment 12 (Plato, *Cratylus*, 402a).
12 Homer, *Iliad*, XXIII, 171f.
13 M.M. Austin and P. Vidal-Nacquet, *Economic and Social History of Ancient Greece*, 1977, pp.221f.
14 Thucydides, VI, 2, 6.
15 Strabo, IV, 1, 5, 179.

Part II: The Classical Greeks

1 Thucydides, II, 65.
2 B.D. Meritt, H.T. Wade-Gery, M.F. McGregor, *The Athenian Tribute-Lists*; Vols I (1939), II (1949), III (1950), IV (1953).
3 Thucydides, II, 41.
4 Herodotus, I, preface.
5 *Ibid*, VII, 152.
6 Thucydides, I, 1.
7 *Ibid*, I, 22.
8 *Ibid*.
9 Pausanias, IX, 13, 3.
10 Theopompus, fragment 27 (F. Jacoby, *Fragmente der Griechischen Historiker*, p.541, no.115).
11 Athenaeus, VIII, 347e.
12 Sophocles, *Oedipus at Colonus*, 913f.

13 Aristotle, *Poetics*, 13, 1453a.
14 Plato, *Protagoras*, 317b.
15 Diogenes Laertius in H. Diels and W. Kranz, *Die Fragmente der Vorsokratiker*, II, 6th ed., 1952, 80B4, 80A1 (Plato, *Theatetus*, 152, 161).
16 Aristotle, *Poetics*, 9, 1452a.
17 Cicero, *Academica*, II, 119.
18 Aristotle, *Poetics*, 2, 1448a.
19 Pausanias, v, 17.
20 Vitruvius, VII, preface 12.
21 Pliny the elder, *Natural History*, XXXVI, 31.
22 Vitruvius, II, 8, 11.
23 Isocrates, *Panegyricus*, 50.
24 Plato, *Laws*, I, 626a.

Part III: The Hellenistic Greeks

1 Pliny the elder, *Natural History*, XXXIV, 19.65.
2 Xenocrates, fragment 4 Heinze.
3 Theocritus, VII, 126.

Part IV: Early Rome and the Republic

1 Herodotus, I, 94.
2 M. Pallottino, *Testimonia Linguae Etruscae*, 2nd ed., 1968, p.109, no.874.
3 Polybius, VI, 11–18.
4 *Ibid*, I, 63.
5 Cato the elder, *On Farming*, II, 7.
6 M.H. Crawford, *Roman Republican Coinage*, I, 1974, pp.489f., nos.6ff.

Part V: Rome under the Emperors

1 Augustus, *Acts of the Divine Augustus* (*Res Gestae*), 34.

2 *Ibid.*, 19–21 (tr. D. Earl).
3 Suetonius, *Augustus*, 29.
4 Strabo, *Geography*, v, 3, 8.
5 Tacitus, *Annals*, iv, 34.
6 C.M. Bowra, *From Virgil to Milton*, 1967 (1945), p.34.
7 Alfred Tennyson, *The Princess*, ii, 355.
8 Ovid, *Tristia*, ii, 207.
9 S. Lauffer, *Diokletians Preisedikt*, 1970 (many fragments).
10 Saint Augustine, *City of God*, xiv, 28; etc.
11 Horace, *Epistles*, ii, 1, 156.
12 Virgil, *Aeneid*, vi, 847–855.

13 M. Grant, *The Fall of the Roman Empire*, 2nd ed. (1990), p.314.
14 Tacitus, *Histories*, iv, 74 (tr. K. Wellesley).

Appendices

1 Pliny the elder, *Natural History*, xxxv, 15.
2 Solon, fragment 5.
3 *Ibid*, fragments 32, 33.
4 Aristotle, *Constitution of Athens*, 20, 1.
5 Y. Meshorer, *Jewish Coins of the Second Temple Period*, 1967, p.116, nos.1–3.

Notes

References to the author's earlier books are abbreviated as follows: *AC*:
From Alexander to Cleopatra, 1982 (The Hellenistic Greeks, 1990);
AM: The Ancient Mediterranean, 1988 (1969); *Caes*: Julius Caesar,
1969; *CG*: The Classical Greeks, 1989; *Cl*: Cleopatra, 1972; *CR*: The
Climax of Rome, 1968; *Etr*: The Etruscans, 1980; *FRE*: Fall of the
Roman Empire, 1990 (1976); *GAW*: Guide to the Ancient World,
1986; *GLA*: Greek and Latin Authors 800 BC–AD 1000, 1980; *HAI*:
History of Ancient Israel, 1984; HR: History of Rome, 1980; *J*: Jesus,
1977; *MGR*: Myths of the Greeks and Romans, 1989 (1962); *RE*: The
Roman Emperors, 1985; *RG*: The Rise of the Greeks, 1987; *RIM*:
Roman Imperial Money, 1954; *SP*: Saint Paul, 1976; *VP*: The Visible
Past: Greek and Roman History from Archaeology 1960–1990, 1990.

Introduction

'Updating'. It is particularly useful to know what, having been tried before, did
not work (R.M. Robbins, *Antiquaries' Journal*, 1989, p.7).
'Classical' originally meant 'first class', *RG*, p.xii, and the term was then applied
generally to the civilization of Greece and Rome. (For its later narrowing to
Greece between its archaic and Hellenistic periods, *see CG*, p.xiii).
Historical method. Despite disagreements on the subject among historians, I
have paid a good deal of attention to individuals, and particularly to those who
shaped and changed the course of history. The observation of Friedrich Engels
that, if Napoleon had not come, another man would have taken his place, seems
to me misguided and inadequate.

The Greeks

PART I: THE RISE OF THE GREEKS

Chapter 1: The Early Greeks and the Near East

Minoans and Mycenaeans. *AM*, pp.87ff., 101ff. For the Mycenaeans' employment of 'Linear B' syllabic script *see RG*, p.331.
Dorians. *RG*, pp.2ff., p.332, notes 5–8.

Emigrations to western Asia Minor. From north to south: Aeolians, Ionians (supposedly led by Athens), Dorians.

Pottery. Protogeometric was preceded by Sub-Mycenaean, *op.cit.* p.3.

Urbanization. By various types of *synoikismos* (amalgamation), ibid.

Epic poems were written in hexameters (six feet of dactyls, long-short-short, and spondees, long-long). The elegiac metre consisted of couplets of hexameters and pentameters (five feet). Lyric metres assumed a number of different forms. *Nonepic poems* referred to in *Iliad* and *Odyssey*: *op.cit.* p.335, note 3.

'Daedalic' style. Named not after the mythical inventor Daedalus but after a seventh-century BC Cretan sculptor of the same name.

Kouroi and Korai. The 'archaic smile' was intended to make the faces look more alive. *See* J. Boardman, *Greek Sculpture: The Archaic Period*, 1978, p.66.

Aristocratic régimes. Popular assemblies existed at an early date, but left all power in the hands of the nobles.

Overpopulation. One cause was the absence of primogeniture, so that properties were divided and allotments became too small and poor.

Coinage. Invented by the Lydians, its primary initial purpose was to facilitate payments by and into governmental treasuries.

Doric and Ionic Orders. *RG*, pp.23f.

Heraclitus's Opposites. Rejected by Parmenides, Chapter 5, section 3.

Chapter 2: Greece

Lefkandi finds. Archaeological Museum, Chalcis.

Chalcidians. In Sicily. Naxos (*c*.734), Leontini (Carlentini), Catana (Catania). In south Italy: Rhegium (Reggio di Calabria).

Origins of Athens. Mythologists pronounced that Ion had settled in Athens and divided the people into its four tribes (named after his sons): the Aigikoreis, Geleontes and Argadeis. The city was described as the 'eldest land of Ionia'.

Dipylon Vase (crater). National Museum, Athens.

Unification of Attica. The sanctuary of Eleusis (Appendix III) was taken over in *c*.675 BC.

Last king of Athens. Believed to have been Acastus.

First archon. Originally appointed for life, later for ten years, and then for one year (*c*.682?). A separate king-archon was retained for religious functions, and, later, the three principal officials (first archon, king-archon, polemarch) were supplemented by six more, the *thesmothetai*, layers down of the law.

Dracon's laws seemed severe to later generations, but were progressive in respect of homicide, since he introduced the concept of intention, distinguishing between murder and accidental (or justifiable) manslaughter.

Solon cancelled the debts of a class of peasants known as the *hektemoroi*, 'sixth-part men', i.e. who handed over to their creditor a sixth part (more probably than five-sixths) of what they earned, an intermediate category between free and slaves, restoring their lands and removing the markers (*horoi*) which creditors had planted on them as a sign of ownership.

Hellespont. *See also* Chapter 3, section 2.

Sigeum. *See GAW*, pp.589f.

Moschophorus (calf-bearer) statue, Acropolis Museum, Athens.

François vase. Museo Archeologico, Florence.

Athenian black-figure painters. Eg Amasis painter (active *c.*561–514) and Exekias.

Athenian factions after Solon. Plainsmen (*pedieis*), old land-owning anti-reformist aristocrats; Coast (*paralia*), middle-class and new-rich business men, led by Alcmaeonid clan but including pro-reformist traders; Hillsmen (*diakria*), or men beyond the Hills (*hyperakria*) mostly shepherds and labourers, who wished that Solon's reforms had gone further.

Pisistratus. He improved law and order by the creation of thirty circuit judges, who superseded the jurisdiction of local aristocracies.

Simonides. *GLA*, pp.393ff.

Red-figure 'pioneers'. Euphronius, Euthymides, Cleophrades painter.

Athenian settlers at Chalcis. Cleruchs, ie holders of *kleroi*, allotments.

Boeotia. The longstanding rival of Thebes was Orchomenus, the chief city of the Cephisus valley, which the Thebans eventually eclipsed.

Corinth's ports. Cenchreae (Saronic Gulf), Lechaeum (Gulf of Corinth). An archaic temple of Poseidon has been found on a plateau overlooking the two seas.

Corinth's Adriatic colonies. Ambracia (Arta), Anactorium (colonized with Corcyra), Leucas (Lefkas).

Dorian tribes. The Hylleis, Dymanes and Pamphyli.

Corinthian ships. Penteconters, which appear on Corinthian vases before 700, were strengthened at the prow by a pointed ram (*embolos*) sheathed in bronze, and accommodated twenty-four rowers, in two lines (with two steering oars at the stern). The twenty-four oarsmen of the biremes (partly based on Assyrian models) sat in two rows of benches, one above the other. Triremes: 27 oarsmen at 2 levels, 31 at top level; three-pronged ram; deck for marines (14 spearsmen and 4 archers).

Seven Sages. Cleobulus the tyrant of Lindus in Rhodes (*c.*580 BC), Solon of Athens, Chilon of Sparta, Thales of Miletus, Pittacus of Mytilene (Lesbos), Bias of Priene (Turunçlar) – its leading man in the mid-sixth century BC – and Periander of Corinth – whose name, however, in the fourth century BC, tyrant-haters struck out in favour of the traditional wise man Myson.

Corinthian architecture. Corcyra, too, had a temple of Artemis of Corinthian type.

Prehistoric Sparta. Embodied in the Homeric figure of Menelaus.

Cleomenes I, opposed by King Demaratus, came to a violent end at Sparta 490.

Chapter 3: East and West

Ten Ionian mainland states. From south to north: Miletus (Yeniköy), Myus (near Avşar), Priene (Turunçlar), Ephesus (Selçuk), Colophon (Değirmendere), Lebedus (Kısık, Xingi), Teos (Sığacık), Erythrae (Ildırı), Clazomenae (Klazümen), Phocaea (Foca).

Homeric poems offer occasional echoes of the Hittite Song of Ullikummi and other near-eastern texts.

Phocaea had originally formed part of Aeolis.

Tartessus. *RG*, pp.150, 176.

Ephesus. The tyrant-dictator Pythagoras once again reorganized the tribal system.

Cyprus. The Greeks of the island spoke a composite dialect (Arcado-Cypriot). For Salamis, *see VP*, pp. 7ff.

Finds from Salamis (Cyprus). Cyprus Museum, Nicosia.

Crete. Sub-Mycenaean twilight: 90 cities (*Iliad*), 100 (*Odyssey*). Cities' subjects included various kinds of dependent, more or less serf-like, communities, some-times similar to the Spartan Helots (listed in Y. Garlan, *Slavery in Ancient Greece*, 1988 pp.93–102). From the late ninth century, metal-workers arrived at Cnossus from northern Syria or Phoenicia. Huge bronze shields of eighth-century date have been found on Mount Ida (the mythical birthplace of Zeus, *cf.* Mt Iouktas). Gortyna was supposedly the home of Daedalus, the seventh century Greek sculptor (*see* note on Chapter 1), and inscriptions of *c*.480–450 have preserved its (much more ancient) laws. Drerus has remains of an early temple (*c*725–700).

Paphos. *GAW*, pp.472ff.

Abdera. A previous attempt to colonize the place by Clazomenae (Klazümen), in the seventh century BC, had been defeated by the Thracians.

Argonauts. *MGR*, pp.289–303.

Calabria in ancient times was the heel of Italy, not the toe as now.

Sybaris. *VP*, pp.15ff.

Colonies of Sybaris on the Tyrrhenian coast: not only Posidonia (Paestum, where three temples survive), but Laus (Lao) and Scidrus (unidentified).

Colonies of Croton at Caulonia and Terina, on the east and west coast of Bruttii respectively.

Setbacks of Croton. Defeat by Locri Epizephyrii (Locri) and Rhegium (Reggio di Calabria) besides the River Sagra (Sagriano or Turbolo) in *c*.540 (?).

Phoenician settlements in W. Sicily. Motya (Mozia), Solus or Soloeis (Solun-tum, Solunto), Panormus (Palermo).

Acragas, Selinus, Segesta. *GAW*, pp.5f., 57f., 572f.

Stesichorus moved to Himera from his south Italian birthplace Mataurus (Gioia Tauro), another of Zancle's colonies.

Gela. *GAW*, p.267.

Colonies of Massalia. In Gaul Monoecus (Monaca), Nicaea (Nice), Antipolis (Antibes), Agathe Tyche (Agde). In Spain: Emporion (Ampurias; a joint colony of Massalia and Phocaea); Hemeroscopion (Gulf of Valencia [Valentia]), Alonae (near Cape Tenebrium [de la Nao]), Maenace (east of Malaca [Malaga]).

PART II: THE CLASSICAL GREEKS

Chapter 4: Against Persia and Carthage

Marathon. One of the Athenian casualties was the polemarch Callimachus.

Athenian 'fifth column' signalling to the Persians after Marathon: identified (dubiously) with treachery by the Alcmaeonid clan.

Athenian plans for 480 BC. *VP*, pp.57ff.

Carthage. *RG*, p.349, n.33; *GAW*, pp.153ff.

Chapter 5: The Classical City States

Pausanias, having been called back from Byzantium to Sparta for trial (in which he avoided conviction for treachery), returned to Byzantium (*c*.477), from which he was dislodged by Cimon in *c*.477/5 or 472/0.

'First Peloponnesian War'. The name sometimes given to Athens's war against the Spartans, Corinthians and Boeotians, including the battles of Tanagra and Oenophyta (457). In the previous year, the Athens had finally subjugated Aegina (of which their possession was confirmed by the Thirty Years' Peace in 445).

Coronea in Boeotia (447). This undid the Athenian victory at Oenophyta.

State-pay. *CG*, p.68.

Early years of the Peloponnesian War. In 429 the Athenian Phormio won two naval victories off Naupactus.

Alcibiades had been one of the commanders of the Sicilian expedition in 415, but was recalled for trial (for alleged profanation and impiety) and escaped to Sparta. After his reappointment in 407 he was dismissed in the following year (a subordinate having been defeated off Notium) and fled into Persian territory, where he was murdered in Phrygia (404).

Athenian support for Amorges, rebellious Persian satrap, began according to Andocides, III. 29, *before* the Sicilian expedition, and contravened the Peace of Epilycus of 424/3 between Athens and Persia (ignored by Thucydides).

Amorges's father Pissuthnes, on the other hand, had supported the rebellion of Samian oligarchs against Athens in 440.

Persian hostility to Sparta in the early 4th century BC. The Spartan king Agesilaus II (444–360) invaded Persian Asia Minor (396–394). Before that, the Spartans had 'unofficially' participated in an attempted *coup* against Artaxerxes II Mnemon (Appendix II) by his brother Cyrus the younger, who was killed, however, at the battle of Cunaxa (Kunish; 401). The expedition was described by the Athenian Xenophon (*c*.428/7–*c*.354) in his *March up Country (Anabasis)*. His numerous other works (*GLA*, pp.472ff.), of second-class quality but historical importance, included the *Hellenica*, a Greek history from 411 to 362, which is mostly lost.

The 'Peace of Callias' (371) was named after the grandson of the man who gave his name to the formal or informal 'Peace of Callias' in 449.

Epaminondas prompted the foundation of new capitals of liberated Arcadia and Messenia, at Megalopolis and Messene (Ithome) respectively.

Second Athenian League. *CG*, p.197.

Isocrates. *Ibid*, pp.220–3.

Philip II in 340–339 led an expedition into Thrace and Scythia, partly in order to gain loot.

Satyr plays. One such play by Sophocles (*Ichneutae*) has largely survived, and the *Cyclops* by Euripides.

Theatre of Dionysus. Constructed of stone at some date after the collapse of the wooden benches of the earlier theatre in c.499 BC, but later rebuilt more than once, notably in the fourth century BC.

Oedipus's marriage to his mother Jocasta. Hence the Freudian 'Oedipus complex'.

Tragic irony. *CG*, p.116.

Old Comedy dramatists. Aristophanes, Cratinus, Eupolis.

Cleon's prosecution of Aristophanes. For passages in his (lost) play *The Babylonians*.

Utopianism of Aristophanes echoed the writings of Hippodamus of Miletus (better known as a town-planner) and was later developed by Phaleas of Calchedon (c.400) and Euhemerus of Messene (c.300).

New Comedy followed the diversified, mythological, socially conscious Middle Comedy (nearly all lost), *CG*, p.301.

Leucippus. Not only Miletus, but also Elea and Abdera, claimed to be his birthplace.

Antiphon. *CG*, pp.74f., 302f.

Hippocrates. Sophists were also believed to have been among his teachers.

Plato's *Meno*. The centre-piece of the dialogue is the weird doctrine of Recollection (*anamnesis*) of a previous condition, by which, as Plato had learnt from the Pythagoreans (through Archytas), all knowledge was said to be transmitted.

Agathon won his first victory at the Lenaea in 416, and came under the influence of the Sophists Gorgias and Prodicus. He went to Archelaus's Macedonian court, and died there in c.401.

Plato in Sicily. In 389 Dion, brother-in-law and son-in-law of Dionysius I, was impressed by Plato's teaching, but Plato's failure to make Dionysius II into a 'philosopher-king' is recorded in the *Seventh Letter*, of doubtful authenticity (*CG*, p.207). After seizing Syracuse in 357, Dion was murdered by Callippus, a member of Plato's Academy, in 354.

Aristotle on the Soul. He does not, like Plato, interpret the soul as immaterial.

Aristotle on education. For his influence on Hellenistic education, *see below*, Chapter 7, section 1.

Aegina pediments. Glyptothek Museum, Munich.

Olympia pediments. Olympia Museum.

Critian Boy. Acropolis Museum, Athens.

Fair-haired Boy. Ditto.

Delphi Charioteer. Delphi Museum.

Bust of Themistocles. Ostia Museum.

Artemisium statue. National Museum, Athens.

Discobolus of Myron. Reconstruction in Museo Nazionale (Terme), Rome.

Riace statues. Reggio di Calabria Museum; but removed temporarily for repairs.

Bust of Pericles by Cresilas of Cydonia (worked c.450–436 BC). Copies in British Museum, London, and Vatican Museums, Rome.

Doryphorus of Polyclitus. Copy in Museo Archeologico Nazionale, Naples.

Diadumenus of Polyclitus. Reconstruction in Metropolitan Museum of Art, New York.

Parthenon sculptures of Phidias, etc. Mostly in British Museum, London.

Phidias's statue of Zeus at Olympia. The other Wonders of the World were the pyramids of Egypt, the Hanging Gardens of Babylon, the Temple of Artemis (Artemisium) at Ephesus, the Mausoleum at Halicarnassus (Bodrum), the colossus of Rhodes (by Chares) and the Pharos (lighthouse) of Alexandria.

Erechtheum Caryatids. Acropolis Museum, Athens (copies in temple).

Hermes of Praxiteles. Olympia Museum.

Temples at Halicarnassus, Eg of Ares, Aphrodite and Hermes (Vitruvius, II, 8, 11).

Mausoleum at Halicarnassus. The building may have been surrounded by two rows of Ionic columns, rather than one. Statue of Mausolus (or ancestor) and reliefs: British Museum, London.

Scopas was the architect of the temple of Athena Alea at Tegea.

Bryaxis of Athens, said to have worked at the Mausoleum, may not be the man of the same name who later made a colossal statue of the god Sarapis (Serapis) for Alexandria.

Timotheus also worked on the temple of Asclepius at Epidaurus.

Leochares, probably Athenian, portrayed Isocrates and Philip II of Macedonia and his family (after the battle of Chaeronea, 338).

PART III: THE HELLENISTIC GREEKS

Chapter 6: Alexander and his Successors

'Hellenistic'. For this term, used to describe the Greeks after Alexander, *see AC*, pp.xii, 283.

Alexander the Great. Outstanding among his historians is Arrian of Bithynia (second century AD). The extent of Greco-Persian collaboration which Alexander had in mind is disputed.

Alexandria. Founded on the site of the fishing village of Rhacotis. Whether Alexander already intended that the place should take over the full commercial role of Tyre in Phoenicia, which he had destroyed, remains uncertain.

Succession Wars after Alexander's death. The contestants included Antipater (*d*.319), his son Cassander (*d*.297), Perdiccas (*d*.321), Craterus (*d*.321), Antigonus the One-Eyed (Monophthalmos, *d*.301), Demetrius the Besieger (Poliorcetes, *d*.283), Lysimachus (*d*.281) and Ptolemy I Soter and Seleucus I Nicator (*see* text).

Minor Hellenistic kingdoms. Bithynia, Pontus, Cappadocia, the Cimmerian Bosphorus, Judaea (see Appendix VI), and the Bactrian and Indo-Greek states, whose monarch Menander Soter Dikaios, in the mid-second century, was the most powerful Greek ruler of his time, placing both Pallas Athene and the Dharma-Chakra (wheel of law) symbol on his coins, and becoming revered as a thinker and sage.

Lamian War. Antipater successfully resisted a Greek siege of Lamia in Malis, commanding the chief route from Thessaly to central Greece.

Chremonidean War. Named after the Athenian politician Chremonides. Athens joined a Peloponnesian anti-Macedonian coalition, supported by Ptolemy II Philadelphus, but had to surrender.

Rhodian philosophers. The Stoic Panaetius (*c*.185–109 BC); his pupil Posidonius of Apamea (*c.*135–51/50) also became a member of the Rhodian school.

Aetolian League. The Assembly could also hold emergency sessions, in addition to its two regular annual meetings.

Chapter 7: Hellenistic Man and Woman

Herophilus's adherents, the Dogmatists, claimed to follow the classic Hippocratic methods of deduction, and were opposed by the Empiricists who rejected such abstract reasoning and preferred direct observation of symptoms.

Epidaurus and Cos. Dietetic régimes, bathing and exercise also played a part in the treatments.

Aristoxenus's forerunners included Ion of Chios (*c.*490), who wrote anecdotal biographic memoirs, and (in the fourth century) Isocrates and Xenophon, who composed *encomia*.

Eminent Hellenistic women. Laia of Cyzicus (portrait painter), Phile of Priene (architect), Polygnota of Thebes (harpist), and the poets Erinna of Telos, Corinna of Tanagra, and Anyte of Tegea.

The Greek novel's origins are much disputed; parts were played in them by the 'fictional history' of Xenophon's *Cyropaedia* (*Education of Cyrus* [II the Great]: especially the tale of Abradates and Panthea) and Ctesias's *History of Persia* (*c.*390 BC). Early novels are the *Ninus Romance* and *Joseph and Aseneth* (written by a Jew), *AC*, pp.139, 211.

Milesian Tales. Inaugurated or popularized by Aristides of Miletus, *c.*100 BC.

Chrysippus. His views are difficult to distinguish from those of his master Zeno.

Diogenes was influenced by Antisthenes of Athens (*c.*495–360) – who maintained that most pleasures are treacherous.

Apoxyomenus of Lysippus. Copy in Vatican Museums, Rome. Restoration in Muzeum Narodowe, Warsaw.

Tyche of Eutychides. Vatican Museums, Rome.

Victory of Samothrace. Louvre, Paris.

Venus of Milo. Louvre, Paris.

Ludovisi Group. Museo Nazionale (Terme), Rome.

Dying Gaul. Capitoline Museum, Rome.

Paintings of the time of Alexander the Great. A wall-painting of early Roman imperial date from Boscoreale near Pompeii (Museo Archeologico Nazionale, Naples) may be a copy of a picture commemorating Alexander's marriage to Barsine Statira in 324.

Stag-hunt mosaic. Pella Museum.

Collapse of Hellenistic states. Hiero II of Syracuse, however, became a client-king of the Romans (263). When they fought against Antiochus III (191–188), they made the Aetolian League their subject ally. They pillaged seventy towns of Epirus after defeating Perseus of Macedonia (167). Outside their sphere, an Indo-Greek state seems to have outlasted even Cleopatra VII of Egypt, *AC*, p.87.

Gigantomachy reliefs from Pergamum. Staatliche Museen, Berlin.

Laocoon group. Vatican Museums, Rome. The group is signed by three Rhodian sculptors (Agesander, Polydorus and Athenodorus). It has recently been inter-

preted as a Pergamene political statement at a time when Roman power seemed menacing. But the work that we have may be a copy of the first century AD.
Portrait of Euthydemus. Torlonia Museum (Villa Albani), Rome.
Wanderings of Odysseus painting. Copy in Vatican Museums, Rome. Wall paintings of Dionysiac scenes (first century AD) in the Villa dei Misteri outside Pompeii are derived from Pergamene or Alexandrian models.
Lost Ram painting. Copy in Museo Archeologico Nazionale, Naples.

The Romans

PART IV: EARLY ROME AND THE REPUBLIC

Chapter 8: The Etruscans and the Rise of Rome

The Etruscan city-states were independent of one another: their league based on Volsinii (Orvieto) was religious and formal.
The Etruscans in Campania. Capua: *Etr*, pp.86–9. Cales: *ibid.*, p.272, note 9. Etruscans also penetrated into much more southerly regions of Campania, eg to Picentia (Pontecagnano), *ibid.*, pp.90, 147, 247, 272.
The Etruscans in northern Italy. They settled Atria and Spina, by the mouths of the Eridanus (Padus, Po), jointly with the Greeks, *ibid.*, pp.106–110.
Aristodemus of Cumae repelled the 'long march' of Etruscan city-state troops from the north in *c*.525–4, and with the help of Latin city-states defeated the Etruscans again at Aricia (Ariccia) in 506/504.
Later Etruscan developments. Wall-paintings from the François Tomb at Vulci (*c*.300 BC; Torlonia Museum [Villa Albani], Rome, *Etr*, pp.169ff.) offer a glimpse of a heroic tradition relating to the city's past, which has, otherwise, vanished, because the Greek and Roman historians remained more or less silent about Etruscan affairs except when they impinged upon Greece and Rome. At Tarquinii (Tarquinia) too, where the construction of lavishly decorated tombs continued, a group of inscriptions of the first century AD offer otherwise unknown information about the exploits of long since dead members of the Spurinna family (*Etr*, p.135). By that time, moreover, individual Etruscans had reached the centre of the Roman scene; thus Augustus's adviser Gaius Maecenas probably originated from Arretium (Arezzo; *Etr*, p.208), and Tiberius's praetorian prefect Lucius Aelius Sejanus came from Volsinii (Orvieto; *Etr*, p.295).
Early inhabitants of Latium. *HR*, p.9.
Early Latin centres. Alba Longa (Castelgandolfo) and Lavinium (Pratica del Mare; *VP*, pp.176ff), were prominent in mythological tradition. Excavations have also shown the significance of Ficana, Politorium (Castel di Decima) and Satricum (Borgo Montello), *GAW*, pp.251, 514, 565f.
Foundation of Rome. Ascribed to various dates, *HR*, p.11.
Septimontium. Not equivalent to the later Seven Hills of Rome, which covered a much more extensive area. Included in the Septimontium was the Caelian Hill, which was settled at an early date, and united with the Palatine and Esquiline in the first part of the seventh century BC.
Early Roman religion. *HR*, pp.19f.

Vulca of Veii. For this sculptural school, which produced a fine terracotta Apollo (Museo della Villa Giulia Rome), *Etr*, pp.223f.

Capitoline Triad. Jupiter, Juno and Minerva were the Greek Zeus, Hera and Athena and the Etruscan Tinia, Uni and Menerva. An earlier triad worshipped at Rome had been Jupiter, Mars (Ares) and Quirinus.

Attempts to reestablish Roman monarchy. *HR*, pp.32f.

Rome's treaty with Aricia. Or with Ardea, or with both?

Celtic-speaking peoples, in the eighth and seventh centuries BC, had moved out of central Europe as far as Spain and Britain, and then during the fifth century they gradually crossed the Alps and expelled the Etruscan settlers from northern Italy – henceforward known as Cisalpine Gaul (Gaul this side of the Alps).

League of Campanian cities. Ruled by Oscan-speaking Samnites (Sabellians) who had merged with the earlier populations but were now threatened by a fresh wave of Samnites.

Via Appia. Constructed by Appius Claudius Caecus, censor 312 BC (*see* next note). He also built an aqueduct to provide Rome with water, the tunnelled Aqua Appia.

Roman government. The censorship was probably created in 443 BC; the censors occupied their office for six months. Dictators, too, who overrode the consuls, held office for six months at most. The dictatorship became obsolete but was temporarily revived in the third century BC, during the Second Punic War, and was later revived again, for autocratic purposes, by Sulla and Julius Caesar.

Concilium plebis. After its decrees (*plebiscita*) had been given equal validity with the laws, the *concilium* became difficult to distinguish from the *comitia plebis tributa*, except that, unlike the latter, it did not include patricians and was presided over by a tribune, instead of a consul or praetor.

Chapter 9: The Imperial Republic

Pyrrhus was killed at Argos in 272 BC.

Early treaties between Rome and Carthage. *HR*, p.82.

Ius gentium. *HR*, p.92.

Second Punic War. The question of 'war guilt' has been greatly disputed.

Plautus. His extant plays are *Amphitryo, Asinaria (Comedy of Asses), Aulularia (Pot of Gold), Bacchides, Captivi, Cistellaria (Casket Comedy), Curculio (Weevil), Epidicus, Menaechmi, Mercator (Merchant), Miles Gloriosus (Braggart Warrior), Mostellaria (Ghost Story), Persa, Poenulus (Little Carthaginian), Pseudolus, Rudens (Rope), Trinummus (Three-Coin Day), Truculentus*. Some passages of the *Vidularia (Travelling Chest)* have also come down to us.

Terence. His surviving comedies are *Andria (Woman of Andros), Heautontimorumenus (Self-Tormentor), Eunuch, Phormio, Adelphi (Brothers)*.

Concrete. *HR*, p.137.

Aemilian Bridge (Ponte Rotto). Constructed by the censors Marcus Aemilius Lepidus and Marcus Fulvius Nobilior.

Aqua Marcia. Constructed by the *praetor urbanus* Quintus Marcius Rex.

Quaestio de repetundis was a lawcourt established in 149 BC as a result of political scandals.

Via Domitia was on the site of an ancient route from the River Rhodanus (Rhône) to Spain.

Concessions in the middle of the Social War. Law of Lucius Julius Caesar (90 BC).

Publius Sulpicius Rufus, as tribune in 88 BC, had tried to carry out Marcus Livius Drusus's ideas by securing a fair distribution of the enfranchised Italians in the Roman tribes.

Cinna. Marius returned to Rome as his ally, but died in 86, his mind unhinged.

Sulla's restoration of the Senate's authority. *HR*, p.162.

Sulla's building programme. The Tabularium (Record-Office), and rebuilding of the Roman Curia (Senate-house) and sanctuary of Fortuna at Praeneste (Palestrina).

Slave rebellions. Before Spartacus, there had been revolts in Sicily in *c.*139–132 and 104–100.

Consulships of Crassus and Pompey in 70. Legally, both were unqualified, because neither had disbanded his army as consular candidates were required to do, and Pompey, who had not even taken his seat as a senator, should have been debarred, according to law, on account of his youth.

Caesar became *pontifex maximus* (chief priest) in 63 – his first political success.

Cicero. Speeches, writings on oratory (*Brutus, Orator* and *About the Orator*), and letters (*To Atticus* and *To Friends*), *GLA* pp.93ff. Political philosophy: *On the State* and *On Laws*. Ethical treatises: *On the Chief Good and Evil* (*De Finibus*), *Discussions at Tusculum* (*Tusculanae Disputationes*), *On the Nature of the Gods, On Old Age, On Friendship, On (Moral) Duties* (*De Officiis*). Cicero also wrote poetry.

Poets of Cisalpine Gaul. Valerius Cato (born *c.*100), Gaius Licinius Calvus (82–47), Gaius Helvius Cinna (*d.*44).

King of Egypt. Ptolemy XII Auletes, father of Cleopatra VII; *Cl*, pp.3–29, *VP*, pp.69ff.

Caesar before Pharsalus. His blockade of Dyrrhachium (Durrës, Durazzo) had been frustrated.

Cleopatra VII's advice on projects at Rome. *Caes*, pp.173f.

Brutus. His original name was Marcus Junius Brutus, and he (significantly) claimed descent from Lucius Junius Brutus, the traditional founder of the Republic. He was adopted by his uncle Quintus Servilius Caepio.

Chapter 10: The Augustan Age

Antony's brother, Lucius Antonius, surrendered to Octavian at Perusia (Perugia) in 40 BC.

Sextus Pompeius, after the battle of Naulochus, fled to Asia, but was put to death at Miletus by Marcus Titius (35), who became proconsul of the province.

Lepidus was allowed to retain the office of chief priest (*pontifex maximus*) until his death in 12 BC.

Augustus's constitution. He retained the consulship from 31 until 23 BC.

Augustus's power over proconsuls. *Imperium maius*, rarely employed.

Tribunician power. Augustus later shared this with Agrippa and Tiberius.

Pater patriae. On the significance of this title, inherited like 'Caesar' and 'Augustus' by later emperors, *HR*, p.211. But Tiberius refused it (*see* note on next Chapter).

Augustus's coinage. Gold, silver, and the novel alloys of *orichalcum* (brass) and copper for token coinage, replacing bronze, which had been discontinued and was discredited in Italy.

Julia (daughter of Augustus). She became estranged from Tiberius and was banished to Pandateria (Ventotene) for adultery in 2 BC, and then moved to Rhegium (Reggio di Calabria) in AD 4. She died in AD 14.

Adoption of Tiberius in AD 4. Agrippa Postumus, the third son of Agrippa and Julia, was adopted with him, but subsequently disgraced (*d*. AD 16).

Tiberius and Nero Drusus (Drusus senior) overran Raetia (parts of Austria, Switzerland and Württemberg), which was annexed (16 BC). Noricum (central Austria and parts of Bavaria) was converted from a client kingdom into a province at the same time or slightly later. (In *c.* AD 9 Illyricum [Yugoslavia] was divided into an Upper Province [Dalmatia] and a Lower Province [Pannonia]. Other expansions: Galatia, in central Asia Minor, had been annexed in 25 BC; Rome's eastern frontier was guaranteed by an agreement with the Parthians (20), which did not, however, last.

Augustus's buildings. D. Earl, *The Age of Augustus*, 1968, pp.107ff. 'My father' in the *Res Gestae*: Augustus's adoptive father, Julius Caesar. The Via Flaminia was the main northern highway of Italy, built by Gaius Flaminius during his censorship (220 BC).

The Milvian Bridge (Pons Mulvius) carried the Via Flaminia across the Tiber north of Rome. Its first surviving mention is in 207 BC.

The Minucian Bridge (Pons Minucius). Its location is not known.

Temple of Apollo. Its colonnades contained Greek and Latin libraries.

The Forum of Caesar contained the temple of Venus Genetrix (the Mother; ie ancestress of Caesar).

Augustus's portraits. Also a varied selection on coins: *RIM*, pp.7ff., 43.

Prose writers under Augustus. Another was Strabo of Amasia (Amasra) in Pontus (*c.*63 BC–at least AD 21), writing in Greek. His *Geography* is the only general study on the subject that has come down to us from the ancient world and is filled with invaluable (if occasionally obsolete) information. Both this seventeen-book work and the forty-seven books of his *Historical Sketches*, which are now almost entirely lost but were intended as a continuation of the work of Polybius, displayed the conviction (derived from the Stoic Posidonius) that Rome fulfilled a necessary and beneficent role as the unifier of the earthly world-state, which reflects the heavenly cosmopolis (Chapter 7, section 2).

Roman epic before Virgil. Naevius, Ennius: Chapter 9, section 1.

Augustan elegiac poetry. Albius Tibullus (55/48–19 BC) was the protégé of Marcus Valerius Messalla Corvinus. He wrote attractively about women, the quiet rural life and the blessings of peace – but remained aloof, like his patron, from the Augustan court.

Chapter 11: Rome After Augustus

Titles of Tiberius. Out of respect for Augustus he did not accept the title 'Father of the Country' (*pater patriae*).

Reign of Tiberius. A crisis was caused by the suspect death of his popular nephew and adopted son Germanicus (AD 19), for which Tiberius was (unjustifiably) blamed.

Philo and his influence. *GLA*, pp.323ff.

Claudius. His generals Aulus Plautius and Ostorius Scapula conquered and annexed Britain, ie the 'Lowland Zone' from Lindum (Lincoln) to South Devon (AD 43–8). (Later, after a revolt by Boudicca [Boadicea] in 60, a succession of Flavian governors extended the conquest to the 'Highland Zone', including eastern Wales [the Silures] and Yorkshire.)

Seneca the younger. Tragedies: *Hercules* (*Furens*), *Trojan Women*, *Phoenician Women*, *Medea*, *Phaedra*, *Oedipus*, *Agamemnon*, *Thyestes*, *Hercules Oetaeus* (of doubtful authenticity). Treatises: *On Anger*, *On Providence*, *On the Steadfastness* (*Constantia*) *of the Wise Man*, *On Leisure*, *On Peace of Mind*, *On the Brevity of Life*, *On Consolation* (*To Marcia*, *Polybius* [*freedman of Claudius*], *Helvia*), *On Clemency*, *On Benefits*.

'Apocolocyntosis' means 'pumpkinification', mocking the deification that had been bestowed on Claudius, as on Julius Caesar and Augustus.

Persius. Rhetorical satires influenced by the Stoic philosopher Lucius Annaeus Cornutus, a freedman of Seneca the younger.

Nero's later advisers. Especially Gaius Ofonius Tigellinus, praetorian prefect from AD 62.

Year of the Four Emperors (AD 69). Galba, Otho, Vitellius, Vespasian. There were two battles of Bedriacum (Calvatone, near Cremona), in which Vitellius's troops (1) defeated Otho's, (2) but were defeated by Vespasian's. Insecurity on the Rhine frontier prompted a Germano-Gallic revolt under Civilis, Classicus and Tutor (see Petillius Cerialis's address to the rebels in Chapter 11, section 3).

First Jewish Revolt (AD 66–73). Celebrated by reliefs on the Arch of Titus at Rome. Masada: *VP* pp.121ff.

Josephus. Works and successive religious positions: *GLA*, pp.237ff.

Pliny the elder. Author of historical works (now lost) and *Natural History* in 37 books.

Martial. Among the targets of his satire were the man who tries to hide his bald patch, and the woman whose hair is artificial or dyed.

Domitianic writers. Also Quintilian of Calagurris (Calahorra) in Spain, who wrote his study of rhetoric (*Institutio Oratoria*) at this time.

Nerva's adoption of Trajan, outside his own family, was a successful repetition of Galba's abortive adoption of Lucius Calpurnius Piso Licinianus (AD 69).

Trajan's Eastern Wars. Hampered by risings of the Jewish Diaspora in Cyrene, Egypt and Cyprus (which provoked anti-Jewish outbursts in Antioch, Damascus and other Syrian cities).

Hadrian's mother was from Gades (Cadiz). His 'adoption' by Trajan was a fake, invented by the latter's widow Plotina.

Plutarch's and Suetonius's careers. *GLA*, pp.349, 409.

Simeon Bar Kosiba came to be known as 'Bar Kochba', Son of a Star, ie Messiah.

Windows at Ostia. Made of selenite (foliated sulphite of lime).

Jurists under Hadrian. Gaius, author of the *Institutes*, was a pupil of Salvius Julianus.

Hadrian's first heir (136). Lucius Aelius Caesar (Lucius Ceionius Commodus, *d*. 138). His adoption meant passing over Hadrian's ninety-year-old brother-in-law Lucius Julius Servianus Ursus and his grandson Cnaeus Pedianus Fuscus Salinator, who were then put to death for alleged sedition.

Antoninus Pius. Builder of the Antonine Wall in Britain from the River Bodotria (Firth of Forth) to the mouth of the River Clota (Clyde) in 141.

Marcus Aurelius. Before adoption by Antoninus Pius (one of whose family names was Aurelius), his name was Marcus Annius Verus.

Epictetus (*c*.AD 55–*c*. 135). From Hierapolis (Pamukkale) in Phrygia. His teachings were preserved by Arrian of Bithynia, the historian of Alexander the Great.

Lucius Verus. Son of Hadrian's first heir Lucius Aelius Caesar.

Cybele. *AC*, p.231.

Mithras. *CR*, pp.183ff.

Civil wars of AD 193–6. The shortlived contestants were Pertinax, Didius Julianus, Pescennius Niger (in the east) and Clodius Albinus (in Gaul).

Law under Septimius Severus. Papinian (Aemilius Papinianus, executed 212), Ulpian (Domitius Ulpianus of Tyre [Sur], killed 223), Paulus (praetorian prefect, perhaps jointly with Ulpian).

Fulvius Plautianus. Father of Caracalla's rejected wife Plautilla.

Caracalla and Elagabalus. The official names of both of them were Marcus Aurelius Antoninus. 'Caracalla' was called this informally, after his long Gallic cloak, and El-Gabal was the name of the Emesan god of whom Elagabalus had been the priest.

Baths of Caracalla. Public Baths at Rome had earlier been constructed by Agrippa, Nero, Titus and Trajan. Notable Baths in the provinces were those at Lepcis Magna (Hadrian), Carthage (Antoninus Pius) and Treviri (Constantine I the Great).

Emperors in AD 238. Maximinus I and his son Maximus (Caesar), Gordianus I and II Africanus (at Carthage), Balbinus and Pupienus, and Gordianus III Pius. *See Scriptores Historiae Augustae*, ss.vv., *RE*, pp.137–151.

Philip was the son of an Arab chieftain Marinus from Trachonitis (east of the River Aulon [Jordan]).

Dissident state in Gaul. Founded by Postumus (259–268).

Dissident state at Palmyra. Zenobia, widow of Odenathus, Rome's semi-independent commander in the east, declared herself Augusta and her son (Vaballathus Athenodorus) Augustus in 270.

Diocletian was known was Jovius (after Jupiter) and Maximian as Herculius (after Hercules).

Persecutions of Christians. Under Marcus Aurelius, Maximinus I, Trajanus Decius, Valerian and Diocletian.

Origins. Maximian from near Sirmium (Sremska Mitrovica), Constantius I from Dardania (Upper Moesia), Galerius from near Florentiana (Dacia Ripensis, Upper Moesia), Licinius I from Dacia Ripensis.

Maximian returned from retirement to support his son Maxentius's claim to the throne, forced another contestant (Severus II) to surrender at Ravenna, was compelled to abdicate again in 308, but after a further rebellion committed suicide in 310.

Licinius I conquered Maximinus II Daia in 313, but was defeated by Constantine I at Hadrianopolis (Adrianople, Edirne) and Chrysopolis (Üsküdar, Scutari).

Constantine I's Christian Councils. Arelate (Arles) 314, Nicaea (Iznik) 325.

Church of Holy Wisdom (Aya Sofya) at Constantinople. Finished under Constantius II (360), and rebuilt by Justinian I (532–537).

Constantine I's family. His wife Fausta and his eldest son Crispus were executed in 326.

Constantine I's successors, Constantine II (337–340), Constantius II, Constans (337–50), Delmatius, Hannibalianus.

Constantius I. Completed the Church of Holy Wisdom (Aya Sofya) at Constantinople, rebuilt by Justinian I in the sixth century. Constantius II overthrew Magnentius (350–3), who came from near Ambiani (Samarobriva, Amiens).

Arians. Founded by Arius (c.260–336), indefatigably opposed by St Athanasius (c.295–373).

St Ambrose. In 338 he compelled Theodosius I to cancel an order requiring the church of Callinicum Nicephorium (Raqqa) on the Euphrates to rebuild a Jewish synagogue burnt down by Christians, *FRE*, pp.156ff.

Writings of Ambrose, Jerome and Augustine. *GLA*, pp.15ff., 230ff., 58ff., *FRE*, Index ss.vv.

Manichaeans. Believers in warring powers of good and evil. *CR*, pp.200–205.

Travelling Bandits in the fifth century. eg the Bagaudae, *HR*, p.338: the presbyter Salvian of Massilia (Marseille) finds their emergence unsurprising, *FRE*, p.66.

Monastic movement. *HR*, pp.345f., *FRE*, pp.145ff.

The last western Roman emperors (455–476). *RE*, pp.308ff. On the last two, *VP*, pp.158ff.

Treviri. A Gallic tribe in the basin of the River Mosella (Moselle). Their chief town became the Roman fortress-city of Augusta Trevirorum (Trier), *VP*, pp.126ff.

Lingones. A Gallic tribe on the border between the provinces of Gallia Lugdunensis and Belgica. Their chief town was Andematunnum (Langres).

Gaius Julius Civilis. A Batavian leader who fomented the Gallo-German war of liberation. The Batavians were a Germanic people living between the Rivers Rhenus (Old Rhine) and Vahalis or Vacalus (Waal).

Tutor and Classicus. Rebel leaders of the tribe of the Treviri (*see above*).

Burgundians. Like the Visigoths, they were Arian Christians.

The conversion of Clovis from paganism to Catholic, rather than Arian, Christianity in 496 or 506 put an end to Arianism in Gaul.

Latin after the fall of the West. At an everyday level Latin was by 700 transforming into vernacular languages.

Constantinople 1204–1261. 'Latin' empire of Crusaders.

Paucity of eastern usurpers. *HR*, p.356, *FRE*, p.204.

NOTES ON APPENDICES

Appendix I: *The Plots of Homer and Hesiod*

Achilles. The only son of the mortal Peleus, king of Phthia in Thessaly, and of the sea-nymph Thetis, daughter of Nereus. The Myrmidons were a people of Phthia.

Occupations of heroes. Oratory, too, was esteemed.

Homeric Gods. For all their power, they are presented, on the whole, as amoral and unedifying. Fate is identified with the gods.

Odysseus's wanderings are mythical and mostly unidentifiable, although many attempts have been made to locate them.

Hesiod's Five Ages. Gold, Silver, Bronze, Heroes (Demigods) and Iron.

Appendix II: *The East*

Phoenicia. Recent archaeological discoveries, Sabatino Moscati observes, have made it possible for us, for the first time, 'to study the origins, character, aim and influences of this previously neglected and lost civilization', which provides a notable bridge between east and west.

Northern Syria. Our knowledge of its civilization has been abruptly thrown far back in time by third millennium discoveries at Ebla (Tell Mardikh).

Posidium and other centres exported bronzework from the middle eastern kingdom of Urartu (*RG*, p.355) to Mediterranean lands.

Carthage, a peninsula projecting from the Gulf of Tunis, only 75 miles from Sicily. The most important of the colonies of the Phoenicians, this 'New City' (Qart Hadasht) was established by settlers from Tyre, traditionally in 814. Virgil's legend of Queen Dido refers to the foundation. During the seventh century Carthage became independent of Tyre, and gradually subjugated the tribes of north Africa. It presided over Phoenician settlements in Sicily, and decisively influenced them. In *c*.535 Carthage and Etruscan Caere (Chapter 8 defeated the Greek (Phocaean) colonists of Alalia (Corsica).

Aramaeans occupied much of Mesopotamia and Syria (eleventh to eighth centuries), taking their name from the north Syrian plain (Aram Naharain, Field of the Rivers). The Aramaic language (north-western Semitic, related to Phoenician) became a *lingua franca*, and under Persian rule 'imperial Aramaic' was official.

Hittites, speaking an Indo-European tongue, came to Asia Minor from the north. The Old Kingdom (*c*.1750–1450) was followed by a Hittite empire (*c*.1450–1200), which was overwhelmed by the Phrygians, a people whose legendary monarch was Midas; but a group of Neo-Hittite states survived in northern Syria.

Hurrians, mountaineers whose language (recorded in a syllabic script) cannot be identified, arrived shortly before 2000 BC in Mesopotamia and spread over Assyria and northern Syria. The Hittites defeated them in *c*.1350 but were influenced by their culture and religion.

Assyrians (N. Iraq), speaking the Semitic Akkadian language, had a powerful monarchy in the thirteenth century BC, and empire under Tiglath-Pileser III

(745–727), including all Syria and Babylonia, which reached its zenith under Sargon II (722–705) and his three successors. The oarsmen of Greek biremes were partly based on Assyrian prototypes.

Babylonians (central Iraq). Classical age of Old Babylonian civilization under Hammurabi (eighteenth century BC). Their power rose vis-à-vis Assyria in the twelfth century. Babylonian conquests obliterated Assyria and absorbed Syria in the later seventh century. The Babylonians were overcome by the Persians (see section (c) of text), who took Babylon in 539, and then Syria. Pythagoras learnt much of his mathematical science from Babylonia.

Necho II of Egypt. 26th (Saite) Dynasty.

Cyrene. Its founder, Aristoteles, took the (Libyan) royal title of Battus (I), and was posthumously worshipped as a hero (*heros*). The Cyrenians defeated the Libyans (reinforced by the Egyptian pharaoh Aphries [Hophra]) at Irasa (*c*.570). The administration of Pheretime (*c*.515) was a rare example, at this date, of Greek female rule. But then the Persians appointed her son Battus IV as puppet ruler of Cyrenaica. The Cyrenians derived revenue from grain, oil, horses, wool and silphium (laserwort?).

Naucratis. *VP*, pp.31ff. Exports included grain, faïence (glazed terracotta), alabaster, linen (for clothing and sails) and papyrus (writing material and ships' ropes). Imports: wine, oil, timber, silver (needed by the pharaohs to pay their mercenaries).

Hellenion at Naucratis. For the nine eastern Greek city-states which combined to found it *see RG*, p.215. Thales learnt much from Egypt, and the roof of the Mausoleum at Halicarnassus was derived from Egyptian models.

Writers at Naucratis. *RG*, p.216.

Artaxerxes II Mnemon disliked the Spartans because they had, unofficially, sent a force to support his rebel brother Cyrus the younger, who was killed at Cunaxa (Kunish) in 401 (*see* Xenophon's *Anabasis*).

Persian influences. The podium of the Mausoleum at Halicarnassus was based on Persian prototypes, via Lycia.

Parthians. For language and religion, *see AC*, p.82.

Persia in 4th century AD. Its outstanding monarch at this period was Shapur (Sapor) II the Great (310–379).

Nestorians were Christians who refused to accept the condemnation, by the Council of Ephesus (431), of Nestorius (*d. c*.451), who had denounced the practice of calling the Virgin Mary Theotokos (God-bearer), on the grounds that the title compromised the full humanity of Jesus.

Firuz was killed by the Hephthalites (white, ie fair-skinned) Huns. The last Sassanian monarch was killed in 651 after Arab victories.

Appendix III: The Principal Greek Shrines

Delphi. The *Homeric Hymn to Apollo* recounts how the god destroyed and superseded various monsters that lurked there.

Statue of Hera at Olympia. Its head has been found and is in the museum there.

The Cyclades, of which Delos was regarded as the centre, were a large group of islands in the middle of the Aegean Sea. During the Bronze Age they enjoyed a distinctive civilization, and in $c.1000$ were occupied by immigrants from continental Greece. Naxos, possessing marble quarries, created the first important school of sculpture (from $c.650$), and was later ruled by a tyrant Lygdamis ($c.545$–$c.525/4$?), after which the Persians destroyed the city for participating in the Ionian Revolt (490). Paros, which likewise quarried its own marble, also produced the seventh-century lyric poet Archilochus, the earliest Greek writer who speaks to us of his own feelings: frankly individual, un-Homeric, self-deprecatory, anti-heroic.

Appendix IV: *Corinth's Neighbours: Megara and Sicyon*

Organization of Megara. The Dorian immigrants, divided into their customary three tribes, reduced the zone's previous inhabitants to serfdom and settled in three villages or groups of villages, which amalgamated into a city ($c.750$). The three tribes were superseded, at some stage, by five new ones, perhaps introducing non-Dorian elements. These tribes appointed five generals, who at first shared their duties with the king and then replaced him. Each tribe presented a squadron to the army.

Megara's loss of Nisaea to Athens in 569/568. Perhaps this was not the first time that the port had been lost – and the loss may not have been final.

Organization of Cleisthenes's Sicyon. It was he who seems to have given the three traditional tribes a new set of names, presumably to get away from narrow Dorian exclusiveness; and it may also have been he who created a fourth tribe, the Aegialeis, perhaps to incorporate part of the non-Dorian serf class.

Pitsa panels. National Museum, Athens.

Appendix V: *Solon and Cleisthenes of Athens*

Athenian metics lacked citizen status, and were not allowed to own land, but paid taxes and were eligible for military service.

The four census classes of Solon. Three of the classes had already existed, less formally, before: *thetes*, mainly hired labourers, who earned less than two hundred bushels of grain or the equivalent; *zeugitai*, from *zeugos* a yoke of oxen, and so mainly farmers; and *hippeis*, knights, who could provide their own horses for military service. At the top, however, Solon added a fourth class, of *pentakosiomedimnoi*, men whose land produced at least five hundred bushels.

Organization of Attica under Cleisthenes. The three *trittyes* in each of his ten new tribes each drew their membership from three different regions of Attica, Town, Coast and Interior, no longer corresponding with the old parties of Plain, Coast and Hill. Demes from each of the three new regions were included in each of the ten tribes.

Appendix VI: *Jews and Christians*

Diaspora. *HAI*, pp.120f. and index (s.v.), *cf* (later) *AC*, pp.75, 77f.
Torah. See *HAI* index, s.v.

Sadducees and Pharisees. *HAI*, pp.216-218.

Jewish (Hasmonaean) independence. A brief intermission under the Seleucid Antiochus VII Sidetes (135/134-129 BC).

Temporary cessation of provincial status. Under Claudius's client-king Agrippa I (AD 41-44).

Judah I ha-Nasi resided first at Beth-Shearim and then at Sepphoris-Diocaesarea (Saffuriya).

Babylonian centres of Judaism: Nehardea, Sura, Pumbeditha. The Babylonian Talmud was more important than its Palestinian counterpart.

Crucifixion of Jesus. *J*, 1977, pp.165ff.

St Paul on Judaism. *SP*, 1976, pp.45ff.

Acts of the Apostles, *ibid.*, index, s.v.

Jewish Christians, like the Jews, were discredited in Roman eyes by the First Jewish Revolt.

Dates of Gospels, *J*, pp.180ff.

Clement and Origen, *GLA*, pp.104ff., 297ff.

Pliny the younger of Comum (Como; *c.*AD 61-*c.*112), nephew and adoptive son of Pliny the elder. Nine books of literary letters, and a tenth containing his official correspondence with Trajan about the administration of Bithynia, including its Christian problem.

Third-century persecutions of Christians. Maximinus I (235-238), Trajanus Decius (249-251), Valerian (253-260). There had been earlier persecutions under Nero (54-68) and Marcus Aurelius (161-180).

Table of Dates*
The Greeks and Others

Greek Lands	Near & Middle East	India & China	America
BC			
2000–1900. Greece invaded from the north (beginning of Middle Helladic or Middle Bronze Age)			
	19th–16th cents (?) Hebrew patriarchs Abraham, Isaac, Jacob		
after 1600. Greece increasingly under Cretan (Minoan) influence	1567. Beginning of Egyptian New Empire	1500. Migration of the 'Aryans' to India	
		1500–after 600. Vedic period of Indian philosophy and religion	
		1500–1030. Shang (Yin) Dynasty (Bronze Age I) in China. Later, capital at Hsiao-Tun (near Anyang)	
	1450–1200. Hittite Empire (Hurrians defeated 1350)		
1400–1200. Mycenaean civilization at height			

* Early dates are approximate

266

BC

Greek Lands	Near & Middle East	India & China	America
	1365–1250. First Assyrian Empire (Tiglath-Pileser I, 1116–1076)		1200–200. Early Horizon period of Andean South America, dominated by Chavin culture
1250. Supposed capture of Troy by Greeks	1300. Departure of Joseph for Egypt		
	13th cent. Moses founds religious community of Israel		1200/800–400/300. Olmec culture (Early-Middle Formative period) based on Gulf Coast of Mexico
late 13th & early 12th cent. Destruction of Mycenaean and other civilizations	13th–12th cents. Invasions by peoples of the Sea, Philistines, Hebrews		
1100–1050. Sub-Mycenaean pottery		1030–771. Early (western) Chou Dynasty (Bronze Age II) in China. Capital in Shensi	1000–300. Adena culture (Woodland stage I) in Ohio, Kentucky, Indiana, Pennsylvania and West Virginia
11th cent. Early Iron Age	11th–8th cents. Aramaeans occupy much of northern Syria		
1075–1000. Dorian invasions and immigrations	1000. Rise of Phoenician city-states		
1050–900. Migrations of Ionians, Aeolians and Dorians to western Asia Minor and islands	1000–965. King David of Israel (Solomon 965–927)		

	Greek Lands	Near & Middle East	India & China	America
BC	1025–900. Protogeometric, 900–700 Geometric pottery	926–722. Kingdoms of Israel (north) and Judah (south)		
		911–745. Assyrian revival (Ashurnasirpal II, 884–859, Shalmaneser III, 859–824)		800. Mexico. Climax of Olmec culture
	900–750. Creation of city-states. Replacement of monarchic by aristocratic governments			
		9th cent. Hebrew prophets Elijah and Elisha		
		9th–7th cents. Empire of Urartu		
		9th–8th cents. Greek coastal markets at Al Mina, Posidium and Paltus		
		850–676. Kingdom of Phrygia (Midas 738–696)		
		814. Traditional foundation date of Carthage, colony of Tyre		

Greek Lands	Near & Middle East	India & China	America
BC			
776. Traditional date of first Olympic (Pan-hellenic) Games		771–249. Later (eastern) Chou Dynasty (Bronze Age III) in China. Capital at Loyang (Honan)	
750–700. *Iliad* and *Odyssey* of Homer; Hesiod			
8th–7th cent. Coloniza-tion under way			
8th–7th cent. Orienta-lizing art			
8th cent. Biremes			
750–650. Major development of metallurgy	745. Second Assyrian Empire founded by Tiglath-Pileser III (745–727)		
750. Adoption of alphabet	742. Isaiah begins to prophesy		
	722. Fall of Israel to Shalmaneser V of Assyria (727–722)		
740/730–720/710. Sparta's First Messenian War			

Greek Lands	Near & Middle East	India & China	America
BC			
late 8th cent. Hoplite revolution			
700. Lelantine War between Chalcis and Euboea			
700–675. First Doric temples			
early 7th cent. First surviving lyric poems	689. Destruction of Babylon by Sennacherib of Assyria (705–681)		
early 7th cent. 'Daedalic' statuettes	687. Kingdom of Lydia founded by Gyges (d.657)		
early 7th cent (?). Pheidon of Argos			
after 700. Samian Heraeum rebuilt (Ephesian Artemisium after 660)			
7th cent (?). Sparta's politico-social system agoge) developed			
7th or 6th cent. Triremes			600. Mexico. Destruction of La Venta, Olmec cultural capital

Greek Lands	Near & Middle East	India & China	America
675–500. Age of 'tyrants' (dictators); often replaced by oligarchies	671. Conquest of Egypt by Esarhaddon of Assyria (681–668)		
669. Argives defeat Spartans at Hysiae			
664 or later. Corcyraeans defeat Corinthians at Sybota	664–526. 26th (Saite) Egyptian Dynasty. Use of Greek and other foreign mercenaries and foundation of Naucratis, etc.		
7th cent. First lawgivers			
shortly before 650. First large-scale statuary	650–550. Kingdom of Media (625–585 Cyaxares)		
650–620. Sparta's Second Messenian War			
640. Perdiccas I of Macedonia moves capital from Lebaea to Aegae	626–539. New Babylonian Empire		
late 7th cent. First Greek coinages	612. Destruction of Nineveh by Medes and Persians		

271

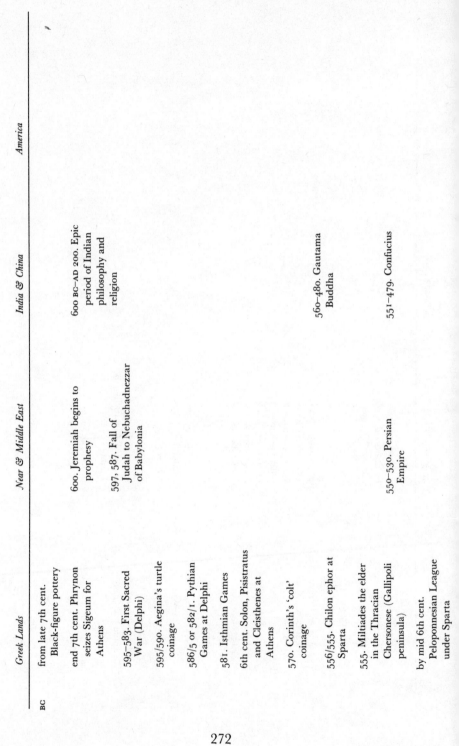

Greek Lands	Near & Middle East	India & China	America
BC			
from late 7th cent. Black-figure pottery			
end 7th cent. Phrynon seizes Sigeum for Athens	600. Jeremiah begins to prophesy	600 BC–AD 200. Epic period of Indian philosophy and religion	
595–583. First Sacred War (Delphi)	597, 587. Fall of Judah to Nebuchadnezzar of Babylonia		
595/590. Aegina's turtle coinage			
586/5 or 582/1. Pythian Games at Delphi			
581. Isthmian Games			
6th cent. Solon, Pisistratus and Cleisthenes at Athens			
570. Corinth's 'colt' coinage		560–480. Gautama Buddha	
556/555. Chilon ephor at Sparta			
555. Miltiades the elder in the Thracian Chersonese (Gallipoli peninsula)	550–530. Persian Empire	551–479. Confucius	
by mid 6th cent. Peloponnesian League under Sparta			

	Greek Lands	Near & Middle East	India & China	America
BC	546. Battle of Champions between Sparta and Argos at Thyrea	546. Conquest of Media and Lydia (Croesus) by Cyrus II the Great (Achaemenid) of Persia (560/559–530)		
	546. Ionia under Persian control			
	540–522. Polycrates tyrant of Samos	539. Conquest of Ionia and Babylonia by Cyrus II the Great of Persia		
	535. Massalians and Phocaeans defeated by Caere and Carthage in battle of Alalia			
	534. First Attic tragedy: Thespis			
	530. Red-figure pottery	525. Conquest of Egypt by Cambyses II of Persia (530–522)		
		522. Oroetes, satrap of Sardis, kills Polycrates of Samos		
	519. Accession of King Cleomenes I at Sparta (d.490/488)		519. Cyrus II the Great of Persia conquers parts of Pakistan	

273

	Greek Lands	Near & Middle East	India & China	America
BC				500. Earliest Zapotec temple at Monte Alban, Oaxaca, Mexico
	516. Miltiades the younger in the Thracian Chersonese	513–512. Expedition of Darius I of Persia (521–486) to Thrace and Scythia		
	510. Destruction of Sybaris by Croton			
	506. Athenians defeat Boeotians and Chalcidians; then 'Heraldless War' against Aegina			
	494. Spartans defeat Argives at Sepeia	499–4. Ionian Revolt against Darius I of Persia		
	493. Themistocles archon at Athens			
	490. Battle of Marathon won by Miltiades the younger of Athens	490, 480, 469/8. Persian Wars against the Greeks by Darius I and Xerxes I (486–465)		
	480s. Archaeanactid rulers in Cimmerian Bosphorus			
	480. Invasion of Greece by Xerxes I of Persia. Battle of Thermopylae (Leonidas I), Artemisium and Salamis (Themistocles)			

Greek Lands	Near & Middle East	India & China	America
BC			
480. Invasion of Sicily by the Carthaginians. Battle of Himera (Gelon of Syracuse and Theron of Acragas)			
479. Battles of Plataea (Pausanias) and Mycale			
478. Athenians form Delian League			
477–463. Campaigns of Cimon transform Delian League into Athenian empire			
475/3. Taras (with Rhegium) defeated by Iapygians; democracy established			
474. Hiero I of Syracuse defeats Etruscans off Cumae			
470s or 460s. Spartans defeat Tegea and Argos at Tegea and the Arcadians at Dipaea			
470–457. Temple of Zeus at Olympia			

275

Greek Lands	Near & Middle East	India & China	America
BC			
469/8. Cimon defeats the Persians at the River Eurymedon			
465. Earthquake at Sparta			
464–420. Activity of the sculptor Polyclitus of Argos			
465/4–461/460. Helots' revolt against Spartans in Messenia			
462. Cimon's expedition to Messenia dismissed by the Spartans			
462/1. Ephialtes's reform of the Areopagus			
461. Cimon ostracized (d.451) and Ephialtes assassinated			
460–445. 'First Peloponnesian War': Athens against Corinth (and later Sparta and Thebes)			
460–454. Athenian expedition to Egypt ends in disaster			

	Greek Lands	Near & Middle East	India & China	America
BC	454/3. Pericles first elected general (d.429)	454. Athenians ejected from Egypt		
	454. Treasury of Delian League transferred to Athens			
	453. Syracusans raid Aethalia (Elba), Corsica and Etruria, and fight the Sicel leader Ducetius (451–450)			
	451. Five Years' Truce between Athens and Sparta			
	451. Thirty Years' Peace between Sparta and Argos			
	450. The Riace bronzes and Myron's Discobolus			
	449/8. Peace of Callias between Athens and Persia	449/8. Peace of Callias arranged by Artaxerxes I Macrocheir of Persia, 465–424		
	447/6–438/2. The Parthenon			
	447. Boeotians defeat Athenians at Coronea and reconstitute League			
	446/5. Revolt against Athens in Euboea			

Greek Lands	Near & Middle East	India & China	America
BC			
445. Thirty Years' Peace between Athens and Sparta			
443. Ostracism of Thucydides the son of Melesias leaves Pericles supreme			
442/1. Sophocles's *Antigone*	440. Pissuthnes, Persian satrap of Sardes, helps Samian revolt against Athens		
440. Revolt of Samos against Athens			
438. Spartocid rulers in Cimmerian Bosphorus			
431–404. Peloponnesian War			
431. Euripides's *Medea*			
425. Aristophanes's *Acharnians*			
	424/3. Treaty between Persia and Athens		
424. The historian Thucydides exiled	423–405/4. Darius II Ochus king of Persia		
422. Brasidas and Cleon killed			
421. The Peace of Nicias			

278

Greek Lands	Near & Middle East	India & China	America
BC			
before 420. Death of Herodotus at Thurii			
415–413. Disastrous Athenian expedition to Sicily	414/412 (or earlier?) Athens aids Persian dissident Amorges in Caria		
413–399. Archelaus of Macedonia moves capital from Aegae to Pella			
411. Governments of Four Hundred and Five Thousand at Athens	408/7. Cyrus the younger in Asia Minor forms alliance with Lysander of Sparta		
406–367. Dionysius I tyrant of Syracuse; fights four Carthaginian wars			
405. Victory of Spartan Lysander at Aegospotami followed by capitulation of Athens and rule of Thirty Tyrants (404)			
400–325. Diogenes (founder of Cynicism)			
399. Trial and death of Socrates	396–4. Campaigns of King Agesilaus II of Sparta against the Persians		
395–387. Corinthian War: coalition against Sparta			

279

	Greek Lands	Near & Middle East	India & China	America
BC	387/6. Peace of Antalcidas or King's Peace	387/6. Peace of Antalcidas or King's Peace, imposed on Greeks by Persian king Artaxerxes II Mnemon (405/4–359/8)		
	385. Jason tyrant of Pherae (ruler of Thessaly 374, d.370)			
	382–378. Spartans seize Thebes and Olynthus and raid Attica			
	first half of 4th cent. Archytas at Taras			
	380s/370s. Plato's *Republic*			
	377. Second Athenian League	371. Persians support (second), abortive, Peace of Callias		
	370s–300. Sculptor Lysippus of Sicyon			
	371. Thebans under Epaminondas defeat Spartans at Leuctra			

Greek Lands	Near & Middle East	India & China	America
BC			
370–288/5. Theophrastus (successor of Aristotle)	367/6. Artaxerxes II Mnemon receives Pelopidas of Thebes and other Greek envoys at Susa		
365/360–275/270. Pyrrho (founder of Scepticism)			
362. Battle of Mantinea between Thebans and Spartans: Epaminondas killed			
359. Accession of Philip II of Macedonia: first successes (359–7)			
357–5. 'Social War': revolt of Athens's subject allies	358. Accession of Artaxerxes III Ochus (d.338), succeeded by Artaxerxes IV Arses, d.336)		
356–346. Third Sacred War between Phocian and Theban coalitions			
351–341. Demosthenes' speeches against Philip II			
345–337. Timoleon at Syracuse			

BC	Greek Lands	Near & Middle East	India & China	America
	338. Philip II defeats Athenians and Thebans at Chaeronea and convenes First Congress of Corinth (Second Congress 337)			
		337. At Second Congress of Corinth Philip II of Macedonia announces expedition against Persian empire, which is launched by Attalus (336)		
	336. Philip II succeeded by Alexander III the Great (d.323)			
		334–330. Alexander III the Great conquers Persian empire; death of Persian king Darius III Codomannus		
			327–5. Alexander III the Great of Macedonia conquers Persian provinces of Pakistan	
	323–283. Reign of Ptolemy I Soter of Egypt (defeats Demetrius I Poliorcetes at Gaza 312)			
	323–2. Antipater defeats Athens in Lamian War			

	Greek Lands	Near & Middle East	India & China	America
BC	301. Antigonus I Monophthalmos died at Ipsus (Phrygia)		321. Accession of Chandragupta, founder of Mauryan Dynasty. Capital at Pataliputra (Patna)	
	late 4th cent. Pytheas of Massalia circumnavigates Britain	late 4th cent. Foundation of Seleucid and Ptolemaic Empires		
	317–289. Agathocles at Syracuse			
	315. Lysimachus in Thrace, etc. (killed by Seleucus I Nicator [founder of Seleucid kingdom] at Corupedium 281)			300 BC–AD 300. Later Pre-Classic and Proto-Classic Maya culture in Yucatan, etc.
	Late 4th and early 3rd centuries. Teaching of Epicurus and Zeno (founder of Stoicism) at Athens			300 BC–AD 400. Hopewell culture (Woodland stage II) in Ohio and Illinois
	295. Foundation of Museum and Library at Alexandria			
	Early 3rd century. Calimachus and Theocritus			

Greek Lands	Near & Middle East	India & China	America
284–239. Antigonus II Gonatas king of Macedonia			
282–263. Philetaerus ruler of Pergamum			
281–261. Seleucid ruler Antiochus I Soter (defeats Gauls [Galatians] 273)		274/268–232/1. Reign of Mauryan Emperor Asoka	
270–215. Hiero II of Syracuse (Roman client)	263. Eumenes I of Pergamum disowns Seleucid suzerainty		
	256/5. Diodotus I Soter, governor of Bactria, breaks away from Seleucid Empire		
251–213. Aratus of Sicyon dominant in the Achaean League (then Philopoemon 192–182)		249–207. Ch'in Dynasty founded by Shih Huang Ti in China. Capital at Hsien-yang, near Sian	
	247. Parthian Arsaces I breaks away from Seleucid Empire		
244–192. Reformist kings at Sparta (Agis IV, Cleomenes III, Nabis)			

	Greek Lands	Near & Middle East	India & China	America
BC	241–197. Attalus I of Pergamum (defeats Gauls 230)	235–200. Euthydemus I Theos, second founder of Bactrian state		
	223–187. Seleucid ruler Antiochus III the Great (defeated by Romans 191–190)			
	221–179. Philip V of Macedonia (defeated by Romans at Cynoscephalae 197)			200 BC. Monte Alban, Oaxaca, Mexico, has population of 16,000 Peru, (Queyash Alto etc; Early Intermediate Period). Heads of kinship groups in power
			206/2 BC–AD 221. Han Dynasty in China. Capital of Former or Western Han at Ch'ang-an (until early 1st century AD)	
			185 BC. Mauryan Empire falls to Sunga Dynasty	
	179–168. Perseus of Macedonia (defeated by Romans at Pydna 168)		170/165. United Indo-Greek kingdom under Eucratides I (d.155), extended by Menander Soter Dikaios (Milinda in Buddhist tradition; 155–140/130)	
		167. Measures of Antiochus IV Epiphanes against Jews lead to Maccabean revolt against Seleucids		

Greek Lands	Near & Middle East	India & China	America
BC			
146. Corinth sacked, Achaean League dissolved, Macedonia and Greece annexed, by Romans	mid-2nd cent. Sadducees and Pharisees in Judaea		
		141–87. Wu Ti enlarges Chinese Empire: travels of explorer Chang Ch'ien (138–125), earliest historian Ssu-ma Ch'ien (100)	
133. Attalus III Philometor Euergetes leaves Pergamum to Rome			
120–63. Mithridates VI Eupator king of Pontus (three Roman wars end in annexation)			
51–30. Cleopatra VII of Egypt (then annexed by Rome)			
	30. Death of Cleopatra VII and Roman annexation of Egypt	40–1. Hermaeus Soter the last Indo-Greek monarch: his state then incorporated in Kushan Empire of Kadjula Kadphises I	

(II) The Romans and Others*

Rome and Italy

BC

1400–1000. 'Apennine Culture' (Bronze Age)

1300–1200. Mycenaean contacts with Sicily

10th cent. Alba Longa centre of association of Latin villages

10th–8th cent. Settlements at Rome

753. Traditional date of foundation of Rome

750–700. Urbanization and new wealth and power of Etruscan city-states in Etruria (first Tarquinii) and north Italy (Felsina)

7th cent. Rise of Etruscan power in Campania

625. Roman Forum drained. First amalgamation of villages

616–579. Tarquinius Priscus founds Etruscan dynasty at Rome

600. Conquest of Alba Longa by the Romans

578–535. Servius Tullius at Rome

550. Carthaginian Malchus in Sicily and Sardinia

6th cent. Etruscans and Greeks at Spina and Atria

535. Caere and Carthage defeat Massalians and Phocaeans in battle of Alalia

525/4. 'Long March' of Etruscans and others repelled by Cumae

late 6th cent. Lars Porsenna of Clusium

late 6th cent. Thefarie Velianas of Caere

late 6th cent. Greek quarter at Graviscae (port of Tarquinii)

* For the Near and Middle East, India and China, and America in early times, *see* Part 1 of Date Table

287

Rome and Italy

BC

507. Deposition of last king of Rome (Tarquinius Superbus), and foundation of Republic

506/4. Cumaeans and Latins defeat Etruscans at Aricia

496. Romans defeat Latins at Lake Regillus

494. First Secession of the Roman plebeians

493. Rome's Cassian Treaty with the Latins

474. Hiero I of Syracuse defeats Etruscans off Cumae

451–450. Decemvirates and Twelve Tables

396. Fall of Veii

387. Gauls defeat Romans on River Allia

383–341, 328–302, 298–290. Samnite Wars (Caudine Forks 321, Sentinum 295)

340–338. Latin and Campanian War

BC	Rome and the West	Near & Middle East*	India & China*	America*
				300 BC–AD 300. Later Pre-Classic and Proto-Classic Maya culture in Yucatan, etc.
				300 BC–AD 400. Hopewell culture (Woodland stage II) in Ohio and Illinois
	280–275. War with Pyrrhus of Epirus			
	264–241. First Punic War (Aegates Islands 241, annexation of Sardinia and Corsica 238)		206/2 BC–AD 221. Han Dynasty in China (expansion of empire under Wu Ti 141–87 BC)	
	218–201. Second Punic War (Trebia 218, Trasimene 217, Cannae 216, Metaurus 207, Ilipa 206, Zama 202)			
	200–196, 171–168 Second and Third Macedonian Wars	192–189. War against Seleucid Antiochus III the Great		
	(see Part I of Date Table)			

* See also Table of Dates (1)

289

Rome and the West	Near & Middle East	India & China	America
BC			
149–146. Third Punic War (destruction of Carthage and Corinth 146)			
139–132, 104–100, 73–71. Slave revolts		138–125. Chinese explorer Chang Ch'ien	
133. Scipio Aemilianus captures Numantia	133–129. Pergamum left to Rome and annexed as province of Asia		
133 and 123–2. Tribunates of Tiberius and Gaius Gracchus			
121. Annexation of Gallia Narbonensis (southern Gaul)			
112–105. Jugurthine War			
102–101. Marius defeats Teutones and Cimbri		100. Chinese historian Ssu-ma Ch'ien	
91–87. Social (Marsian) War			
81. Dictatorship of Sulla			
81–72. Revolt of Sertorius in Spain			
70. Consulships of Pompey and Crassus			

BC

Rome and the West	Near & Middle East	India & China	America
	66. Surrender of Tigranes I the Great of Armenia (95–56) to Pompey		
63. 'Conspiracy' of Catiline. Cicero's *Catilinarian Orations*	66–63. After suppression of pirates (66) Pompey converts remnant of Seleucid empire into Roman province of Syria, and Judaea becomes Roman client		
60. 'First Triumvirate' of Pompey, Crassus and Caesar, followed by first consulship of Caesar (59)		50 BC–AD 100. Roman trade with south India	
58–51. Caesar's Gallic War	53. Crassus defeated by Parthians near Carrhae and killed		
49–45. Civil War. Caesar's victories at Pharsalus (and the subsequent death of Pompey), Thapsus and Munda, followed by his perpetual dictatorship and assassination (44)	48–47. Caesar's Alexandrian War and defeat of Pharnaces II of the (Cimmerian) Bosphorus (63–47) at Zela		

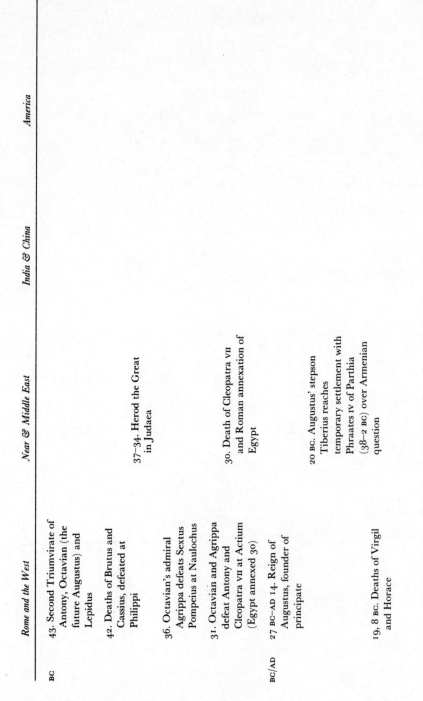

	Rome and the West	Near & Middle East	India & China	America
BC	43. Second Triumvirate of Antony, Octavian (the future Augustus) and Lepidus			
	42. Deaths of Brutus and Cassius, defeated at Philippi	37–34. Herod the Great in Judaea		
	36. Octavian's admiral Agrippa defeats Sextus Pompeius at Naulochus			
	31. Octavian and Agrippa defeat Antony and Cleopatra VII at Actium (Egypt annexed 30)	30. Death of Cleopatra VII and Roman annexation of Egypt		
BC/AD	27 BC–AD 14. Reign of Augustus, founder of principate	20 BC. Augustus' stepson Tiberius reaches temporary settlement with Phraates IV of Parthia (38–2 BC) over Armenian question		
	19, 8 BC. Deaths of Virgil and Horace			

292

AD

Rome and the West	Near & Middle East	India & China	America
	6–14. and from 44. Judaea a Roman province (30 or 33 crucifixion of Jesus, 64 execution of St Paul)	early 1st century AD. Capital of Latter or Eastern Han at Lo-yang	1–600. Moche culture on northern Peruvian coast
9. Arminius defeats and kills Varus in Teutoburg Forest			1–5000. Basketmaker II culture (hamlets of circular houses) in south-western United States
14–68. Julio-Claudian dynasty (Tiberius 14–37, Gaius [Caligula] 37–41, Claudius 41–54, Nero 54–68)	36. Settlement with Artabanus III of Parthia (12–38)		1st cent AD. Major urbanization at Teotihuacán, which controlled central Mexico (population of 200,000 in AD 500)
43–46. Annexation of Britain (revolt of Boudicca 61)			
	58–63. Wars of Corbulo against Vologeses I of Parthia (51–78), followed by further settlement		
65. Deaths of Seneca and Petronius			
68–69. Civil Wars (Galba, Otho, Vitellius)	66–73. First Jewish Revolt (Roman War): fall of Jerusalem (70) and Masada (73)		

Rome and the West	Near & Middle East	India & China	America
69–96. Flavian dynasty (Vespasian 69–79, Titus 79–81, Domitian 81–96)			
79. Destruction of Pompeii and Herculaneum by eruption of Vesuvius			
96–98. Nerva: adopts Trajan (98–117); further adoptive emperors, Hadrian (117–138), Antoninus Pius (138–161), Marcus Aurelius (161–180)		100 (?). Accession of Kushan king Kanishka. Capital at Purushapura (Peshawar)	100. Peru. Moche tomb of 'Old Lord of Sipán'
104, 117 (?), after 120, after 127. Deaths of Martial, Tacitus, Plutarch, Juvenal	113–117. Trajan's attempt to extend Roman Empire to Persian Gulf. War against Pacorus II (78–115/6), Revolt of Jewish Dispersion		
122, 142. Walls of Hadrian and Antoninus Pius in Britain			

Rome and the West	Near & Middle East	India & China	America
	132–5. Second Jewish Revolt (Roman War)		
	162–176. War of Lucius Verus (*d.* 169, colleague of Marcus Aurelius) against Vologeses III of Parthia (148–192)		
166–172, 177–180. Wars against Marcomanni and Sarmatians			
193–7. Rival emperors after murder of Commodus (180–192)			
193–235. Severan dynasty ('Military Monarchy'): Septimius Severus 193–211, Caracalla 211–217, Elagabalus 218–222, Severus Alexander 222–235	197–9. War of Septimius Severus (after defeating Pescennius Niger at Issus, 194) against Vologeses IV of Parthia (191–198/9)		
		200. The Six Systems of Indian philosophy	
212. *Constitutio Antoniniana* conferring general citizenship		221–589. The Six Dynasties in China, split into several states	
	224/6. Persian (Sassanian) Ardashir I overthrows Parthian state (Artabanus V)	224–271. P'ei Hsiu, who made a map of China in 18 sections	
235–268. 'Military Anarchy': many rulers at Rome and elsewhere			

AD

295

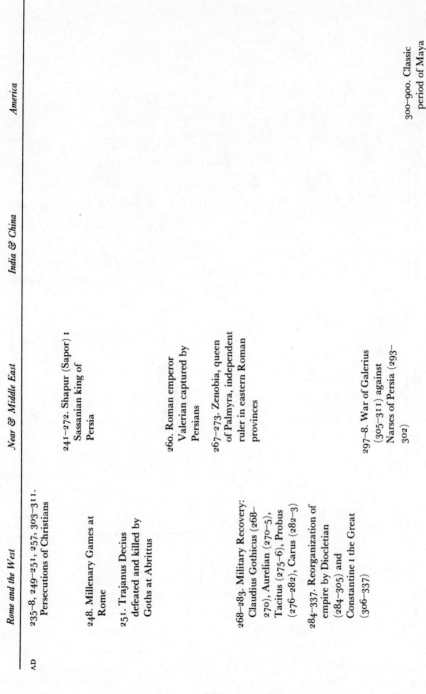

Rome and the West	Near & Middle East	India & China	America
AD			
235–8, 249–251, 257, 303–311. Persecutions of Christians			
	241–272. Shapur (Sapor) I Sassanian king of Persia		
248. Millenary Games at Rome			
251. Trajanus Decius defeated and killed by Goths at Abritus			
	260. Roman emperor Valerian captured by Persians		
	267–273. Zenobia, queen of Palmyra, independent ruler in eastern Roman provinces		
268–283. Military Recovery: Claudius Gothicus (268–270), Aurelian (270–5), Tacitus (275–6), Probus (276–282), Carus (282–3)			
284–337. Reorganization of empire by Diocletian (284–305) and Constantine I the Great (306–337)	297–8. War of Galerius (305–311) against Narses of Persia (293–302)		300–900. Classic period of Maya culture

Rome and the West	Near & Middle East	India & China	America
AD			300. Peru Moche tomb of 'Lord of Sipán'
313. Edict of Mediolanum in favour of the Christians (paganism briefly restored by Julian the Apostate, 361–3)			
		319/320. Accession of Chandra Gupta I, founder of the Gupta Dynasty in north India (335 Samudra Gupta, 375 Chandra Gupta II). Capital at Pataliputra (Patna)	
324–330. Foundation of Constantinople on site of Byzantium			
	338–350. Wars of Constantius II (337–361) against Sapor II of Persia (309–379)		
	363. Julian the Apostate dies of wounds during Persian War and Jovian negotiates unfavourable peace		
364. Division of empire; Valentinian I in west (capital Mediolanum, d.375)	364. Division of empire: Valens in east (capital Constantinople), killed by Goths at Hadrianapolis 378		

297

AD	Rome and the West	Near & Middle East	India & China	America
		378–395. Theodosius I the Great		
	373–397– (St Ambrose bishop of Mediolanum)			
	387, 394 Theodosius I defeats Magnus Maximus and Eugenius	387. Armenia divided between the eastern Roman and Persian Empires		
	395. Accession of Honorius (in western empire (*d.*423)	395. Accession of Arcadius in eastern empire (*d.*408)		
	395–408. Stilicho commander-in-chief in the west (then Aetius 432–454. Ricimer 456–472)			
	395–430. St Augustine bishop of Hippo Regius			
	404. Western capital moved from Mediolanum to Ravenna			
		408–450 Theodosius II eastern emperor (438 the Theodosian Code)		
	410. Capture of Rome by Alaric I the Visigoth			
	425–455. Valentinian III emperor in west			

Rome and the West	Near & Middle East	India & China	America
428–477. Gaiseric king of the Vandals (captures Carthage 439, sacks Rome 455)			
445–453. Attila sole king of the Huns (defeated by Aetius and Visigoths at Catalaunian Plains 451)			
474–5, 476–480. Julius Nepos western emperor at Ravenna, then in Dalmatia			
475–476. Romulus Augustulus the last western emperor at Ravenna, overthrown by Odoacer the Herulian, who becomes king of Italy (476–493)			

Bibliography

I ANCIENT WRITERS

(A) *Greek writers*

AESCHYLUS, of Eleusis, 525/524–456 BC. Athenian tragic dramatist.

ALCAEUS, of Mytilene (Lesbos), *c.*620 BC. Lyric poet.

ALCMAEON, of Croton, later 5th century BC. Natural scientist and physician.

ALCMAN, worked at Sparta, later 7th century BC. Lyric poet.

ANAXAGORAS, of Clazomenae, *c.*500–*c.*428 BC. Pre-Socratic philosopher.

ANAXIMANDER, of Miletus, *c.*610–after 546 BC. Pre-Socratic philosopher.

ANAXIMENES, of Miletus, after 600–528/525 BC. Pre-Socratic philosopher.

ANDOCIDES, of Athens, *c.*440–390 BC. Orator.

ANTIGONUS, of Carystus, *c.*240 BC. Biographer.

ANTISTHENES, of Athens, *c.*445–360 BC. Founder or forerunner of Cynic school of philosophy.

ANYTE, of Tegea, *c.*300 BC. Woman poet.

APOLLONIUS RHODIUS, of Egypt, *c.*295–*c.*215 BC. Epic poet.

ARATUS, of Sicyon, 271–213 BC. Statesman and autobiographer.

ARATUS, of Soli in Cilicia, *c.*315–240/329 BC. Writer of astronomical poem.

ARCHELAUS, of Athens, 5th century BC. Pre-Socratic philosopher.

ARCHILOCHUS, of Paros, *c.*710–after 648 BC (?). Poet.

ARCHYTAS, of Taras, 4th century BC. Statesman, mathematician and Pythagorean philosopher.

ARISTARCHUS, of Samos, early 3rd century BC. Astronomer.

ARISTOPHANES, of Athens, 457/445–before 385 BC. Dramatist (Old Comedy).

ARISTOTLE, of Stagirus, 384–322 BC. Philosopher and scientist.

ARRIAN, of Bithynia, 2nd century AD. Historian (of Alexander, etc.) and preserver of Epictetus (q.v.).

ASCLEPIADES, of Samos, early 3rd century BC. Epigrammatist.

AURELIUS, MARCUS, *see* MARCUS AURELIUS.

BACCHYLIDES, of Iulis (Ceos), *c.*524/521(?)–after 452 BC. Lyric poet.

BION, of Borysthenes (Olbia), *c.*325–after 239 BC.

CALLICLES, later 5th century BC. Sophist.

CALLIMACHUS, of Cyrene (lived at Alexandria), c.310/305–240 BC. Poet.

CERCIDAS, of Megalopolis, *c.*290–220 BC. Statesman, general, Cynic philosopher and poet.

300

CLEMENT, SAINT, born at Athens (?) (lived at Alexandria), *c.*AD 150–211/216. Christian theologian.

CORINNA, of Tanagra, *c.*200 BC (?). Woman lyric poet.

CRATES, of Thebes, *c.*365–285 BC. Cynic philosopher and poet.

CRATINUS, of Athens, later 5th century BC. Dramatist (Old Comedy).

CTESIBIUS, of Alexandria, *c.*270 BC. Mechanical inventor.

DEMETRIUS, of Phaleron, later 4th century BC. Athenian statesman and Peripatetic philosopher.

DEMOCRITUS, of Abdera, 5th century BC. Philosopher and scientist (atomist).

DEMOSTHENES, of Athens, 384–322 BC. Orator and statesman.

DIO CASSIUS, of Nicaea, *c.*AD 155–235. Historian of Rome.

DIOGENES, of Sinope, *c.*400–*c.*325 BC. Cynic philosopher.

DIOGENES LAERTIUS, 1st half of 3rd century AD. Summarizer of ancient philosophies.

DIONYSIUS I, of Syracuse, *c.*430–367 BC. Ruler and tragic dramatist.

EMPEDOCLES, of Acragas, *c.*493–*c.*433 BC. Pre-Socratic philosopher-poet and statesman.

EPICHARMUS, of Syracuse (?), early 5th century BC. Comic dramatist.

EPICTETUS, of Hierapolis (Phrygia), *c.*AD 55–*c.*135. Stoic philosopher (*Discourses*).

EPICURUS, of Samos, 341–270 BC. Founder of Epicurean school of philosophy.

ERASISTRATUS, of Ceos (lived at Alexandria), earlier 3rd century BC. Physician.

ERATOSTHENES, of Cyrene (lived at Alexandria), *c.*275–194 BC. Mathematician and geographer.

ERINNA, of Telos, *c.*300 BC. Woman poet.

EUCLIDES, of Megara, *c.*450–380 BC. Founder of Megarian school of philosophy.

EUPOLIS, of Athens, later 5th century BC. Dramatist (Old Comedy).

EURIPIDES, of Phlya (Attica), *c.*485/480–*c.*406 BC. Athenian tragic dramatist.

GORGIAS, of Leontini, *c.*483–376 BC. Sophist.

GOSPELS, *see* JOHN, LUKE, MARK, MATTHEW.

HECATAEUS, of Miletus, *c.*500 BC. Geographer and historian.

HERACLITUS, of Ephesus, *c.*500 BC. Pre-Socratic philosopher.

HERODAS (Herondas), of Cos (?), later 3rd century BC. Writer of mimes.

HERODOTUS, of Halicarnassus, *c.*480–*c.*425 BC. Historian.

HEROPHILUS, of Calchedon (lived at Alexandria), earlier 3rd century BC. Physician.

HESIOD, of Cyme (Aeolis) (lived at Ascra), 8th century BC.

HIPPARCHUS, of Nicaea (lived at Rhodes), *c.*190–after 126 BC. Astronomer.

HIPPIAS, of Elis, 5th century BC. Sophist.

HIPPOCRATES, of Cos, 5th century BC. Physician.

HIPPODAMUS, of Miletus, 5th century BC. Town-planner and political theorist.

HOMER, of Chios (lived at Smyrna), 8th century BC. Epic poet (*Iliad* and *Odyssey*).

HOMERIC HYMNS (not by Homer), 8th–6th centuries BC.

ION, of Chios (lived at Athens), 5th century BC. Poet, historian and autobiographer.

ISOCRATES, of Athens, 436–338 BC. Rhetorician, educationalist and political theorist.

JOHN, SAINT, Gospel of. Written in early 2nd century AD (uncertain authorship).

JOSEPHUS, of Jerusalem (later lived at Rome), AD 37/38–after 94/95. Historian of the Jews.

LEUCIPPUS, of Miletus, later 5th century BC. Philosopher and scientist (atomist).

LUKE, SAINT, Gospel of. Written in later 1st century AD (uncertain authorship).

MARCUS AURELIUS. Roman emperor (AD 161–180) and Stoic philosopher.

MARK, SAINT, Gospel of. Probably written soon after First Jewish Revolt (AD 66–73) (authorship uncertain).

MATTHEW, SAINT, Gospel of. Written in later 1st century AD (authorship uncertain).

MELEAGER, of Gadara, c.100 BC. Epigrammatist and Cynic satirist.

MENANDER, of Athens, c.342–292 BC. Dramatist (New Comedy).

MENIPPUS, of Gadara, earlier 3rd century BC. Satirist.

NESTORIUS, died c.AD 451, patriarch of Constantinople and Christian theologian.

ORIGEN, of Alexandria, c.AD 185/186–254/255. Christian theologian.

PANAETIUS, of Rhodes (lived at Athens and Rome), c.185/180–109 BC. Stoic philosopher.

PARMENIDES, of Elea, 6th–5th centuries BC. Pre-Socratic philosopher.

PAUL, SAINT, of Tarsus, died c.AD 62/64. Christian theologian and missionary.

PAUSANIAS, of Lydia, 2nd century AD. Travel-writer.

PHALEAS, of Calchedon, 5th century BC. Political theorist.

PHILO JUDAEUS, of Alexandria, c.30 BC–AD 45. Jewish theologian and philosopher.

PHRYNICHUS, of Athens, 6th–5th centuries BC. Tragic dramatist.

PINDAR, of Cynoscephalae, c.518–c.438 BC. Lyric poet.

PLATO, of Athens, c.429–347 BC. Philosopher.

PLUTARCH, of Chaeronea, before AD 50–after 120. Philosopher and biographer.

POLYBIUS, of Megalopolis (later lived at Rome), c.200–after 118 BC. Historian.

POLYCLITUS, of Sicyon and Argos, later 5th century BC. Sculptor and writer on sculpture.

POSIDONIUS, of Apamea (Syria), c.135–c.51/50 BC. Historian and polymath.

PROTAGORAS, of Abdera, 5th century BC. Sophist.

SAPPHO, of Eresus (Lesbos) (lived at Mytilene), born c.612 BC. Woman lyric poet.

SEMONIDES, of Samos (lived on Amorgos), 7th or 6th century BC. Iambic and elegiac poet.

SIMONIDES, of Iulis (Ceos), c.556–468 BC. Lyric and elegiac poet and epigrammatist.

SIMPLICIUS, of Cilicia, 6th century AD. Commentator on Aristotle.

SOLON, of Athens, early 6th century BC. Statesman and poet.

SOPHOCLES, of Colonus (Attica), c.496–406 BC. Athenian tragic dramatist.

STESICHORUS, of Mataurus (lived at Himera), c.632/629–c.556/553 BC (?). Lyric poet.

STRABO, of Amasia, c.63 BC–at least AD 21. Geographer and historian.

STRATO, of Lampsacus, later 3rd and earlier 2nd centuries BC. Scientist and Peripatetic (Aristotelian) philosopher.

THEOCRITUS, of Syracuse (lived at Cos and Alexandria), c.300–260 (?) BC. Bucolic (pastoral) poet and writer of mimes.

THEOPHRASTUS, of Eresus (Lesbos) (lived at Athens), *c.*370–288/285 BC. Peripatetic (Aristotelian) philosopher, scientist and polymath.

THEOPOMPUS, of Chios, 4th century BC. Historian.

THRASYMACHUS, of Calchedon, later 5th century BC. Sophist and rhetorician.

THUCYDIDES, of Athens, *c.*460/455–*c.*400 BC. Historian.

TIMON, of Phlius, *c.*320–230 BC. Sceptic philosopher and poet.

TYRTAEUS, of Sparta, 7th century BC. Elegiac poet.

XENOCRATES, of Calchedon, later 4th century BC. Platonic philosopher.

XENOPHANES, of Colophon, 6th–5th centuries BC. Pre-Socratic philosopher.

XENOPHON, of Erchia (Attica) (lived at Scillus in Elis), *c.*428–*c.*354 BC. Soldier, man of letters, historian.

ZENO, of Citium (Cyprus), 335–263 BC. Founder of the Stoic school of philosophy.

(B) *Latin Writers*

AMBROSE, SAINT, of Treviri (bishop of Mediolanum), *c.*AD 339–397. Theologian and letter-writer.

AMMIANUS MARCELLINUS, of Antioch (Antakya), *c.*AD 330–395. Historian.

APULEIUS, of Madaurus (N. Africa), 2nd century AD. Novelist.

AUGUSTINE, SAINT, of Thagaste (N. Africa) (bishop of Hippo Regius), AD 354–430. Theologian.

AUGUSTUS. First Roman *princeps* or emperor (31 BC–AD 14). Left autobiographical *Res Gestae Divi Augusti* (*Monumentum Ancyranum*).

BOETHIUS, *c.*AD 480–524. Consul, commentator, writer on mathematics and music and theology.

CAESAR, Gaius Julius, 100–44 BC. Dictator, writer of *Commentaries* (*Gallic War, Civil War*).

CASSIODORUS, of Scylacium, *c.*AD 490–583. Statesman, historian, writer of monastic manual.

CATO THE ELDER (the Censor), of Tusculum, 234–149 BC. Statesman, encyclopaedist, writer on agriculture.

CATULLUS, of Verona, *c.*84–54 BC. Poet.

CICERO, of Arpinum, 106–43 BC. Orator, writer on oratory and philosophy, letter-writer, statesman.

CORNUTUS, of Lepcis Magna, 1st century AD. Stoic philosopher and rhetorician.

ENNIUS, of Rudiae, 239–169 BC. Historical poet and dramatist.

GAIUS, 2nd century AD. Jurist.

HORACE, of Venusia, 65–8 BC. Lyric, satirical and philosophical poet.

JEROME, SAINT, of Stridon (on borders of Dalmatia and Pannonia), *c.*AD 348–420. Theologian.

JUVENAL, of Aquinum, earlier 2nd century AD. Satirical poet.

LIVIUS ANDRONICUS, of Tarentum, 3rd century BC. Tragic and comic dramatist and adapter of Homer.

LIVY, of Patavium, 64/59 BC–AD 12/17. Historian.

LUCAN, of Corduba, AD 39–65. Historical poet.

LUCILIUS, of Suessa Aurunca, later 2nd century BC. Satirical poet.

LUCRETIUS, *c.*94–55 BC. Philosophical (Epicurean) poet.

NAEVIUS, of Capua, later 2nd century BC. Tragic and comic dramatist and historical poet.

OVID, of Sulmo, 43 BC–AD 17. Poet.

PAPINIAN, executed AD 212. Jurist (*Quaestiones, Responsa*, etc.).

PERSIUS, AD 34–62. Philosophical (Stoic) and satirical poet.

PETRONIUS ARBITER, Titus Petronius Niger, consul AD 61. Novelist.

PLAUTUS, of Sarsina, later 3rd and earlier 2nd century BC. Comic dramatist.

PLINY THE ELDER, of Comum, AD 23/24–79. Officer, administrator, historian, scientist.

PLINY THE YOUNGER, of Comum, c.AD 61–c.112. Literary letter-writer.

PROPERTIUS, of Asisium, 54/47–before 2 BC. Elegiac love-poet.

QUINTILIAN, of Calagurris, c.AD 30/35–100 (?). Rhetorician and literary critic.

SALLUST, of Amiternum, c.86–c.35 BC. Historian.

SALVIAN, of Treviri (presbyter at Massilia), c.AD 400–480. Theologian.

SENECA THE YOUNGER, of Corduba, 4 BC/AD 1–AD 65. Statesman, Stoic philosopher, tragic dramatist, literary letter-writer.

SUETONIUS, of Hippo Regius, c.AD 69–after AD 121/122. Biographer.

TACITUS, of Gaul (German frontier?) or north Italy, c.AD 56–c.116 (?). Historian, biographer, ethnologist and writer on oratory.

TERENCE, of north Africa, c.190–159 BC. Comic dramatist.

TERTULLIAN, of Carthage, c.AD 160–c.240. Christian theologian.

TIBULLUS, later 1st century BC. Elegiac love-poet.

ULPIAN, of Tyre (Sur), killed AD 223. Jurist.

VARRO, of Reate, 116–27 BC. Encyclopaedic scholar, historian, biographer, geographer, writer on agriculture, philosophical (Cynic) satirist.

VIRGIL, of Mantua, 70–19 BC. Poet (Eclogues, Georgics, Aeneid).

VITRUVIUS, 1st century BC. Architect, military engineer, writer on architecture.

II MODERN WRITERS

General

L.J. ARCHER (ed.), Slavery and Other Forms of Unfree Labour, 1988

A.H. ARMSTRONG (ed.), Classical Mediterranean Spirituality, 1986

A. BENJAMIN (ed.), Post-Structuralist Classics, 1988

E.J. BICKERMAN, Chronology of the Ancient World, 1980 (1968)

L.R. BINFORD, Debating Archaeology, 1989

L.R. BINFORD, In Pursuit of the Past: Decoding the Archaeological Record, 1988 (1983)

R.R. BOLGAR, The Classical Heritage and its Beneficiaries, 1977 (1954)

R. BROEK, etc. (eds), Knowledge of God in the Graeco-Roman World, 1988

A. CAMERON and A. KUHRT (eds), Images of Women in Antiquity, 1983

E. CANTARELLA, Pandora's Daughter: The Role and Status of Women in Greek and Roman Antiquity, 1987

R.A.G. CARSON, Coins of Greece and Rome, 1971 (1962)

M. CRAWFORD, Sources for Ancient History, 1983

D. DAICHES and A. THORLBY (eds), The Classical World, 1972

J. FERGUSON (ed.), Greek and Roman Religion: A Source Book, 1988

M.I. FINLEY, Ancient History: Evidence and Models, 1985

M.I. FINLEY, Ancient Slavery and Modern Ideology, 1983 (1980)

M.I. FINLEY, *Politics in the Ancient World*, 1983

M.I. FINLEY, *The Ancient Economy*, 1985 (1973)

H.P. FOLEY (ed.), *Reflections of Women in Antiquity*, 1981

C.W. FORNARA, *The Nature of History in Ancient Greece and Rome*, 1988

Y. GARLAN, *War in the Ancient World: A Social History*, 1975

P.D.A. GARNSEY (ed.), *Non-Slave Labour in the Greco-Roman World*, 1980

P.D.A. GARNSEY and C.R. WHITTAKER (eds), *Imperialism in the Ancient World*, 1979

M. GRANT, *A Guide to the Ancient World: A Dictionary of Classical Place Names*, 1986

M. GRANT, *Greek and Latin Authors 800 BC–AD 1000*, 1980

M. GRANT, *Myths of the Greeks and Romans*, 1989 (1962)

M. GRANT, *The Visible Past: Greek and Roman History from Archaeology 1960–1990*, 1990

M. GRANT (ed.), *Greece and Rome: The Birth of Western Civilization*, 1986 (1964)

M. GRANT and R. KITZINGER (eds), *Civilization of the Ancient Mediterranean: Greece and Rome*, 3 vols, 1988

P. GREEN, *Classical Bearings: Interpreting Ancient History and Culture*, 1989

J. HIGGINBOTHAM (ed.), *Greek and Latin Literature: A Comparative Literature*, 1969

G. HIGHET, *The Classical Tradition*, 1967 (1949)

M.C. HOWATSON (ed.), *The Oxford Companion to Classical Literature*, 1989 (1937)

T. IRWIN, *Classical Thought*, 1989

A.W. LAWRENCE, *Greek and Roman Sculpture*, 1972

P. LEKAS, *Marx on Classical Antiquity: Problems of Historical Methodology*, 1989

T.J. LUCE (ed.), *Ancient Writers: Greece and Rome*, 2 vols, 1982

H.I. MARROU, *A History of Education in Antiquity*, 1977 (1956)

M. MASSEY, *Women in Ancient Greece and Rome*, 1988

F. MEIJER and H. MULDER, *Trade and Transport in the Ancient World*, 1988

R.B. ONIANS (ed.), *The Origins of European Thought*, 1988 (1951)

J. PERADOTTO and J.P. SULLIVAN, *Women in the Ancient World*, 1984

S.B. POMEROY, *Goddesses, Whores, Wives and Slaves: Women in Classical Antiquity*, 1975

M. REINHOLD, *Diaspora: The Jews Among the Greeks and Romans*, 1983

A.E. SAMUEL, *The Promise of the West: The Greek World, Rome and Judaism*, 1989

C. SCARRE (ed.), *Past Worlds: The Times Atlas of Archaeology*, 1988

A. SHERRATT (ed.), *The Cambridge Encyclopaedia of Archaeology*, 1980

E. SIMON, *The Ancient Theatre*, 1982

C.G. STARR, *History of the Ancient World*, 3rd ed., 1983

C.G. STARR, *The Influence of Sea-Power on Ancient History*, 1989

H. TEMPORINI, W. HAASE, etc. (eds), *Aufstieg und Niedergang der antiken Welt*, many vols, 1972– .

A. WALLACE-HADRILL (ed.), *Patronage in Ancient Society*, 1990 (1989)

A. WEDBERG, *A History of Philosophy in Antiquity and the Middle Ages*, 1982

T. WIEDEMANN, *Greek and Roman Slavery*, 1981

S. WOODFORD, *The Art of Greece and Rome*, 1982

The Greeks

A.W.H. ADKINS and P. WHITE (eds), *Readings in Western Civilization, I: The Greek Polis*, 1986

A.H. ARMSTRONG, *Introduction to Ancient Philosophy*, 1965 (1947)

J. BARNES, *The Presocratic Philosophers*, 2 vols, 1979

J. BARNES (ed.), *Early Greek Philosophy*, 1987

H. BARRETT, *The Sophists: Rhetoric, Democracy and Plato's Idea of Sophistry*, 1987

H. BENGTSSON, *History of Greece from the Beginnings to the Byzantine Era* (ed. E.F. Bloedow), 1988 (1969)

M. BERNAL, *The Afroasiatic Roots of Classical Civilization, I: The Fabrication of Ancient Greece 1785–1985*, 1988

C.R. BEYE, *Ancient Greek Literature and Society*, 1987 (1975)

R. BICHLER, *Hellenismus*, 1983

M. BIEBER, *The Sculpture of the Hellenistic Age*, 1981 (1955)

W.R. BIERS, *The Archaeology of Greece: An Introduction*, 1987 (1980)

J. BOARDMAN, *Greek Art*, 1985 (1964)

J. BOARDMAN, *Pre-Classical*, 1978 (1967)

J. BOARDMAN, *The Greeks Overseas*, 1984 (1964)

J. BOARDMAN, etc. (eds), *The Cambridge Ancient History, III, Part 3: The Expansion of the Greek World 8th to 6th Centuries BC*, 2nd ed., 1982

J. BOARDMAN, etc. (eds), *The Oxford History of the Classical World, I: Greece and the Hellenistic World*, 1988 (1966)

A.R. BOSWORTH, *Conquest and Empire: The Reign of Alexander the Great*, 1988

C.M. BOWRA, *The Greek Experience*, 1985 (1957)

R. BROWNING (ed.), *The Greek World: Classical, Byzantine and Modern*, 1985

W. BURKERT, *Greek Religion: Archaic and Classical*, 1985

A.R. BURN, *The Pelican History of Greece*, 1982 (1966)

J.B. BURY and R. MEIGGS, *A History of Greece*, 1987 (1990)

I. CARRADICE and M. PRICE, *Coinage in the Greek World*, 1988

M. CARY, *History of the Greek World from 353 to 146 BC*, 1977 (1951)

G.A. CHRISTOPOULOS and J.C. BASTIAS (eds.), *History of the Hellenic World*, 2 vols, 1975

G.W. CLARKE (ed.), *Rediscovering Hellenism: The Hellenic Inheritance and the English Imagination*, 1989

J.N. COLDSTREAM, *Geometric Greece*, 1977

B.F. COOK, *Greek Inscriptions*, 1987

R.M. COOK, *Greek Art*, 1976 (1972)

R.M. COOK, *Greek Painted Pottery*, 1972 (1960)

J.J. COULTON, *Ancient Greek Architects at Work*, 1988 (1982)

J.K. DAVIS, *Democracy and Classical Greece*, 1978

L. DE CRESCENZO, *The History of Greek Philosophy: The Pre-Socratics*, 1988

G.E.M. DE SAINTE CROIX, *The Classical Struggle in the Ancient World*, 1983 (1981)

W.B. DINSMOOR, *The Architecture of Ancient Greece*, 1975 (1950)

K.J. DOVER, *Greek and the Greeks, I: Language, Poetry, Drama*, 1987

K.J. DOVER, *The Greeks and Their Legacy*, 2 vols, 1989

P.E. EASTERLING and B.M.W. KNOX (eds), *The Cambridge History of Classical Literature, I: Greek Literature*, 1989 (1985)

P.E. EASTERLING and J.V. MUIR, *Greek Religion and Society*, 1985

V. EHRENBERG, *The Greek State*, 1974 (1960)

J. FERGUSON, *Among the Gods: An Archaeological Exploration of Ancient Greek Religion*, 1989

J. FERGUSON, *The Heritage of Hellenism*, 1973

J.V.A. FINE, *The Ancient Greeks*, 1983

M.I. FINLEY, *Democracy Ancient and Modern*, 1985 (1973)

M.I. FINLEY, *Economy and Society in Ancient Greece*, 1983 (1981)

M.I. FINLEY, *The Ancient Greeks*, 1977 (1963)

M.I. FINLEY (ed.), *The Legacy of Greece: A New Appraisal*, 1981

F.J. FROST, *Greek Society*, 1971

Y. GARLAN, *Slavery in Ancient Greece*, 1988 (1982)

M. GRANT, *From Alexander to Cleopatra: The Hellenistic World*, 1990 (1982)

M. GRANT, *The Classical Greeks*, 1989

M. GRANT, *The Rise of the Greeks*, 1987

P. GREEN, *Alexander to Actium: the Hellenistic Age*, 1990

E.S. GRUEN, *The Hellenistic World and the Coming of Rome*, 1984

W.K.C. GUTHRIE, *History of Greek Philosophy*, 6 vols, 1962–1986 (1981)

N.G.L. HAMMOND, *History of Greece to 322 BC*, 1986 (1959)

N.G.L. HAMMOND, *History of Macedonia*, III (336–167 BC), 1988

N.G.L. HAMMOND, *The Classical Age of Greece*, 1975

N.G.L. HAMMOND, *The Macedonian State: Origins, Institutions and History*, 1990

V.D. HANSON, *The Western Way of War: Infantry Battle in Classical Greece*, 1990 (1989)

C.M. HAVELOCK, *Hellenistic Art*, 1971

R.J. HOPPER, *The Early Greeks*, 1976

S.C. HUMPHREYS, *Anthropology and the Greeks*, 1983 (1978)

L.H. JEFFREY, *Archaic Greece: The City-States c.700–500 BC*, 1978

G.K. JENKINS, *Ancient Greek Coins*, 1972

A.H.M. JONES, *Athenian Democracy*, 1987 (1957)

A.H.M. JONES, *The Greek City from Alexander to Justinian*, 1981 (1940)

R. JUST, *Women in Athenian Law and Life*, 1989

H. KOESTER, *History, Culture and Religion in the Hellenistic Age*, 1982

A.W. LAWRENCE, *Greek Architecture*, 4th ed. (ed. R.A. Tomlinson), 1983 (1957)

A. LESKY, *A History of Greek Literature*, 1966

P. LEVI, *The Pelican History of Greek Literature*, 1985

D.M. LEWIS and R. MEIGGS (eds), *A Selection of Greek Historical Inscriptions to the end of the Fifth Century BC*, 1988 (1969)

R. LING, *The Greek World*, 1988 (1976)

G.E.R. LLOYD, *The Revelations of Wisdom*, 1987

H. LLOYD-JONES (ed.), *The Greeks*, 1975 (1962)

A.A. LONG, *The Hellenistic Philosophers*, I, 1987

A.A. LONG and D.N. SEDLEY, *The Hellenistic Philosophers*, 2 vols, 1989 (1987)

P. MACKENDRICK, *The Greek Stones Speak*, 1981 (1962)

O. MURRAY, *Early Greece*, 1980

O. MURRAY and S. PRICE (eds.), *The Greek City: From Homer to Alexander*, 1990

D. MUSTI, *Storia Greca*, 1989

J. OBER, *Mass and Élite in Democratic Athens*, 1989

J. ONIANS, *Art and Thought in the Hellenistic Age*, 1982 (1979)

J.J. POLLITT, *Art and Experience in Ancient Greece*, 1972

J.J. POLLITT, *Art in the Hellenistic Age*, 1986

J.J. POLLITT, *The Art of Ancient Greece: Sources and Documents*, 1990

A. POWELL, *Athens and Sparta: Constructing Greek Political and Social History 478–371 BC*, 1988

P.J. RHODES, *The Athenian Empire*, 1985

P.J. RHODES, *The Greek City-States: A Source Book*, 1986

G.M.A. RICHTER, *A Handbook of Greek Art*, 9th ed., 1987 (1959)

J.W. ROBERTS, *City of Socrates: An Introduction to Classical Athens*, 1984

C.M. ROBERTSON, *A Shorter History of Greek Art*, 1981

N.K. RUTTER, *Greek Coinage*, 1983

M.B. SAKELLARIOU, *The Polis-State: Definition and Origin*, 1989

H. SANCISI-WEERDENBURG and A. KUHRT (eds), *Achaemenid History*, 3 vols, 1989

D. SANSONE, *Greek Athletics and the Genesis of Sport*, 1988

R. SEALEY, *A History of the Greek City-States 700–338 BC*, 1976

R. SEALEY, *Women and Law in Classical Greece*, 1990

R.K. SINCLAIR, *Democracy and Participation in Athens*, 1988

A.M. SNODGRASS, *An Archaeology of Greece*, 1988

C.G. STARR, *The Birth of Athenian Democracy: The Assembly in the Fifth Century BC*, 1990

A. STEWART, *Greek Sculpture: An Exploration*, 1990

D. STOCKTON, *The Classical Athenian Democracy*, 1990

O. TAPLIN, *Greek Fire*, 1990

W.W. TARN and G.T. GRIFFITH, *Hellenistic Civilisation*, 1974 (1927)

J.P. VERNANT, *Myth and Society in Ancient Greece*, 1982 (1980)

P. WALCOT (ed.), *The Ancient World: Source Books*, 4 vols (Greece), 1973–6

F.W. WALBANK, *The Hellenistic World*, 1981

F.W. WALBANK, etc. (eds), *The Cambridge Ancient History, VII, Part I: The Hellenistic World*, 2nd ed., 1984

L. WHIBLEY, *A Companion to Greek Studies*, 1968 (1931)

C.D. WILCOXON, *Athens Ascendant*, 1979

E. WILL, *Histoire politique du monde hellénistique*, 2 vols, 1981, 1982 (1979)

D. WILLIAMS, *Greek Vases*, 1985

J.J. WINKLER and F.I. ZEITLIN, *Nothing to do with Dionysus? Athenian Drama in its Social Context*, 1990

E.M. WOOD, *Peasant-Citizen and Slave: The Foundations of Athenian Democracy*, 1988

S. WOODFORD, *An Introduction to Greek Art*, 1988 (1986)

A.G. WOODHEAD, *The Study of Greek Inscriptions*, 1981 (1959)

F.J. YARTZ, *Ancient Greek Philosophy: Sourcebook and Perspective*, 1984

The Romans

G. ALFÖLDY, *The Social History of Rome*, 1988 (1985, 1975)

P.D. ARNOTT, *An Introduction to the Roman World*, 1976

A.E. ASTIN, etc. (eds), *The Cambridge Ancient History, VIII: Rome and the Mediterranean to 133 BC*, 2nd ed., 1989

E. BADIAN, *Roman Imperialism in the Late Republic*, 1968 (1967)

B. BALDWIN, *An Anthology of Later Latin Literature*, 1987

J.P.V.D. BALSDON (ed.), *The Romans*, 1965

T. BLAGG and M. MILLETT (eds), *The Early Roman Empire in the West*, 1990

A.E.R. BOAK and W.G. SINNIGEN, *History of Rome to AD 565*, 5th ed., 1969

J. BOARDMAN, etc. (eds), *The Oxford History of the Classical World, II: The Roman World*, 1988 (1986)

K.R. BRADLEY, *Slavery and Rebellion in the Roman Empire 140–70 BC*, 1990.

K.R. BRADLEY, *Slaves and Masters in the Roman Empire*, 1987, (1984)

D.C. BRAUND, *Rome and the Friendly King*, 1984

D.C. BRAUND (ed.), *The Administration of the Roman Empire 241 BC–AD 193*, 1988

P.A. BRUNT, *The Fall of the Roman Republic and Related Essays*, 1988

A. BURNETT, *Coinage in the Roman World*, 1987

J.B. CAMPBELL, *The Emperor and the Roman Army 31 BC–AD 235*, 1984

H. CARCOPINO, *Daily Life in Ancient Rome*, 1956

R.A.G. CARSON, *Coins of the Roman Empire*, 1990

M. CARY and H.H. SCULLARD, *A History of Rome*, 1975 (1935)

H. CHADWICK, *Early Christian Thought and the Christian Tradition*, 1984 (1966)

R. CHEVALLIER, *Roman Roads*, 1976

K. CHRIST, *The Romans: An Introduction to their History and Civilization*, 1984

F.M. CLOVER and R.S. HUMPHREYS (eds), *Tradition and Innovation in Late Antiquity*, 1989

O.A.W. DILKE, *The Ancient Romans: How they Lived and Worked*, 1975

D.R. DUDLEY, *Roman Society*, 1975

A.M. DUFF, *Freedmen in the Early Roman Empire*, 1958

R. DUNCAN JONES, *The Economy of the Roman Empire*, 1982

R. DUNCAN JONES, *Structure and Scale in the Roman Economy*, 1990

D.C. EARL, *The Moral and Political Tradition of Rome*, 1984 (1967)

J. FERGUSON, *The Religions of the Roman Empire*, 1982 (1970)

A. FERRILL, *The Fall of the Roman Empire: The Military Explanation*, 1988 (1983)

R. LANE FOX, *Pagans and Christians*, 1990

J.F. GARDNER, *Women in Roman Law and Society*, 1986

P. GARNSEY and R. SALLER, *The Roman Empire: Economy, Society and Culture*, 1987

W. GOFFART, *Barbarians and Romans AD 418–584: The Technique of Accommodation*, 1980

W. GOFFART, *Rome's Fall and After*, 1989

M. GRANT, *History of Rome*, 1987 (1978)

M. GRANT, *The Climax of Rome*, 1974 (1968)

M. GRANT, *Roman History from Coins*, 1968 (1958)

M. GRANT, *The Army of the Caesars*, 1974

M. GRANT, *The Etruscans*, 1980

M. GRANT, *The Fall of the Roman Empire*, 1990 (1976)

M. GRANT, *The Jews in the Roman World*, 1984 (1973)

M. GRANT, *The Roman Emperors*, 1985

M. GRANT, *The World of Rome*, 1987 (1960)

R.M. GRANT, *Augustus to Constantine: The Rise and Triumph of the Christian Movement in the Roman World*, 1990 ed.

K. GREENE, *The Archaeology of the Roman Economy*, 1986

E.S. GRUEN, *Studies in Greek Culture and Roman Policy*, 1990

N. HANNESTAD, *Roman Art and Imperial Policy*, 1986

M. HENIG (ed.), *A Handbook of Roman Art*, 1983

S. JOHNSON, *Rome and its Empire*, 1989

A.H.M. JONES, *A History of Rome through the Fifth Century*, 1968

A.H.M. JONES, *The Decline of the Ancient World*, 1966

A.H.M. JONES, *The Later Roman Empire*, 1989 (1964)

A.H.M. JONES, *The Roman Economy: Studies in Ancient Economic and Administrative History*, 1974

A. KEAVENEY, *Rome and the Unification of Italy*, 1988

E.J. KENNEY and W.V. CLAUSEN, *The Cambridge History of Classical Literature, II: Latin Literature*, 1982 (also in five separate parts, 1983)

A. KING, *The Archaeology of the Roman Empire*, 1982

W. KUNKEL, *An Introduction to Roman Legal and Constitutional History*, 1973 (1966)

B. LEVICK, *The Government of the Roman Empire: A Sourcebook*, 1985

N. LEWIS, *The Roman Principate 27 BC–285 AD*

E.N. LUTTWAK, *The Grand Strategy of the Roman Empire from the First Century AD to the Third*, 1976

P. MACKENDRICK, *The Mute Stones Speak*, 1983 (1960)

W.L. MACDONALD, *The Architecture of the Roman Empire*, 2 vols, 1982 (1956), 1986

A.H. MCDONALD, *Republican Rome*, 1966

R. MACMULLEN, *Changes in the Roman Empire*, 1990

R. MACMULLEN, *Corruption and the Decline of Rome*, 1988

R. MACMULLEN, *Roman Social Relations 50 BC–AD 284*, 1981 (1974)

F.B. MARSH, *A History of the Roman World 146 to 30 BC*, 1971 (1935)

H. MARSH, *The Caesars*, 1972

A. MASSIE, *The Caesars*, 1988 (1983)

H. MATTINGLY, *Roman Coins*, 1962 (1928)

F. MILLAR, *The Emperor in the Roman World*, 1977

C. NICOLET, *Rome et la conquête du monde méditerranéen*, 1977

C. NICOLET, *The World of the Citizen in Republican Rome*, 1980

R.M. OGILVIE, *Roman Literature and Society*, 1984 (1980)

R.M. OGILVIE, *The Romans and their Gods*, 1969

V.E. PAOLI, *Rome: Its People, Life and Customs*, 1963

J. PELIKAN, *The Excellent Empire: The Fall of Rome and the Triumph of the Church*, 1990

T.W. POTTER, *Roman Italy*, 1987

J.D. RANDERS-PEHRSON, *Barbarians and Romans: The Birth-Struggle to Europe AD 400–700*, 1983

M. ROSTOVTZEFF, *Social and Economic History of the Roman Empire* (ed. P.M. Fraser), 1979 (1926)

E.T. SALMON, *A History of the Roman World: 30 BC to AD 138*, 1990 (1944)

H.H. SCULLARD, *A History of the Roman World: 753 to 146 BC*, 1980 (1935)

H.H. SCULLARD, *From the Gracchi to Nero*, 1990 (1959)

F.B. SEAR, *Roman Achitecture*, 1989

H. SHELTON, *As the Romans Did: A Sourcebook in Roman Social History*, 1988

M. SORDI, *The Christians and the Roman Empire*, 1986

J.E. STAMBAUGH, *The Ancient Roman City*, 1988

C.G. STARR, *The Beginnings of Imperial Rome: Rome in the Mid-Republic*, 1980

R. SYME, *Roman Papers*, 7 vols, 1979–1990

R. SYME, *The Roman Revolution*, 1960 (1939)

R.J.A. TALBERT, *The Senate of Imperial Rome*, 1984

M. VICKERS, *Ancient Rome*, 1989 (1977)

J. WACHER, *The Roman Empire*, 1987

J. WACHER (ed.), *The Roman World*, 2 vols, 1988, 1990

F.W. WALBANK, etc. (eds), *The Cambridge Ancient History, Vol. VII, Part 2, The Rise of Rome to 220 BC*, 2nd ed., 1989

A. WARDMAN, *Rome's Debt to Greece*, 1976

G.R. WATSON, *The Roman Soldier*, 1983 (1969)

G. WEBSTER, *The Roman Imperial Army*, 1985 (1969)

C. WELLS, *The Roman Empire*, 1984

L.P. WILKINSON, *The Roman Experience*, 1975

G. WILLIAMS, *The Nature of Roman Poetry*, 1983 (1970)

Z. YAVETZ, *Slaves and Slavery in Ancient Rome*, 1988

MAPS

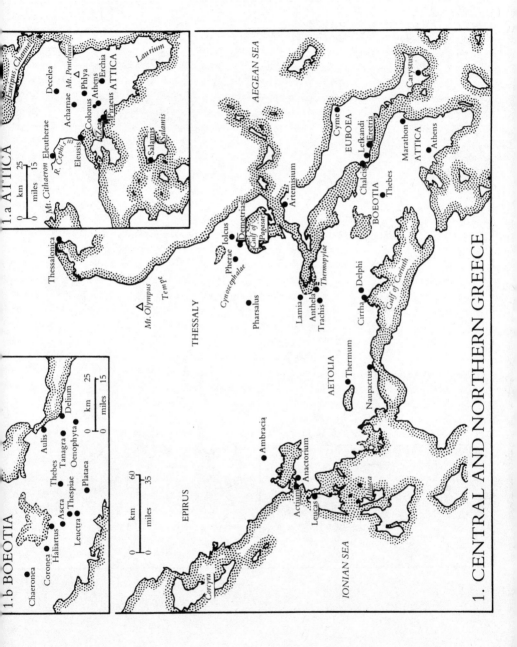

1.a ATTICA

Euripus Channel

Decelea
Acharnae *Mt. Pentelicus*
Phlya
Athens
Erchia
*R. Cephis*is
Eleusis
Colonus
Piraeus ATTICA
Ceos
Salamis
Salamis
Laurium

Mt. Cithaeron Eleutherae

km   25
     15
miles
0

1.b BOEOTIA

Chaeronea
Coronea
Haliartus
Ascra
Thebes
Tanagra
Aulis
Delium
Leuctra
Thespiae
Oenophyta
Plataea

km   25
     15
miles
0

1. CENTRAL AND NORTHERN GREECE

AEGEAN SEA

Cyme

EUBOEA
Lefkandi
Chalcis
Eretria

Marathon
ATTICA
Athens

Carystus

BOEOTIA
Thebes

Artemisium

Thessalonica

Mt. Olympus
Tempe

Pherae
Iolcus
Demetrias
Gulf of Pagasae

THESSALY

Cynoscephalae

Pharsalus

Lamia
Anthela
Trachis
Thermopylae

Delphi
Cirrha
Gulf of Corinth

AETOLIA
Thermum

Naupactus

Ambracia

EPIRUS

Anactorium
Actium
Leucas
Ithaca

IONIAN SEA

Corcyra

km   60
     35
miles
0

311

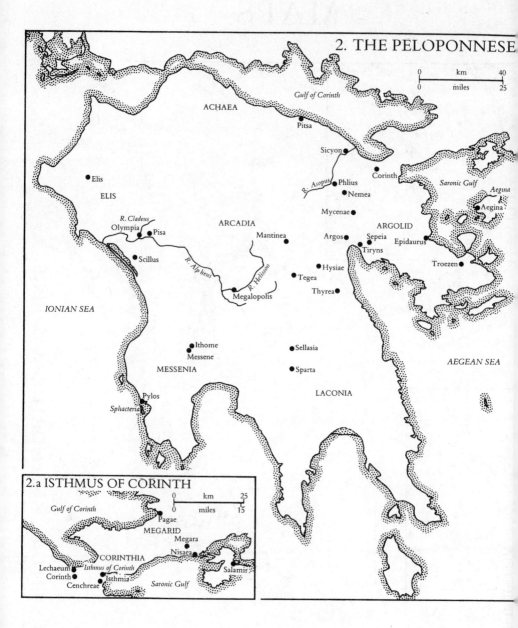

2. THE PELOPONNESE

km 40
miles 25

ACHAEA

Gulf of Corinth

Pitsa

Sicyon

R. Asopus Phlius

Corinth

Saronic Gulf

Aegina

Elis

ELIS

Nemea

Mycenae

Aegina

ARCADIA

R. Cladeus

Olympia Pisa

Mantinea

Argos Sepeia

ARGOLID

Epidaurus

Scillus

R. Alpheus

Tiryns

R. Helisson

Hysiae

Troezen

IONIAN SEA

Megalopolis

Tegea

Thyrea

Ithome

Messene

Sellasia

AEGEAN SEA

MESSENIA

Sparta

Pylos

LACONIA

Sphacteria

2.a ISTHMUS OF CORINTH

Gulf of Corinth

km 25
miles 15

Pagae

MEGARID

Megara

CORINTHIA

Nisaea

Lechaeum *Isthmus of Corinth*

Corinth

Isthmia

Salamis

Cenchreae

Saronic Gulf

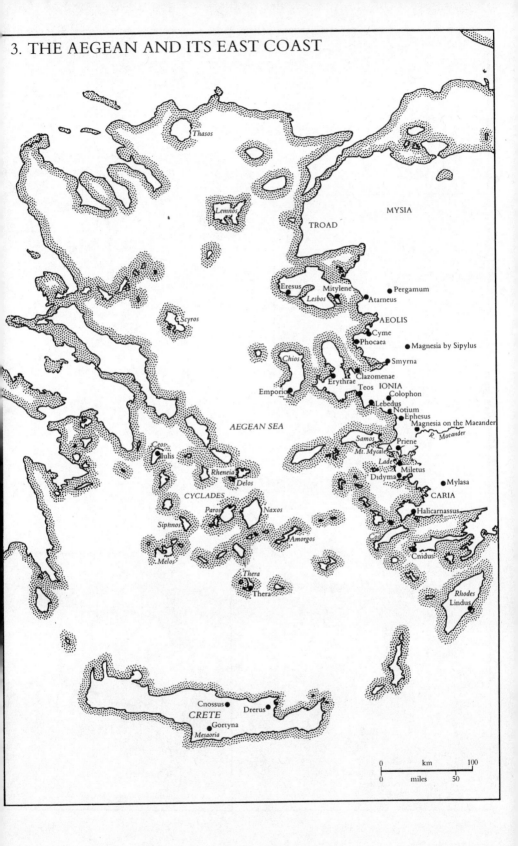

3. THE AEGEAN AND ITS EAST COAST

Thasos

Lemnos

MYSIA

TROAD

Eresus Mitylene ● Pergamum
Lesbos Atarneus

Scyros AEOLIS
Cyme
Phocaea ● Magnesia by Sipylus

Chios Smyrna

Clazomenae
Erythrae Teos IONIA
Emporio Colophon
Lebedus
Notium
● Ephesus
Magnesia on the Maeander

AEGEAN SEA *R. Maeander*

Samos Priene
Ceos Mt. Mycale
Iulis Lade
Rheneia Miletus
Delos Didyma ● Mylasa

CYCLADES CARIA
Paros
Naxos Halicarnassus
Siphnos
Cos
Amorgos
Melos Cnidus

Thera
Rhodes
Thera Lindus

Cnossus ● Drerus
CRETE
Gortyna
Mesaoria

0   km   100
0   miles   50

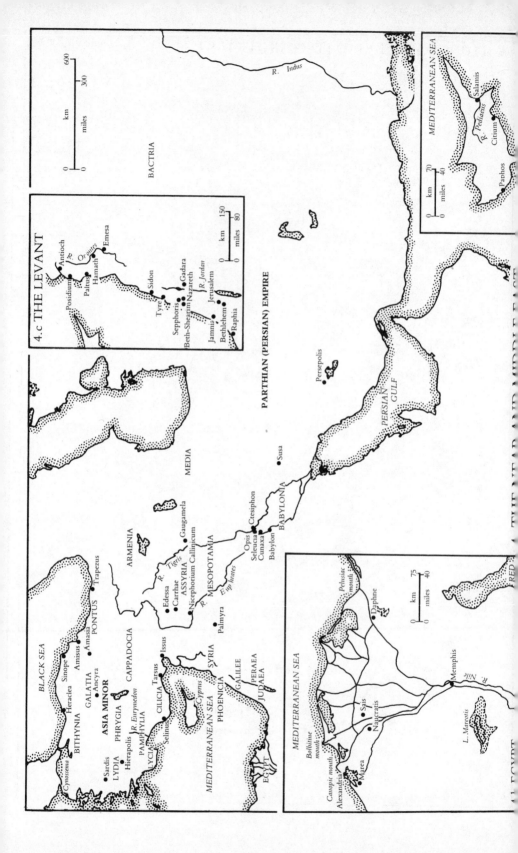

4.c THE LEVANT

Antioch
R. Orontes
Posidium
Paltus
Hamath
Emesa
Sidon
Sepphoris
Beth-Shearim Nazareth
Gadara
Tyre
R. Jordan
Jammia
Jerusalem
Bethlehem
Raphia

km 150
miles 80

PARTHIAN (PERSIAN) EMPIRE

Persepolis

PERSIAN GULF

MEDIA

Susa

BABYLONIA

Opis
Seleucia Ctesiphon
Cunaxa
Babylon

ARMENIA

R. Tigris
Gaugamela

Edessa
Carrhae
Nicephorium Callinicum

MESOPOTAMIA

R. Euphrates

Palmyra

BLACK SEA

Sinope
Heraclea
Amisus
Amasia
Trapezus

BITHYNIA
GALATIA
Ancyra
PONTUS

PHRYGIA
CAPPADOCIA

Hierapolis
R. Eurymedon
Sardis
LYDIA
PAMPHYLIA
LYCIA
Selinus
CILICIA
Tarsus
Issus

Cynossema

ASIA MINOR

Cyprus

SYRIA

PHOENICIA
GALILEE
PERAEA
JUDAEA

MEDITERRANEAN SEA

EGYPT

R. Indus

BACTRIA

600
300
km
miles
0
0

MEDITERRANEAN SEA

Salamis
R. Pediaeus
Citium
Paphos

km 70
miles 40
0
0

MEDITERRANEAN SEA

Pelusiac mouth

Daphne

Bolbitine mouth

Canopic mouth
Alexandria
Marea
Sais
Naucratis
Memphis
R. Nile
L. Mareotis

km 75
miles 40
0
0

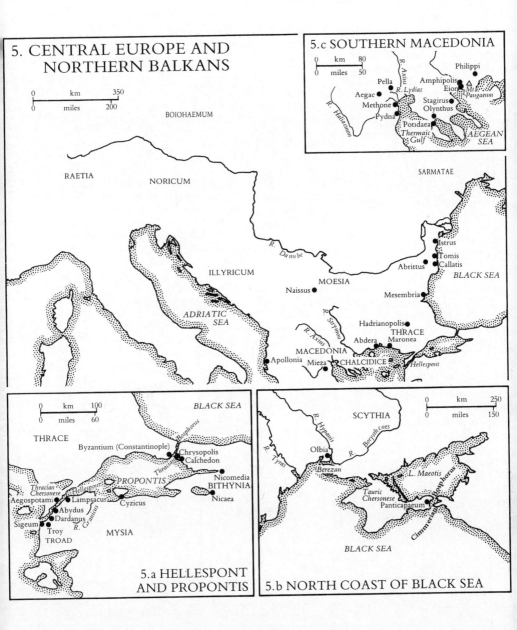

5. CENTRAL EUROPE AND
NORTHERN BALKANS

0 | km | 350
0 | miles | 200

BOIOHAEMUM

RAETIA

NORICUM

SARMATAE

ILLYRICUM

R. Danube

MOESIA

Naissus

Istrus
Tomis
Abrittus
Callatis

BLACK SEA

Mesembria

ADRIATIC
SEA

R. Strymon

R. Axius

Hadrianopolis

THRACE

Abdera
Maronea

MACEDONIA

Apollonia
Mieza

CHALCIDICE

Hellespont

5.c SOUTHERN MACEDONIA

0 | km | 80
0 | miles | 50

R. Axius

Philippi

Pella
Amphipolis
Eion
Mt. Pangaeum

Aegae
R. Lydias

Methone
Stagirus
Olynthus

Pydna

Potidaea

Thermaic
Gulf

AEGEAN
SEA

R. Haliacmon

5.a HELLESPONT
AND PROPONTIS

0 | km | 100
0 | miles | 60

BLACK SEA

THRACE

Byzantium (Constantinople)
Bosphorus
Chrysopolis
Calchedon

Thracian
Hellespont

PROPONTIS

Nicomedia

BITHYNIA

Thracian
Chersonese

Hellespont

Nicaea

Aegospotami
Lampsacus
Cyzicus

R. Granicus

Abydus
Dardanus

Sigeum

Troy

TROAD

MYSIA

5.b NORTH COAST OF BLACK SEA

0 | km | 250
0 | miles | 150

SCYTHIA

R. Hypanis

R. Borysthenes

Olbia

R. Tyras

Berezan

L. Maeotis

Tauric
Chersonese

Panticapaeum

Cimmerian Bosphorus

BLACK SEA

315

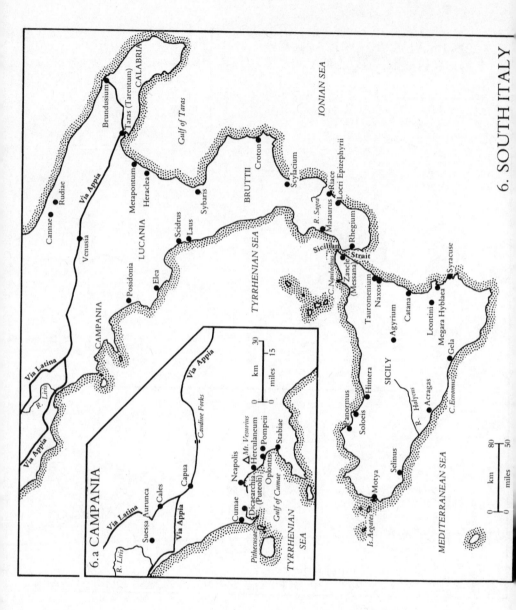

6. SOUTH ITALY

IONIAN SEA

CALABRIA

Brundusium

Taras (Tarentum)

Gulf of Taras

Metapontum

Heraclea

Rudiae

Cannae

Via Appia

Venusia

Sybaris

Croton

Scylacium

BRUTTII

Posidonia

LUCANIA

Scidrus

Laus

Elea

R. Sagra

Mataurus

Locri Epizephyrii

Rhegium

Sicillum

Zancle (Messana)

Strait

C. Naulochus

Tauromenium

Naxos

Catana

CAMPANIA

Agyrium

Leontini

TYRRHENIAN SEA

Megara Hyblaea

Syracuse

Via Latina

R. Liris

Via Appia

Panormus

Soloeis

Himera

SICILY

Gela

R. Halycus

Acragas

Selinus

C. Ecnomus

Motya

Is. Aegates

MEDITERRANEAN SEA

0   km   80
0   miles   50

6.a CAMPANIA

Via Latina

R. Liris

Suessa Aurunca

Cales

Via Appia

Capua

Candine Forks

Via Appia

Cumae

Neapolis

Pithecusae

Dicaearchia (Puteoli)

Herculaneum

△*Mt. Vesuvius*

Pompeii

Oplontis

Stabiae

Gulf of Cumae

TYRRHENIAN SEA

0   km   30
0   miles   15

7. CENTRAL AND NORTHERN ITALY

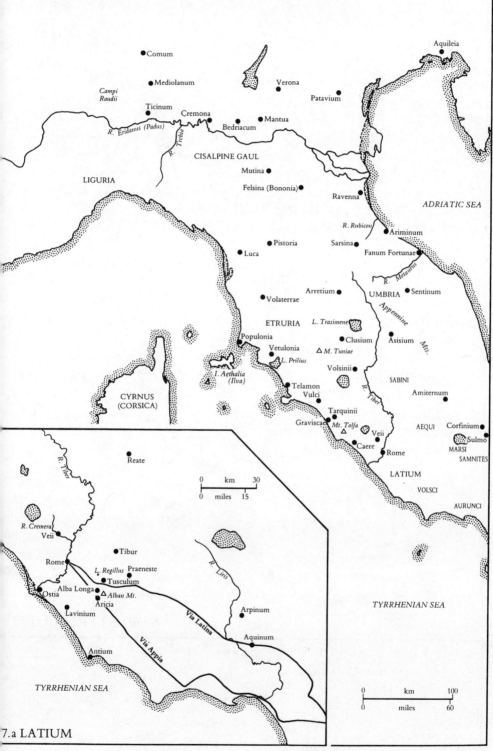

Comum

Mediolanum

Campi Raudii

Ticinum

Cremona

Verona

Patavium

Aquileia

Bedriacum

Mantua

R. *Eridanus (Padus)*

R. *Trebia*

CISALPINE GAUL

LIGURIA

Mutina

Felsina (Bononia)

Ravenna

ADRIATIC SEA

R. *Rubicon*

Ariminum

Pistoria

Sarsina

Fanum Fortunae

Luca

R. *Metaurus*

Arretium

UMBRIA

Sentinum

Volaterrae

Appennine

ETRURIA

L. *Trasimene*

Populonia

Clusium

Asisium

Mts.

Vetulonia

△ M. *Tuniae*

L. *Prilius*

Volsinii

I. *Aethalia (Ilva)*

Telamon

Vulci

SABINI

Amiternum

CYRNUS (CORSICA)

R. *Tiber*

Tarquinii

Graviscae

Mt. *Tolfa*

Veii

AEQUI

Corfinium

△

Sulmo

Caere

MARSI

Reate

Rome

SAMNITES

LATIUM

VOLSCI

| 0 | km | 30 |
| 0 | miles | 15 |

AURUNCI

R. *Tiber*

R. *Cremera*

Veii

Tibur

Rome

L. *Regillus*

Praeneste

Tusculum

R. *Liris*

Alba Longa

△ *Alban Mt.*

Aricia

Arpinum

Lavinium

Via Latina

Aquinum

TYRRHENIAN SEA

Antium

Via Appia

| 0 | km | 100 |
| 0 | miles | 60 |

TYRRHENIAN SEA

7.a **LATIUM**

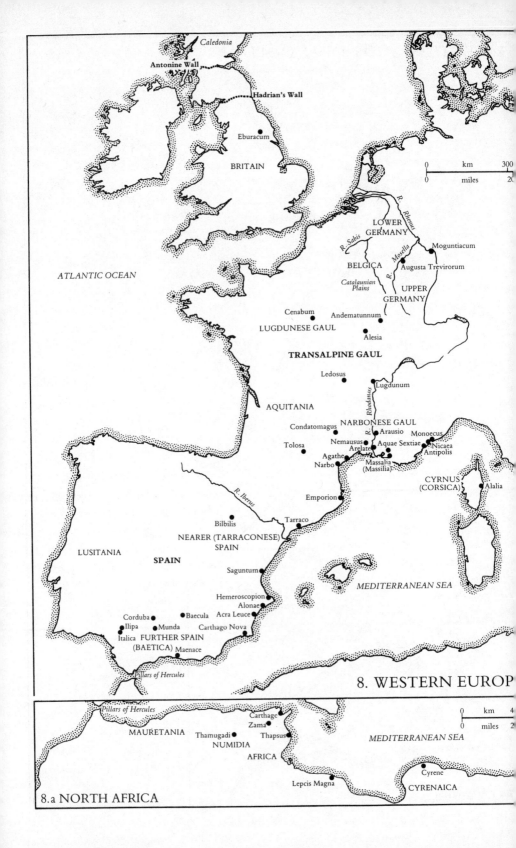

Caledonia

Antonine Wall

Hadrian's Wall

Eburacum

BRITAIN

ATLANTIC OCEAN

LOWER
GERMANY

R. Sabis

R. Rhenus

Moguntiacum

BELGICA

R. Mosella

Augusta Trevirorum

*Catalaunian
Plains*

UPPER
GERMANY

Cenabum   Andematunnum

LUGDUNESE GAUL

Alesia

TRANSALPINE GAUL

Ledosus

Lugdunum

R. Rhodanus

AQUITANIA

NARBONESE GAUL

Condatomagus

Arausio   Monoecus

Nemausus
Aquae Sextiae   Nicaea

Tolosa   *R.*   Arelate   Antipolis

Agathe

Narbo   Massalia
(Massilia)

CYRNUS
(CORSICA)   Alalia

Emporion

R. Iberus

Bilbilis   Tarraco

NEARER (TARRACONESE)
SPAIN

LUSITANIA

SPAIN

Saguntum

MEDITERRANEAN SEA

Hemeroscopion
Alonae

Corduba   Baecula   Acra Leuce

Ilipa   Munda   Carthago Nova

Italica   FURTHER SPAIN
(BAETICA)   Maenace

Pillars of Hercules

8. WESTERN EUROP

Pillars of Hercules   Carthage

Zama

km

miles

MAURETANIA   Thamugadi   Thapsus

NUMIDIA

AFRICA   *MEDITERRANEAN SEA*

Lepcis Magna

Cyrene

CYRENAICA

8.a NORTH AFRICA

km   300

miles   20

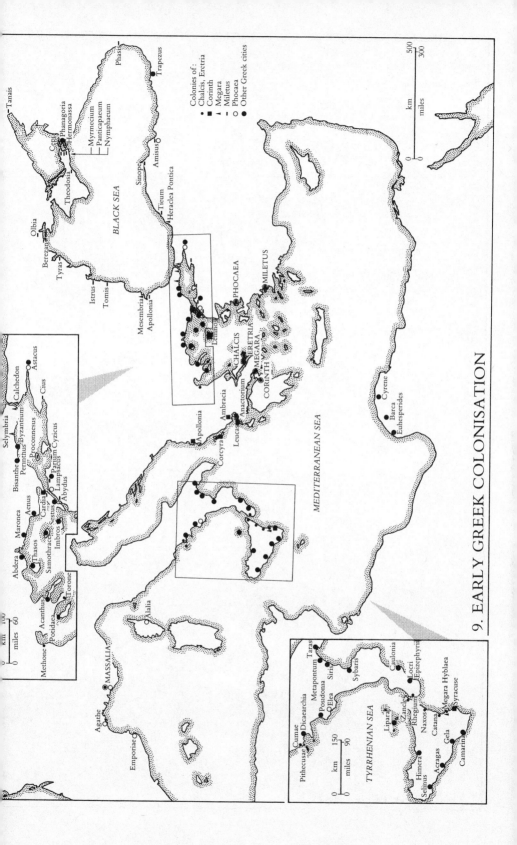

9. EARLY GREEK COLONISATION

Colonies of:

- ● Chalcis, Eretria
- ■ Corinth
- ◄ Megara
- ○ Miletus
- ○ Phocaea
- ● Other Greek cities

BLACK SEA

Tanais
Phanagoria
Cepi
Hermonassa
Myrmecium
Panticapaeum
Nymphaeum
Theodosia
Phasis
Trapezus
Sinope
Amisus
Olbia
Berezan
Tyras
Tieum
Heraclea Pontica
Istrus
Tomis
Mesembria
Apollonia
Selymbria
Bisanthe
Perinthus
Byzantium
Calchedon
Astacus
Proconnesus
Cius
Parium
Cyzicus
Lampsacus
Abydos
Cardia
Sestus
Imbros
Samothrace
Maronea
Aenus
Abdera
Thasos
Acanthus
Potidaea
Methone
Torone
Agathe
MASSALIA
Emporiae
Alalia
Apollonia
Corcyra
Ambracia
Leucas
Anactorium
CHALCIS
ERETRIA
MEGARA
CORINTH
PHOCAEA
MILETUS
Cyrene
Barca
Euhesperides

MEDITERRANEAN SEA

TYRRHENIAN SEA

Cumae
Pithecusae
Dicaearchia
Metapontum
Taras
Posidonia
Siris
OElea
Sybaris
Caulonia
Locri
Epizephyrii
Lipara
Zancle
Rhegium
Naxos
Catana
Megara Hyblaea
Syracuse
Himera
Selinus
Acragas
Gela
Camarina

10. THE CONQUESTS OF ALEXANDER THE GREAT

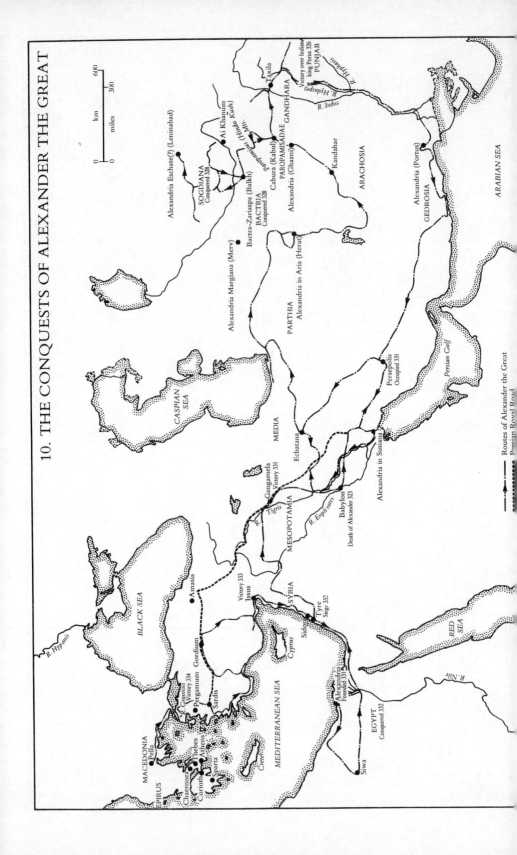

EPIRUS
MACEDONIA
Pella
Chaeronea 338
Thebes
Athens
Corinth
Sparta
R. Hypanis
BLACK SEA
Amasia
Pergamum
Granicus Victory 334
Sardis
Gordium
Crete
MEDITERRANEAN SEA
Cyprus
Sidon
Tyre Siege 332
Victory 333 Issus
SYRIA
Alexandria Founded 331
EGYPT Conquered 332
Siwa
RED SEA
R. Nile

CASPIAN SEA

Alexandria Eschate(?) (Leninabad)
SOGDIANA Conquered 328
Ai Khanum
Maracanda (Samarkand)
(Hindu Kush)
Bactra-Zariaspa (Balkh)
BACTRIA Conquered 328
Alexandria Margiana (Merv)
PARTHIA
Alexandria in Aria (Herat)
Cabura (Kabul)
PAROPAMISADAE GANDHARA
Alexandria (Ghazni)
Kandahar
ARACHOSIA
Alexandria (Portus)
GEDROSIA
ARABIAN SEA

Taxila
Victory over Indian king Porus 326
PUNJAB
R. Hydaspes
R. Hyphasis
R. Indus

MEDIA
Ecbatana
Gaugamela Victory 331
R. Tigris
MESOPOTAMIA
R. Euphrates
Babylon
Death of Alexander 323
Alexandria in Susiana
Persepolis Occupied 331
Persian Gulf

km
miles
0   300   600

━━━▶ Routes of Alexander the Great
∙∙∙∙∙∙ Persian Royal Road

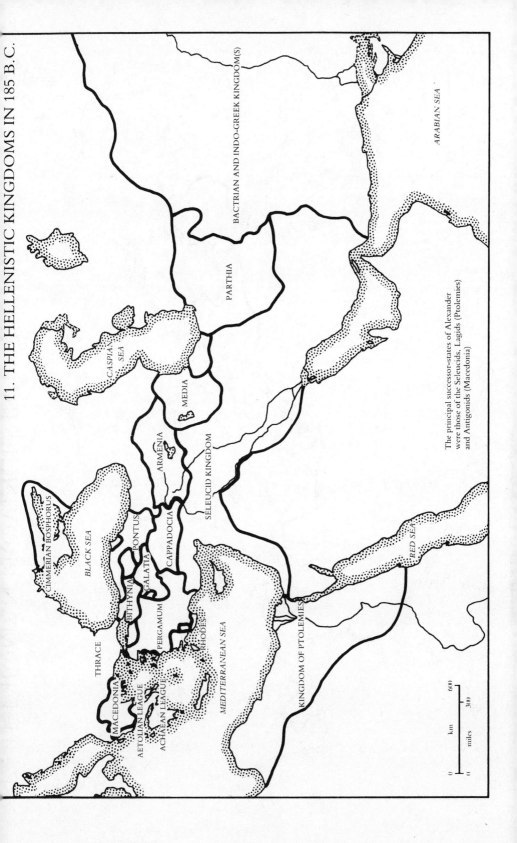

11. THE HELLENISTIC KINGDOMS IN 185 B.C.

ARABIAN SEA

BACTRIAN AND INDO-GREEK KINGDOM(S)

PARTHIA

CASPIAN SEA

MEDIA

ARMENIA

SELEUCID KINGDOM

CAPPADOCIA

PONTUS

GALATIA

BITHYNIA

CIMMERIAN BOSPHORUS

BLACK SEA

THRACE

PERGAMUM

MACEDONIA

AETOLIAN LEAGUE

ACHAEAN LEAGUE

RHODES

MEDITERRANEAN SEA

KINGDOM OF PTOLEMIES

RED SEA

The principal successor-states of Alexander were those of the Seleucids, Lagids (Ptolemies) and Antigonids (Macedonia)

km   0   300   600

miles

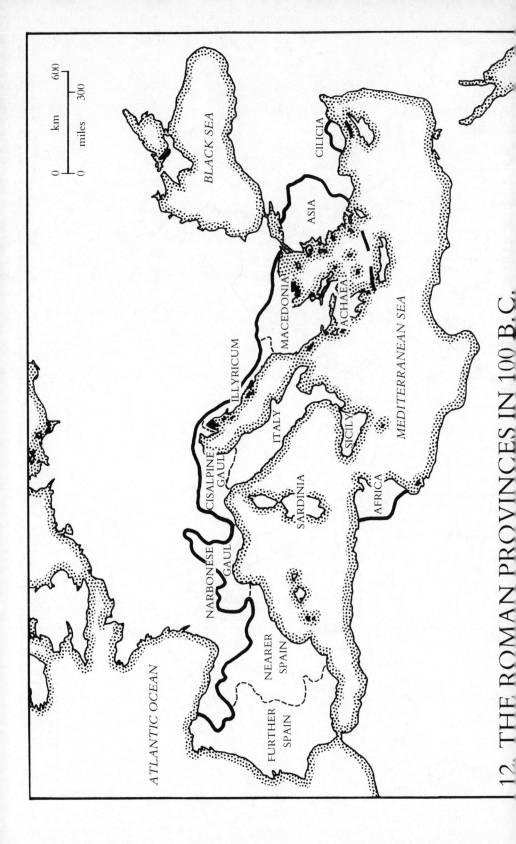

12. THE ROMAN PROVINCES IN 100 B.C.

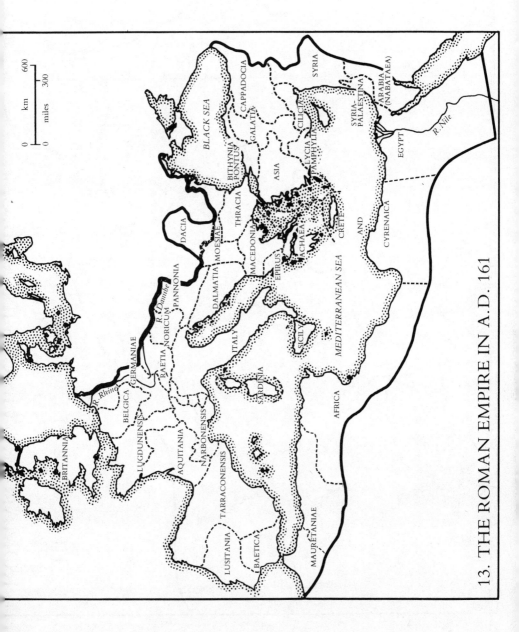

13. THE ROMAN EMPIRE IN A.D. 161

BRITANNIA

R. Rhine

BELGICA
GERMANIAE
LUGDUNENSIS
NARBONENSIS
AQUITANIA
RAETIA NORICUM
PANNONIA
DALMATIA
ITALY
TARRACONENSIS
LUSITANIA
BAETICA
SARDINIA
SICILY
MAURETANIAE
AFRICA

R. Danube

DACIA
MOESIAE
MACEDONIA
THRACIA
EPIRUS
ACHAEA
CRETE

BLACK SEA

BITHYNIA
PONTUS
GALATIA
CAPPADOCIA
ASIA
LYCIA
PAMPHYLIA
CILICIA
SYRIA
SYRIA-
PALAESTINA
ARABIA
(NABATAEA)

AND

MEDITERRANEAN SEA

CYRENAICA

EGYPT

R. Nile

km   600
      300
miles
0
0

323

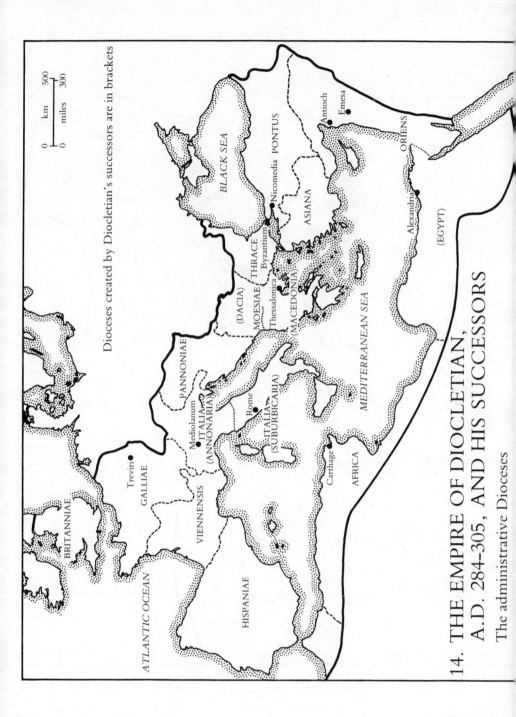

14. THE EMPIRE OF DIOCLETIAN,
A.D. 284-305, AND HIS SUCCESSORS

The administrative Dioceses

Dioceses created by Diocletian's successors are in brackets

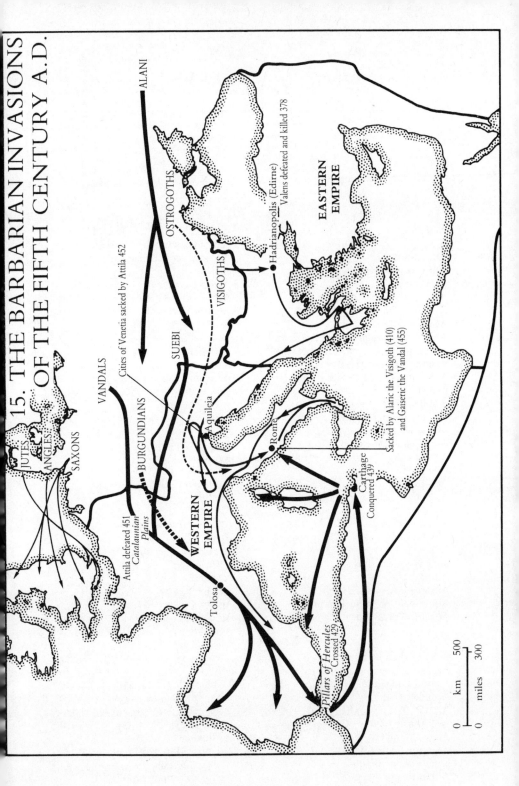

15. THE BARBARIAN INVASIONS OF THE FIFTH CENTURY A.D.

ALANI

OSTROGOTHS

VISIGOTHS

Hadrianopolis (Edirne)
Valens defeated and killed 378

EASTERN EMPIRE

Cities of Venetia sacked by Attila 452

SUEBI

Aquileia

VANDALS

BURGUNDIANS

Rome

Sacked by Alaric the Visigoth (410)
and Gaiseric the Vandal (455)

JUTES
ANGLES
SAXONS

Attila defeated 451
Catalaunian Plains

WESTERN EMPIRE

Carthage
Conquered 439

Tolosa

Pillars of Hercules
Crossed 429

0   500
km

0   300
miles

INDEX

Abdera (Avdira) 46, 89f., 92, 130, 250, 252
Abradates 254
Abrittus (Razgrad) 204
Absyrtus 82
Abydus (Nağara) 46
Academy, Platonic 94, 98, 130, 252
Acastus 248
Achaea (N. Peloponnese), Achaean League 49f., 119ff., 128, 133, 160
Achaeans (Homeric) 8, 225
Achaemenids, see Persia
Acharnae 86
Achilles 36, 79, 81, 83, 225, 262
Achilles painter 107f.
Acilia, see Ficana
Acra Leuce (Alicante) 158
Acragas (Agrigentum Agrigento) 53, 60, 88, 250
Acrocorinth 29, 236
Acropolis (Athens) 77, 87, 104, 106
Actium 178, 186
Adam 243
Admetus 82
Adonis 128
adoptive succession 195, 202, 259f.
Adratus 83, 236
Adria, see Atria
Adrianople, see Hadrianopolis
Adriatic Sea 28, 30, 115, 120, 156, 249
Aeaea 226
Aeetes 82
Aegates (Egadi) Is. 157
Aegean Sea 20, 23, 28, 31, 35, 37, 44, 46, 63, 80, 144, 230, 234, 264
Aegialeis 264
Aegina 21, 25, 28, 58, 75, 101, 235, 251f.
Aegisthus 77, 80
Aegospotami 69
Aegyptus, son of Belus 77
Aegyptus, see Egypt
Aeinautai 39f.

Aelia Capitolina, see Jerusalem
Aelius Caesar 260
Aenaria, see Pithecusae
Aeneas 185f.
Aeolis 26, 35, 43f., 69, 248f., 254
Aequi 150
Aesarus (Esaro) R. 50
Aeschylus 76–80, 86
Aesculapius, see Asclepius
Aethalia (Ilva, Elba) I. 67
Aetius 214
Aetolian League 119f., 254
Africa, north 161, 172, 198ff., 203, 214, 221, 228, 262
Africa (Roman province) 160, 179, 183
Agamemnon 77, 80, 84, 225
Agariste 236
Agatharchus 108
Agathe Tyche (Agde) 250
Agathocles 120
Agathon 95, 252
Agave 85
Agde, see Agathe Tyche
Ager Gallicus 158
ager publicus (common land) 155, 158, 162f., 165
Agesander 254
Agesilaus II 72, 251
Agiads 31, 59
Agira, see Agyrium
Agis IV 119
agoge 33
Agricola, Cnaeus Julius 195
agriculture, farming, grain 9, 13, 19–23, 26f., 29ff., 37, 41, 46, 48f., 54, 66–69, 73, 117, 119, 142, 144f., 153, 162f., 185, 187, 200, 208, 229, 235, 248, 263: see also ager publicus
Agrippa I 265
Agrippa, Marcus Vipsanius 178, 181, 183, 198, 258, 260
Agrippa Postumus 258

Agrippina the younger 192f.
Ahenobarbus, Lucius Domitius 172
Aigikoreis 248
Ajax 73
Akkadian 262
Al-Suriyya, see Sura
alabaster 263
Alalia (Aleria) 42, 54, 61, 143, 262
Alamanni 205
Alaric I 212f., 215
Alba Longa (Castelgandolfo) 147, 149, 255
Alban Mount 144, 147, 149
Albinus, Clodius, see Clodius Albinus
Albis (Elbe) R. 181
Alcaeus 44, 187
Alcalá del Rio, see Ilipa
Alcestis 82
Alcibiades 67f., 251
Alcinous 226
Alcmaeon 51, 91
Alcmaeonids 25, 249f.
Alcman, 32
Aleria, see Alalia
Alesia (Alise-Ste.-Reine) 170
Alexander I 59, 73
Alexander III the Great 73f., 98, 114f., 117–120, 124, 127f., 156, 173, 195, 229f., 241, 253f., 260
Alexander, Severus 204
Alexandria 115f., 123ff., 129, 132, 135, 171f., 177, 185–189, 199, 229, 241, 243, 253, 255
Algidus (Algido) Mt. 150
Alicante, see Acra Leuce
aliens, resident, see metics
Allia (Bettina) R. 150
Al Mina 228
Alonae 250
alphabet, writing, scripts, 10f., 26, 49, 229, 237, 247
Alpheus R. 233
Alps Mts. 166, 201, 253
Altat of Augustan Peace, see Ara Pacis
Altis, see Olympia
Amasia (Amasra) 258
Amasis 229
Amasis painter 249
Amazons 83, 104, 110
amber 54
Ambiani (Samarobriva, Amiens) 261
Ambracia (Arta) 178, 249

Ambrose, St. 211, 216, 261
Amiata, Mt., see Tuniae
Amisus (Samsun) 47
Ammianus Marcellinus 211f.
Amorges 68, 251
Amorgos 16
Amphictyonies 232ff.
Amphipolis 66f., 70, 73
Amphitheus 86
Ampurias, see Emporion
Amyntas I 72f.
Amyntas III 98
Anabasis, see Xenophon
Anacreon 38f.
Anactorium 249
anamnesis (recollection) 252
Anatolia, see Asia Minor
Anaxagoras 89, 92
Anaxilas 60
Anaximander 15, 40f., 43
Anaximenes 15, 41
Anchises 186
Andematunnum (Langres) 261
Andocides 251
Andocides painter 24
Andromache 83
Anio (Aniene) R. 151
Annaba, see Hippo Regius
annona militaris, see taxes
Antakya, see Antioch
Antalcidas 230
Anthela 232
Antibes, see Antipolis
Antigone 77, 79, 81
Antigonids 115, 160
Antigonus I Monophthalmos (the One-Eyed) 115, 253
Antigonus II Gonatas 115, 118
Antigonus III Doson 119, 121
Antigonus of Carystus 128
Antimachus I Theos Nicephorus 135
Antioch (Antakya) 117, 126, 209, 211, 259
Antiochus I Soter 117
Antiochus II Theos 118
Antiochus III the Great 117, 133, 160, 241, 254
Antiochus IV Epiphanes 241
Antiochus VII Sidetes 265
Antiochus, see Eunus
Antipas, Herod, see Herod Antipas
Antipater 74, 115, 118f., 253

Antiphon 91, 252
Antipolis (Antibes) 250
Antisthenes 130, 152
Antium (Anzio) 150, 152
Antonine Age 200
Antoninus Pius 199, 201, 203, 260
Antonius, Lucius 177, 257
Antonius, Marcus (Mark Anthony) 176ff., 183ff., 257
Anyte 254
Apamea (Qalaat al-Mudik) 124, 254
apatheia, see *ataraxia*
apella, see Assembly
Apelles 127
Apennines Mts. 142, 149f.
Aphaea 101
Aphries (Hophra) 263
Aphrodite 44f., 83, 109, 126, 253f.: see also Venus
Apocolocyntosis, see Seneca the Younger
apoikiai, see colonization
apokletoi, see *prytaneis*
Apollo 12, 14, 19, 23, 31, 36, 51f., 54, 77, 80, 82, 84f., 87, 101f., 110, 135, 154, 182f., 232, 234, 256, 258, 263
Apollodorus (architect) 195
Apollodorus (painter) 108
Apollonia (Pojani) 30
Apollonius Rhodius 129, 132
Apoxyomenus (Man Scraping Himself) 125, 254
Appian Way, see roads
Apuleius 202
Aqua Appia, Marcia, see aqueducts
Aquae Sextiae (Aix-en-Provence) 165
aqueducts 162, 182, 256
Aquileia 201
Aquinum (Aquino) 197
Ara Pacis (Altar of Peace) 183
Arabia, Arabs 204, 263; see also Philip
Aram Naharain 262
Aramaeans 228, 262
Aramaic 193, 262
Aratus of Sicyon 121, 128
Arausio (Orange) 165
Arcadia 31, 33, 67, 72, 121, 185, 251
Arcadius 212
'archaic smile' 248
Archelaus (king of Macedonia) 73, 82, 108, 252
Archelaus (philosopher) 92
Archilochus 11, 264

Archimedes 124
architecture 11, 13f., 29, 110, 128, 182f., 194, 198f., 209, 216f., 229, 249
archons 21f., 56, 239, 248; see also polemarch
Archytas 93f., 97, 252
Ardashir (Artaxerxes) 231
Ardea 256
Arelate (Arles) 261
Areopagus 21f., 64, 77, 238f.
Areas 253; see also Mars
areta, arete (virtue) 76, 90, 93
Areus 119
Arezzo, see Arretium
Argadeis 248
Argeads 72
Arginusae 69
Argolid 8, 27f.
Argonauts 47, 52, 82, 250
Argos 12, 21, 27f., 30, 32ff., 58, 72, 77, 79f., 83, 85, 103, 105, 236, 256
Arians, see Christianity
Aricia (Ariccia) 148f., 152, 255f.
Ariminum (Rimini) 182
Ariovistus 170
Aristarchus 124
Aristides (of Athens) 63
Aristides (of Miletus) 254
atistocrats (nobles) 9f., 12f., 22f., 27, 29f., 35, 37f., 42, 44, 52ff., 60f., 67, 72, 118, 120, 170, 180, 197, 210f., 235f., 238, 240, 248f.: see also Basilidae, Eupatrids, *gamoroi, geomoroi, hippeis, patricians*
Aristodemus the Effeminate, 49, 144, 148f., 255
Aristonicus 162
Aristoteles, see Battus I
Aristotle 9, 74, 86, 98ff., 122ff., 126, 129, 131, 240, 252
Aristoxenus 127, 254
Arius 261
Arles, see Arelate
Armenia 177f., 230f.
Arminius 181
Arpinum (Arpino) 165, 168
Arretium (Arezzo) 200, 255
Arrian 253, 260
Arsaces I, Arsacids 118, 230
Arsinoe II 128
Arta, see Ambracia
Artabazus 59

Artaphernes 56
Artaxerxes I Macrocheir 230
Artaxerxes II Mnemon 72, 230, 251, 263
Artaxerxes III Ochus 230
Artaxerxes, see Ardashir
Artemis 11, 14, 42, 52, 54, 83f., 104, 148,
    234, 249, 253; see also Diana
Artemisia II 109
Artemisium 58, 102, 252: see also Ephesus
Arverni 170
Asclepiads 92
Asclepius (Aesculapius) 92, 124, 253
Ascoli Satriano, see Ausculum
Ascra 26
Aseneth 254
Asia 85, 117, 168, 234
Asia Minor 8f., 13f., 16, 20, 25f., 35, 37,
    42f., 46, 56f., 59, 63, 69, 108, 114, 118f.,
    126, 133, 135, 160, 166, 168, 200, 206,
    210, 228, 230ff., 235, 243, 251, 253,
    257, 262: see also Aeolis, Bithynia,
    Cappadocia, Caria, Cilicia, Galatia,
    Lycia, Lydia, Mysia, Pamphylia,
    Paphlagonia, Phrygia, Pontus
Asia (Roman province) 164, 166, 179
Asisium (Assisi) 188
Asius 38
Asophus R. 236
Aspasia 65, 94
Assemblies 13, 21f., 25, 31, 33, 64, 67, 78,
    87, 112, 120f., 147, 153, 163f., 238f.,
    248, 254, 256: see also democracy
Assisi, see Asisium
Assyria 9, 45, 229, 262f.
ataraxia, apatheia, hasuchia, serenity 130ff.,
    136, 187
Atarneus (Dikili) 98
Ataulf 212
Athanasius, St. 261
Athena (Pallas Athene) 24, 77, 104ff.,
    126, 134f., 226, 253: see also Minerva
Athenodorus 254: see also Vaballathus
Athens 8f., 14ff., 19–27, 29f., 34–38, 44,
    46, 56–59, 63–68, 90ff., 98, 101, 104–
    108, 111f., 116, 118, 122, 124f., 127,
    130, 134, 154, 160, 168, 183, 187, 230,
    232, 234, 236, 238ff., 248, 250f., 253f.,
    264
athletics 75, 91, 102, 233f.: see also
    Isthmian, Nemean, Olympian,
    Pythian Games
atonists, atoms 89, 172

Atossa 77
Atreus 77, 84
Atria (Adria) 255
Attalus I Soter 118, 126, 135
Attalus III Philopator 133, 160, 162f.
Attalus (general) 73
Attica 18–21, 24f., 35, 56f., 59, 64, 68, 77,
    234, 238, 248, 264
Atticus, Titus Pomponius 168f.
Attila 214
Augusta Trevirorum (Treviri, Trier) 206,
    260f.
Augustine, St. 213f., 216, 261
Augustus (Octavian) 133, 176-191, 194,
    200, 206, 217, 230, 241, 255, 257ff.: see
    also Pax Augusta
Aulis (sacrifice of Iphigenia) 77, 84f.
Aulon R., see Jordan
Aurelian 206
Aurelius, Marcus 201f., 231, 260, 265
Ausculum (Ascoli Satriano) 156
autocrats, see tyrants
Avdira, see Abdera
Aventine Hill 147f., 153f.
Avidius Cassius 231
Avsar, see Myus
Axius, R. 72
Aya Sofya (Haghia Sophia), Church of
    Holy Wisdom 209, 261

Babylon, Babylonia 50, 114, 117, 228–
    231, 242, 252f., 263, 265
Bacchae, Bacchants, see Maenads
Bacchis, Bacchiads 29f.
Bacchylides 61
Bactria 118, 135, 230, 253
Baecula 159
Baetica, see Spain
Bagaudae 216, 261
Bahram V Gor 231
Balbinus 260
Baltic Sea 214
banking 117, 119, 168
Banyas, see Panion
Bar Kosiba (Kochba), Simeon 198, 242,
    259
Barsine Statira 114, 254
Basilicas, Christian 209
Basilicas, pagan 162, 182, 195, 209
Basilidae 42
Batavians 220, 261
Baths 203, 206, 254, 260

Batrachois (Frogs), see Aristophanes
Battus I (Aristoteles) 263
Battus IV 263
Bedriacum (Calvatone) 259
Belgae 170
Belkis, see Cyzicus
Benacus (Garda) L. 206
Berezan 48
Bergama, see Pergamum
Beth Shearim 265
Bethlehem 213, 242
Bettina R., see Allia
Bias 249
Bibracte (Mont Beuvray) 170
Bilbilis (Calatayud) 194
bilocation 51
Bion 131
bireme, see ships
Bisanthe (Rhadaestus, Rodosto) 38
Bithynia 236, 243, 253, 260, 265
Black (Euxine) Sea 21, 30, 39, 46ff., 66–69, 73, 189, 235f.
Boadicea, see Boudicca
Bodotria, R. (Firth of Forth) 260
Bodrum, see Halicarnassus
Boethius 221
Boeotia, Boeotian League 11, 18ff., 25ff., 43, 57ff., 65, 67, 72f., 75, 120, 249, 251
Boiohaemum (Bohemia) 181, 202
Bologna, see Bononia, Felsina
Boniface 214
Bononia (Bologna) 176: see also Felsina
Borysthenes (Danapris, Dnieper) R. 47, 131
Boscoreale 254
Bosphorus, Cimmerian (Strait of Kerch) 48
Bosphorus, Kingdom of (Cimmerian) 48, 253
Bosphorus, Thracian 46, 235
Boudicca (Boadicea) 259
Boule, see Council
Branchidae 234
Brasidas 67, 70
Brennus 150f.
Brettioi, (Bruttii, Calabria) 49, 102, 250
bridges, Roman 162, 167, 182, 208, 256, 258
Brindisi, see Brundusium
Britain 42, 170, 192, 195, 203, 220, 256, 260
bronze, Bronze Age 18, 20, 26f., 29, 31f.,
38f., 42, 44, 49, 102f., 126, 183, 200, 232, 236, 250, 264
brotherhood (*phratria*) 21, 25
Brotherhood of Man 130
Brundusium (Brindisi) 177
Bruttii, see Brettioi
Brutus, Lucius Junius 257
Brutus, Quintus Caepio (Marcus Junius) 174, 176f., 187, 257
Bryaxis 110, 253
Bryges painter 107
bucolic poetry, see pastoral
Bug R., see Hypanis
Bulda, see Paltus
Burgandians 221, 261
burials, graves, tombs, funerals 12, 18, 20, 45, 79, 143f., 146, 225, 255: see also Mausoleum
Byzantine empire 217, 221f., 242
Byzantium (Istanbul) 46f., 63, 72f., 208, 235, 251: see also Constantinople

Cadiz, see Gades
Cadmeia 26
Caecilius Metellus Pius Scipio, Quintus, see Scipio
Caelian Hill 146, 255
Caepio, see Brutus, Servilius
Caere (Cerveteri) 42, 54, 143, 146, 151, 157, 262
Caesar, Gaius (grandson of Augustus), see Gaius Caesar
Caesar, Gaius Julius (dictator) 168–174, 176–179, 182ff., 192, 198, 256–259
Caesar, Lucius (grandson of Augustus), see Lucius Caesar
Caesar, Lucius Julius 257
Caiaphas 242
Calabria, see Brettioi
Calagurris (Calahorra) 259
Calchedon (Kadıköy) 46f., 91, 124, 235, 252
Caledonia (Scotland) 203
Cales (Calvi) 61, 143, 255
Caligula, see Gaius
Callatis Pontica (Mangalia) 127
Callias (grandson of next) 72, 251
Callias (son of Hipponicus) 65, 230, 251
Callicles 91
Callicrates 104
Callimachus (poet) 132
Callimachus (polemarch) 56, 250

Callinicum Nicephorium (Raqqa) 261
Callippus 252
Calpurnius Piso Frugi, Lucius, see Piso
Calvi, see Cales
Calvus, Gaius Licinius 257
Calypso 225f.
Cambyses II 230
Camillus, Marcus Furius 150
Campania 48f., 61, 142ff., 151, 160ff.,
    193, 228, 255f.
Campi Raudii (near Rovigo?) 165
Campus Martius 183, 198
Çan Çayı R., see Granicus
Canachus 236
Cannae (Canne) 159
Canon 103
Capitohne Hill 146, 149
Capitoline Triad, Capitol 148, 182, 256
Cappadocia 253
Capreae (Capri) 191
Capua (S. Marioa Capua Vetere) 61,
    143f., 152, 159f., 163, 167, 200, 255
Caracalla 203, 260
Caria 68f.
Carlentini, see Leontini
Carnutes 170
Carolingians 221
Carrhae (Harran) 170, 230
Cartagena, see Carthago Nova
Carthage, Punic Wars 42, 54, 60f., 120,
    143, 157–160, 162ff., 172, 186, 214,
    228, 251, 256, 260, 262
Carthago Nova (Cartagena) 158
Carus 206
Caryatids 106, 253
Carystus 63, 128
Caspian Sea 230
Cassander 115, 118, 253
Cassandra 77
Cassandrea 115: see also Potidaea
Cassiodorus 221
Cassius, Avidius, see Avidius Cassius
Cassius Longinus, Gaius 174, 176f.,
    187
Cassivellaunus 170
Castel di Decima, see Politorium
Castellamare di Brucia, see Elea
Castor 182
Catalaunian Plains (near Châlons-sur-
    Marne) 214
Catana (Catania) 53, 248
Catilina, Lucius Sergius 168f., 176

Cato, Marcus Porcius the elder (censor)
    161f.
Cato, Marcus Porcius the younger
    (Uticensis) 169, 177
Cato, Valerius, see Valerius
cattle 48, 79, 146, 235: see also sheep
Catullus 171
Catuvellauni 170
Cauca (Coca) 211
Caucasus Mts. 78, 82
Caudine Forks 152
Caulonia 250
cavalry, see horses
Cavo, Mt., see Alban Mount
Cayster (Küçük Menderes), R. 42
Celts, see Gaul
Cenabum (Orléans) 170
Cenchreae 249
censors 154, 161, 256
Centaurs 101, 104, 110
Ceos 24, 91
Cephisus, R. 20, 249
Ceramicus 24
Ceres, see Demeter
Cerialis, Quintus Petillius
Cerveteri, see Caere
Chaeronea 73f., 118f., 253
Chalcidian League, Chalcidice 19, 46, 73,
    98
Chalcidiceum 182
Chalcis 18f., 25, 27, 46, 49, 52, 98, 142f.,
    228f., 248
Champions, Battle of the, see Thyrea
Chance, see Fortuna, Tyche
Chandragupta Maurya 117
Chares 126, 253
Charlemagne 221
Charmides, see Plato
Chersonese, Tauric (Crimea) 84f.
Chersonese, Thracian (Gallipoli
    peninsula) 23f. 46, 68f., 83
Cherusci 181
chief priest, see religion
Chilon 33, 249
Chios 35ff., 43, 254
Chiusi, see Clusium
Choephori, see Aeschylus
Chremonidean War, Chremonides 118f.,
    253
Chremylus 87
Christianity, Christians 185, 207–214,
    216, 218, 221, 231, 242f., 260f., 263ff.

Chrysippus 130, 254
Chrysopolis (Scutari, Üsküdar) 261
Cicero 100, 168f., 176, 257
Cilicia 114, 195, 243
Cimon 63ff., 107, 251
Cinna, Gaius Helvius 257
Cinna, Lucius Cornelius 166, 257
Circe, 226
Circus Flaminius 182
Cirrha 232
Cisalpine Gaul, see Gaul Cisalpine
Cithaeron, Mt. 85
Citium 130
city-state, see polis
Civilis, Gaius Julius 220, 259, 261
Cladeus R. 233
clan (genos) 13, 21f., 25, 44
Classical age 110ff., 137, 217, 247: see also
    Early, High, Late Classical styles
Classicus, Julius 220, 259, 261
Claudius 192, 199, 259, 265
Claudius, Appius 154
Claudius Caecus, Appius 154, 256
Claudius II Gothicus 205
Claudius Pulcher, Appius 163
Clazomenae (Klazümen) 89, 249f.
Cleisthenes (Athenian) 25, 236, 239f., 264
Cleisthenes (tyrant of Sicyon) 236, 264
Clement, St. 243, 265
Cleobulus 249
Cleomenes I 24f., 33f., 58, 249
Cleomenes III 119, 121
Cleon 67, 86f., 252
Cleopatra VII 133, 172, 177f., 186, 229,
    254, 257
Cleophon 68
Cleophrades painter 249
cleruchs, see colonization
client-kings 157, 179, 241f., 254, 258, 265
clients (clientela) 153, 155, 161, 163
Clitias 22
Clodia 171
Clodius Albinus 260
Clodius Pulcher, Publius 171
Clota (Clyde), R. 260
Cloudcuckooland, see Nephelococcygia
Clouds, see Aristophanes
Clovis 221, 261
clubs (hetaireiai) 44, 53, 127
Clusium (Chiusi) 150
Clyde R., see Clota
Clytemnestra 77, 80, 84

Cnidus (Reşadiye peninsula) 92, 109,
    230
Cnossus 250
Coast, see paralia
Coes 44
coinage, coins, money 13ff., 19, 24, 27,
    31, 33, 52, 135, 161, 173, 198, 200, 205,
    248, 253, 258
Colaeus 37
Colchis 82
Colline Gate 166
colonization 10, 21, 25, 28, 37ff., 42, 46f.,
    49f., 52f., 60, 66, 72, 98, 106, 117f.,
    142f., 149, 152, 156, 163, 172f., 178,
    232, 234f., 242, 249f.
Colonus 79, 81
Colophon (Değirmendere) 15, 53, 69,
    127, 249
Colosseum (Flavian Amphitheatre) 194
Colossus of Rhodes 126, 253
Comedy 52, 112, 160f., 236: see also
    Middle, New, Old Comedy, Plautus,
    Terence
comitatenses 207
comitia, see Assembly
commerce, see trade
Commodus 202
common land, see ager publicus
Comum (Como) 265
concilium plebis, see Assembly
Concordia (Homonoia) 154, 169
Condatomagus (La Graufesenque) 200
Congresses, Panhellenic 58, 73
Constans 261
Constanţa, see Tomis
Constantine I the Great 137, 208f., 211,
    242f., 260f.
Constantine II 261
Constantinople (Istanbul) 137, 208f.,
    214, 216, 222, 235, 261: see also
    Byzantine empire, Byzantium
Constantius I Chlorus 206, 208, 260
Constantius II 209, 261
Constitutio Antoniniana 203
consuls 148, 153f., 158f., 167, 176, 182,
    256f.
copper 44, 49, 228: see also bronze
Corbulo, Cnaeus Domitius 230
Corcyra (Corfu) 29f., 52, 120, 249
Corduba (Cordoba) 192
Corfinium (Corfinio) 165
Corfu, see Corcyra

Corinna (in Ovid) 188
Corinna (poet) 254
Corinth 9, 13f., 22, 28–31, 52, 59, 65ff., 72f., 79, 82, 121, 143, 160, 172, 229, 235ff., 249, 251, 264: see also Gulf of Corinth, Isthmus of Corinth, Protocorinthian
Corinthian War 72, 94
corn, see agriculture
Cornelia 170
Cornutus, Lucius Annaeus 259
Coronea 65, 251
Corsica (Cyrnus) 42, 54, 67, 157, 262
Cos 52, 92, 124f., 254
Councils, Greek (Boule etc) 21f., 25, 37, 39, 52, 54, 64, 97, 120f., 238: see also Areopagus, gerousia
Crassus, Marcus Licinius 167–170, 230, 257
Craterus 253
Crates 131
Crathis (Crati) R. 49
Cratinus 252
Cratylus, see Plato
cremation, see burials
Cremera (Valchetta) R. 150
Cremona 250
Crenides, see Philippi
Creon (Corinth) 82
Creon (Thebes) 79, 81
Cresilas 103, 252
Crete 8, 16, 18, 45, 236, 250
Creusa (Athens) 84
Creusa (Corinth) 82
Crispus 261
'Critian Boy' 102, 252
Crito, see Plato
Croesus 40
Cronus 233: see also Saturn
Croton (Crotone) 15, 50f., 91, 93, 250
Crusaders 221f., 261
Ctesias 254
Ctesibius 123
Ctesiphon (Taysafun) 231
Cumae (Cuma) 19, 49, 54, 61, 142, 144, 148, 186, 228, 255: see also Gulf of Cumae
Cunaxa (Kunish) 251, 263
Cupid 202
curia, see Senate House
curiae (wards) 147
Cyaxares 229

Cybele 129, 202, 260
Cyclades Is. 234, 263f.
Cyclops, see Polyphemus
Cydonia 252
Cylon 21
Cyme (Aeolis; Namurtköy) 26
Cyme (Campania), see Cumae
Cynics 130ff.
Cynoscephalae 75, 160
Cynossema (Kılıdülbehar) 68
Cynthia 188
Cynthus Mt. 234
Cyprus 8, 44f., 130, 228, 230, 250, 259
Cypselus 30
Cyrene (Shahhat) Cyrenaica 124, 132, 229, 259, 263
Cyrnus, see Corsica
Cyrus II the Great 16, 37, 41, 229f., 254
Cyrus the younger 69, 230, 251, 263
Cyzicus (Belkis) 46f., 68, 254

Dacia (Rumania) 194f., 206, 210
Dacia Ripensis (Upper Moesia) 260
Daedalus (mythical inventor) 248
Daedalus (sculptor), Daedalic style 14, 236, 248, 250
daimonion 93
Dalmatia 170, 206, 213, 215, 258
Damascus 195, 259
Danapris (Dnieper) R., see Borysthenes
dancing, see music
Danube (Ister) R., 24, 47, 200ff., 204ff., 208ff., 214
Dardanelles, see Hellespont
Dardania (Upper Moesia) 260
Dardanus (Maltepe) 166
Darius I 16, 24f., 43, 46f., 56, 58, 69, 73, 77, 230, 234
Darius II Ochus 68f., 230
Darius III Cadomannus 114, 230
'Dark Age' 8, 18, 45
Datis 56
David 242
Death (Thanatos) 82
debt 22, 154, 162, 166, 173, 238, 248
Decebalus 194f.
Decelea 68
decemviri 154
Decius, Trajanus 204, 260, 265
Değirmendere, see Colophon
Deianira 80
deification 177, 179, 182, 259

Deinomenids 60
Delium 67
Delmatius 261
Delos, Delian League 23, 38, 63, 65, 72, 234, 263f.
Delphi 10, 25, 29, 54, 58, 73, 77, 80, 84, 87, 102, 120, 232f., 236, 252, 263: see also Pythian Games
Demaratus 143, 249
demes 25
Demeter 11f., 87, 129, 202, 234
Demetrias (Pagasae, near Volo) 115
Demetrius I the Besieger (Poliorcetes) 115, 118, 253
Demetrius of Phaleron 118
Demetrius (painter) 135
democracy 13, 22, 24f., 32, 52, 56, 64ff., 72, 76, 78f., 86, 93, 97, 111f., 118, 147, 153f., 203, 235, 238ff.
Democritus 89, 92, 130
Demos 86
Demosthenes (general) 68
Demosthenes (orator) 73ff.
deus ex machina 86
Dharma-Chakra 253
Diadumenus (Youth binding a Fillet) 103, 252
diakria (Hill) 23, 249, 264
dialects (Greek) 26, 36, 43, 250
Diana (Artemis) 147ff.
Diaspora (Jewish Dispersion), see Jews
diatribes 131
Dicaearchia (Puteoli, Pozzuoli) 38, 49
Dicaeopolis 86
dictators 155, 166f., 173, 179, 256: see also tyrants
didactic poetry 227
Didius Julianus 260
Dido 186, 262
Didyma 39, 234
Dike (Justice) 226f.
Dikili, see Atarneus
Diocaesarea, see Sepphoris
Diocletian 206ff., 210, 243, 260
Diodotus I 118
Diogenes 131, 254
diolkos, draw-way 30
Dion 252
Dionysia, Great 23, 86
Dionysius I 94, 252
Dionysius II 94, 252
Dionysius (Phocaean) 42

Dionysus 12, 23, 77, 85, 109, 129, 202, 236, 251f., 255
Diotima 95
Dipoenus 236
Dipylon painter 20f., 248
Dirce R. 26
Discobolus 102, 252
Dispersion, Jewish, see Jews
divi, see deification
Dnieper R., see Borysthenes
Dobrogea (Dobruja) 47
Dogmatists 254
Domitian 194ff., 198
Domna, Julia, see Julia Domna
Domus Aurea, see Golden House
Dorians 8, 13, 20, 27f., 30ff., 35, 225, 232, 235f., 247ff., 264
Doric Order 13, 29, 31, 52, 101, 104, 106, 248
Doryphorus (Youth holding Spear) 103, 252
Dracon 21, 248
drawing, see painting
draw-way, see diolkos
Drerus 250
Drusus the elder, see Nero Drusus
Durazzo, Dürrës, see Dyrrhachium
Dying Gaul 126f., 254
Dymanes 249
Dyrrhachium (Durazzo, Durrës) 257

Early Classical (Severe) style 101ff., 107
Earth Goddess, see Mother Goddess
earthquakes 64
Ebla 262
Eburacum (York) 203
Ecclesia, see Assembly
Ecclesiazusae, see Aristophanes
Ecnomus (Monte S. Angelo or Cufino) 157
Ed-Dimas, see Thapsus
Edessa (Urfa) 204
Edirne, see Hadrianopolis
education 33, 71, 73, 90, 97, 100, 118, 122f., 133, 187, 252
Egadi Is, see Aegates
Egypt 9, 13, 29, 39f., 65, 68, 84, 110, 114–117, 119, 129, 133, 160, 169, 172, 177f., 180, 229f., 241, 253., 259, 263
Eion 63
Elagabalus 204, 260
Elba I., see Aethalia

Elbe, R., see Albis
Elea (Vella, Castellamare di Brucia) 42, 88, 96, 252
Electra 80, 84f.
elegiac poetry 32, 128f., 188ff., 258
elephants 117, 156
Eleusis 12, 77, 202, 234, 248
Eleutherae 102
Elijah 242
Elis 28, 132, 233
Elisha 242
Elymians 53
Emesa (Homs) 260
Empedocles 88f.
Empiricists 254
emporia (markets, trading posts) 9, 19, 39, 47ff., 228f.
Emporio 35
Emporion (Emporiae, Ampurias) 42, 250
enfranchisement 61, 107, 164f., 243, 257
Enkomi 45
Enoch 242
entasis 104
Epaminondas 72f., 251
ephebes 122f.
Ephesus (Seçuk) 14, 42f., 54, 88, 104, 108, 148, 234, 249f., 253, 263
Ephialtes 64
ephors 31, 33, 119
epic poetry, see Apokonius Rhodius, Ennius, Hesiod, Homer, Lucan, Naevius, Virgil
Epicharmus 52
Epictetus 201, 260
Epicurus 89, 130f., 171f.
Epidaurus 124, 253f.
epidemic, pestilence, plague 66f., 80, 154, 204
epigram 86, 128f., 194
Epilycus 251
Epirus 29, 156f., 254
equites, see knights
Erasistratus 124
Eratosthenes 124
Ercolano, see Herculaneum
Erechtheum (Athens), 106, 253
Eregli, see Heraclea Pontica
Eresus 44, 123
Eretria 17ff., 46, 49, 56, 228f.
Ergotimus 22
Eridanus (Po) R., see Padus
Erinna 254

Erinyes, see Furies
Eros, see Cupid, love
Erythrae (Ildırı) 249
Esarhaddon 45
Esaro R., see Aesarus
Esquiline Hill 135, 146, 255
Eteocles 77, 79
Etruscans, Etruria 29, 42,49f., 54, 61, 106f., 142–151, 168, 184, 191, 216, 228, 255f.
Euboea 8, 17ff., 25, 45f., 49, 52, 56, 58, 63, 65, 68, 98, 102, 142, 228
Euclid 123
Euclides 93
Eudemus 99
Euelpides 86
Euelthon 45
Euhemerus 252
Eumenes I 118
Eumenes II Soter 134f.
Eumenides, see Aeschylus, Furies
eunomia (order) 76, 240
Eunus (Antiochus) 162
Eupalinus 38
Eupatridai 21, 24, 238
Euphrates R. 170, 197, 208, 261
Euphronius 249
Eupolis 252
Euripides 73, 76, 82–87, 122, 124, 128, 251
Euripus strait 18, 58
Eurotas R. 31
Eurydice 79
Eurymedon (Köprü Çayı) R. 63, 230
Eurypontids 31
Eurystheus 82
Euthydemus I Theos 135, 255
Euthydemus, see Plato
Euthymides 249
Euthyphro, see Plato
Eutychides 126, 254
Euxine Sea, see Black Sea
Exekias 24, 249
ex-slaves, see freedmen

Fabii 150
faction, internal warfare (stasis) 13, 23, 40, 51f., 61f., 67f., 71, 100, 235
faience 263
'Fair-Haired Boy' 102
Fall of Western Roman Empire 210, 215, 218, 252
Famagusta, see Salamis (Cyprus)

Fanum Fortunes (Fano) 206
farmers, see agriculture
Farther Spain (Baetica), see Spain
Fates (Moirai), Fate, Destiny 82, 129f.,
133, 196, 262
Father of the Country, see *pater patriae*
Fausta 261
Felsina (Bologna) 144: see also Bononia
festivals 12f., 16, 23f., 32, 38, 77, 86f.,
104f., 116, 128, 149, 232ff., 252
Ficana (near Acilia) 255
field force, see *comitatenses*
Field of Mars, see Campus Martius
First Jewish Revolt (First Roman War)
193, 241, 243
First Peloponnesian War 251
First Triumvirate 169
Firth of Forth, see Bodotria R.
Firuz 231, 263
fisheries 39, 48f., 115, 235
Five Ages 262
Five Hundred, see Councils
Five Thousand 68
Five Years' Truce 65
Flaccus, Marcus Fulvius, see Fulvius
Flaminius, Gaius 158, 163, 258
Flavian Amphitheatre, see Colosseum
Flavian dynasty 194
Florentiana (Florentin) 260
Florian 206
Forms (*ideai*) 96, 98f.
Fort of the Mulesians 39
Forth, Firth of, see Bodotria R.
Fortuna (Fors) 151, 257
Forum Boarium 146
Forum (Constantinople) 208
Forum Julium (of Caesar) 182f., 258
Forum of Augustus 182f.
Forum of Trajan 195
Forum Romanum 146, 183
Four Hundred 68: see also Councils
Four Regions (Rome) 147
France, see Gaul
François Vase 22, 248, 255
Franks 221
freedmen, ex-slaves, emancipation 23,
119, 193, 201, 203, 259
Fritigern 210
Frogs. see Aristophanes
frontier force, see *limitanei*
Fulvius Flaccus, Marcus 164
Fulvius Nobilior, Marcus 256

funerals, see burials
Furies (Erinyes, Eumenides) 77

Gadara (Umm Qeis) 131
Gades (Cadiz) 259
Gaiseric (Gebseric) 214f.
Gaius (Caligula) 191f.
Gaius (jurist) 260
Gaius Caesar 181
Galatia, Galatians, see Gaul, Gauls
Galatia (province) 258
Galba 193, 259
Galerius 206, 208, 231, 260
Galilee 242
Gallia, see Gaul
Gallic Gulf (Golfe du Lion) 53
Gallienus 204f.
Gallipoli, see Chersonese (Thracian)
Gallus, Trebonianus, see Trebonianus
Gallus
gamoroi 52, 60
Gandhara 135
Garda L., see Benacus
Gaugamela (Gomal) 114, 230
Gaul, Gauls (Celts) 42, 53f., 115, 118,
120, 126, 135, 150, 158, 164f., 170, 176,
193, 205f., 212, 214f., 219ff., 256,
259ff.: see also Ager Gallicus, Dying
Gaul, Ludovisi Group
Gaul, Cisalpine (North Italy) 158, 169,
171, 256f.
Gediz Çayı R., see Hermus
Gela 52, 60, 68, 77, 250
Geleontes 248
Gelon 60f.
gems 14
generals, Greek (*strategoi*) 56f., 64, 69f.,
73, 121, 239, 264
genos, see clan
Genseric, see Gaiseric
Geometric 9, 20, 27, 29
geometry, see mathematics
geomoroi 38
geonim 242
Germanicus 259
Germans, Germany 170, 181f., 194f.,
201f., 206, 210, 212, 214ff., 218f., 259:
see also Alamanni, Batavians,
Burgundians, Cherusci, Cimbri,
Franks, Goths, Marcomanni,
Ostrogoths, Suebi, Teutones, Vandals,
Visigoths

gerousia 31f.
Geta 203
giants, Gigantomachy 134, 254
Giardini Naxos, see Naxos (Sicily)
Gibraltar, Strait of, see Pillars of Hercules
gift exchanges 10, 226
Gioia Tauro, see Mataurus
gladiators 157
Gnosis 127
gold 19, 47ff.,103, 228
Golden Ass 202
Golden Fleece 82
Golden Horn, see Byzantium
Golden House (*Domus Aurea*) 192
Golden Octagon, see Antioch
Golfe du Lion, see Gallic Gulf
Gomal, see Gaugamela
Gordianus I, II Africanus 260
Gordianus III Pius 204, 260
Gorgias 91, 95, 252
Gortyna 250
Gospels, Four, see Christianity
Goths 204ff., 210: see also Ostrogoths, Visigoths
Gracchus, Gaius Sempronius 162–165
Gracchus, Tiberius Sempronius 162ff.
grain, see agriculture
Granicus (Çan Çayı) R.
Gratian 210
Graufescenque, La, see Condatomagus
graves, see burials
Graviscae 143
Great Goddess, see Mother Goddess
Gulf of Ambracia 178
Gulf of Corinth 15, 28, 30, 120, 232, 235, 249
Gulf of Cumae (Bay of Naples) 49
Gulf of Pagasae 115
Gulf of Taras 48f.
Gulf of Tunis 262
Gulf of Valentia 250
gymnasium 123

Hades (Pluto) 234
Hadrian 197ff., 202f., 242, 259f.
Hadrianopolis (Adrianople, Edirne) 210, 261
Haemon 79
Haghia Sophia, see Aya Sofya
Haliacmon R. 72
Haliartus 72

Halicarnassus (Bodrum) 69, 109f., 253, 263
Hamath 228
Hamilcar 60
Hamilcar Barca 158
Hammurabi 263
Hannibal 158ff., 231
Hannibalianus 261
Harran, see Carrhae
Hasdrubal 158
Hasdrubal Barca 159
Hasidim 241
Hasmonaeans 241, 265
hasuchia, see *ataraxia*
Hebrews, see Jews
Hecabe, Hecuba 83
Hecataeus 41, 69
Hecatomnus 109
Hector 225
Helen 52f., 84f., 225
Heliaea 238f.
Helicon, Mt. 26
Helios, see Sun
Helisson R. 236
Hellenion, see Naucratis
Hellenism, 58, 104, 117, 123, 161, 198, 205, 216f.: see also Panhellenism
Hellenistic epoch, art 110, 115–137, 160, 167, 171, 178, 183, 187ff., 191f., 252ff.
hellenotamiai 63
Hellespont (Dardanelles) 21, 39, 46, 58, 69, 114, 248
Helots 16, 32, 59, 64, 119, 236, 250: see also serfs
Helviaus Cinna, Gaius, see Cinna
Hemeroscopion 250
Hephaestus 105: see also Vulcan
Hephthalites (White Huns) 263
Hera 11, 27, 38, 84, 103, 105, 109, 143, 233, 263: see also Juno
Heraclea in Lucania (Policoro) 108, 156
Heraclea Pontica (Ereğli) 236
Heracles (Hercules) 80–84, 101, 148, 233, 260
Heracles, Pillars of, see Pillars of Heracles
Heraclidae, see Euripides
Heraclitus 43, 88f., 92, 248
Heraeum (Argos) 27, 103
Heraeum (Samos) 38, 43
Heraldless War, see Aegina
Herculaneum (Ercolano) 194
Hermes 84, 109, 253: see also Mercury

Hermias 98
Hermione 85
Hermocrates 68
Hermus (Gediz Çayı) R. 41
Herod Antipas 242
Herod I the Great 241f.
Herodas 125
Herodotus 17, 69ff., 142
heroes, heroines 11f., 36f., 41, 79f., 85,
    184, 189, 196, 225f., 236, 255,
    262ff.
Herophilus 124, 254
Hesiod 11, 15f., 26f., 53, 226f., 262
hetaireiai, see clubs
Hierapolis (Pamukkale) 260
Hiero I 60ff., 75, 102, 144
Hiero II 120, 157, 254
High Classical style 103, 105, 108
High Priests, see Jews
Hill, see diakria
Himera (Imera) 52, 60, 250
Hipparchus (astronomer) 124
Hipparchus (son of Pisistratus) 24
hippeis (knights) 10, 86, 264: see also
    Aristophanes
Hippias (son of Pisistratus) 24, 34, 56
Hippias (sophist) 91, 95
Hippo Regius (Annaba) 198, 213
Hippocrates (of Gela) 52, 60
Hippocrates (physician) 71, 92, 252, 254
Hippodamia 101
Hippodamus 252
Hippolyte 83
Hippolytus 83
Hipponax 43
Hispania, see Spain
Histria, see Istrus
Hittites 26, 228f., 249, 262: see also Neo-
    Hittite
Holy Sepulchre, see Jerusalem
Homer (Iliad Odyssey) 8, 11, 15f., 24, 26,
    28, 36f., 45, 52f., 70, 78, 122, 185f.,
    225f., 234, 248ff., 262, 264
Homeric Hymns 232, 234, 263
Homeridae 37
homoioi 32
Homonoia, see Concordia
homosexuality 16, 33, 44, 95, 128, 193,
    204, 235, 239
Homs, see Emesa
Honorius 212f.
Hophra, see Aphries

hoplites, phalanx 10, 13, 28, 30, 32, 57f.,
    64, 73, 147, 152, 156
Horace 187f., 217
Horrea Agrippiana 183
horses, cavalry 18, 26, 45, 56, 59f., 73,
    205, 210, 214, 263
Hortensius, Quintus 155
Hostia 188
hubris 12, 70f., 78–81, 235
humanitas 169, 185f.
Huns 210, 214: see also Hephthalites
Hurrians 26, 228, 262
Hylleis 249
Hyllus 80
Hymns, Homeric, see Homeric Hymns
Hypanis (Bug) R. 47
hyperakria 249
Hysiae 28

Iberus (Ebro) R. 158f.
Ibycus 39
Ichneutae (Trackers), see Sophocles
Ictinus 104
Ida, Mt. 250
ideai, see Forms
Ildïrï, see Erythrae
Ilerda (Lerida) 172
Iliad, see Homer
Ilipa (Alcalá del Rio) 159
Ilium, see Troy
Illyricum (Yugoslavia), Illyrians 30, 73,
    170, 181ff., 213, 258
Ilva (Elba) I., see Aethalia
Imera, see Himera
imperator, imperium 173, 257
India (and Pakistan) 114f., 117f., 156
Indo-Greeks 118, 135, 253f.
inflation 205, 207
inhumation, see burials
Io 78
Iolcus 82
Iole 80
Ion 84, 248, 254
Ionia, Ionians, Ionian Revolt 13f., 16f.,
    19f., 23, 25, 35–43, 46f., 51, 53, 56, 63,
    69, 89, 92, 98, 127, 143, 229f., 234, 248,
    264
Ionian Sea 28, 233
Ionic Order 14, 43, 106, 109, 248, 253
Iouktas, Mt. 250
Iphigenia 77, 84f.
Iran 114, 118: see also Persia

Iraq, see Assyria, Babylonia, Mesopotamia
Irasa 263
iron, Iron Age 9, 20, 33, 45, 49, 144, 146, 228
Ischia, see Pithecusae
Isis 116, 128, 202
Islam 221
Ismenus R. 26
Isocrates 73, 111, 122, 251, 253f.
isonomia 92, 240
Israel, see Judaea
Issus 114, 230
Istanbul, see Byzantium, Constantinople
Ister R., see Danube
Isthmia, Isthmian Games 31, 233
Isthmus of Corinth 27, 29, 58f., 235
Istrus (Histria) 47
Italica 195
Ithaca 36, 225f.
Ithome, see Messene
Ituna R. (Solway Forth) 198
Iulis 24
ivory 29, 32, 38, 103, 183, 228
Izmit, see Nicomedia
Iznik, see Nicaea

Jamnia (Yavneh) 241f.
Jason (Argonaut) 82, 129
Jason (Joshua, High Priest) 241
Jehovah, see Jews
Jerome, St. 213, 261
Jerusalem 193, 209, 241f.
Jesus Christ 185, 209: see also Christianity
Jews, Judaism 116, 191ff., 198, 211, 241ff., 254, 259, 261, 264ff.: see also Judaea and First, Second, Jewish Revolts
Job 226
Jocasta 80, 252
John the Baptist, St. 242
Jordan (Aulon) R. 242, 260
Joseph 254
Josephus 193, 259
Joshua, see Jason
Jovian 209, 231
Judaea (Israel, Palestine, Yehud) 241f., 253: see also Jews
Judaism, see Jews
Judas Maccabaeus 241
Jugurtha 165, 177
Julia (daughter of Augustus) 181, 189, 258

Julia (daughter of Julius Caesar) 169f.
Julia (grand-daughter of Augustus) 189
Julia Domna 203
Julia Maesa 204
Julia Mamaea 204
Julian the Apostate 209, 212
Julianus, Didius, see Didius Julianus
Julianus, Salvius, see Salvius Julianus
Julio-Claudian dynasty 181, 193
Julius Caesar, Gaius, Lucius, see Caesar
Julius Nepos 215
Juno (Hera) 148, 182, 256
Jupiter (Zeus) 144, 147f., 161, 182, 186, 256, 260
jurists, see law
ius gentium, see law
Justice, see Dike
Justinian I 221, 261
Jutland 165
Juvenal 197, 200
Juventas (Youth) 182

Kadıköy, see Calchedon
Kerch, see Panticapaeum
Kerch, Strait of, see Bosphorus Cimmerian
Kılıdülbehar, see Cynossema
Klazümen, see Clazomenae
Kings, see monarchies
King's Peace, see Peace of Antalcidas
Kısık, see Lebedus
klerouchoi, see colonization
knights, Greek, see *hippeis*
knights, Roman (*equites*) 163f., 166, 168f., 176, 180, 203
Kniva 204
Kochba, Bar, see Bar Kosiba
Kom Gieif, see Naucratis
Köprü, Çayı, see Eurymedon R.
korai, see sculpture
Korakou 28
Kore, see Persephone
Kosiba, Bar, see Bar Kosiba
Kouklia, see Paphos
kouroi, see sculpture
Küçük Menderes R., see Cayster
Kyllyrioi 52

Lacedaemon, see Sparta
Laches, see Plato
Laconia 31f., 64, 229
Lacydon, see Massalia

Lade, 39, 43, 230
Laetus, Quintus Aemilius 202
Laia 254
Laius 80
Lamia 253
Lamian War 118, 253
Lampsacus (Lapseki) 46, 123
landscape, see nature
Langres, see Andematunnum
Laocoon 135, 254
Lapiths 101, 104, 110
Lapseki, see Lampsacus
Lares 182
Lares Parsenna 144
Later Classical Style 108
Lateranus, Lucius Sextius 154
Latin Right (*ius Latii*) 164, 166
Latium, Latin League 142, 144–152, 156,
    255
Laurium 20, 57, 68, 118
Laus 250
Lavinia 186
Lavinium (Pratica del Mare) 149, 255
laws, legislation, edicts, jurists, law courts
    10, 21f., 30, 33, 64, 67, 79, 81, 86, 90f.,
    97, 112, 154f., 157f., 163, 166f., 180,
    183, 198, 202, 207ff., 218, 238, 248ff.,
    253, 256f., 260
Lebda, see Lepcis Magna
Lebedus (on Kısık peninsula) 249
Lechaeum 249
Lechova R., see Helisson
Ledosus (Lezoux) 200
Lefkandi 8, 18f., 45, 248
Lefkas, see Leucas
Lelantine plain 18f.
Lelanton R. 18
Lemnos 80
Lenaea, see festivals
Leo I (pope) 214
Leo III (pope) 221
Leochares 110, 253
Leonidas I 58
Leontini (Carlentini) 91, 248
Lepcis Magna (Lebda) 199, 260
Lepidus, Marcus Aemilius (censor 179
    B.C.) 256
Lepidus, Marcus Aemilius (consul 78
    B.C.) 167
Lepidus Marcus, Aemilius (triumvir)
    176, 178, 187, 257
Lerida, see Ilerda

Lesbia 171
Lesbos 16, 43f., 67, 123, 249
Leucas (Lefkas) 249
Leucippus 89, 131, 252
Leuctra 72
Lezoux, see Ledosus
Libation-Bearers (*Choephori*), see Aeschylus
Libo Visolus, Gaius Poetelius, see
    Poetelius
Libon 101
Library, see Alexandria
Libya, Libyans 229, 263
Licinius I 208, 260f.
liman (river-mouth) 47f.
limitanei 207
Lindum (Lincoln) 259
Lindus 249
linen 263
Lingones 219, 261
Liris (Garigliano) R. 150
Livia 181
Livius Andronicus 157, 160
Livius Drusus, Marcus 165, 257
Livy 184
Locri Epizephyrii 95, 250
Love (Eros), love poetry 38f., 44, 85, 89,
    95, 128f., 187f.: see also Cupid
Luca (Lucca) 170
Lucan 192
Lucania 108, 156, 167
Lucilius 161, 187
Lucius Caesar 181
Lucius (in Apuleius) 202
Lucius Verus, see Verus
Lucretius 171f.
Lucullus, Lucius Licinius 168
Ludi Saeculares, see Secular Games
Ludovisi Group 126, 254
Lugdunensis, Galia, see Gaul
Luna (Luni, Carrara) 183
Lupercal 182
Lyceum 98, 123: see also Peripatetics
Lycia 110, 263
Lycurgus 33, 119
Lycus 84
Lydia 16, 40f., 43, 142, 160, 229, 248
Lydias R. 72
Lygdamis 234, 264
lyric poetry, lyre 11, 24, 32, 38, 44, 75f.,
    86, 187ff., 248, 264
Lysander 69, 71f., 230
Lysimachus 253

Lysippus 125f., 128, 254
Lysistrata 87

Maccabees, see Hasmonaeans, Judas
  Maccabaeus
Macedonia 19, 23f., 30, 45f., 56, 58f., 66f.,
  72ff., 82, 98, 108, 111, 114–119, 121,
  127, 133, 160, 177, 230, 252ff.
Macrinus 203
Madaurus (Mdaourouch) 202
Maeander (Menderes) R. 39
Maecenas, Gaius 184f., 187f., 255
Maenace (Torre del Mar) 250
Maenads (Bacchae, Bacchants) 85
Maesa, Julia, see Julia Maesa
Magnentius 261
Magnesia beside Sipylus (Manisa) 160
Magnesia on the Maeander (near
  Ortaklar) 102
Mainz, see Moguntiacum
Malaca (Malaga) 250
Malis 253
Malkepe, see Dardanus
Mamaea, Julia, see Julia Mamaea
Mangalia, see Callatis Pontica
Manichaeans 213, 261
Manisa, see Magnesia beside Sipylus
Mantinea 67, 72, 95
Mantua (Mantova) 184
Marathon 46, 56–59, 77, 104, 230, 250
marble, see stone
Marcellus, Marcus Claudius 181f.
Marcius Rex, Quintus 256
Marcomanni 181, 202
Marcus Aurelius, see Aurelius
Mardonius 56, 59
Mareotis L. 116
Marinus 260
Marius, Gaius 165f., 168, 177, 257
Market of Tragjan, 195
Marmara, Sea of, see Propontis
Marmarereğlisi, see Perinthus
Maronea 37
Mars (Ares) 182f., 256
Marseille, see Massalia
Martial 194f., 259
Masada 193, 259
Masinissa 159
Massalia (Massilia, Marseille) 42, 53f.,
  143, 147f., 164, 250, 261
Mataurus (Gioia Tauro) 250
mathematics 15, 40, 50, 93, 123f.

Mauretania (Morocco) 203, 214
Mausoleum (Halicathassus) 109f., 253,
  263
Mausoleum of Augustus 183
Mausolus 109f, 253
Maxentius 208, 260f.
Maximian 206, 208, 260f.
Maximinus I Thrax 204, 260, 265
Maximinus II Daia 261
Maximus 260
Mdaourouch, see Madaurus
Mean, the 99f.
Medea 82, 129
Media 114, 229f.
medicine 51, 71, 91f., 98, 124, 154
Mediolanum (Milan) 205f., 208, 210ff,
  214
Medontids 21
Megalopolis 121, 133, 251
Megara 19, 21f., 28, 38, 93, 235f., 264
Megara Hyblaea 255f.
Megarid 235
Meidias painter 108
Melanchrus 44
Melos (Milo) 126, 254
Memphis 116f., 229
Menander (comic dramatist) 84, 87, 125,
  128,160
Menander Soter Dikaius (Indo-Greek
  king) 253
Menelaus 83ff., 225, 249
Menexenus, see Plato
Menippus 131
Meno, see Plato
Mercato Saraceno, see Sarsina
mercenaries 23, 38, 60f., 156, 263
merchants, see trade
Mercury, see Hermes
Merovingians 221
Mesaoria plain 44
Mesembria (Messebur) 47
Mesopotamia 114, 204, 231, 262
Messalla Corvinus, Marcus Valerius 258
Messana (Messina) 157: see also Zancle
Messene 251f.
Messenia, 31f., 64, 72, 251
Messiah, Messianism 185, 242f., 259
Messina, Strait of, see Sicilian Strait
metals, mines 10, 15, 18f., 23, 27, 29, 31,
  37, 42, 45, 60, 64, 66, 73, 118, 143, 146,
  200, 228, 250: see also bronze, copper,
  gold, iron, silver, tin

Metapontum (Metaponto) 50f.
Metaurus (Metauro) R. 159
Metallus Pius Scipio, Quintus Caecilius, see Scipio
metempsychosis 51
Methone 46
metics (metoikoi), resident aliens 15, 29, 238, 264
Mezitli, see Soli
Midacritus 42, 54
Midas 262
Middle Comedy 252
Mieza 98
Milan, see Mediolanum
Milas, see Mylasa
Milesian Tales 129, 254
Miletus (Yeniköy) 15, 37–41, 43, 46f., 50, 66, 69, 89, 123, 229, 234, 249, 252, 254, 257
Military Anarchy 204
Military Monarchy 203f.
Miltiades the elder 23, 46
Miltiades the younger 24, 46, 56f.
Milvian bridge, see bridges
mime 125, 132
Minerva (Athena) 148, 182, 256
mines, see metals
Minoans, Minos 8, 11, 247
Minucian Bridge, see bridges
'miserabilistic' style 127
Mishnah 242
misthosis (state pay) 65, 251
Mithras, Mithraism 202, 260
Mithridates I of Parthia 230
Mithridates VI the Great of Pontus 133, 166, 168, 172
Mitylene, see Mytilene
Mnesicles 106
Modena, see Mutina
Moesia, see Dacia Ripensis, Dardania
Moguntiacum (Mainz) 210
Mohammed (prophet) 221
Mohammed (Mehmet) II the Conqueror 222
Moirai, see Fates
Molossus 83
monarchies, kings, 8ff., 12, 21, 28, 30–33, 35, 38, 42, 44f., 115–119, 128, 137, 146, 173, 183, 236, 248, 256, 264
money, see coinage
monks 216, 261
Monoecus (Monaco) 250

Mont-Beuvray, see Bibracte
Montagnone, Mt. 49
Monte S. Angelo, Cufino, see Ecnomus
mosaics 127, 254
Moschophorus 22, 248
Mosello (Moselle) R. 261
Moses 242
Mother, Earth, Great Goddess 11, 45, 182
Motya (Mozia) 250
Munda 172
Muses 226f.
Museum, see Alexandria
music, dancing 23f., 32, 38, 75f., 86, 97, 125, 128, 160, 233, 254
Mutina (Modena) 176
Mycale, Mt. 35ff.
Mycenae, Mycenaeans 8f., 11ff., 18f., 26f., 31, 36, 39, 44f., 80, 83, 225, 228f., 236, 247: see also Argos
Mylasa (Milas) 109
Myrmidons 225, 262
Myron 102, 252
Mysia 98
Myson 249
Mystery religions 12, 202f., 234
Myths, mythology 12, 26, 40f., 75, 85, 101, 105, 107, 135, 146, 161, 184ff., 188f., 227f., 233, 248, 252, 255, 262
Mytilene 44, 67, 249
Myus (near Avşar) 249

Nabis 119
Nabopolassar 229
Naevius, Cnaeus 160f., 258
Nağara, see Abydus
Nahra el-Asi R., see Orontes
Naissus (Niş) 205
Namurtköy, see Cyme
Não de la, C., see Tenebrium
Naples, see Neapolis
Naples, Bay of, see Gulf of Cumae
Narses 231
nature, landscape 108, 135f., 185: see also physis
Naucratis (Kom Gieif) 39, 229, 263
Naulochus (Venetico) C. 178, 257
Naupactus 120, 251
Nausicaa 226
navies, naval forces, fleets, see ships
Naxos (island of Cyclades) 14, 38, 63, 234, 264

Naxos (Sicily) (Giardini Naxos) 52, 248
Nazareth 242
Neapolis (Naples) 49, 184
Nearer Spain (Tarraconensis), see Spain
Necho II 229, 263
Nehardea 265
Nemausus (Nîmes) 199
Nemea, Nemean Games 28, 233
Nemesis 71
Neo-Hittite 228, 262
Neoptolemus 81, 83
Neoteric movement 171
Nephelai (*Clouds*), see Aristophanes
Nephelococcygia (Cloudcuckooland) 86f.
Nepos, Julius, see Julius Nepos
Neptune, see Poseidon
Nereus 262
Nero 192f., 196, 230, 260, 265
Nero Drusus (Drusus the elder) 181, 258
Nerva 195, 211, 259
Nervii 170
Nessebur, see Mesembria
Nestorius 263
New Comedy 84, 87, 125, 160, 252: see also Menander
new man, see *novus homo*
Nicaea (Iznik) 124, 209, 261
Nicaea (Nice) 250
Nicephorium, see Callinicum Nicephorium
Nicias, 67f.: see also Peace of Nicias
Nicomedia (Izmit) 206
Niger, Pescennius, see Pescennius Niger
Nike, see Victory
Nîmes, see Nemausus
Ninevah 229
Ninus 254
Niobid painter 107
Niş, see Naissus
Nisaea 235f., 264
Nobilior, Marcus Fulvius, see Fulvius
noblemen, see aristocrats
nomoi, see laws
Noricum 258
Notium 69, 251
novels, romance 129, 193, 202, 254
novus homo (new man) 158, 161, 165, 168, 180f.
Nubia 229
Numidia (E. Algeria) 159, 165, 214

Octavia 177
Octavian, see Augustus
Octavius, Marcus 163
Odenathus 260
Odoacer 215, 221
Odysseus 36, 81, 135, 225f., 255, 262
Odyssey, see Homer
Oedipus 26, 52, 77, 79ff., 252
Oenomaus 101
Oenophyta 65, 251
oikos (family) 21
oil, see olives
Olbia (Olvia) 47f., 131
Old Comedy 86ff., 125
Old Rhine, R, see Rhenus
oligarchy, timocracy, *optimates* 13, 22, 31, 40, 54, 60, 66, 68, 71, 76, 164, 177ff., 235f., 238, 251
olives, oil 20, 26, 48f., 54, 200, 233, 238, 263
Olorus 70
Olympia, Olympic Games 28, 101, 104, 106f., 109, 233f., 236, 252, 263
Olympias 73
Olympus Mt. 233
Olynthus 73f.
Opimius, Lucius 164
Opis 114: see also Seleucia on the Tigris
Oplontis (Torre Annunziata) 194
optimates, see oligarchy
oracles, prophecies, seers 10, 25, 29, 39, 75, 78–81, 87, 232
oratory 32, 64f., 74f., 130, 168, 176, 192, 195, 218, 239, 262: see also rhetoric
orchestra 24
Orchomenus 249
order, see *eunomia*
Orestes (German general) 215
Orestes (sculptor) 134
Orestes (son of Agamemnon) 77, 80, 84f.
orientalizing style 9, 19, 229
Origen 243, 265
originality 11, 110f., 137, 187, 217
Orléans, see Cenabum
Orodes II 230
Oroetes 39
Orontes (Nahrel-Asi) R. 228
Orpheus 51
Ortaklar, see Magnesia on the Maeander
Orthagoras 236
Ortygia, see Syracuse
Orvieto, see Volsinii

Oscan language 256
Ostia 152, 199, 215, 252, 260
Ostorius Scapula, Publius 259
ostracism 64, 239
Ostrogoths 210, 221
Otho 259
Ovid 188ff.

Padua, see Patavium
Padus (Eridanus, Po) R., 145, 150, 158,
    165f., 255
Paestum, see Posidonia
Pagasae, Gulf of, see Gulf of Pagasae
Painted Portico (Stoa Poikile), see Stoics
painting, drawing 8f., 14, 20, 22, 24, 27,
    29, 31, 105–108, 128, 135f., 143, 194,
    236f., 249, 254f.
Pakistan, see India
Palatine Hill 146, 182f., 255
Palermo, see Panormus
Palestine, see Judaea
Palestrina, see Praeneste
Pallas Athene, see Athena
Palmyra (Tadmor) 205f., 260
Paltus (Tell Sukas, Bulda) 228
Pamphyli 249
Pamphylia 63
Pamukkale, see Hierapolis
Panaetius 134, 253
Panathenaia 23f., 104f.
Pandateria (Ventotene) 258
Pandora 16, 226
Pangaeum, Mt. 23f., 46, 72f.
Panhellenism 12, 28, 58f., 69, 73, 91,
    232ff: see also Congresses, Hellenism
Panion (Banyas) 241
Panionion, Pan-Ionian League 35f.
Pannonia 178, 181, 213, 258
Panormus (Palermo) 60, 250
Panthea 254
Pantheon 198
Panticapaeum (Kerch) 48
Panzano Secco, see Regillus L.
Paphlagonia 86
Paphos (Kouklia) 45, 250
Papinianus, Aemilius 260
papyrus 263
paralia (Coast) 249, 264
Paris 52, 84, 225
Parmenides 88, 95f., 248
Parmenio 73
Parnassus Mt. 232

Parnon Mt. 31
Paros 11, 14, 46, 57, 110, 264
Parrhasius 108
Parthenon 104f., 108, 112, 134, 252
Parthia 118, 170, 177f., 195, 201, 204,
    230f., 242, 258, 263
pastoral, bucolic poetry 132, 184f.
Patavium (Padua) 184
pater patriae (Father of the Country)
    179f., 258f.
patricians 153, 166, 256
Patroclus 45, 225
Paul (Saul), St: 242f, 265
Paulus, Julius 260
Pausanias (son of Cleombrotus) 59, 63,
    251
Pausanias (grandson of last) 72
Pausanias (travel writer) 109
Pavia, see Ticinum
Pax Augusta, Romana 180, 183–186,
    188, 199f., 219f., 258
Peace of Antalcidas (King's Peace) 72,
    230
Peace of Callias (449 B.C.) 65, 230, 251
Peace of Callias (371 B.C.) 72, 251
Peace of Epilycus 251
Peace of Nicias 67, 86
Peace of Philocrates 73
Pediaeus (Pidias) R. 45
Pedianus Fuscus Salinator, Cnaeus 260
pedieis (Plainsman) 249, 264
Pegae 235
Pegasus 31
Peisthetaerus 86
Peleus 262
Pella 73, 115, 127, 254
Peloponnese, Peloponnesian League 8,
    21, 26–34, 58f., 72, 101, 120, 233, 236,
    253
Peloponnesian War 66–71, 73, 81, 83,
    86f., 93, 112, 230, 251
Pelops 101, 233
Penates 182
Penelope 225f.
pentakosiomedimnoi 264
Pentateuch, see Torah
penteconter, see ships
Pentelicus Mt. 20
Penthelids 44
Pentheus 85
Peraea 242
Perdiccas II 73

Perdiccas III 73
Perdiccas (general) 253
Pergamum (Bergama) 118, 123, 126, 133f., 160, 162ff., 166, 254f.
Periander 30f., 249
Pericles 64–67, 71, 79, 89f., 92, 94, 103f, 106, 252
Perinthus (Marmaraereğlisi) 38, 73
perioikoi 15f., 27, 32, 59
Peripatetics 98: see also Lyceum
Persephone (Kore) 234
Persepolis 114
Perses 226
Perseus 133, 160, 254
Persia, Persian Wars 13f., 16f., 19, 24f., 37, 39, 41, 46, 56–60, 63, 65f., 68–74, 77, 87f., 102, 104, 110, 114, 204, 209, 212, 228–232, 234, 241f., 251, 253f., 262ff.
Persian Gulf 195, 197, 202
Persius 192, 259
Pertinax 260
Perusia (Perugia) 259
Pescennius Niger 260
pestilence, see epidemics
Peter, St. 209
Petronius Arbiter (Titus Petronius Niger) 192f., 202
Phaeacians 226
Phaedo, see Plato
Phaedra 83
Phaedriades (Shining Cliffs) 232
Phaedrus, see Plato
phalanx, see hoplites
Phaleas 250
Phaleron 20
Pharisees 241, 243, 265
Pharnaces II 172
Pharos, see Alexandria
Pharsalus 172, 192, 257
Pheidon 12, 27–30
Pherae 82
Pheretime 263
Phidias 104ff., 109, 252
Phile 254
Philebus, see Plato
Philip II 72ff., 98, 111f., 114, 118f., 230, 251, 253
Philip V 133, 160
Philip the Arabian 204, 260
Philippi (Crenides) 73, 177, 187
Philo Judaeus 191f., 241, 259

Philocrates 73
Philoctetes 80f.
Philius 11, 132
philosophy 11, 15, 40f., 43, 71, 88–100, 112, 119, 123, 127, 129ff., 136f., 161, 171f., 183, 187, 191f., 202, 259
Phocaea 41f., 46f., 53f., 143, 249f., 262
Phocis 73, 232
Phoenicia 9f., 14, 18, 45, 51f., 60f., 84, 228f., 250, 253, 262
Phormio 251
phratria, see brotherhood
Phrygia 201, 251, 260, 262
Phrynichus 24
Phthia 262
physicians, see medicine
physis (nature) 79, 90f.
Picentia (Pontecagnano) 255
Pidias R., see Pediaeus
Pilatus, Pontius 242
Pillars of Heracles 37, 54
Pindar 61, 75f.
Piraeus 20, 25
pirates 120, 168, 177
Pisa 101, 233
Pisciatello, R., see Rubican
Pisistratus 23f., 44, 46, 76, 234, 249
Piso Frugi Licinianus, Lucius Calpurnius 259
Pissuthnes 66, 68, 251
Pistoria (Pistoia) 168
Pithecusae (Aenaria, Ischia) 19, 49, 54, 142, 228
Pitsa 236f., 264
Pittacus 44, 249
Placidia, Galla 212, 214
plague, see epidemics
Plainsmen, see *pedieis*
Plataea 27, 57, 59, 63, 230
Plato 10, 74, 92–100, 112, 123, 134, 252
Plautianus, Gaius Fulvius 203, 260
Plautilla 260
Plautius Aulus 259
Plautus 87, 160f., 256
Pliny the elder 110, 194, 236, 259, 265
Pliny the younger 197, 243, 265
Plotina 259
Plutarch 196f., 259
Pluto, see Hades
Plutus, see Aristophanes
Po (Eridanus) R., see Padus
Poetelias Libo Visolus, Gaius 154

Pojani, see Apollonia
polemarch 21, 56, 239, 248, 250
polis (city-state) 9–12, 14ff., 49, 71, 74,
    79, 81, 90f., 97, 99f., 111f., 118, 143,
    155, 227
Politorium (Castel di Decima) 255
Pollio, Gaius Asinius 184
Polybius 133f., 153, 153, 155, 157, 258
Polybus 80
Polyclitus 103ff., 109, 252
Polycrates 38f., 44, 234
Polycrates junior 39
Polydorus (sculptor) 254
Polydorus (son of Priam and Hecabe) 83
Polygnota 254
Polygnotus 106f.
Polymestor 83
Polynices 77, 79, 83
Polyphemus (Cyclops) 226, 251
Polyzalus 102
Pompeii 162, 194, 199, 254f.
Pompeius, Cnaeus, junior 172
Pompeius Magnus, Cnaeus (Pompey the
    great) 167–172, 174, 179, 182, 184,
    192, 257
Pompeius, Sextus 172, 177f.
Pons Aemilius, Minucius, Sublicius,
    Ponte Rotto, see bridges
Pontecagnano, see Picentia
Pontius Pilatus, see Pilatus
Pontus 133, 166, 168, 172, 253, 258
populares 164, 177
Populonia 143
Porticus Aemilia 161
Porticus Octavia 182
portraits, see coinage, sculpture
Poseidon (Neptune) 31, 83, 102, 105, 226,
    249
Posidium (Ras-el-Bassit) 228, 262
Posidonia (Paestum) 50, 250
Posidonius 124, 134, 253f., 258
Postumus 260
Potidaea 30: see also Cassandrea
pottery, vases 8f., 14, 20, 22, 24, 27, 29,
    31f., 107f., 143, 146, 200, 239, 248
Pozzuoli, see Dicaearchia
Praeneste (Palestrina) 151f., 257
praetorian prefects 191, 204, 255, 259f.
praetors 154, 158, 174, 256
Pratica del Mare, see Lavinium
Praxagora 87
Praxiteles, 108f., 126, 253

Priam 83, 135, 225
Priene (Turunçlar) 249, 254
Prilius L. 143
princeps civitatis, principate 179, 181
Probus 206
procurators 180, 195
Prodicus 91, 252
prokrisis 239
Prometheus 78, 226
Propertius 188, 190
prophecies, see oracles
Propontis (Sea of Marmara) 39, 46
Propylaea (Athens) 106
Protagoras 90f., 94, 132
Protocorinthian pottery 29
Protogeometric pottery 8, 20, 27, 31, 248
prytaneis (steering committee) 54, 120, 239
Psammetichus I 229
Psyche 202
Ptolemies 115, 123, 128, 160, 172, 229,
    241
Ptolemy I Soter 116, 127, 253
Ptolemy II Philadelphus 116f., 128, 253
Ptolemy III Euergetes 118
Ptolemy IV Philopator 117
Ptolemy V Epiphanes 117
Ptolemy XII Auletes (Father of
    Cleopatra VII) 178, 257
public land, see *ager publicus publicani*, see
    taxes
Pulcher, Appius Claudius, see Claudius
Pumbeditha 265
Punic Wars, see Carthage
Punjab 114, 135
Pupienus 260
Puteoli, see Dicaearchia
Pydna 160
Pylades 80, 84
Pylos 67
pyramids 253
Pyrgi 143, 157
Pyrrho 132
Pyrrhus 156f., 256
Pythagorus (philosopher) 15, 50f., 93f.,
    252, 263
Pythagorus (tyrant of Ephesus) 42, 250
Pythia 232
Pythian games 102, 233
Pytho, see Delphi

quaestiones, see law
Qart Hadasht, see Carthage

Quintilian 259
Quirinal Hill 146
Quirinus 182, 256

rabbis, see Jews
Raetia 258
Raphia (Tell Rafah) 117
Raqqa, see Callinicum Nicephorium
Ras-el-Bassit, see Posidium
Ravenna 212, 214ff., 261
Razgrad, see Abrittus
Reccared 221
recollection, see *anamnesis*
Record Office, see Tabularium
recusatio 188
Regillus L. (Panzano Secco) 149
religion, Christian, see Christianity
religion, pagan 11ff., 16, 23, 35, 43, 51,
    53, 70f., 75–82, 85, 87, 93, 95f., 98f.,
    105f., 130f., 147f., 176ff., 182f., 186,
    189–192, 202f., 207, 211ff., 216, 227,
    229, 232ff., 236, 239, 248, 255, 257,
    260–263: see also festivals
Res Gestae Divi Augusti 182f.
Resadiye peninsula, see Cnidus
revolution, see faction
Rhacotis 253
Rhadaestus, see Bisanthe
rhapsodes 37
Rhegium (Reggio di Calabria) 39, 49, 60,
    248, 250, 258
Rheneia I. 38
Rhenus (Rhine) R. 195, 200, 204, 210,
    212, 220, 261
rhetoric 111, 122f., 192, 259: see also
    oratory
Rhodanus (Rhône) R. 54, 165, 237
Riace 102, 252
Ricimer 215
Rimini, see Ariminum
roads 152, 164f., 182, 234, 256ff.
Roman Wars (of Jews), see First, Second
    Jewish Revolts
romances, see novels
Rome 54, 102f., 133–223, 241ff., 255–261,
    265
Romulus Augustulus 215
Roselle, see Rusellae
Rovigo, see Campi Raudii
Roxane 114
Rubicon (Pisciatello?) R. 172
Rudiae 161

Rufinus 212
Rumania, see Dacia
Rusellae (Roselle) 143

Sabellians, Sabines 149ff., 167
Sabis (Sambre) R. 170
Sacred War, First 232
Sacred War, Third 73
Sacred Way, see roads
Sadducees 241, 265
Saffuriya, see Seppheris
Sages, Seven, see Seven Sages
Sagra (Sagriano or Turbolo) R. 250
Saguntum (Sagunto) 159
Saida, see Sidon
Salamis (Cyprus) 8, 45, 250
Salamis (island) 21, 23, 58f., 77, 82, 230,
    235f.
Sallust 176f.
Salonica, see Thessalonica
salt 54, 144f., 150
Salvian 261
Salvius Julianus 198, 260
Samarobriva, see Ambiani
Sambre R., see Sabis
Samnites, Samnite Wars 144, 151f., 154,
    156, 165f., 256
Samos 15, 35, 42ff., 50, 66, 108, 124,
    129ff., 229, 234, 251
Samothrace 126, 254
Samsun, see Amisus
sanctuaries, see temples
Sanhedrin 242
Santorini, see Thera
San Vittorino, see Amiternum
Sant' Eufernia, see Terina
Sappho 16, 44, 187
Sapor (Shapur) I 204, 231
Sapor (Shapur) II the Great 263
Sarapis (Serapis) 116, 253
Sardinia 157, 161, 228
Sardis (Sart) 39, 56, 66
Sargon II 263
Sarmatia 202
Saronic Gulf 20, 28, 30, 235, 249
Sarsina (Mercato Saraceno) 160
Sassanians, see Persia
Sassoferrato, see Sentinum
satire 43, 125, 131, 161, 187, 194f., 197,
    259
Satricum (Borgo Montello) 255
Saturn 182

Saturninus, Lucius Appuleius 165
satyr-plays 76, 79, 251
Satyrican, see Petronius
Satyrus (biographer) 127
Satyrus (sculptor) 110
Saul, see Paul, St.
Sceptics 132
Scheria 226
Scidrus 250
science 40, 50, 53, 91, 93, 98f., 123f., 135f.,
    192, 259
Scipio, Cnaeus Cornelius 159
Scipio, Publius Cornelius 159
Scipio Africanus the elder, Publius
    Cornelius 159ff.
Scipio Africanus the younger
    (Aemilianus), Publius Cornelius 161ff.
Scipio, Quintus Caeceilius Metellus Pius
    170
Scopas 110, 253
Scotland, see Caledonia
scripts, see alphabets
sculpture 13f., 22f., 38, 42, 101–107, 110,
    119, 125–128, 134f., 143, 173, 183,
    193ff., 229, 233f., 248, 250, 252–256,
    258f., 264
Scutari (Üsküdar) see Chrysopolis
Scyllis 236
Scyros 63
Scythia, Scythians 48, 51, 230, 251
Sebaa Biar, see Zama
Secessions, see plebeians
Second Jewish Revolt 198, 242
Second Triumvirate 176f., 184, 187, 230
Secular Games (*Ludi Saeculares*) 188
Segesta 53, 250
Sejanus, Lucius Aelius 191, 255
Selçuk, see Ephesus
selenite 199, 260
Seleucia on the Tigris 117, 231: see also
    Opis
Seleucids 115, 117f., 133, 160, 230, 265
Seleucus I Nicator 117, 234, 253
Selinus (Selindi, Cilicia) 195
Selinus (Selinunte, Sicily) 53, 250
Sellasia 119, 121
Semonides 16, 37
Senate (Constantinople) 208
Senate (Rome), senators 153, 155, 158f.,
    161, 163f., 166–169, 173f., 176, 179f.,
    182f., 191, 194f., 197f., 202f., 206, 210,
    215, 257

Senate House (*curia*) 182, 211, 257
Seneca the elder, Lucius Annaeus
    192
Seneca the younger, Lucius Annaeus 192,
    201, 259
Senegal, R. 54
Sentinum (Sassoferrato) 152
Sepeia 28, 34
Sepphoris-Diocaesarea (Saffuriya,
    Zippori) 265
Septimius Severus, see Severus
Septimontium, see Seven Hills of Rome
    (early)
Serapis, see Sarapis
Serdaiol 49
serfs 16, 28, 32, 52, 236, 250, 264: see also
    Helots
Sertorius, Quintus 167
Servianus Ursus, Lucius Julius 260
Servilius Caepio, Quintus 257
Servius Tullius 147: see also Wall
Sessa, see Suessa Aurunca
Seven Against Thebes, see Aeschylus
Seven Hills of Rome (early:
    Septimontium) 146, 255
Seven Hills of Rome (later) 255
Seven Sages 30f., 33, 40, 249
Seven Wonders of the World 43, 106, 110,
    116, 252f.
Severe style, see Early Classical
Severus Alexander, see Alexander
Severus, Septimius 203f., 207, 231,
    260
Severus II 261
Seville, see Italica
shamans 51
Shapur, see Sapor
sheep, wool 38f., 46, 50, 235, 263
Shining Cliffs, see Phaedriades
ships, navies, fleets 10, 30, 37ff., 42, 46,
    54, 56–60, 63, 65ff., 72, 84, 116, 119,
    126, 145, 148, 156f., 178, 194, 215,
    225f., 229, 249, 263
shrines, see temples
Sibari, see Sybaris
Sibyl 49, 186
Sicilian Strait (Strait of Messina) 48f., 51,
    157
Sicily 13, 19, 29, 48, 51ff., 60ff., 67f., 75,
    78, 86, 88, 90f., 94, 96, 119f., 142, 156f.,
    160, 162, 172, 177, 185, 228, 235, 251f.,
    257, 262

Sicyon 13, 28, 103, 125, 128, 232, 236f., 264
Sidon (Saida) 10, 228
Sığacık, see Teos
Sigeum (near Yenisehir) 21, 23, 44, 248
Sillua, Sillume 45
silphium 263
Silures 259
silver 19f., 24, 27, 47, 52, 57, 68, 118, 263
Simeon Bar Kosiba (Kochba), see Bar Kosiba
Simonides 24, 61, 249
Sinope (Sinop) 47, 131
Siphnos 38
Sirmium (Sremska Mitrovica) 260
Siscia (Sisak) 178
slaves 15, 19, 23, 32, 37, 39, 43, 48, 54, 68, 111, 161f., 167, 193, 199f., 203, 228, 257
Smyrna (Izmir) 36
Social War 165f., 257
Socrates 86, 92–97, 169
Sogdiana 118
Sol, see Sun
Solus, Soloeis (Soluntum, Solunto) 250
Solway Firth, see Ituna
sophists 89ff., 132, 202, 252
Sophocles 76f., 79–82, 86, 251
Soukh-Aras, see Thagaste
Spain (Hispania) 37, 42, 54, 60, 159, 165, 167, 169f., 179, 181, 192–195, 197, 200, 211, 221, 228, 256f., 259
Sparta 13, 16, 24f., 27f., 31–34, 53, 57ff., 63–67, 70ff., 83, 86, 119ff., 225, 230, 236, 249ff., 263
Spartacus 167, 257
Sphacteria 67
Sphinx 80
Spina 255
Spurinna family 255
Stabiae (Castellamare di Stabia) 194
Stagirus 98
stasis, see faction
state pay (*misthosis*)
Statira, see Barsine
Stesichorus 52f., 84, 250
Stilicho 212
Stoics (Stoa Poikile, Painted Portico) 130, 134, 169, 192, 197, 201
Stolo, Gaius Licinius 154
stone, marble 20, 29, 38, 43, 102, 126, 162, 182f., 199, 251, 264

Strabo 54, 183, 258
strategoi, see generals
Strato 123f.
Stridon 213
Strymon (Struma) R. 63
Sublician Bridge, see bridges
Subura 183
Suebi (Suevi) 181
Suessa Aurunca (Sessa) 161
Suetonius 183, 198, 259
Sulla, Lucius Cornelius 166f., 173, 256f.
Sulmo (Sulmona) 188
Sulpicius Rufus, Publius 166, 257
Sun (Helios, Sol) 82, 110, 126, 202, 208f.
Sunium, C. 57
Sur, see Tyre
Sura (Al-Suriyya) 265
Susa 114
Sybaris (Sibari) 49–52, 69, 250: see also Thurii
Sybaris, R. 49
Sybota Is. 30
Symmachus 211
synoikismos, see urbanization
Syracuse (Siracusa) 29, 52, 60ff., 67f., 75, 77, 94, 102, 116, 119f., 124f., 144, 157, 159, 230, 252, 254
Syria 9, 14, 18f., 29, 45, 114, 124, 142, 200, 203, 205, 228f., 231, 250, 259, 262f.

Tabularium (Record Office) 257
Tacitus (emperor) 206
Tacitus (historian) 191, 195f., 198, 219f.
Tadmor, see Palmyra
Talamone, see Telamon
Talmud 242, 265
Tanagra 65, 127, 251, 254
Taras (Tarentum, Taranto) 32, 48, 93, 127, 130, 156f., 159, 163, 177: see also Gulf of Taras
Tarik 221
Tarquinii (Tarquinia) 143, 146, 255
Tarquinius Priscus 143, 146ff.
Tarquinius Superbus 144, 147f.
Tarracina. (Terracina) 152
Tarraconensis, Hispania, see Spain
Tarsus 243
Tartessus 37, 42, 249
Tauris, see Chersonese, Tauric
taxes, taxation, tolls 13, 115, 117, 151, 161, 163f., 169, 203, 205, 207f., 215, 220, 232, 264

Taygetus, Mt. 31
Taysafun, see Ctesiphon
Tegea 33, 253f.
Telamon (Talamone) 158
Telemachus 226
teleology 93, 96, 99, 123
Telesterion, see Eleusis
Tell Mardikh, see Ebla
Tell Rafah, see Raphia
Tell Sukas, see Paltus
Telos 254
Tempe 58, 233
temples, shrines, sanctuaries 10, 12, 14,
   27, 31, 38f., 42f., 52f., 101, 104ff., 116f.,
   124, 143f., 147f., 153f., 182f., 229,
   232ff., 241, 248ff., 253, 257f.
Tenebrium (de la Nao) C. 250
Teos (Sığacık) 38, 46, 249
Terence 87, 161, 256
Terillus 60
Terina (S. Eufemia) 250
Terracina, see Tarracina
Tertullian 243
tetrarchy 206ff.
Tetricus 206
Teutoburg Forest (near Detmold or
   Osnabruck? Death of Varus) 181
Teutones 165
Thagaste (Soukh-el-Aras) 213
Thales 15, 40, 249, 263
Thamugadi (Timgad) 199
Thapsus (Ed-Dimas) 172
Thasos 46, 64, 107
Theaetetus, see Plato
Theagenes 21, 235
Theatre of Dionysus (Athens) 77, 251f.
Theatre of Marcellus (Rome) 182
Theatre of Pompey (Rome) 174, 182
Thebes 26, 52, 72f., 77, 80f., 83ff., 120,
   131, 249, 254
Thefarie Velianas, see Velianas
Themistocles 57ff., 71, 102, 252
Theocritus 125, 128f., 132, 185
Theoderic the Great (Ostrogoth) 221
Theodosius I the Great 210ff., 261
Theodosius II 231
Theognis 235
Theogony, see Hesiod
Theophrastus 99, 123ff., 127
Theopompus 73
Thera (Santorini) 8, 60, 229
Thermaic Gulf 46, 72f.

Thermopylae 58
Thermum 120
Theseus 81, 83f.
thesmoi, thesmothetai, see laws
Thesmophoria, see festivals
Thesmophoriazusae, see Aristophanes
Thespiae 26
Thespis 24, 76
Thessalonica (Salonica) 115, 206, 211
Thessaly 27, 43, 47, 58, 82, 101, 160, 172,
   253, 262
thetes 264
Thetis 262
Third Sacred War 73
Thirty Years' Peace 251
Thrace 23ff., 37f., 46, 51, 56, 66f., 70,
   72f., 89f., 167, 230, 235, 250f.: see also
   Bosphorus Chersonese (Thracian)
Thrasymachus 91
Thucydides (historian) 30f., 52, 64–71,
   251
Thucydides (son of Melesias) 65
Thurii 69, 90, 156: see also Sybaris
Thyrea 28, 33
Tiber R. 142, 144f., 148, 150, 199, 217,
   258: see also bridges
Tiberius 181f., 191. 196, 255, 258f.
Tibullus 258
Tibur (Tivoli) 151f., 198
Ticinum (Pavia) 206
Tigellinus, Gaius Ofonius 259
Tiglath-Pileser III 262f.
Tigranes I the Great 230
Tigris R. 114, 117, 231
Timaeus (of Locri Epizephyrii) 95f.
timber, see wood
Timesitheus 204
Timgad, see Thamugadi
timocracy, see oligarchy
Timoleon 119f.
Timon 132
Timotheus 110, 253
tin 42, 54
Tinea (Tyne) R. 198
Tiresias 79f.
Tiryns 27
Titius, Marcus 257
Titus 193f., 241, 259
Tolfa Mt. 143
Tolosa (Toulouse) 212
tombs, see burials
Tomis (Constanța) 189

Torah 241, 243, 264
Torre Annunziata, see Oplontis
Torre del Mar, see Maenace
Toulouse, see Tolosa
Trabzon, see Trapezus
Trachis 80
Trachonitis 260
trade, commerce, merchants 10, 13, 22f.,
    29, 33, 37, 39ff., 43, 48f., 54, 63, 116,
    118f., 142f., 148, 150, 153f., 166, 199f.,
    238, 241
trading posts, see emporia
tragedy 16, 23f., 71, 76–86, 95, 100, 107,
    112, 160, 192, 196, 236, 259
Trajan 195ff., 199, 231, 242f., 259f., 265
Trajanus Decius, see Decius
Trapezus (Trebizond, Trabzon) 47
Trasimene, L. 159
Trebia (Trebbia) R. 159
Trebizond, see Trapezus
Trebonianus Gallus 204
Treviri (city), see Augusta Trevirorum
Treviri (tribe) 219, 261
tribes (foreign) 149, 170, 215, 259, 261,
    264: see also Germans
tribes (within community) 21, 25, 28,
    30, 35, 42, 147, 236, 248, 250, 257,
    264
tribuni plenis 154, 158, 162–168, 256
tribunicia potestas (tribunician power) 179,
    258
Tribute Lists 65
Trimalchio 193
trireme, see ship
trittyes 264
Triumvirate, First, Second, see First,
    Second Triumvirate
Troad 166
Troezen 58
Troy (Ilium), Trojans 8, 20, 36, 44, 52f.,
    77, 79ff., 83f., 101, 107, 135, 185f.,
    225
Tullius, Servius, see Servius Tullius
Tuniae (Amiata) Mt. 143
Turbolo R., see Sagra
Turunçlar, see Priene
Tusculum 149, 151f.
Tutor, Julius 220, 259, 261
Twelve Tables 154
Tyche (Chance) 126, 129f., 133, 254; see
    also Fortuna
Tyne R., see Tinea

'tyrants' dictators, autocrats 12f., 21f.,
    28f., 31, 33, 38, 40, 42, 44, 49, 52, 56,
    60f., 67, 78, 97, 120, 136, 169, 173,
    235f., 249, 264
Tyre (Sur) 10, 114, 228, 253, 260, 262
Tyrrhenian Sea 50, 250
Tyrrhenoi, see Etruria, Etruscans
Tyrtaeus 32

Ukraine 39, 47, 210
Ullikummi 249
Ulpianus, Domitius 260
Ulysses, see Odysseus
Umbria 159f.
Umbricius 197
Umm Qeis, see Gadara
updating 1f., 218f., 222f., 247
Urartu 262
urbanization 9, 21, 29, 31, 35, 109, 143,
    146, 199, 248, 251, 264
Urfa, see Edessa
Üsküdar (Scutari), see Chrysopolis

Vaballathus Athenodorus 260
Vahalis (Waal) R. 261
Valchetta, R., see Cremera
Valens 210f.
Valentia (Valencia), Gulf of, see Gulf of
    Valentia
Valentinian I 209f., 212
Valentinian II 211
Valentinian III 214f.
Valerian 204, 231, 260, 265
Valerius Cato 257
Valerius Messala Corvinus, Marcus, see
    Messala
Vallia, see Wallia
Vandals 214f., 221
Varro, Marcus, Terentius 103
Varus, Publius Quinctilius 181
vases, see pottery
Veii (Veio) 144, 146, 148, 150f., 256
Velia, see Elea
Velianas, Thefarie 143
Venetico (Naulochus) C., see Naulochus
Ventotene, see Pandateria
Venus 126, 254, 258; see also Aphrodite
Venusia (Venosa) 156, 187
Vergil, see Virgil
Verona 171
Verus, Lucius 201, 231, 260
Vespasian 193f., 241, 259

Vestal Virgins 182
Vesuvius, Mt. 194
Vetulonia 143
Via Appia (Appian Way), Domitia, Flaminia, Sacra, see roads
Vico, Mt. 49
Victory (Nike, Victoria) 106, 126, 211, 254
Vieux Port, see Massalia
Viminal Hill 146
Vindex, Gaius Julius 193
vines, wine 20, 37f., 48f., 54, 200, 263
Virgil 184–188, 217, 258, 262
virtue, see *arete*
Visigoths 210–215, 221
Vitellius 259
Vitruvius 110, 253
Volaterrae (Volterra) 143f.
Volo, see Demetrias
Vologeses I 230
Vologeses III 231
Volsinii (Orvieto) 191, 255
Vulca 148, 256
Vulcan (Hephaestus) 186
Vulci 143, 255
Waal, R., see Valhalis
'Wall of Servius Tullius' 151
Wallia (Vallia) 212
wards, see *curiae*
White Huns, see Hephthalites
White Plain 235
women 14, 16 32f., 37, 44, 51, 53, 70, 80, 85, 87, 109, 127ff., 137, 161, 178, 189, 192, 197, 226f., 233ff., 238f., 254, 258f., 263: see also love, love poetry
Wonders of the World, Seven, see Seven Wonders of the World

wood, timber 27, 44, 46, 48, 66, 72, 103, 106, 148, 236, 252, 263
wool, see sheep
Works and Days, see Hesiod
writing, see alphabets

Xenocrates 98, 130
Xenophanes 15, 53
Xenophon 92, 251, 254, 263
Xerxes I 58ff., 69, 77f., 230, 234
Xuthus 84

Yahweh, see Jews
Yavneh, see Jamnia
Year of the Four Emperors 193, 196, 203f., 259
Yehud, see Judaea
Yenişehir, see Sigeum
York, see Eburacum
Youth, see Juventas
Yugoslavia, see Illyricum

Zama (Sebaa Biar?) 159
Zancle (Messana, Messina) 49, 52, 250
Zea 20
Zela (Zile) 172
Zeno (emperor) 215
Zeno (founder of Stoicism) 130, 254
Zenobia 206, 260
zeugitai 264
Zeus 11f., 43, 76, 78, 81, 101, 105f., 134, 225f., 232f., 241, 250, 252: see also Jupiter
Zeuxis 73, 108
Zile, see Zela
Zippori, see Sepphoris